The BBQ Queens' Big Book of Barbecue

THE BBQ Queens' Big Book OF BARBECUE

Karen Adler AND Judith Fertig

The Harvard Common Press · Boston, Massachusetts

The Harvard Common Press
535 Albany Street
Boston, Massachusetts 02118
www.harvardcommonpress.com

Printed in the United States of America

LIBRARY OF CONGRESS CATALOGING-IN-PUBLICATION DATA

Adler, Karen.
    The bbq queens' big book of barbecue / Karen Adler and Judith M. Fertig.
        p. cm.
    Includes index.
    ISBN 1-55832-296-5 (hc : alk. paper) — ISBN 1-55832-297-3 (pbk : alk. paper)
1. Barbecue cookery. I. Fertig, Judith M. II. Title.
    TX840.B3A32 2005
    641.5'784—dc22

                                                                    2004029897

Special bulk-order discounts are available on this and other Harvard Common Press books. Companies and organizations may purchase books for premiums or resale, or may arrange a custom edition, by contacting the Marketing Director at the address above.

Cover and interior design by Richard Oriolo
Illustrations by Laura Tedeschi
Grill photograph courtesy of Bob Lyon
Cover photography by Terri Voyles with Omni Images

10 9 8 7 6 5 4 3 2 1

To our families,

especially Karen's husband, Dick,

and Judith's children, Sarah and Nick,

who are always ready to praise and encourage us

and to taste a tender morsel or two and say,

"That's not bad!"

Contents

ACKNOWLEDGMENTS ▪ ix

Meet the BBQ Queens ▪ xiii

The BBQ Queens on the Basics ▪ 1

Sprinkle, Slather, Soak, and Drizzle:
Rubs, Marinades, Vinaigrettes, and Sauces ▪ 45

An A to Z of Grilled and Smoked Veggies, Cheeses, and Pizza ▪ 113

Taking Wing: Poultry and Game Birds ▪ 187

In the Swim: Fish and Shellfish ▪ 251

Here's the Beef ▪ 299

Bringing Home the Bacon: Pork ▪ 361

A Little Lamb ▪ 417

RESOURCE GUIDE ▪ 443
MEASUREMENT EQUIVALENTS ▪ 448
INDEX ▪ 449

Acknowledgments

We love to cook outdoors because it's relaxing and a great way to share techniques, recipes, great food, and cool drinks. Whether it's schmoozing with friends and family on a deck or patio, conversing over a smoker at a barbecue competition, or shootin' the bull at a tailgate, count us in! Although this book is a salute to women who sizzle and smoke, we also owe a lot to the men in our lives. Karen's son-in-law Brian Young's experimentation with smoking wild game has been inspiring. Her other son-in-law, Jimmy Donnici, is also an ace at the grill and has shared many recipes with her. Good friend Don Coffey is an exceptional cook and outdoor smoker who has a special way with wild duck.

Judith's father, Jack Merkle, learned the meat trade from his generations-old family business and has taught her a lot.

We want to thank the staff of the many cooking schools where we have enjoyed teaching and meeting new food friends, including Larry Oates, owner of KitchenArt in West Lafayette, Indiana; Priscilla Barnes, owner of Cook's Nook in McPherson, Kansas; Deb Lackey at Dorothy Lane School of Cooking in Dayton, Ohio; Viking Culinary Centers all across the country; Carol Tabone at Jungle Jim's Cooking School in Fairfield, Ohio; Marilyn Markel at A Southern Season in Chapel Hill, North Carolina; Kitchen Conservatory and Dierberg's in St. Louis; Kathleen Craig and the great staff at Cooks of Crocus Hill in Minneapolis and St. Paul; Byerly's in Minneapolis and St. Paul; Chef's Gallery in Stillwater, Minnesota; Marshall Field's Culinary Studio in Chicago; Debbie Meyer at Market Street in Dallas; Central Market's Cooking School at various locations in Texas; Cooks Warehouse in Atlanta; Sur La Table Cooking Schools throughout the United States; Hall's Crown Center in Kansas City, Missouri; Culinary Center of Kansas City in Overland Park, Kansas; Rebecca Miller at Whole Foods Market in Overland Park, Kansas; and Denise Manu at Roth Concept Center in Lenexa, Kansas.

Special venues where we have met great people while we cooked up a royal feast include the Seattle Grillfest in Seattle and Charlie Trotter's To Go in Chicago. Special people include Cheryl Parker at the American Royal Barbecue Cooking Stage in Kansas City, Missouri, and Mark Dressler and Matt Sutherland, who supported and promoted the BBQ Queens at the First Annual Traverse Epicurean Festival in Traverse City, Michigan.

The Kansas City Barbeque Society, under the guidance of cofounder and executive director Carolyn Wells, has guided so many of us toward true slow-smoked American barbecue. The society promotes good food with good friends and emphasizes "having fun while doing so!" We hope that we live up to the honors that have been bestowed on us by our friend Ardie Davis, a.k.a. Remus Powers, Ph.B.: Karen's Master of Barbecue from Greasehouse University and Judith's place in the Order of the Magic Mop.

We thank all of our friends and colleagues in Les Dames d'Escoffier International and charter members of the Kansas City chapter for their encouragement and support. Our involvement with the International Association of Culinary Professionals has helped steer our culinary careers to new vistas. We have enjoyed all the good people from our Slow Foods Convivium in Kansas City, led by Jasper Mirabile Jr. Our involvement with the American Barbecue Hall of Fame and Museum is in its infancy, but we hope that the vision of our chairman, George Vesel, has us cooking at a venue solely dedicated to barbecue in the near future.

We're grateful for the wonderful recipes submitted by our friends the BBQ Babes and the Grill Gals: Carolyn Wells, Cheryl Alters Jamison, Diane Phillips, Dotty Griffith, Paula Lambert, Karen Putman, Candy Weaver, Janeyce Michel-Cupito, Beckie Baker, Julie Fox, Kathy Smith, Celina Tio, Bonnie Tandy Leblang, Rozane Miceli Prather, Latifa Raoufi, Debbie Moose, and Lisa Readie Mayer. Additional barbecue friends and companies that have helped us include Donna Myers, Paul Kirk, Dennis Hayes, Steve Raichlen, Nick Nicholas, Jim Eber, Dave Eckert, KitchenAid, Traeger, and Cookshack.

Special thanks goes to our many "foodie" friends, including the Kansas City Cookbook Club (Dee Barwick, Liz Benson, Vicki Johnson, Gayle Parnow, Mary Pfeifer, Kathy Smith, and Roxanne Wyss) and all the 'Que Queens (Beckie Baker, Dee Barwick, Janeyce Michel-Cupito, Cathy Jones, Ronna Keck, Kathy Smith, Jean Tamburello, Lou Jane Temple, Bunny Tuttle, and Carolyn Wells).

Of course, we want to thank everyone at The Harvard Common Press, from publisher Bruce Shaw to editors Pam Hoenig and Valerie Cimino to P.R. experts Skye Stewart and Liza Beth—and everyone else there. Special recognition goes to our agent, Lisa Ekus, and her able staff—and to the radio DJ who said that women couldn't barbecue!

Last, we would be remiss to leave out two women—our mentors—whose wacky partnership keeps on inspiring us: Lucy Ricardo and Ethel Mertz.

Thanks, everybody!

Meet the BBQ Queens

Some women wear false eyelashes. Some women wear purple. The BBQ Queens wear tiaras and beauty queen sashes, lots of jewelry, and sometimes even big hair. It's all for a good cause, though—getting people excited about the thrill of the grill and the art of slow smoking. We, Karen Adler and Judith Fertig, the BBQ Queens, are cookbook authors, culinary instructors, and members of an all-girl barbecue team that was formed when a local Kansas City DJ infamously proclaimed, "Women can't barbecue!" Those were fightin' words to us. In response, we didn't burn our bras or wring our hands. We stepped up to the grill and smoker and let the power of sizzle and smoke do our talking at the legendary Battle of the Sexes Barbecue Contest in Kansas City.

We had so much fun and so much success that we felt like royalty. We decided we should be BBQ Queens and that was that.

From our first flimsy dime store glitter tiaras, we've moved up the royal chain to real rhinestones and even a working tiara that doubles as a sun visor. Someday, we're gonna have tiaras bedecked with cubic zirconias (but only if lots of people buy this book, so spread the word). Believe us, everything looks and tastes better when you're wearing a tiara.

So the tiara-totin' BBQ Queens are here to tell you that women *can* barbecue. They can also grill, smoke, rotisserie cook, plank, stir-grill, and yadda, yadda, yadda. From sea to shining sea, we've met lots of Grill Gals, BBQ Babes, and even a Silver Queen Corn Queen who all reinforce that idea, and you'll meet them in the pages of this book.

We're here to share our expertise at the grill and smoker with you. We'll even tell you how to do the four queen waves (see page 224), a life skill you definitely should have. Who else is gonna show you that? After all, you never know when sudden fame could be thrust upon you and somehow you have to cope. We know all about that. We sleep much better at night knowing that we know how to wave like the really royal people we are. You will, too.

And for those who say they can never figure women out, here's how we explain ourselves.

The BBQ Queen Philosophy

1. We grill and smoke like girls. Is there a gender difference in the way people approach grilling and smoking? You bet.

Like the best-selling self-help series states, men *are* from Mars, even at the grill and smoker. They might single-mindedly grill or smoke part of the meal, sitting outside with a frosty beer, watching the world go by as they wait for their barbecued brisket or ribs or grilled chicken wings to get done. Our dads grilled fabulous steaks and burgers over charcoal when we were growing up. Karen's husband, Dick, grills thick and juicy strip steaks to perfection. Judith's dad grills a wonderful beef tenderloin that has become the centerpiece of family celebrations. And Judith's son, Nick, grills a mean hamburger stuffed with blue cheese as well as a moist and delicious beer can chicken.

Women, on the other hand, are from Venus, and they usually plan the menu, shop, prepare the food for the grill or smoker, cook it, serve it, and clean up. No wonder we deserve tiaras!

When we say we grill and smoke like girls, we mean that we like to grill or smoke more than one thing at a time and think about the big picture—the whole meal—not just one part. We can grill great steaks and burgers and smoke divinely delicious ribs or briskets. But we also think about the rest of the meal—and actually prepare it. Oooh, a sauce would be good with this. Which side dish? How about dessert?

The instructions we give for each master recipe sometimes encourage you to add something else to the grill or smoker to make the most of your time and streamline dinner preparation. We suggest some "crowning glories" to finish off the dish or serve on the side. We also encourage cooking for leftovers, as you'll see in many recipes, and urge you to grill or smoke foods to use as condiments, saving you time down the road.

Besides thinking about the total menu rather than one component, women exhibit other differences at the grill and smoker. According to our informal backyard research, women tend to be more experimental in what they grill or smoke at home. Women are more likely to grill fish or vegetables or pizza, for instance, or to try smoked goat cheese. Men tend to rely on that old saw "If it ain't broke, don't fix it" and stick to the things they do well, such as great grilled steak or smoked brisket. *Vive la différence!*

Woman also tend to want things neat and tidy, even in the backyard. That's why women are more likely to flip on the switch to a gas grill rather than take the time to build a charcoal fire. (See page 8 for how to build a charcoal fire using a charcoal chimney. It's really easy.) The BBQ Queens love the convenience of gas grills, but a hot hardwood lump charcoal fire is hard to beat for searing and charring with lots of extra flavor.

And last, time is of the essence to the fairer sex. Unless women are competing in a barbecue contest, they're not likely to baby-sit a smoking brisket for 12 hours, as a lot of guys do. Although the BBQ Queens do traditional slow-smoked brisket, we offer choices such as smoking in an electric water smoker or smoke-roasting meats using the smoker and the oven to produce delicious results in only 5 hours. Likewise, we show how to use the indoor stovetop smoker pan that literally flies off the shelves every time we talk about it in a class. (We wish we had stock in that company.)

2. Grilling and smoking are meant to be fun. As our culinary school students have heard us say time and time again, relax and have fun at the grill or smoker. This is not rocket science.

You don't need calipers or a stopwatch to cook a great meal on the grill or smoker. (An instant-read meat thermometer is sure handy, though.) You just need to pay attention to your food. If you know what to look for (and each of our recipes will tell you), you'll know when your food is done. The more you grill or smoke, the more relaxed you'll be.

3. Make "rustic" part of your food vocabulary. Your food doesn't have to be absolutely perfect to be really good. That's why "rustic" is our favorite word. If your burgers aren't exactly the same size and shape, so what? That's rustic. If your grilled food doesn't look as if a chef towered it into heights of glory, so what? That's rustic, and that's charming, we think. Rustic food looks like it's homemade, and that's very appealing. Casually arranged on a plate or platter, garnished simply with fresh herbs or other natural ingredients, grilled or smoked food can look great as well as taste great.

The rustic approach can shorten prep time in the kitchen, too. Instead of fine mincing, simple chopping saves time with the same taste results.

4. A recipe is a general blueprint. Another key component to our relaxed philosophy is that every recipe is a blueprint, not an immutable law carved in stone. (We guess that means we're type B people at heart.) Just as you probably wouldn't build a new house without changing at least one thing in the architect's plans—more closet space, please!—you should feel free to change these recipes to suit your own taste. We encourage you to experiment.

We always cringe when we read recipes for "perfectly grilled" steak (or perfectly grilled anything). Perfect according to whom? A perfect steak, to us, means a little char on the exterior and medium-rare on the inside. To others, it might mean less char, more smoke flavor, and medium on the inside. It's all a matter of personal taste.

That's why we start you off with a master recipe, then suggest ways that you could modify it if you like your food done a different way.

5. Start simple, then get frilly. After you feel comfortable with the master grilled or smoked recipe, it's time to branch out with other versions or riffs on leftovers. Basically, we start you off with a simple recipe, then jazz it up as we go along. No matter which food you want to grill or smoke, you'll find lots of ways to enjoy it.

For instance, you'll find Grilled Asparagus on page 117, a master recipe. When you've grilled asparagus simply and find you want a new twist, then you can try Grilled Asparagus with Shaved Parmigiano-Reggiano or even Asian-Style Asparagus with Peanut Butter Dipping Sauce. If you have leftovers, you can make our Grilled Asparagus Frittata.

So put on your imaginary tiara and get grilling and smoking with the BBQ Queens!

The BBQ Queens on the Basics

Checking out at the grocery store should be simple, right? But no, it's a litany of questions: Paper or plastic? Credit or debit? Drive up or carry out? 👑 This chapter is about answering those kinds of questions for cooking with fire. 👑 What kind of grill or smoker do you have or do you want? How do you want to cook—grill, smoke, rotisserie, plank, or stir-grill? What type of fire do you need to prepare? How do you get the temperature you need? How long do you grill or smoke something? How do you know when your food is done?

The Difference Between Grilling and Smoking

Is grilling from Mars, smoking from Venus? Nah. Although grilling and smoking seem to be very opposite cooking techniques, they're actually similar. Just like going from white to black involves ever-darkening shades of gray, going from grilling to smoking involves ever-cooling degrees of temperature, moving foods from directly over the fire to farther away from it.

Grilled foods cook fast over a medium to hot fire (300 to 500°F or more) to char them slightly and give them a robust flavor. Because the foods cook fast, you usually grill foods that are already fairly tender, such as chicken breasts, pork chops, pork tenderloin, steaks, fish fillets, shellfish, and vegetables.

Slow-smoked foods, also known as true barbecue, cook slowly and indirectly—next to (not over) a low fire, perhaps with fragrant wood added. For that reason, smoked foods take on a heavier wood smoke flavor. Because the foods cook low (200 to 250°F) and slow, you usually smoke foods that need a longer cooking time, such as beef brisket, pork loin, spareribs, and pork shoulder or butt. The great thing about smoking, however, is that you can also smoke foods that you normally grill.

In between simple grilling and simple smoking are all kinds of specialty techniques, such as stir-grilling, planking, rotisserie cooking, and stovetop smoking, all of which we will cover later on in this chapter.

Which Grill Is Right for You?

People always ask us whether we grill with charcoal or gas, to which we answer yes— we swing both ways, as they say. The majority of American households have at least one outdoor grill, which, more often than not, is gas rather than charcoal. Although Grill Gals are more likely to use a gas grill, there are those among us who swear by charcoal. As far as we're concerned, to get great flavor and char, charcoal is the way to go— in particular, hardwood lump charcoal, which burns really hot for a terrific sear. But there are pluses to gas grilling as well, not the least of which is you just flip a switch and it's on. You can add wood smoke to a gas grill, too, as we'll show you later on. Just make sure you buy a unit with enough BTUs for hot surface searing.

Barbecue expert Donna Myers is president of DHM Group, a public relations company specializing in the barbecue industry. In the 1990s, she conducted biannual surveys with the Barbecue Industry Association (now the Hearth, Patio, and Barbecue Association). One of those surveys reported that the average American household owns 1.6 grills. In fact, 20 million households own two grills and 9.8 million households own three or more grills.

The BBQ Queens have eleven different kinds of outdoor grills and smokers. Karen has large and small kettle charcoal grills, a gas grill, a kamado-style ceramic grill, and an electric smoker oven; all her equipment can also be used for slow smoking. Her husband, Dick, owns a portable gas grill. Judith has a medium-size gas grill with one burner (for grilling only), as well as a charcoal grill and an electric-fired wood pellet–fueled grill, both of which can be used for smoking and grilling. We both have electric bullet-shaped water smokers. Plus, for indoor use, we have Camerons Stovetop Smokers and an assortment of grill pans and electric grills / griddles.

The kind of grill *you* choose should be determined by the space you have, the kind of fuel you want to use, the amount of cooking surface you need, the look of the grill (hey, it should look as good as you do!), and how much money you want to spend.

In addition to the grills and smokers we own and cook on, we have also cooked on a whole assortment of others, including various models made by Cookshack, Traeger, BeefEater, Big Green Egg, Grill Dome, Weber, Viking, KitchenAid, Wolf, Char-Broil, Sunshine, Fire Magic, Sunbeam, Ducane, Hasty-Bake, Napoleon, Brinkmann, and Charmglow—and we'll be adding more to this list. Check out our guide to grilling and smoking equipment on pages 3–5 and 18–21.

Gas Grills

So many choices abound in this category that we can't begin to list them all here. But go to our resource guide for a detailed look at gas grill manufacturers. The biggest decision to make is whether you want to buy a unit that uses propane fuel or natural gas. Most propane grills are movable, unless you have them built in. A movable grill means that if it is a windy or rainy day, you can pick up your grill and drag it to a place of shelter (but never indoors or in the garage, unless you want to leave this life prematurely). Natural gas units must be hooked up to your gas line, which will make the grill stationary.

Once you've decided which kind of gas you want, the next step is to go shopping at your local grill store. Most grill retailers go to trade shows, where they must choose from hundreds of gas grill models, trying to purchase a variety of grills from reputable manufacturers that will satisfy their customers' needs. Our best advice is make friends with your local grill retailer and find out how he (or she) stands behind his products, whether he makes service calls, and whether the grills have warranties. Another big plus is buying from a store that will preassemble and deliver the grill. But you need to ask!

You want to buy a gas grill with at least two separate burners so you can turn off one of the burners to cook indirectly and smoke on the grill. The burners need to heat the entire surface, so if you have a fairly large cooking surface, you will need four or more burners. If you don't have enough burners, there may not be enough heat coverage, and you will have hot and cold spots on your grill. Go for more burners if you can afford it, because the more burners you have, the more temperature selections you have, allowing you to grill several items that may need different levels of heat at the same time.

If you can afford it, buy a grill that is rust-resistant (or get a cover for it) and on which you can crank up the heat level to at least 36,000 BTUs. Make sure the cooking surface is large enough for your needs. (Manufacturers often include the warming rack and side burners in their total cooking surface dimensions, so you need to make sure how much of that space is actual cooking surface.)

Charcoal Grills

Charcoal grills come in all sizes and shapes, with or without lids. The big choices with a charcoal grill are the amount of cooking surface on the grill rack, how far the grill grates are from the fire, and whether you have a lid or not. Also, check for sturdy legs and heavy metal construction. Cheaper grills are often not the bargain they seem to be. Many of the kettle-shaped grills of lesser quality are imitating the popular Weber kettle grills first introduced to Americans by George Stephen in 1951. Both of the BBQ Queens own Webers. Karen recently replaced her Weber after more than 15 years of use. Her investment added up to about $5 a year. Now *that's* a bargain!

If you grill a lot or entertain and grill, you may want a large cooking surface. If you're in a small apartment (make sure the fire codes allow you to operate an outdoor grill on your balcony), opt for a hibachi. With charcoal, no matter the size of your grill, you get great flavor in your food, especially if you burn hardwood lump charcoal, which is irregularly shaped and made only from hardwoods, unlike charcoal briquettes, which have a uniform shape and are made from several different materials.

Electric Grills

Electric grills are available for indoor and outdoor use. The heat level of these grills is usually not high enough for great searing. Some outdoor models are ideal for homes and apartments with small patios that might not allow for gas or charcoal grills. One of the most popular indoor electric grills is the George Foreman. It has heating elements on both sides of the grill, which cooks foods extremely fast and eliminates the need to turn them.

Wood Pellet Grills

Wood pellet grills combine the ease of an electric starter with the flavor of compressed wood pellets. These grills need to be plugged into an electrical outlet. Wood pellets are added to the hopper, which feeds the pellets down a chute to burn and smoke. Because the pellets are compressed, they take up much less storage space than charcoal, while still imparting a wonderful wood flavor to foods. You can buy different flavors of pellets and mix and match them for your own custom wood taste. The leader in making this kind of grill is Traeger.

Kamado Grills

Kamado porcelain cookers are Asian-style cookers shaped like an egg, similar to ancient clay vessels such as the tandoor. Kamados are very heavy and usually sold on either a metal base with wheels or a heavy-duty wooden cart with wheels. When the lid is clamped shut, the kamado cooks like a pressure cooker, quicker than a regular smoker. With the lid open, it works well as a grill, nice and hot. Big Green Egg offers a lifetime guarantee on their grills that can't be beat.

Water Smokers

The bullet-shaped water smoker is about 18 inches in diameter and 3 to 4 feet tall. The unit is relatively small but has enough cooking space to smoke two big hams or a couple of turkeys at once. The choices for fuel are charcoal, electricity, and gas. Prices range

Utensils for Grilling and Smoking

Several basic tools make grilling and smoking easier. Kitchen shops, hardware stores, restaurant supply stores, and barbecue and grill retailers are good sources for the items listed below. Professional utensils are superior in quality and durability and worth the extra money. Long handles are preferable on everything, to keep you a safe distance from the fire.

- A *stiff wire brush* with a scraper makes cleaning the grill easy. Tackle this while the grill is still warm.

- One *natural-bristle basting brush* can be used to apply oil to the grill and a second to baste food during grilling or smoking.

- *Grate Chef Grill Wipes* are small pads saturated with high-temperature cooking oil. You can use them for oiling the grill grates prior to cooking, then turn them over to clean the grill when you're finished cooking. The high-temperature oil doesn't smoke, and it doesn't drip from the pads, which prevents flare-ups.

- *Perforated grill racks* are placed on top of the grill grates to accommodate small or delicate food items, such as chicken wings, fish fillets, shellfish, and vegetables, which might fall through the grates. Always oil the grill rack before using so that the food won't stick.

- *Hinged grill baskets* hold food in place and make turning easy.

- *Grill woks and metal baskets* with perforated holes let in smoky flavor while sitting directly on top of the grill. Stir-grill fish, chicken, shellfish, or vegetables by tossing them with long-handled wooden paddles.

- *Heat-resistant oven or grill mitts* offer the best hand protection, especially when you need to touch any hot metal, such as skewers, during the grilling process.

- *Long-handled, spring-loaded tongs* are easier to use than the scissors type. They are great for turning shellfish, sliced vegetables, and skewers. Buy two sets of tongs—one for raw meats and the other for cooked meats.

- *Long-handled offset spatulas* with extra-long spatula surfaces are great for turning large pieces of food.

- A *long, wooden-handled offset fish spatula* with a 5- to 6-inch blade is essential for turning fish fillets. Oil it well to avoid sticking.

- Keep a *spray bottle or pan filled with water* handy to douse flare-ups. A garden hose within easy reach can substitute, but make sure the water is turned on!

- *Skewers*—wooden or metal—allow smaller items to be threaded loosely together and then placed on the grill to cook. Wooden or bamboo skewers should be soaked for at least 30 minutes before using so that the ends won't char during grilling. Flat wooden or metal skewers are preferred, so that cubed food doesn't spin while turning. Or use double skewers to keep cubed food from spinning.

- *Disposable aluminum pans* hold meats or vegetables and their natural juices or sauces for basting. Place small vegetables, shellfish, or cheese in them to smoke. The pans can be bent and shaped to fit in a small grill or smoker. Or use one as a tent to create a mini oven for thick meats that need a longer cooking time.

- We suggest using two *professional baking sheets*, double-stacked, to carry foods to and from the grill. Place the raw food on the top sheet and carry it out to the grill. Use the clean sheet to receive the cooked food off the grill.

- We like to have an *instant-read meat thermometer* handy by the grill. A *heatproof meat thermometer* is great to place in a leg of lamb, a whole chicken, a pork loin, or another roast before putting it on the rotisserie. For smoking on a charcoal or gas grill, a *grill thermometer* inserted through a small hole (you may have to drill the hole yourself) in the dome of the grill will tell you the internal temperature; 225 to 250°F is the optimum temperature for slow smoking.

- A *charcoal chimney or electric fire starter* is key for starting a charcoal fire.

- A good-quality *chef's knife* is essential for slicing meat.

from $50 to $250, with charcoal smokers being the least expensive and gas the most expensive. A water smoker is a vertical smoker with two or three chambers. The bottom holds the heating unit, whether it's the fire grate for charcoal, the electric coil, or the gas burners. This is where you add your wood chunks or pellets for smoking. The next cylinder holds the water pan, with either one or two racks above it. The water pan shields the food you are cooking from the fire. Manufacturers claim that you can use these units as grills by placing one of the grill grates over the fire grate. However, many of the electric and gas units can reach only about 250°F—perfect for smoking but not hot enough for grilling. Charcoal units are better for grilling. That being said, the BBQ Queens prefer to use this small but mighty piece of equipment as a smoker, with electricity as our choice of fuel. Electric smokers cost just a bit more than charcoal units, but all you have to do is plug them in and add the wood. You'll save oodles in operating expenses, too.

▬▬

Grilling 101

Lighting the Fire

In each grilling recipe in this book, we tell you to "prepare a (medium to hot) fire in a grill." This means "direct heat," with the flames under the food you're cooking. Preparing a direct-heat fire is done differently depending on the type of equipment you have.

CHARCOAL GRILLS

A charcoal fire can be started in any of several safe, ecologically sound ways. We prefer using real hardwood lump charcoal instead of compressed charcoal briquettes. Hardwood lump charcoal gives a better flavor and is an all-natural product without chemical additives. Hardwood lump charcoal is labeled as such. It is readily available at most barbecue and grill shops, hardware stores with large grill departments, and some grocery stores. Start your hardwood lump charcoal in a metal charcoal chimney with an electric fire starter, or with solid fire starters made with paraffin, also available at hardware, discount, and home improvement stores. Start a charcoal grill about 30 minutes before you're ready to grill.

Lighting the fire with a charcoal chimney With a charcoal grill, you'll want to buy a charcoal chimney, which lets you start a fire using only a match, newspaper, and charcoal. The chimney is an upright cylindrical metal canister, like a large metal coffee can with a handle. Fill it with 15 to 20 pieces of hardwood lump charcoal, then place it on a non-flammable surface, such as concrete or the grill rack. Slightly tip the chimney over and stuff one or two crumpled sheets of newspaper in the convex-shaped bottom. Light the paper with a match. After about 15 minutes, the coals will be hot and starting to ash over, signaling that you can get a hot fire going. Be sure to check it after the first 5 minutes to make sure the charcoal has caught fire, or you may need to light another piece of newspaper.

Making fire with electricity An electric fire starter is another easy way to start a fire in a charcoal grill. You'll need an outdoor electrical outlet or extension cord. Place the coil on the lower rack of the grill and stack charcoal on top of it. Plug it in and the fire will start in 10 to 15 minutes. Remove the coil and let the starter cool on a nonflammable surface, out of the reach of children and pets.

Lighting the fire with solid starters Solid starters are compressed wood blocks or sticks treated with a flammable substance such as paraffin. They are easy to ignite and don't give off a chemical odor. Solid starters are great to have on hand if you absolutely must start a fire regardless of the weather. Competition barbecuers always have these in their toolboxes, at the ready in case of inclement weather. Two or three will easily light the charcoal; set them on top of or beside the charcoal and ignite.

GAS GRILLS

Follow the manufacturer's directions for starting your gas grill. You'll need at least 36,000 combined BTUs (which measure the maximum heat output of a burner) to sear a steak, burger, or chop effectively. That means if each gas burner has a maximum of 25,000 BTUs, you'll need to turn both burners to medium-high or high and close the grill lid to let the grill reach 50,000 BTUs. Then open the lid and immediately place the food to sear on the hot grate. Again, check with the manufacturer or grill store retailer for heating information. The manufacturer's directions will tell you how long your grill takes to reach the temperature you want. Newer grills have inset thermometers that register the temperature inside the grill.

ELECTRIC GRILLS, WOOD PELLET GRILLS, SMOKER OVENS, AND WATER SMOKERS

Electric grills need to be plugged into an electrical outlet. Electric units vary in the kinds of temperature controls they have, so read the manufacturer's directions.

An electric-fired wood pellet grill is as easy to use as a gas grill, but prevention is worth a pound of cure, as the saying goes. If wood pellets get damp, they turn to mush, which can clog the ignition and keep the grill from lighting. If this happens, remove the grill grate. Remove the sliding barrier tray and cover with aluminum foil. Check to make sure that nothing is clogging the electric ignition in the bottom of the grill. Make sure the wood pellets in the hopper are dry. Replace the barrier tray and grill grate. Plug the grill into an outdoor electrical outlet and turn on the grill. Hold your hand over the grill rack to make sure the grill is heating up, then set the desired temperature.

Electric smoker ovens and water smokers need to be plugged into an outlet. Then you add the kind of wood you want and follow the manufacturer's directions for direct and indirect cooking.

KAMADO GRILLS

Kamado grills have a ceramic firebox for the charcoal at the grill's inner base. The charcoal can be started by placing two or three crumpled pieces of newspaper on the bottom and placing enough charcoal on top so that when the paper burns and the charcoal settles, it is just below the air holes in the firebox. You may use an electric fire starter for this kind of grill, but never use lighter fluid.

Fueling the Fire: Direct Versus Indirect Heat

Okay, you have your fire lit. Now what?

It's time to build the fire to the desired temperature, and for that you need fuel. In a charcoal grill, that means more charcoal. In a gas grill, it means propane or natural gas. In an electric grill, it means electricity. And in an electric-fired wood pellet grill, it means wood pellets.

You also have to decide which type of fire you need to make a particular recipe. Your choices are direct or indirect.

Knowing how to cook over direct and indirect heat will allow you to get the most flavor out of your food. Direct heat means that you're cooking directly over the heat source, whether it be coals in a charcoal grill or lit burners in a gas grill. Indirect heat means that you're cooking away from the source of heat, whether your food is off to the side of the heat source, in the center of the grill with the fire banked on both sides, or at a distance above the fire. If you own or cook on a pit barbecue, the indirect fire is in an offset firebox.

Here's how to prepare direct and indirect fires in both charcoal and gas grills.

CHARCOAL GRILLS

Direct Fire First, make sure the bottom vents of the grill are open, because fire needs oxygen. Next, start a fire in a charcoal chimney using hardwood lump charcoal and newspaper. Or use an electric fire starter or solid starters. Place more hardwood charcoal in the bottom of the grill. Your fire should extend out about 2 inches beyond the space you will need for the food you plan to grill. When the coals are hot in the charcoal chimney, dump them on top of the charcoal in the bottom of the grill and wait for all the coals to catch fire and ash over. When they've just begun to ash over and turn a whitish gray, replace the grill grate. When you put the food on the grate, it will be directly over the coals.

Indirect Fire Prepare a direct fire first. Once your hot coals are in the bottom of the grill, there are two ways you can create an indirect fire. First, using a long-handled grill spatula, push the coals over to one side of the grill to provide direct heat there. The other side of the grill will now have indirect heat. Second, bank the coals on both sides of the grill. The center of the grill will then be the indirect cooking area. For smoking, carefully place a disposable aluminum pan filled with water on the indirect side, next to the hot coals on the bottom of the grill or smoker. (Smoking is longer and slower, so you need the extra moisture from the water.) Place the hardwood chunks, chips, or pellets (for wood smoke flavoring) on top of the coals. Replace the grill grate. With an indirect fire, you can grill directly over the hot coals while you smoke over the indirect side. When cooking indirectly, close the grill lid and use the vents on the top and bottom of the grill to adjust the fire temperature. Open vents allow more oxygen in and make the fire hotter, partially closed vents lower the heat, and closed vents extinguish the fire.

GAS GRILLS

Direct Fire Turn on the burners. Place the food on the grill grate directly over the hot burner, and that is direct heat. To cook this way, ideally leave the grill lid up. When it is raining or snowing, however, closing the lid is preferable. This will essentially turn the hot grill into a hot oven, meaning you'll actually be grill-roasting. Also, because you can't see the food, it is easier to overcook it with the lid down.

Grill with the Lid Open or Shut?

Traditionally, grilling was done over an open fire or flame. Think about Wild West cattle drives and big Texas barbecue parties. Steaks were grilled on open brazier grills, while whole goats and quarters or sides of beef were smoked by digging a hole or pit in the ground. Thus, many grillers believe that *true* grilling is with the lid open.

If you are using hardwood lump charcoal and if you add wood chips or pellets to your fire (gas or charcoal), you will probably get more smokiness if you grill with the lid closed. Also, a thicker piece of meat will cook to the desired doneness faster with the lid closed. And if it is very cold, windy, rainy, or snowy, closing the lid makes good sense.

So should you grill with the lid open or shut? It's your choice.

Indirect Fire Your grill must have at least two burners for indirect grilling. Fire up the burner on one half of the grill only. The side of the grill with the burner off is for indirect cooking. For smoking, add water-soaked wood chips or dry compressed wood pellets to a smoker box or in an aluminum foil packet pierced with holes. Also, place a disposable aluminum pan filled with water over the direct heat. To cook this way, close the grill lid. If you have three or more burners, you may also set up your grill with the two outer burners on and the center of your grill used for indirect cooking. Adjust the burners to regulate the level of heat.

WOOD PELLET GRILLS

Wood pellet grills are constructed so that they provide only indirect fire, although you can adjust the temperature from low smoking at 250°F to indirect grilling at 500°F.

KAMADO GRILLS

Follow the manufacturer's directions, which usually recommend using hardwood lump charcoal placed just below the air holes in the firebox. The temperature is regulated by the amount of air allowed to flow in. More air means a hotter fire. The lid clamps down and seals tightly for smoking. With the lid open, you can grill directly. Smoking in a kamado is more like roasting in an oven. A water pan is not used.

WATER SMOKERS

Bullet-shaped water smokers fueled with charcoal work best for grilling. Place the grill rack over the hot fire in the firebox and grill. Remember that the grill rack is very close to the fire, so it grills hot and fast. The gas and electric models don't get hot enough for grilling. All the models use a vertical indirect grilling setup. For smoking, three or four chunks of water-soaked wood or a foil packet of wood pellets is placed in the firebox at the base. Next, the cylinder that holds the water pan is set on top, followed by the grill rack. The water pan separates the grill rack from the fire; thus the fire is indirect. The lid closes loosely, and now you're smoking.

ELECTRIC OVENS

This is similar in concept to the water smoker. The BBQ Queens are most familiar with the Cookshack Smokette, which Karen has. The oven box is a bit smaller than bullet-shaped water smokers and can smoke about 22 pounds of meat. The tight construction of this unit allows the food to smoke without a water pan, if you like. Because it is electric and the construction is tight, meaning the smoke does not escape, this unit is very popular with restaurant kitchens. The ease of these electrical units is that they use wood for the wood smoke flavor, but the fire is controlled by a thermostat. You can time your food (45 to 60 minutes per pound in the smoker) and do other things while the food is smoking.

Grilling Temperature

Most food is grilled directly over a medium-hot to hot fire, depending on the distance your grill rack sits from the fire and the heat of the fire itself.

In a charcoal grill, the fire is ready when the flames have subsided and the coals are glowing red and just beginning to ash over. This is a hot fire. You can recognize a medium-hot fire when the coals are no longer red but instead are ashen.

For a gas grill, read the manufacturer's directions for the time it takes the grill to reach the desired temperature. Or use the hand method (see box, right) or a grill thermometer to judge the grill's temperature.

ADJUSTING YOUR GRILL'S TEMPERATURE

On a charcoal grill, always begin the fire with the bottom or side vents open. Lower the temperature by partially closing the vents, and raise the temperature by opening the vents or by adding more charcoal to ratchet up the fire. More air means the fire will burn faster and hotter; less air makes for a slower and lower fire.

On a gas grill, adjust the heat by turning the heat control knobs to the desired level. Most heat control knobs are marked "high," "medium," and "low," although some are marked only "high" and "low." On some models, you can control the temperature by turning the temperature dial.

On a wood pellet grill, you just turn the dial to the temperature you want. Other electric units may produce only one temperature or have a temperature dial for adjusting the temperature.

Gas Grilling with a Kiss of Smoke

A gas grill is very easy to use but does not impart the flavor that hardwood charcoal or wood pellets do. To get more wood smoke flavor on a gas grill, moisten the wood chips

---

The Hand Method for Judging a Grill's Temperature

Hold your hand 5 inches above the heat source. If you can hold it there for about 2 seconds, your fire is hot (about 500°F or more) and perfect for grilling. Being able to hold your hand there for 3 seconds indicates a medium-hot fire (about 400°F), good for grilling; 4 seconds indicates a medium fire (about 350°F), for grilling or higher-heat indirect cooking; and 5 to 6 seconds indicates a low fire (200 to 250°F), ideal for slow smoking.

or place dry wood pellets in an aluminum foil packet. Poke holes in the packet and place on the grill rack directly over the heat. The wood chips or pellets will smolder rather than burn, adding smoky flavor. Do not put chips or pellets directly on the lava rock, metal flame guard, or ceramic plates in the bottom of the grill, because the residue could block the holes in the gas burners. This is definitely *not* a good thing.

Getting Ready to Grill

The grill should be clean and the grill rack lightly oiled prior to starting the fire. We like to use Grate Chef Grill Wipes, premoistened towelettes for oiling and cleaning the grill.

Have all your equipment handy.

Decide whether you are going to cook with the grill lid closed, which will allow you to cook your food faster and conserve fuel, or with the lid open, which will require a hot fire to sear the food you are grilling.

Preparing Food for Grilling

Preparing food for grilling can be as simple as brushing it with olive oil and seasoning it with salt and pepper or applying a marinade, sauce, or rub beforehand. Preparing food in these ways will help it stay juicier and more flavorful when grilled. Avoid rubs, marinades, or sauces with a high sugar content, because the sugar will burn as it grills. Also, remove any excess marinade or sauce that might drip onto the heat source and flare up.

How to Grill

Once your grill is at the proper temperature, place the food on the hot grill grate. Let it sear and char before turning it with grill tongs or a grill spatula. We prefer not to use a grill fork, because it pokes holes in the food and causes the juices to escape. Avoid turning the food unless the recipe says to do so. The food needs to sit undisturbed for a time to get those lovely grill marks.

BASTING

Some foods that tend to dry out with the hot, fast searing of the grill—such as boneless, skinless chicken breasts; thin, butterflied pork chops; and fish or shellfish—might benefit from the moisture and flavor of basting. A baste can be any liquid that will provide moisture, from fruit juice to a vinaigrette to a melted butter- or olive oil–based sauce. A baste also adds flavor to food. Use a basting brush to coat food during grilling. Always make sure that the basting sauce is cooked off—meaning that if you baste the top of the chicken breast, for example, you turn it to cook the baste, which may have come in contact with the raw meat when it was first placed on the grill.

An eye-catching way to baste is to use an herb brush. Gather together a small bouquet of fresh mint, lavender, rosemary, thyme, or other herb. Tie the stems together tightly with kitchen twine or a twist tie. Dip your brush into the basting liquid and baste as described above. Mint brushes are delicious with lamb; rosemary brushes work well with pork and poultry.

GLAZING

A glaze usually contains sugar, which will burn if left too long over a hot fire. To avoid scorching your food, apply the glaze during the last 5 to 10 minutes of grilling.

Sweet tomato-based barbecue sauce is probably the most popular glaze used in American backyard grilling. Barbecue sauce gives food a pretty sheen and color. Jams, jellies, and preserves, which are heated to melt them before they are applied, add a sheen and sweet flavor to grilled poultry and pork. A grilled ham steak glazed with apricot preserves or chicken paillards glazed with cherry preserves are both pretty and delicious.

Grilling Times

Estimated grilling times are just that—estimates, not hard and fast rules. In every recipe, we give you an estimate of how long something will take to grill, but we also give you a doneness signal—an internal temperature or appearance—that will let you know when the food is done. When you cook outdoors, the weather is a big factor in cooking time. Things grill faster on hot days than on cold ones.

People in our cooking classes always seem to worry that foods won't be cooked properly on a grill. Don't worry about undercooking food. If you want to fret about something, fret about overcooking it. Undercooked food can always be put back on the grill, or you can finish cooking it by zapping it in the microwave for a few seconds or putting it in the oven. If food is undercooked, you can always rescue it. If food is overcooked, you've got nowhere to go but the grilling doghouse.

GRILLING TIMETABLE

People usually grill small, thin cuts of meat. For these, we prefer a hot fire, around 500°F, because we like a little char. If you don't, cook over a medium to medium-hot fire and increase the cooking time by 2 to 3 minutes. We recommend turning meat or fish once, halfway through the total cooking time.

Beefsteak	1 inch thick	8 minutes for rare
Burger	½ inch thick	8 minutes for rare
Chicken breast paillard	½ inch thick	4 minutes for done
Chicken leg or thigh	5 to 8 ounces each	8 to 12 minutes for done
Fish fillet or steak	5 to 8 ounces each	10 minutes per inch of thickness
Lamb chop	1 inch thick	8 minutes for rare
Pork loin or rib chop	1 inch thick	8 minutes for rare
Pork steak or blade	1 inch thick	8 minutes for rare
Pork tenderloin	2 inches thick	12 to 15 minutes for rare

WHEN TO PULL FOOD OFF THE GRILL

We recommend that if you're just starting to grill, you use an instant-read meat thermometer to test the doneness of grilled chicken, pork, beef, veal, lamb, and game. Insert the thermometer in the thickest part of the meat and read the temperature. After a while, you'll be able to tell the doneness of grilled meats by touch alone. When you touch a pork tenderloin with tongs and it's soft and wiggly, it's too rare. When the tenderloin begins to offer some resistance, it's rare to medium-rare. When it just begins to firm up, it's medium. When it feels solid, it's well done. You can also tell how red meat is cooked by its color. When the internal temperature of red meat is under 140°F, it is red; from 140 to 160°F, the color ranges from red to pink; at 175°F, the meat is brown or gray and very well done.

Fish doneness is best judged by appearance. Fish is done when it begins to flake when tested with a fork in the thickest part. Shellfish is done when it is opaque and somewhat firm to the touch. Vegetables are done when they look done and are cooked to your preferred degree of tenderness. Breads are done when they have risen and browned.

Foods continue to cook for a few minutes after they're taken off the grill, raising the internal temperature another 5 to 10°F. Use our doneness chart (see page 17) as a guideline in helping you choose the desired degree of doneness you prefer. Take the internal temperature of meat while it is on the grill and consider that the temperature will continue to rise off the grill. If a pork loin registers an internal temperature of 145°F on the grill, it will go up to 150 to 155°F while resting for 10 to 15 minutes before slicing. If you leave the pork loin on the grill or smoker until it reaches 155°F, it will be 160 to 165°F once it has rested. By the time meat reaches 175°F, it is too well done, making it dry and less appetizing. For more information about safe meat temperatures, call the USDA Meat and Poultry Hotline at (888) 674-6854.

Burgers can be made from beef, chicken, lamb, pork, or even tuna. Because they're all ground and have a similar texture and volume, they follow the same doneness guidelines. The Centers for Disease Control and Prevention does not recommend eating undercooked (pink) ground beef, but hey, you're the grill mistress; you make the call.

DONENESS CHART FOR GRILLING

Personal preferences run the gamut from very rare to very well done. Use this chart as a guideline for your outdoor grilling.

Beefsteak	125°F for rare, 140°F for medium, 160°F for well done
Burger	140°F for medium, 160°F for well done
Chicken breast	160°F
Chicken leg or thigh	165°F
Fish fillet or steak	Begins to flake when tested with a fork in thickest part
Lamb chop	125°F for rare, 140°F for medium
Pork loin or rib chop	140°F for medium
Pork tenderloin	140°F for medium, 160°F for well done
Shellfish	Opaque and somewhat firm to the touch
Turkey breast	165°F
Turkey leg or thigh	175 to 180°F
Veal chop	125°F for rare, 140°F for medium, 160°F for well done
Vegetables	Cooked to your liking

Smoking 101

With most types of grills or smokers—including gas grills—you can slow smoke almost any food for delicious barbecue in your own backyard. Most grills can be set up to function as a smoker, as long as they have a lid that can be closed. Some smokers can function as a grill, too, while others can function only as a smoker. Be aware of this and ask the right questions for the kind of grilling or smoking you want to do.

People who sell smoking equipment will ask whether you're a "backyarder," meaning that you barbecue only in your own backyard for friends and family, or a "competitor," meaning that you participate in barbecue contests. Backyarders can use just about any kind of smoker, including those that run on electricity, but competitors rely mainly on the charcoal type.

The Best Smoker for You

The kind of smoker you choose is determined by the space you have, the kind of fuel you want to use, the amount of cooking surface you need, and how much money you want to spend. The fuel choices are gas, electric, charcoal, and hardwood. Some of the most popular units for home use are Weber kettle-shaped charcoal grills, the charcoal Weber Smokey Mountain Cooker, and the Brinkmann, Weber, and Char-Broil bullet-shaped water smokers, which are variously fueled by charcoal, electricity, or gas. These units are moderately priced, ranging from under $50 to $250, and can be used for grilling and smoking. Backyarders also can use wood pellet grills, ceramic smokers, smoker ovens, and gas grills with two or more burners for smoking. Some gas grills can even be adapted to cook with charcoal or charcoal and gas at the same time. Passionate backyarders may even use medium to large smoking rigs or pit smokers with a firebox on the side.

Competition barbecuers usually start out small with a Weber charcoal grill or a Weber Smokey Mountain Cooker, then graduate to bigger smoking rigs. Our barbecue buddy Paul Kirk has a special rig costing around $18,000 that he hauls on a trailer to barbecue events. This type of smoker uses both charcoal and "sticks," or pieces of hardwood cut to fit the width of the firebox.

Preparing Your "Pit," Equipment, and Utensils

Your grill or smoker should be clean, and your fuel should be handy. Wood chips should be soaked in water for at least 30 minutes before smoking. Wood chunks need to be soaked for at least an hour. If you're using flavored wood pellets, use them dry; when wet, wood pellets turn to mush. If you prepare your food and have all your equipment ready, your smoking experience will be relaxing and enjoyable.

Lighting and Fueling the Fire

You light the fire for the smoker in the same way you do for grilling, whether you're using a charcoal, gas, wood pellet, electric, or kamado grill or a big smoker rig. The difference is that you prepare an indirect fire and keep the temperature lower, around 200 to 250°F.

CHARCOAL GRILLS

Use a charcoal chimney, electric fire starter, or solid starters to light the hardwood lump charcoal. When the coals have ashed over, position the coals on one or both sides of the grill, so that the other side of the grill or the center section is indirect. Place a metal or disposable aluminum pan of water beside the coals. Place the grill rack over the top. The section(s) with the coals is direct heat; the section with the water is indirect heat. Use grill thermometers to monitor the temperature in both sections. Ideally, smoking is done at a temperature (measured in the indirect section) of 200 to 250°F.

CHARCOAL WATER SMOKERS

Start your charcoal in a charcoal chimney. Place the coals in the bottom third of the smoker (the firebox). Place wood chunks or chips or aluminum foil packets of wood pellets on the coals for optimum smoke flavor. Fill the water pan and place it in the second chamber of the smoker. The grill racks (usually two) fit directly above the water pan. Close the lid and monitor the fire until it is about 275°F. (*Note:* The lid on this type of smoker does not fit tightly, allowing for air and smoke to circulate.) When the food is placed in the smoker, it will probably lower the temperature to the desired 200 to 250°F. You can grill on a charcoal water smoker by placing the grill rack directly over the charcoal fire in the firebox. You do not use the other chambers for grilling.

ELECTRIC AND GAS WATER SMOKERS

Like a charcoal water smoker, electric and gas smokers are usually built in three sections. In an electric model, the bottom section is a bed of lava rock on which an electric coil rests. Gas smokers have a covered gas flame unit. Add an aluminum foil packet of water-soaked wood chips or dry wood pellets near but not touching the heating elements. The next section of the smoker contains the water pan and the smoker racks, on which you place the food to be smoked. The third portion of the smoker is the lid. Cover the smoker, plug it in or turn on the gas, and set the thermostat (if it has one) to 200 to 250°F. Then leave it alone. Resist the urge to lift the lid and keep checking the meat or food you are smoking. The more you lift the lid, the longer the food will take to smoke. The temperature should remain at a fairly constant 200 to 250°F.

These are the BBQ Queens' favorite smokers. We call them outdoor slow cookers. You turn them on and almost forget about them, which frees you to make the rest of the meal (or do your nails, read a book, whatever).

COMPETITION-STYLE SMOKERS

A big smoker rig usually has a large cooking chamber with a firebox attached to the side. This offset firebox is where the charcoal fire is built. The food smokes in the main chamber from the indirect heat produced in the firebox. The firebox has its own door, so you can add more charcoal or wood when necessary, without having to open the door to the large smoking chamber. A venting system with dampers between the firebox and the main chamber helps control the heat and the amount of smoke flowing into the main chamber. Smaller models can use charcoal or wood chunks. Larger models might rely on hickory, oak, cherry, or apple logs for both heat and smoke. The food is smoked on racks in the larger chamber.

GAS GRILLS

To prepare an indirect fire on a gas grill, you need one with two or more burners. Turn one burner on and leave the other one off. The side with the burner on is direct heat; the side with the burner off is indirect heat. You may place a water pan in the back of the grill on the direct side. Add water-soaked wood chips or dry wood pellets to the direct side of the grill above the fire by placing the wood in a metal smoker box or in an aluminum foil packet that has been poked with holes. The presoaked wood chips or dry wood pellets will smolder and smoke and give the food a luscious smoky flavor. Some gas grills have a built-in smoker box, to which you can add water-soaked wood chips or dry wood pellets and even regulate the heat.

WOOD PELLET GRILLS

Wood pellet grills are designed for indirect cooking only. The ignition and flame are about a foot below the grill rack where the food is placed. To turn this type of grill into a smoker, set the temperature at 200 to 250°F and close the lid. Wood pellets are available in more than a dozen different flavors, from alder and mesquite to mulberry and sassafras.

KAMADO GRILLS

Kamado smokers have a ceramic firebox for the charcoal at the inner base. The charcoal can be started by placing two or three crumpled pieces of newspaper on the bottom and placing enough charcoal on top so that when the paper burns and the charcoal settles, it is just below the air holes in the firebox. You may use an electric fire starter, but never use lighter fluid for this kind of grill. The kamado does not need very much charcoal, so start with a small amount as you learn to regulate the heat a small fire can produce. Again, aim for a temperature of 200 to 250°F for slow smoking.

ADDING WOOD FOR SMOKE FLAVOR

When you're slow smoking at a low temperature, the flavor comes from smoldering aromatic woods—hickory, cherry, oak, mesquite, pecan, and others—that are placed on or near the fire. But beware: most slow smokers agree that there is nothing worse than too much smoke. When the BBQ Queens were learning how to barbecue, we both made the mistake of thinking, "If three chunks of wood are good, maybe five are better," and ended up with inedibly bitter food. Err on the side of too little smoke. You can always put the food back in for more smoking, but oversmoked food can't be rescued.

You may use several different types of woods, depending on the type of smoking equipment you have.

Fine wood chips: For the stovetop smoker. These chips are a little bigger than sawdust. You use them dry and in small amounts—1 to 2 tablespoons placed in the middle of the bottom of the smoker. When you place the smoker over a heat source, these fine chips smolder and burn, giving off aromatic smoke. Medium-high heat is used for stovetop smoking, which means that the food cooks quite fast. The smoke is able to penetrate the food well because the unit itself is very small and the smoke quite intense.

Shredded wood chips: For charcoal and gas grills or smokers. These small pieces of wood should be soaked in water for at least 30 minutes before using. You want them to smolder, not burn. Use about 1 cup at a time and replenish them every hour or so. In a charcoal grill or smoker, scatter them directly on the coals. In a gas grill or in an electric bullet

Great Smoke Flavors

WOOD FLAVORS

Whether you use logs, sticks, chunks, pellets, shreds, sawdust, vines, or chips, hardwoods can infuse foods with great smoke flavor. From common hardwoods such as hickory and oak to grapevines and sassafras, the variety of woods for smoking is wide and delicious. Many woods are synonymous with regional barbecuing, such as hickory smoke from the South, where hickory trees are plentiful, mesquite smoke from the Southwest, and alder from the Northwest. A word of caution: do not use resinous or sappy softwoods such as pine, or your food will be inedible.

- **Alder:** Gives a light, aromatic flavor. Alder and seafood are a match made in heaven.

- **Apple:** Provides a sweeter, aromatic flavor that is good with chicken or pork. It's also used in combination with hickory and oak by competition barbecuers.

- **Black walnut:** Lends a strong smoke flavor that is delicious with game, pork, and beef.

- **Cedar:** Provides a strong flavor that is good with salmon, chicken, and shrimp. Usually used as planks for wood planking.

- **Cherry:** Lends a deeper, sweeter note to smoked foods. Cherry is delicious with beef tenderloin, pork, chicken, and lamb.

- **Citrus:** Gives a moderate fruit flavor that is great with fish, seafood, poultry, and fruit.

- **Grapevines:** Provides a medium fruit flavor that pairs well with game, lamb, and poultry.

- **Hickory:** Gives a strong, hearty smoke flavor that is perfect for beef, pork, and chicken.

- **Maple:** Lends a mild flavor to ham, pork, and poultry.

- **Mesquite:** Provides the strongest, smokiest flavor and is best suited to beef, especially brisket. Make sure you don't use too much, or your food will taste acrid.

- **Mulberry:** Gives a flavor similar to grapevine smoke and works nicely with pork, poultry, ham, and game birds.

- **Oak:** Provides a medium smoke flavor without being bitter and goes well with any food.

- **Oak barrel wood:** Provides a unique smoke flavor similar to "oaky" wines, such as some Chardonnays. These wood chunks and chips are made from oak barrels used to age wine.

- **Orange:** Gives a moderate fruit flavor that is great with fish, seafood, poultry, and fruit.

- **Peach:** Lends a moderate fruit flavor to fish, seafood, poultry, and fruit.

- **Pear:** Provides a moderate fruit flavor that's nice with fish, seafood, poultry, and fruit.

- **Pecan:** Creates a medium smoke flavor that is less pronounced than hickory but more pronounced than oak. Pecan is great to use for grilling fish, poultry, and pork with a kiss of smoke.

- **Sassafras:** Lends a musky flavor that is good with lamb, pork, and poultry.

OTHER SMOKE FLAVORS

Smoke flavor also comes from a variety of other flora. Fresh herbs on the fire emit a fragrant scent. When herb leaves die off in the fall, those woody stems (from lavender, rosemary, thyme, or lemon balm) are perfect for adding smoky flavor. We like the flavor of mint stalks and lemon balm thrown on the fire. Try branches of rosemary while grilling or smoking lamb. Dried corncobs, ground up or not, can be thrown on a hot fire to create a sweet smokiness. Cornhusks add a smoky flavor as well. A little bit of hay can make a sweet, smoky difference (see Prairie-Style Hay-Smoked Steak on page 326). The shells of pecans, peanuts, almonds, walnuts, and other nuts add flavor, too. Even fruit tree leaves can be used on a fire for an interesting smoke flavor. And if you live by the coast, seaweed may be your ticket to a tempting smoky meal.

The BBQ Queens agree that slow smoking enhances meats and vegetables with a deeper smoke flavor than grilling. However, we have a theory about adding various woods, herbs, and the like to a hot grill fire. Although this smoke may not have enough time to penetrate the meat, the smoke does permeate the air around you, your clothes, and your skin. So when you throw aromatics on the fire, even for just a short time, the aroma will be part of the sensual experience as you devour your grilled foods.

smoker, place them in an aluminum foil packet, poke holes in the packet, and place it on the grill rack over the heat (in a gas grill) or near the electric coil (in an electric smoker). You also may use a metal smoker box instead of a foil packet.

Wood pellets: For charcoal, gas, electric, and wood pellet grills or smokers. These are basically pellet-shaped bits of compressed sawdust used in wood pellet grills for fuel and wood smoke flavor. You can also use them with other grills or smokers. Wood pellets must be used dry; if you moisten them, they turn into a mushy sawdust. Because you don't have to soak them, they are always ready to go. Plus, because they are compressed, they take up less space than other wood products. For smoking, use $1/3$ cup at a time. For a charcoal grill or smoker, place the pellets in an aluminum foil packet, poke holes in the packet, and place it directly on the coals. For a gas grill or an electric bullet smoker, place the packet on the grill rack over the heat (in a gas grill) or near the electric coil (in an electric smoker). A metal smoker box may be used instead of the foil packets. Wood pellets must be replenished about every hour (the wood pellet grill does this automatically).

Wood chunks: For charcoal and electric smokers. These are bigger pieces of aromatic wood, 3 to 4 inches long and wide. You need to soak them for at least 1 hour before using. Wood chunks are most often placed directly on hot coals or near but not touching the electric coil. We don't recommend using wood chunks with a gas grill because they're not as effective as wood pellets or chips. Three or four wood chunks will last 2 to 3 hours when you're slow smoking.

Wood "sticks" or logs: For big smoker rigs. These are even bigger pieces of wood, cut to fit the diameter of the firebox and placed right on the hot coals. Use three sticks to start and replenish them as necessary.

Getting Ready to Smoke

The smoker should be clean and the rack(s) lightly oiled. Have all your equipment handy. If you are using charcoal, have plenty on hand. If you are using gas, make sure your tanks are full. Soak wood chips or chunks in water (at least 30 minutes for chips, an hour for chunks) or have dry wood pellets handy.

Place the wood of your choice on or near the heat source, according to the kind of smoker you have, and follow the manufacturer's directions. The directions may or may not tell you the amount of wood to use. Our recommendation is to use wood during the first 2 to 3 hours of cooking. Different smokers burn wood at different rates, so you will have to check the smoker and replenish the wood as necessary. For foods that take longer to smoke, such as brisket or pork butt, check to see whether the food has a good smoky aroma before adding more wood during the longer cooking time. It may not need more smoke flavor.

Smoke with the lid or hood closed. This will trap the heat and smoke, allowing greater circulation and a steadier temperature.

Adjusting Your Smoker's Temperature

On a charcoal grill, lower the temperature by closing the vents; raise the temperature by opening the vents or adding more charcoal. Keeping the lid on the smoker closed will also help maintain a steady temperature.

On a gas grill, adjust the heat by turning the control knobs to the desired level. For smoking, adjust the heat control on one burner while leaving the other burner(s) off. Some models allow you to control the temperature by turning a temperature dial. You can also crack the lid slightly to lower the temperature.

On an electric grill, turn the temperature dial to 200 to 250°F.

> ## The Hand Method for Judging a Smoker's Temperature
>
> If your unit has a temperature gauge, set the temperature to 200 to 250°F. If it does not, hold your hand 5 inches above the indirect section of a grill or over the rack in a smoker. If you can hold it there for only 5 to 6 seconds, the fire is ideal for slow smoking.

Preparing Food for Smoking

Preparing food for smoking can be as simple as brushing it with olive oil and seasoning it with salt and pepper. Foods for the smoker stay more juicy and flavorful when marinated, slathered, or rubbed beforehand. Even delicate foods such as cheese need to be brushed or sprayed with olive oil, or they may develop an unappetizing bronze "skin."

How to Smoke

When your smoker is at the proper temperature of 200 to 250°F, place the food on the grill racks or in a disposable aluminum pan, set in the smoker, and close the lid. Let the food cook and smoke for about half of the total cooking time before checking it. Remember, the more you open the smoker, the more the temperature will drop, the more smoke you will lose, and the longer your food will take to get done.

When the BBQ Queens smoke on an electric bullet-shaped water smoker, which registers a constant 225°F, this is how we figure our cooking time. In moderate, calm weather with an outside temperature of 60 to 75°F, we estimate our smoking time at 20 to 30 minutes per pound, with at least 3 to 4 pounds of food on the smoker. For instance, a 12-pound whole turkey will take 4 to 6 hours to smoke. For a turkey, we stoke the smoker with three to five chunks of wood, fill the water pan, close the lid, and smoke for 2 to 3 hours without lifting the lid. If you have a charcoal smoker, you may have to check on the food sooner to add more fuel to the fire.

BASTING

Some foods, such as ribs, brisket, and pork butt, which take several hours to smoke, can benefit from basting. A baste can be any liquid that will provide moisture, from black coffee, cider vinegar, or apple juice to flavorful mixtures such as Rosemary, Garlic, and Lemon Baste (page 68), Homemade Teriyaki Marinade (page 69), and Lemon Butter Drizzle (page 87). A baste adds moisture and flavor to smoked foods. Traditionally, fatty foods such as pork butt or brisket get a bracing, somewhat acidic baste with coffee, vinegar, or apple juice to help cut the fat. Nonfatty foods such as fish or shellfish are more likely to get a moistening baste of butter or olive oil.

Thin basting mixtures, especially those with some sugar in them, also can add a sheen to foods. Homemade Teriyaki Marinade (page 69) is terrific for adding a "lacquered" finish to grilled or smoked foods.

Let the food smoke for an hour or so before basting. Remember to allow more cooking time when basting because opening the lid for basting will lower the temperature inside.

GLAZING

Glazing is done during the last 30 to 60 minutes of smoking. This process also adds a sheen to smoked or grilled foods. Glazing is usually done with barbecue sauce, which contains some sugar or corn syrup and thus creates a burnished, satin finish. Fruit preserves and glazes made with preserves are popular for pork, poultry, and ham.

To glaze foods such as ribs or chicken, turn them bottom side up and brush with barbecue sauce or another glaze. Cover the smoker and let the sauce set for 15 to 30 minutes. Then turn the food over, brush with glaze, close the lid, and let the sauce set for another 15 to 30 minutes. Serve more sauce at the table.

Smoking Times

Smoking times vary based on the heat of the fire, the temperature outdoors, and whether the day is windy, sunny, overcast, or rainy. The better you can control the temperature of your smoker, the easier it is to estimate the cooking time and the better your barbecue will be.

Exact time is less crucial with smoking than with grilling, because smoking is a gentler cooking process. But smoking foods too long will give them a bitter flavor. Use the suggested cooking time given in each recipe as a guide, but also watch your food while it's smoking and use an instant-read meat thermometer inserted in the thickest part to gauge doneness. To be on the safe side, we recommend allowing about an hour extra when smoking any food.

SMOKING TIMETABLE

This chart provides some idea of how long foods will take to smoke at 200 to 250°F. The better you can control your fire, and thus the temperature, the more reliable these cooking times will be.

Beef brisket (trimmed)	10 to 12 lbs.	12 to 15 hours
Chicken (whole)	4 to 5 lbs.	2$\frac{1}{2}$ to 3 hours
Chicken breast (bone-in)	4 lbs.	1$\frac{1}{2}$ to 2$\frac{1}{2}$ hours
Lamb (leg)	6 to 8 lbs.	3 to 4$\frac{1}{2}$ hours
Pork (Boston) butt	6 to 7 lbs.	8 to 12 hours
Pork loin roast	4 to 5 lbs.	3 to 3$\frac{1}{2}$ hours
Pork ribs (2 slabs at a time)		
Baby back	3 to 4 lbs.	3$\frac{1}{2}$ to 4 hours
Spareribs	5 to 6 lbs.	4 to 6 hours
Pork sausage	1$\frac{1}{2}$ to 2$\frac{1}{2}$ in. diam.	1 to 3 hours
Turkey (whole)	10 to 12 lbs.	5 to 6 hours
Turkey breast (boneless)	3 lbs.	1$\frac{1}{2}$ to 2 hours

DONENESS CHART FOR SMOKING

Knowing at what temperature your smoked food is done is crucial. You want succulent, moist, tender barbecue—not dried-out jerky. For ribs, the doneness test is visual—when the rib meat has pulled back about an inch from the bones. The BBQ Queens use both heat-safe meat thermometers (inserted in brisket or pork butt and left in during smoking) and instant-read meat thermometers (quickly inserted in foods and then removed).

Beef brisket (trimmed)	10 to 12 lbs.	160°F
Chicken (whole)	4 to 5 lbs.	175°F
Chicken breast (bone-in)	4 lbs.	165°F
Lamb (leg)	6 to 8 lbs.	140 to 145°F
Pork (Boston) butt	6 to 7 lbs.	160°F
Pork loin roast	4 to 5 lbs.	145 to 155°F
Pork ribs (2 slabs at a time)		
Baby back	3 to 4 lbs.	Meat pulls back from bone
Spareribs	5 to 6 lbs.	Meat pulls back from bone
Pork sausage	1½ to 2½ in. diam.	150 to 155°F
Turkey (whole)	10 to 12 lbs.	175 to 180°F
Turkey breast (boneless)	3 lbs.	170 to 175°F

Now Let's Have Some Fun!

Want to add even more pizzazz to your outdoor cooking repertoire? We like to wow family, friends, and other foodies with skewers of all kinds, wok baskets made specifically for the grill, stovetop smoking, rotisserie meat preparation, and wood plank cooking.

Skewering on all kinds of sticks, from traditional wooden skewers to herb stalks and even sugar cane, is fun indeed. A whole meal prepared in a grill wok is simplicity at its best. (Try shrimp with seasonal fresh vegetables for a winner every time.) Similarly, a stovetop smoker can give you great smoke flavor all year-round in any kind of weather. Move over rotisserie chicken! A pork loin roast or beef tenderloin is succulent when spit roasted. And there's nothing prettier than a salmon fillet planked on cedar. The combination of pink salmon and burnished wood looks great and tastes even better.

The Art of the Skewer

Sometimes BBQ Queens just wanna have fun. We always have fun out at the grill or smoker, where everyone seems to gather. When we want to have even more fun, we grill something a little unexpected. Our new fun favorite is arranging food on skewers, in unusual, eye-catching ways. Think "stick" in its many forms: fresh rosemary or lavender branches, sugar cane, lemongrass, bamboo, or the old campfire standard, the twig. Or how about round skewers? Those new coiled metal skewers produced by Charcoal Companion look snazzy served on dinner plates.

SKEWERING 101

The first decision is the skewer itself, and you have lots of choices here.

Wooden skewers, which come in packages at the grocery store, need to be soaked in water for at least 30 minutes before threading them with food and grilling. After grilling, you just throw the charred skewers away.

Reusable metal skewers, some with prongs on both ends, or the new metal coil skewers can be easily cleaned with soapy water after grilling , then towel-dried so they don't get water spots. We generally prefer flat metal skewers to wooden ones (see page 32).

Kabob baskets—some long and cylindrical, others wide and flat to hold several metal skewers at a time—are a good choice if you like to grill skewers a lot and want more control when grilling. You need to spray or brush the baskets with oil before grilling so the food doesn't stick. When you're ready to turn the skewers, you just flip the entire basket.

Finally, there are natural skewers, such as herb stalks. Fresh rosemary and lavender branches, bamboo, lemongrass, sugar cane, and twigs from the yard are all safe for food to touch. Before you branch out into the unknown, however, check to make sure that natural skewers are safe to use. Poisoning your barbecue guests with mystery skewers is not a queenly thing to do.

We've found that the best way to make sure all the food gets done at the same time is to avoid those 1950s-style kabobs, with meat or chicken and vegetables all on one stick. We think it's better to have all vegetables, meat, fish, or fruit on one skewer so that every-

Herb Grilling

In an old nursery rhyme and children's song, the king was in his countinghouse, counting all his money. The queen was in the parlor, eating bread and honey. In real time, the men in our lives watch the daily rise and fall of the stock market (more rise than fall, we hope). And we, the BBQ Queens, would rather putter around in our herb gardens than eat bread and honey.

A few years ago, Karen laid out four formal raised beds in her backyard, where a profusion of herbs (basil, Italian parsley, lemon balm, tarragon, and oregano) grows along with her beloved heirloom tomatoes. Judith practices container gardening for herbs that can't withstand the extremes of Kansas weather—bay, scented geranium (Rober's Lemon Rose is her favorite), lemon verbena, and lemongrass.

We wish we could say that we summon various vassals to do the transplanting, weeding, and watering, but not so. We're hands-on queens, so we put on our working tiaras (black sun visors with a glittery tiara design—very chic) and head outdoors.

We both love the fresh scent and taste of herbs and use them whenever we can. Fresh or dried, herbs can really enhance the flavor of foods before, during, or even after grilling. Here's how you do it.

Before grilling: Slather Rosemary Pesto (page 62) on beef or pork tenderloin or boneless chicken breasts, then grill over medium heat. Infuse fish and shellfish with aromatic Lemongrass Marinade (page 74). Use marinades with lots of herbs, such as Amogio (page 72), Chimichurri Sauce (page 346), and Aromatic Lemon-Herb Marinade (page 68), for fish, poultry, and pork.

Use fresh herb stalks as skewers for grilled foods of all kinds. Thread shrimp or scallops on slender but sturdy stalks of lemongrass or lemon verbena. Thread chunks of

thing cooks evenly and you don't have a charred cherry tomato next to a bloody chunk of beef. Leave about 1/8 inch of space between foods on a skewer. If the pieces are squashed together, the inside surfaces where they touch will not cook as fast as the outside surfaces. And goodness knows you don't want chicken sushi on a stick.

beef, pork, or parboiled new potatoes on fresh rosemary stalks. Thread fresh peach or nectarine halves on sturdy lavender stalks. Sandwich fresh scented geranium leaves between nectarine or peach halves or large, pitted sweet cherries on a metal or pre-soaked wooden skewer.

During grilling: Stir-grill cherry tomatoes with fresh basil and mint in a grill wok. Grill chicken breasts or portobello mushrooms on a hinged grill rack with fresh herb branches sandwiched inside. Or try our favorite Silver Queen Corn Queen's Rosemary-Scented Grilled Butterflied Chicken (page 205), grilled over a bed of fresh rosemary.

Thinly slice potatoes lengthwise, then sandwich a fresh sage leaf between two potato slices, brush with olive oil, and grill. Use fresh herb branches to baste foods during grilling. When you cut back your woody herbs in the fall, save the trimmings and place them on a charcoal fire for grilling fish, chicken, or a boneless leg of lamb—in the Provençal way. Wrap fingers of bread dough in large leafy herbs, brush with olive oil, and grill, as in Grilled Leaf-Wrapped Bread Sticks (page 181). Simmer apple jelly or a mild honey with fresh or dried herbs to use as a glaze during the last minutes of grilling chicken breasts, pork tenderloin, or lamb chops.

After grilling: Serve Rustic Béarnaise Sauce (page 98) with grilled shrimp, salmon, or chicken. Make a simple Gremolata (page 274) with freshly grated lemon zest, Italian parsley, and garlic. Swirl together butter, tomato *concassé*, fresh basil, and fresh lemon juice for an aromatically wonderful finishing touch over grilled veggies, chicken, or fish. Or serve Thousand-Herb Sauce (page 192) over grilled chicken, fish, shellfish, pork, or lamb.

When you grill skewers, try to arrange them so that they are not in danger of falling through the grill grate. If we can, we place them horizontally and turn them with grill tongs. If you're really worried about your food falling though the grate, use a kabob basket or place the skewers on a perforated grill rack, then on the grate.

Food on a skewer will take anywhere from 20 seconds to 10 minutes to grill, so grilling skewers is fast, fast, fast—perfect for Grill Gals on the move.

Wok on the Wild Side

Stir-grilling foods over a hot fire is a great way to make lowfat, one-dish meals on the grill—and no mess in the kitchen! You can, if you wish, serve stir-grilled dishes with steamed rice, soba noodles, pasta ribbons, or couscous, but they're also terrific on their own. Stir-grilled meals add lots of big flavor but few calories to any healthy eating plan.

STIR-GRILLING 101

To stir-grill, you need a grill wok, a hexagonal metal wok with perforations (they usually cost less than $30), along with wooden spoons, paddles, or long-handled spatulas. The perforations in the wok allow for more of the wood and charcoal flavors to penetrate the food. The standard wok is 12 inches, but some manufacturers also make a 15-inch wok. The BBQ Queens prefer a bigger wok because more space means potentially more char and more room for a larger quantity of food. We like to use long-handled wooden paddles or spoons to toss the food in a grill wok. We call this technique "stir-grilling," a similar but healthier alternative to stir-frying.

To stir-grill, first marinate the food—sometimes overnight, sometimes just for 30 minutes—in a sealable plastic bag in the refrigerator. Then prepare a hot fire in the grill and coat the inside of the grill wok with nonstick cooking spray. Place the prepared wok in the sink and dump the bag of marinated food into the wok. The marinade will drain away. Place the wok on a baking sheet and take it outside to the grill. Place the wok over direct heat and stir-grill the food, using wooden paddles or long-handled spoons or metal grill spatulas, until done.

When choosing what to stir-grill, think like a gal—fresh, colorful vegetables cut into interesting sizes and shapes and tender cuts of meat, such as chicken breasts and pork or beef tenderloin. The finished dish will have great eye appeal, as well as being healthy and delicious.

Burnin' Ring of Fire: Rotisserie Cooking

Rotisserie cooking, or spit roasting, is habit-forming. Once you do it, you're hooked. Just ask Diane Phillips, a BBQ Babe (see page 434) whose specialty is rotisserie cooking. Check out her book *The Ultimate Rotisserie Cookbook* (The Harvard Common Press, 2002).

What hooks you with rotisserie cooking is the flavor. As the spit constantly turns, the food bastes in its own juices, producing an exceptionally tender and moist result. (And don't you know, the BBQ Queens love tender!) Whole birds; beef, lamb, veal, and pork roasts; and ribs are all excellent candidates for the outdoor rotisserie. (See the box on page 40 for information about rotisserie cooking fish and vegetables.) This is certainly a nice alternative to have in your culinary arsenal.

THE RIGHT ROTISSERIE FOR THE JOB

When you buy an electric rotisserie for your grill, make sure the motor has adequate power to turn the size and weight of food you want to cook. The manufacturer's directions should make this clear for a whole turkey (10 to 12 pounds), a boneless prime rib roast (9 to 14 pounds), a whole pork loin roast (5 to 6 pounds), and a whole chicken (4 to 5 pounds).

ROTISSERIE COOKING 101

First, set up your rotisserie on the grill. On charcoal grills, the rotisserie unit is often an add-on product that needs to be clamped to the sides of the grill. We recommend that you follow the manufacturer's directions for doing this and for placing the drip pan beneath the meat. On some gas grills, the cooking grate(s) must be removed and the lava rock moved aside so a drip pan can be placed on the rock grate directly beneath where the meat will sit on the spit. In either case, the drip pan should contain about an inch of liquid—a marinade, vinegar, juice, beer, wine, or just plain water. This liquid will steam up into the meat, adding moisture and a wonderful aroma as the meat turns and cooks.

Do not skewer the meat and place it on a lit grill until you are certain that everything is set up properly. With the grill off or unlit, measure the meat over the drip pan. The pan will prevent flare-ups, so make sure the meat is not larger than the drip pan you plan to use. If it is, use either a larger pan or two pans. For easy cleanup, the BBQ Queens prefer to use a disposable aluminum pan.

Trim the meat, then season it. Use pliers to tighten the thumbscrews on the spit forks to prevent loosening during the rotisserie process. Slide the meat onto the spit rod and push it into the secured spit fork so that it is held firmly by the fork's tines. Slide the

When Karen first heard about the stovetop smoker, she scoffed. After all, she is from Missouri, the Show Me State. How good could food that received only a short shot of smoke really be? Show me the smoke!

Well, Karen tried this gadget, then Judith tried it, and the BBQ Queens now decree: The stovetop smoker is great! Long live the stovetop smoker!

With the stovetop smoker, you can get great smoke flavor under certain conditions and with certain foods. It certainly doesn't replace the art of slow-smoked barbecue, but it does have a place in our fast-paced, sometimes even frenetic, kitchens.

Basically, the stovetop smoker (which usually costs less than $50), looks like an old-fashioned popcorn popper—the kind folks used to hold over a flame and shake to keep the kernels from burning. Of course, we use the smoker in our own inimitable way, as we'll explain.

STOVETOP SMOKING 101

Made of stainless steel, the stovetop smoker is designed to trap and smolder tiny wood particles away from the food so the resulting smoke permeates the food but doesn't make your kitchen smoke alarm go crazy.

To use it, place about 1 tablespoon of very fine wood chips in the center of the base of the smoker. These chips are available in many different varieties, including alder, apple, cherry, corncob, hickory, maple, mesquite, oak, and pecan. Make sure the chips are dry when you put them in the smoker so that they will smolder effectively.

A metal drip tray fits snugly on top of the chips, then a coated, footed wire rack is placed on the tray. Coat or brush whatever food you're smoking with olive oil, then season it with salt and pepper. If you wish, you can marinate the food first and pat it dry, or sprinkle on a rub, before smoking. You can also use up to 1/4 cup of a slather, but that's as fancy as we get. We don't use any concoctions that may drip and burn, affecting the taste of the food. Arrange your food in a single layer on the rack, so you have the most surface area exposed to the smoke. (If you want to double our recipes, smoke the food in two batches.) Slide the metal lid closed, extend the handles, and place the smoker over one burner. Gas or electric coil burners work just fine, but flat ceramic burners require 20 percent more cooking time.

Turn the burner to medium (375°F), medium-high (400°F), or high (450°F-plus) heat. Although the instructions enclosed with the smoker say to keep the heat on medium, we don't. We mainly use medium-high or high heat so that the food gets cooked fast and doesn't dry out. Your stovetop smoker won't be in perfect alignment after placing it over high heat, but who cares? Ours still work just fine.

Start keeping track of the cooking time when you see the first hint of smoke escaping from the smoker.

Although the instruction booklet enclosed with the smoker says that you can smoke a whole turkey, brisket, or rack of spareribs by tenting foil over the smoker (without the metal lid), we prefer smoking already-tender foods with shorter cooking times. Fish and shellfish, chicken, pork and beef tenderloin, soft and semisoft cheeses, and vegetables work well. We think that cuts of meat such as brisket, pork butt, and pork loin roast, which need long, slow cooking to tenderize, taste better cooked in a "real" smoker, on a rotisserie, or over indirect heat on a grill.

It's easy to tell when your food is done. Fish and shellfish should have a bronzish cast and be opaque all the way through. Chicken, beef, and pork also will have a bronzish color and can be checked for doneness with an instant-read meat thermometer. Vegetables and cheeses are done when they have the amount of smoky taste you desire.

We start meats such as pork or beef tenderloin on an outdoor grill or in an indoor grill pan, then finish them in the stovetop smoker. That way, we get a slight caramelization and grill marks on the exterior and a smoky and juicy interior. Perfect!

After you've finished smoking (you can check your food periodically by sliding the lid back), remove the smoker from the heat. Be careful: the smoker will be very hot. Let it sit for a minute or two, then remove the food and let the smoker cool. After the charred wood chips have cooled completely, rinse them down the drain (so you don't start a fire in your wastebasket).

The stovetop smoker can be cleaned with hot soapy water or placed in the dishwasher. The bottom of the smoker will become discolored after the first use because of the direct heat, but you didn't want to display your smoker in your china cabinet anyway, did you?

Try some of the following recipes, and you'll be a stovetop smoker convert in no time flat. Smoke a variety of foods, then accompany them with any of the "crowning glories" in other smoked recipes that suit your fancy.

Stovetop Smoked Soft Cheese

Smoked soft cheese—such as cream cheese or fresh goat cheese—is one of our favorite goodies, delicious in spreads, crumbled over grilled vegetable salads, or sitting atop a simply dressed salad of baby greens. The crimped foil "tray" keeps the cheese from melting on the rack, because the stovetop smoker cooks food at a higher temperature than an outdoor smoker does. SERVES 4

SUGGESTED WOOD: Apple, cherry, hickory, or pecan

One 8-ounce package cream cheese or one 6- to 9-ounce piece fresh goat cheese
Olive oil

1. Remove the cheese from the package, brush or spray with olive oil, and place on a double thickness of aluminum foil. Crimp the edges to make a "tray" and place on the smoker pan rack. Secure the lid.

2. Place the smoker over one burner on the stove, set at medium heat. When a wisp of smoke escapes from the smoker, start the timer for 10 minutes. Slide open the lid to check for doneness. When the cheese has a smoky aroma and a bronzed appearance, remove the smoker from the heat but keep the lid closed for another minute. Serve hot, at room temperature, or cold.

Stovetop Smoked Shrimp

This has become the BBQ Queens' favorite appetizer to serve at home or bring to a gathering. In about 8 minutes, you have a fabulously smoky dish. How easy is that? Serve the shrimp with your favorite cocktail sauce. The same amount of large sea scallops will smoke in the same amount of time. SERVES 12 AS AN APPETIZER

SUGGESTED WOOD: Hickory or pecan

1 pound large shrimp, peeled and deveined
Olive oil
Fine kosher or sea salt and freshly ground black pepper to taste

1. Rinse the shrimp under cold running water, drain, and pat dry with paper towels. Arrange on the smoker pan rack, drizzle with olive oil, and sprinkle with salt and pepper. Close the lid.

2. Place the smoker over one burner on the stove, set at high heat. When a wisp of smoke escapes from the smoker, start the timer for 6 minutes. Slide open the lid to check for doneness. When the shrimp are bronzish pink, opaque, and somewhat firm to the touch, remove the smoker from the heat but keep the lid closed for another 2 minutes. Serve hot, at room temperature, or cold.

Stovetop Smoked Tomatoes

You can use either large beefsteak or smaller Roma tomatoes, whichever you have on hand. Add them to sauces or the sublime Smoked Tomato Grits (page 164). SERVES 4

SUGGESTED WOOD: Hickory or pecan

4 large beefsteak tomatoes, cored, or 12 Roma tomatoes, cut in half
Olive oil
Fine kosher or sea salt and freshly ground black pepper to taste

1. Arrange the tomatoes on the smoker pan rack, cut sides up. Drizzle with olive oil and sprinkle with salt and pepper. Close the lid.

2. Place the smoker over one burner on the stove, set at medium-high heat. When a wisp of smoke escapes from the smoker, start the timer for 8 to 10 minutes. Slide open the lid to check for doneness. When the tomatoes have cracked skins and are soft to the touch, remove the smoker from the heat but keep the lid closed for another minute. Serve hot, at room temperature, or cold.

Stovetop Double-Smoked Ham

When Judith lived in Vermont, she and her family enjoyed the local corncob-smoked cheddar and ham. Now you can do the same at home. The smoked ham is delicious sliced and served as an entrée. But, oh my, what wonderful grilled smoked ham and cheese sandwiches, smoked ham club sandwiches, and diced smoked ham and bean soup this makes. SERVES 12

SUGGESTED WOOD: Apple, cherry, or oak with a pinch (about ¹/₂ teaspoon) of corncob; or use plain hickory

1 spiral-sliced or whole boneless ham

1. Place the ham on the smoker pan rack and tent with a double thickness of aluminum foil, securing it tightly around the rim of the smoker.

2. Place the smoker over one burner on the stove, set at medium heat. When a wisp of smoke escapes from the smoker, start the timer for 30 minutes. When the ham has a smoky aroma, remove the smoker from the heat but keep the lid closed for another minute. Serve hot, at room temperature, or cold.

Stovetop Smoked Pork Tenderloin

We like to lay some grill marks on the tenderloin first, then smoke it to medium doneness. We slice the pork and serve it with a variety of dipping sauces, such as Cilantro-Peanut Dipping Sauce (page 389), Spicy Lemon-Soy Sauce (page 312), and Picadillo Olive Salsa (page 192). Sliced smoked pork tenderloin is great platter food to serve at a party. SERVES 6 TO 8

SUGGESTED WOOD: Apple, cherry, or oak

Two 1¹/₂-pound pork tenderloins

Olive oil

Fine kosher or sea salt and freshly ground black pepper to taste

1.   Brush or spray the pork tenderloin with olive oil. Heat an indoor grill pan over high heat and sear the meat on all sides, 2 to 3 minutes per side. Season with salt and pepper, then place the seared tenderloins on the smoker pan rack. Secure the lid.

2.   Place the smoker over one burner on the stove, set at high heat. When a wisp of smoke escapes from the smoker, start the timer for 8 to 10 minutes. Slide open the lid to check for doneness. When an instant-read meat thermometer inserted in the center registers 145°F for medium, remove the smoker from the heat but keep the lid closed for another minute. Serve hot, at room temperature, or cold.

Stovetop Smoked Beef Tenderloin

Get fancy with Tricolored Peppercorn Rub (page 62) instead of plain salt and pepper, then accompany with Peppercorn Beurre Blanc (page 102) or Smoked Chile Beurre Blanc (page 99) for heavenly eating. SERVES 8

SUGGESTED WOOD: Hickory or mesquite

One 4-pound beef tenderloin, trimmed of any fat and silverskin

Olive oil

Fine kosher or sea salt and freshly ground black pepper to taste

1.   Brush or spray the tenderloin with olive oil. Heat an indoor grill pan over high heat and sear the meat on all sides until you have good grill marks, about 5 minutes per side. Season with salt and pepper, then place the seared tenderloin on the smoker pan rack. Secure the lid.

2.   Place the smoker over one burner on the stove, set at high heat. When a wisp of smoke escapes from the smoker, start the timer for 15 minutes. Slide open the lid to check for doneness. When an instant-read meat thermometer inserted in the center registers 135°F for rare, remove the smoker from the heat but keep the lid closed for another minute. Serve hot, at room temperature, or cold.

other fork onto the spit so that it also holds the meat securely and tighten its thumbscrew with the pliers.

It's very important to balance the meat on the spit so it can turn easily. If the meat is not balanced, it could shorten the life of your rotisserie. To balance the rod, hold it so that the ends lay across the palms of your hands. Position the meat on the rod so that there is no heavy side; otherwise, the heavy side will rotate down. Tie any loose bits to the body of the meat with kitchen twine. Insert a heatproof meat thermometer in the thickest part of the meat, away from any bone(s) and positioned so that it will turn freely with the meat and you can read it. Place the spit on the rotisserie. Start the rotisserie, letting it rotate enough times until you're sure the meat turns easily.

Check to make sure the grill's lid will close while the rotisserie is on. If necessary, you can prop the grill lid open a bit with bricks or metal cans.

Now prepare a medium-hot fire in your grill. You want to cook the meat at 300 to 350°F, which is measured at a distance above the coals, so the actual fire has to be a little hotter.

Cover and cook, checking the meat, the fire, and the drip pan at least every hour. Sometimes the thumbscrews will loosen, or the meat may shrink and the forks may need to be adjusted, so keep a clean pair of pliers handy. Keep checking the meat thermometer so that you know when the meat is done. During the last hour of cooking, apply any finishing sauce or glaze every 30 minutes.

When the meat is done, remove it from the spit and let it rest for at least 15 minutes before slicing.

Now you've got some mighty fine eatin', and your guests will sing your praises. Brush up on the four queen waves (see page 224) so that you're ready for the accolades.

Serving It Up on a Shingle

As BBQ Queens, we certainly get a lot of attention when we wear our tiaras out in public. But at home, it's another story.

Tooling Around with the BBQ Queens

We both have our own BBQ toolboxes—small plastic storage boxes for all our grill necessities. That way, we can take everything outside at once—or to a TV station to do an on-air demo.

Here's some of the stuff we won't leave home without.

Needle-nose pliers: Useful for pulling the membrane off the back of a slab of ribs or to fine-tune the apparatus on a rotisserie.

Instant-read meat thermometer: A must for checking the doneness of meat and poultry.

Grill utensils: Long-handled grill tongs, a grill spatula, a wide-bladed fish spatula, and a wire grill brush.

Newspaper and long matches: For starting the charcoal chimney.

Aluminum foil: For lining the bottom of a charcoal grill; wrapping up packets of wood chips or pellets; and protecting food from the heat of a grill, smoker, or rotisserie.

Kitchen twine: For tying up roasts or whole birds for the grill, smoker, or rotisserie.

Disposable aluminum pans: Buy these in several sizes for grilling or smoking; they make for easy cleanup.

Paper towels: For cleaning up.

Empty spray bottles: You may want two, one filled with water to douse excessive flare-ups (remember—we like char) and the other filled with a marinade you can just spritz on.

Brushes and dish mops: Indispensable for basting and slathering.

Grate Chef Grill Wipes: Great for oiling the grill grates without having excessive oil drip onto the flames.

Flavored wood pellets: We love the herb-, mulberry-, and orange-flavored wood pellets available from BBQr's Delight (sold in small packages, perfect for our toolboxes).

Extra tiaras: Just in case!

You know how you hate it when you get a new haircut or hair color and no one in your family notices? Or when you ask your partner or children to do something and they just don't seem to hear you? (Judith swears that she has a voice with a frequency that only dogs can hear. Karen knows that her husband, Dick, would hear just fine if she asked him to build a duck blind in their backyard, but somehow he misses her request to take out the trash or mow the lawn.) Well, say goodbye to their "see no evil, hear no evil" ways. We guarantee that if you serve your friends and family dinner on a wooden plank, they *will* notice.

Plank cooking is an ancient culinary art originating with Native Americans on both coasts. When the shad ran in New England rivers and the salmon in Pacific Northwest waters, these fish were caught, then pegged to maple or alder planks, which were placed upright around a bonfire to cook. Planking is currently experiencing a revival as Americans explore all the possibilities of cooking on the backyard grill. Once your guests see—and taste—your planked entrées, they'll understand why. The secret to great flavor is to keep the food on the plank in one layer—the more food touching the plank, the more aromatic the taste.

Everything from tuna to tenderloin has a certain "wow" factor when it's cooked and served on a plank. Whereas grilled foods slightly char to take on a robust flavor, and smoked foods have a heavier wood smoke taste, planked foods absorb the gentle aroma and flavor of the wood they are cooked on.

PLANKING 101

Plank cooking is easy. We suggest that you buy untreated hardwood planks. The most important consideration in choosing a plank is to make sure it fits inside your grill. Planks are commonly 15 to 16 inches long, 6 to 7 inches wide, and $1/4$ to $1/2$ inch thick. The BBQ Queens also use those 2- to 3-inch-thick reinforced cedar baking planks, which are available at gourmet or barbecue and grill shops. They last a long time and are slightly hollowed out, keeping any sauce on the plank. You can also buy commercial-grade 1- to 2-inch-thick untreated hardwood planks at the lumberyard and cut them to fit your grill rack. Food cooks the same on thinner or thicker planks, but thicker planks last longer. Planks can be reused until they're either too charred or too brittle to hold food.

Although planking on cedar is the universal favorite because it gives the best aromatic flavor, any regional hardwood—such as alder, hickory, maple, oak, or pecan—available in barbecue and grill shops will produce great-tasting planked food, too.

Submerge the plank in water for at least 1 hour before using. A deep sink or a large rectangular container that you can fill with water works well. Use a heavy can to weight down the plank. A water-soaked plank produces maximum smoke flavor and is more resistant to charring on the grill.

Prepare an indirect fire in a grill, with a hot fire on one side and a medium fire on the other. You can do this in a gas grill with dual burners or in a charcoal grill by massing two-thirds of the hot coals on the "hot" side and one-third on the "medium" side.

Now here's where Karen and Judith agree to disagree. Judith prefers to season the presoaked plank over hot coals. She places the plank over high heat for about 5 minutes. When the plank starts to char and pop, she turns it over so the charred side is up, then arranges the food in a single layer on that side. Karen doesn't like to season her planks. Both produce great-tasting food. You decide which method you prefer.

Don't crowd the food on the plank. Arrange it in a single layer to ensure the best flavor. Use two planks, if necessary.

Place the plank(s) on the grill grate and close the lid. Cook for 12 to 20 minutes, depending on the amount of food. (Each of our recipes tells you how long.) Stay close by, in case of flare-ups, for which you should keep a spray bottle filled with water handy.

For a rustic and restaurant-style effect, serve the food right on the plank, like a platter. After you've cooked and served on the plank, cleanup couldn't be easier—a little hot soapy water and a good rinse. Eighty-grit sandpaper may be used to spruce up the plank, too.

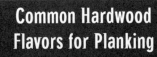

Common Hardwood Flavors for Planking

- **ALDER:** Gives a light, aromatic flavor. Alder and seafood are a match made in heaven.

- **CEDAR:** Probably the most aromatic wood, it lends a deep but gentle flavor to planked food of all kinds.

- **HICKORY:** Supplies a strong, hearty wood flavor that is wonderful with beef, pork, and chicken.

- **MAPLE:** Smolders to a sweet, mild flavor that pairs well with chicken, vegetables, and fish.

- **OAK:** Provides a medium woodsy aroma without being bitter. It goes well with any food.

Greasehouse University and the Order of the Magic Mop: The Kansas City Barbeque Society

Although Karen is the more certified barbecue cook—she has attained an M.B. (Master of Barbecue) at the esteemed and fictional Greasehouse University, but she hasn't yet taken her oral exams for the Ph.B. (Doctor of Barbecue Philosophy)—it was Judith who was inducted into the Order of the Magic Mop.

The honor could have been awarded for her service to the barbecue world in helping Paul Kirk whip his manuscript into shape for his gargantuan *Paul Kirk's Championship Barbecue* (The Harvard Common Press, 2004); her work as coauthor with Karen of *Fish & Shellfish, Grilled & Smoked* (The Harvard Common Press, 2002) and *Easy Grilling & Simple Smoking with the BBQ Queens* (Pig Out Publications, 1997); her how-to barbecue classes that she teaches with Karen; or because she's friends with Ardie Davis, a.k.a. Remus Powers, Ph.B., in the colorful world of competition barbecue. Ardie is the bestower of the mop.

The barbecue ritual involves the lowly dish mop, that wood-handled, yarn-headed tool used to clean dishes and "mop" basting liquid on slow-smoking meats. Ardie's dish mop, however, is a special kind that he buys only at Piggly Wiggly grocery stores in the Memphis area for $1.49. "It's got a plain wood handle, no glue at all, just fastened together with a wire and a nail. The top is Egyptian cotton," Ardie says.

Ardie uses his mop to "bless" barbecue rigs or induct barbecuers into the Order of the Magic Mop by the simple gift of a new mop, autographed by Remus Powers himself. He flicks the mop over your rig, your food, and you, while intoning, "In the name of the steer and the hog and the holy smoke, you are now a member of the Order of the Magic Mop."

Like Tinker Bell's pixie dust, it's magic if you think it is. The BBQ Queens believe!

Sprinkle, Slather, Soak, and Drizzle: Rubs, Marinades, Vinaigrettes, and Sauces

Adding another flavor element to foods that are grilled or smoked can be done at two different times—before or after cooking. Foods cooked on the grill or in the smoker will already be getting a slightly charred, caramelized, or wood smoke flavor. The addition of citrus, garlic, fresh or dried herbs, spices, wine, or aromatic vegetables can further enhance the flavor. Think of basic grilled or smoked foods as clear polish on your nails—classic and in good taste. Rubs, pastes, slathers, and marinades applied before cooking, and vinaigrettes, drizzles, and sauces used after cooking, are more like a French manicure—a lot more sophisticated and quietly wow-y. You can't go wrong with either.

The BBQ Queens promise that you won't find recipe versions of iridescent, grunge-blue polish painted on talon-like nails here. After all, we don't wear real rhinestone tiaras for our health. We wear them because we have good taste. So you can trust us, girlfriend. You won't catch us in bright blue eye shadow. Nnnuh-uh.

Dry Rubs, Pastes, and Slathers

9 n cosmetic makeup terms, olive oil, salt, and pepper function as the flavor foundation for grilled foods of all kinds. Sure you could go without them and be totally plain-Jane, but we don't recommend it. Beyond the basic olive oil, salt, and pepper are dry rubs, pastes, and slathers.

Dry rubs are dry herb and spice mixtures that are sprinkled on the surface of fish, poultry, meat, or vegetables before grilling or smoking. Like Tinker Bell's fairy dust, you sprinkle on a rub for some culinary magic.

Rubs can be as simple as salt and pepper or as complex as a mixture of 12 ingredients. The key is that everything going into a rub should be dry, so that the rub stays in suspension. If you even think about adding fresh garlic or herbs, then you no longer have a dry rub. (Not that there's anything wrong with that—it's just not a rub and it will keep refrigerated for only a few days.) Rubs are used on both grilled and smoked foods.

Wow-factor pastes, such as those with fresh garlic or smoke-roasted red bell peppers, add a big burst of flavor to food destined for the grill. They're like all-in-one cosmetics—a foundation that's also a bronzer, a lipstick that's also a balm. You get the picture: no need for a separate foundation of olive oil, salt, and pepper when you use a paste because they're already in the paste. Pastes need to be brushed on the surface of food, then left to sit for about 30 minutes before cooking to let the flavors develop.

The idea for slathers comes from our Kansas City barbecue buddy Paul Kirk, author of *Paul Kirk's Championship Barbecue* (The Harvard Common Press, 2004). Basically, a slather is a mustard-based mixture—or just plain American or Dijon mustard—spread over a food before slow smoking or planking. The slather is then sprinkled with a rub and left to sit until it gets tacky to the touch, about 15 minutes. The combination of the slather and the rub makes a kind of savory bark on the food, keeping it moist and flavorful. We use slathers on slow-smoked pork loin roasts, pork butts, and planked salmon fillets.

BBQ Queens' All-Purpose Rub 49

Memphis Blue-Ribbon Rib Rub 49

Prizewinning Rib Rub 50

Fair for Fowl Rub 51

Spicy Orange Rub 51

Zesty Sugar and Spice Rub 52

Spicy Red-Hot Lemon Pepper Rub 53

SALTS OF THE EARTH
Lavender Salt 55
Rosemary Salt 56
Fennel Salt 56
Spicy, Savory Seasoned Salt 56
Smoked Hickory Salt 57

Cajun Steak Rub 58

BBQ Queens' Photo Op Barbecue Rub 58

Texas Two-Steppin' Mesquite Rub 59

Fireworks Rub 60

Ole Hickory Rub 60

Dukka 61

Tricolored Peppercorn Rub 62

Rosemary Pesto 62

Chive Pesto 64

Five-Spice Asian Paste 64

Porcini Paste 65

Mustard-Mayo Slather 66
Mustard-Mayo-Dill Slather 66
Mustard-Mayo-Orange Slather 66
Mustard-Mayo-Tarragon Slather 66

Rosemary, Garlic, and Lemon Baste 68

Aromatic Lemon-Herb Marinade 68

Homemade Teriyaki Marinade 69

Garlic-Citrus Marinade 70

Provençal Red Wine Marinade 70

Rosemary-Mustard Marinade 71

Amogio 72

Fennel and Orange Marinade 72
Fennel and Orange Drizzling Sauce 73

Tequila-Lime Marinade 73

Lemongrass Marinade 74

Tandoori Marinade 74

Lemon-Tarragon Vinaigrette 75

Saffron Vinaigrette 76

Wheat Beer Vinaigrette 77

THEY DUBBED IT . . . COLESLAW
Blue Cheese Coleslaw 79
Crunchy Broccoli Slaw with Thai Chile-Peanut Dressing 80
Layered Vinegar Slaw 80
Mediterranean Summer Squash Slaw 81
Frozen Asset Slaw 82
Red Cabbage and Apple Slaw 83

Citrus Caesar Vinaigrette 84

Balsamic-Thyme Vinaigrette 84

Fresh Basil Vinaigrette 85

Hot Shallot Vinaigrette 85

Chipotle Vinaigrette 86

Lemon Butter Drizzle 87

Vietnamese Drizzle 87

Honey-Almond Grilling Glaze 88

BBQ Queens' Love Potion for the Swine 89

The Doctor Is In Apricot-Bourbon Barbecue Sauce 90

Simply Delicious Bordelaise Sauce 91

Mango-Lemon Sauce 92

Raspberry and Blood Orange Sauce 92

Poblano Cream Sauce 93

Smoked Garlic and Cilantro Cream Sauce 93

Roasted Red Pepper Sauce 94

Tomato-Fennel Sauce 95

Pistachio-Pomegranate Sauce 96

Food Processor or Blender Hollandaise 97

Rustic Béarnaise Sauce 98

Smoked Chile Beurre Blanc 99

Mustard-Cornichon Beurre Blanc 100

Raspberry Beurre Blanc 101

Peppercorn Beurre Blanc 102

Kimizu 103

Lemon-Garlic Mayonnaise 103

Rustic Aioli 104

White Truffle Aioli 105

BAKED OR BARBECUED BEANS

Texas-Style Pinto Beans 106

*BBQ Queens'
Barbecued Beans* 107

Jazzy Java Baked Beans 108

*Easy Southern-Style
Baked Beans* 109

The Doctor Is In Easy Aioli 110

**Creamy Blue
Cheese Dressing** 111

Tzatziki 112

BBQ Queens' All-Purpose Rub

As the title of this recipe suggests, you can use this on just about anything you grill or smoke—from flatbreads and cheese to veggies, fish, chicken, and meats. This spice mixture provides a sweet (from the celery seeds) and hot (from the black pepper) one-two punch with a savory underlayer (from the garlic powder and onion salt). MAKES ABOUT 2 CUPS

$1/2$ cup freshly ground black pepper

$1/2$ cup sweet Hungarian paprika

$1/4$ cup garlic powder

$1/4$ cup onion salt

3 tablespoons dry mustard

3 tablespoons celery seeds

3 tablespoons chili powder

Combine all the ingredients in a large glass jar with a tight-fitting lid. Secure the lid and shake to blend. This rub will keep in the cupboard for several months.

Memphis Blue-Ribbon Rib Rub

This is delicious on pork ribs, pork butt, pork loin, pork chops, and pork steaks. We sound like that shrimp character in *Forrest Gump*, don't we? MAKES ABOUT 3 CUPS

1 cup sweet Hungarian paprika

$1/2$ cup lemon pepper seasoning

$1/2$ cup freshly ground black pepper

$1/4$ cup garlic salt

$1/4$ cup chili powder

$1/2$ cup firmly packed light or dark brown sugar, spread on a baking sheet and left to dry for 1 hour

Combine all the ingredients in a large glass jar with a tight-fitting lid. Secure the lid and shake to blend. This rub will keep in the cupboard for several months.

Prizewinning Rib Rub

The celery salt in this seasoning adds a slightly sweet flavor that's perfect with pork, chicken, and fish. **MAKES ABOUT ³/₄ CUP**

> ¹/₄ cup sugar
>
> 2 tablespoons garlic salt
>
> 2 tablespoons freshly ground black pepper
>
> 2 tablespoons sweet Hungarian paprika
>
> 2 tablespoons celery salt

Combine all the ingredients in a small glass jar with a tight-fitting lid. Secure the lid and shake to blend. This rub will keep in the cupboard for several months.

BBQ Queens' Rub Pantry

A rub is always made with dry ingredients, so the following spices, seasonings, and herbs are all dried. The list can be endless, so decide on the number of seasonings you like best and enjoy!

THE BASICS

Brown sugar, light and dark	Onion powder	Salt: kosher or sea salt, garlic salt, onion salt
Celery seeds or salt	Paprika, sweet Hungarian	
Chili powder	Pepper: freshly ground black, lemon, seasoned	
Garlic powder		
Mustard, dry	Red pepper flakes	

BBQ QUEENS' FANCY RUB PANTRY

Anise seeds	Cumin, ground or seeds	Rosemary
Basil	Fennel seeds	Tarragon
Cayenne pepper	Garlic, granulated	Thyme
Citrus peel, ground dried	Lavender	White pepper, ground
Coriander, ground or seeds	Onion, granulated	

Fair for Fowl Rub

A former chef at Kansas City's Peppercorn Duck Club developed this rub, which he used on a hickory-smoked duck he entered in the American Royal Barbecue Contest. It's not limited to duck, of course. Try it if you want on rotisserie or slow-smoked fowl of any kind, from chicken and turkey to Cornish game hens and duck. This recipe makes enough to rub one 4-pound chicken or duck. Multiply it about three times to use on a turkey. MAKES ABOUT $2/3$ CUP

> $1/2$ cup coarse kosher or sea salt
>
> 1 teaspoon dried rosemary
>
> 1 teaspoon fennel seeds
>
> 1 teaspoon anise seeds
>
> 1 teaspoon garlic powder
>
> 1 teaspoon ground white pepper
>
> 1 teaspoon sweet Hungarian paprika

Combine all the ingredients in a small glass jar with a tight-fitting lid. Secure the lid and shake to blend. This rub will keep in the cupboard for several months.

Spicy Orange Rub

S avory, spicy, and zesty, this is great on grilled fish, chicken, duck, turkey, or pork. Pair this pretty orange rub with a darker one, such as Fireworks Rub (page 60), sprinkling alternating 1-inch stripes of the rubs on a raw fish fillet. It's beautiful and tasty, too. MAKES ABOUT $1/3$ CUP

> 3 tablespoons ground dried orange peel
>
> 1 tablespoon onion powder
>
> $1 1/2$ teaspoons ground ginger
>
> 1 tablespoon red pepper flakes

Combine all the ingredients in a glass jar with a tight-fitting lid. Secure the lid and shake to blend. This rub will keep in the cupboard for several months.

Zesty Sugar and Spice Rub

Five-spice powder, available at better grocery stores and Asian markets, sets the tone here, joined by allspice, coriander, cinnamon, sugar, and dried orange peel to make a heady and aromatic rub that is fabulous on duck, turkey, game birds, and pork. We also like it sprinkled on fresh apple or pear slices used raw in a salad or sautéed in butter for a side dish. MAKES ABOUT ²/₃ CUP

2 teaspoons five-spice powder

2 teaspoons ground allspice

2 teaspoons ground coriander

2 teaspoons ground cinnamon

2 tablespoons sugar

2 tablespoons ground dried orange peel

Combine all the ingredients in a glass jar with a tight-fitting lid. Secure the lid and shake to blend. This rub will keep in the cupboard for several months.

Spicy Red-Hot Lemon Pepper Rub

This hot and lemony rub is very versatile. Try it on poultry, pork, fish, and vegetables. **MAKES ABOUT 1 CUP**

1/2 cup lemon pepper seasoning

2 tablespoons chili powder

2 tablespoons ground cumin

2 tablespoons ground coriander

1 tablespoon firmly packed light or dark brown sugar

1 1/2 teaspoons fine kosher or sea salt

1 1/2 teaspoons red pepper flakes

1 tablespoon freshly ground black pepper

Combine all the ingredients in a small jar with a tight-fitting lid. Secure the lid and shake to blend. This rub will keep in the cupboard for several months.

‣‣‣‣‣

Chefs—as well as avid backyard cooks and competition barbecuers—are always after that signature flavor, that certain something you can't quite put your finger on that elevates a dish to fantastic. In this quest, they're rediscovering, of all things, salt.

Not just any salt, of course, but specialty salts, either naturally flavorful or helped along with the addition of smoke, herbs, or other seasonings. As an article in the *New York Times Magazine* recently related, "A sprinkle of these rare, natural salts from the sea brings out the best (flavor, that is) in just about any food—even sweets." (Note that all salt is sea salt. Even if it is found inland, it was created from long-ago seas.)

A few of these "new" old salts have been harvested since around the eighth century B.C. The most basic is *fleur de sel*, or "flower of the sea." This salt is made when sun and wind conditions are ideal on the coasts of Normandy and Brittany, France, where it is hand-harvested from salt ponds. Douglas Rodriguez, author of *Latin Flavors on the Grill* (Ten Speed Press, 2000), sprinkles *fleur de sel* over cantaloupe seared in caramelized sugar. Petrossian, the caviar emporium and specialty bakery, serves it on chocolate cake.

Another specialty salt is Hawaiian red alae salt. After drying, it is combined with Hawaiian red clay for added minerals and a somewhat flinty taste. Tom Colicchio of New York City's Gramercy Tavern uses it over grilled turbot.

Peruvian pink sea salt comes from an ancient ocean trapped underground. The salt dissolves into a spring located high in the Andes, and the spring water is collected in terraced ponds in the Sacred Valley of the Incas. According to chef Michael Mischan of Aspen, Colorado, this salt's mineral quality is "unbelievable on sliced ripe tomatoes."

In *Saveur* magazine, editor Colman Andrews has raved about Danish smoked salt, an ancient Viking seasoning (needed, we guess, to make all the wind-dried cod more palatable after months of eating it). Seawater is boiled in a cauldron over a fire of cherry, elm, juniper, beech, and oak until the water evaporates, and the resulting salt "tastes like a bonfire," Andrews says. This salt gives an instant rich, smoky flavor to any food.

Rosemary and lavender salts are produced by Eatwell Farm, an organic farm in northern California that grows organic herbs and mixes them with gray French sea salt.

Eatwell Farm products are available from the Cooking School of Aspen (www.salt-traders.com or 800-641-7258).

In most recipes in this book, we recommend "kosher or sea salt." According to Robert Wolke in his book *What Einstein Told His Cooks* (W. W. Norton, 2002), kosher salt is distinguished by its coarse, irregular crystals and the rabbinical supervision of its manufacture. Kosher salt is pure and clean with no additives (except that Morton Coarse Kosher Salt lists a trace amount of anticaking agent). Its coarse crystals are well suited to adhering to foods.

Using one or more of these salts can elevate your food to the celestial—nothing to sneeze at if you're working on the title of culinary goddess. Hawaiian red alae salt, Peruvian pink sea salt, and other more arcane salts, such as South African sea salt, Japanese nazuna, Hawaiian black lava salt, and Mexican *benequenes*, are available from the Cooking School of Aspen (see above). Danish smoked salt is carried by several different spice emporiums, or you can make your own Smoked Hickory Salt (below). It's also very easy to make your own lavender, rosemary, or fennel salt or a special seasoned salt, as described below.

Lavender Salt

This coarse salt blend is meant to be sprinkled on lamb, beef, and pork before grilling. Use unsprayed lavender buds from your garden, as Judith does, or buy organic lavender buds from a health food store. For the best flavor, rub the salt mixture between your hands before sprinkling it on food to release the natural oils in the lavender.
MAKES ABOUT 1/4 CUP

> 2 tablespoons dried lavender buds
> 2 tablespoons best-quality coarse sea salt, preferably *fleur de sel*

Combine the ingredients in a small glass jar with a tight-fitting lid. Cover and shake to blend. This salt will keep in the cupboard for up to 1 year.

Rosemary Salt

Sprinkle this salt on lamb, beef, and pork before grilling. It's also great over vegetables, grilled fish, or steak. For the best flavor, rub the salt mixture between your hands before sprinkling it on food to release the natural oils in the rosemary. MAKES ABOUT $1/4$ CUP

>   2 tablespoons dried rosemary
>   2 tablespoons best-quality coarse sea salt, preferably *fleur de sel*

Combine the ingredients in a small glass jar with a tight-fitting lid. Cover and shake to blend. This salt will keep in the cupboard for several months.

Fennel Salt

Use this salt on lamb, fish, or pork before grilling, then finish the dish with Fennel and Orange Drizzling Sauce (page 73). For the best flavor, rub the salt mixture between your hands before sprinkling it on food to release the natural oils in the fennel seeds. MAKES ABOUT $1/4$ CUP

>   2 tablespoons fennel seeds
>   2 tablespoons best-quality coarse sea salt, preferably *fleur de sel*

Combine the ingredients in a small glass jar with a tight-fitting lid. Cover and shake to blend. This salt will keep in the cupboard for several months.

Spicy, Savory Seasoned Salt

This all-purpose salt and spice blend can go on anything before grilling or smoking. MAKES ABOUT $3/4$ CUP

> $1/2$ cup fine sea salt
>   2 tablespoons sweet Hungarian paprika
>   1 tablespoon dry mustard

1 teaspoon crumbled dried thyme

1 teaspoon crumbled dried marjoram

1 teaspoon garlic powder

1 teaspoon ground celery seeds

1 teaspoon onion powder

1 teaspoon dillweed

Combine all the ingredients in a small glass jar with a tight-fitting lid. Cover and shake to blend. This salt will keep in the cupboard for several months.

Smoked Hickory Salt

The BBQ Queens have been intrigued by all the fancy salts from around the world. The smoked salts really caught our eye but distressed our pocketbooks. Not willing to spend $10 to $20 for a few ounces, we thought we could smoke our own and put the money we saved into dazzling cubic zirconia tiaras. And so we did. This recipe was tested in a Camerons Stovetop Smoker. You can also use other woods, such as mesquite, pecan, or oak. Heavier smoke flavors work best. MAKES ABOUT 1 CUP

2 tablespoons hickory wood chips made for a stovetop smoker

1 cup coarse kosher salt

1. Place the wood chips in the center of the smoker pan. Place the drip pan and rack in the pan.

2. Spread the salt evenly in a Pyrex baking dish that fits in the smoker pan. The layer of salt should be about $1/8$ inch thick, so that the smoke can penetrate it easily. Place the dish on top of the rack and close the lid. (If the dish is too deep to allow the lid to slide closed, cover the pan with a sheet of heavy-duty aluminum foil crimped tightly around the pan.) Place the smoker over medium-high heat and smoke the salt for 15 to 20 minutes.

3. Turn off the heat and let the smoke dissipate before opening the lid, 10 to 15 minutes. The salt will be lightly browned and taste of hickory. Store in a glass jar with a tight-fitting lid. It will keep indefinitely in the cupboard.

Cajun Steak Rub

This rub is great on steaks, hamburgers, pork tenderloin, chops, even chicken breasts. Spray or brush light olive or vegetable oil evenly on the surface of the food, then sprinkle it with the rub before grilling. MAKES ABOUT 1/4 CUP

- 1 tablespoon garlic powder
- 1 tablespoon freshly ground black pepper
- 1 tablespoon sweet Hungarian paprika
- 1 1/2 teaspoons cayenne pepper
- 1 teaspoon fine kosher or sea salt
- 1/2 teaspoon ground white pepper

Combine all the ingredients in a small glass jar with a tight-fitting lid. Secure the lid and shake to blend. This rub will keep in the cupboard for several months.

BBQ Queens' Photo Op Barbecue Rub

While photographing gadgets, grills, and spices for this book, we arranged different-colored dried herbs and spices on a white plate. We thought, "Wonder what it would taste like if we combined them all in a rub?" We did, and it was pretty darn good. Try this on chicken, pork, or even fish, then smile for the camera. MAKES ABOUT 1 CUP

- 3 tablespoons firmly packed dark brown sugar
- 2 tablespoons chili powder
- 2 tablespoons ground ancho chile (see box on page 59)
- 2 tablespoons ground chipotle chile (see box on page 59)
- 2 tablespoons lemon pepper seasoning
- 2 tablespoons sweet Hungarian paprika

2 tablespoons dillweed

2 tablespoons granulated onion

2 tablespoons celery seeds

Combine all the ingredients in a large glass jar with a tight-fitting lid. Secure the lid and shake to blend. This rub will keep in the cupboard for several months.

Texas Two-Steppin' Mesquite Rub

Try this rub on brisket. It makes lots—remember, we're talkin' Texas. **MAKES ABOUT 2 CUPS**

1/2 cup coarse kosher salt

1/4 cup garlic powder

1/4 cup lemon pepper seasoning

1/4 cup firmly packed light or dark brown sugar

3 tablespoons ground chipotle or ancho chile (see box)

3 tablespoons mesquite seasoning (see box)

3 tablespoons dried thyme

3 tablespoons ground cumin

Combine all the ingredients in a large glass jar with a tight-fitting lid. Secure the lid and shake to blend. This rub will keep in the cupboard for several months.

McCormick Seasonings

If you want to add some great ready-made rubs to your pantry, we recommend McCormick Grill Mates. Flavors include Barbecue Seasoning, Mesquite Seasoning, Montreal Steak Seasoning, and Spicy Montreal Steak Seasoning. For your "fancy" rub pantry, try McCormick Chipotle Chile Pepper and Ancho Chile Pepper. They are fine alone, but we like to doctor them up, too.

Fireworks Rub

The spiciness and heat of this rub makes it a good seasoning for just about anything. We use it on grilled fish for fish tacos, smoked brisket, grilled chicken wings, and even grilled pork tenderloin. If you like really hot stuff, double the amount of red pepper flakes. MAKES ABOUT 1 CUP

1/4 cup chili powder

1/4 cup ground cumin

1/4 cup ground coriander

2 tablespoons firmly packed light or dark brown sugar

2 tablespoons red pepper flakes

2 tablespoons freshly ground black pepper

1 tablespoon coarse kosher salt

Combine all the ingredients in a large glass jar with a tight-fitting lid. Secure the lid and shake to blend. This rub will keep in the cupboard for several months.

Ole Hickory Rub

This southern-style rub has hickory salt as the key ingredient. It is delicious on pork—shoulder, butt, ribs, chops, and tenderloin. MAKES ABOUT 2 CUPS

1/2 cup store-bought hickory salt or Smoked Hickory Salt (page 57)

1/4 cup garlic powder or granulated garlic

1/4 cup onion powder

1/4 cup chili powder

3 tablespoons sweet Hungarian paprika

3 tablespoons firmly packed light or dark brown sugar

3 tablespoons dry mustard

1¹/₂ tablespoons ground ginger

1¹/₂ tablespoons red pepper flakes

Combine all the ingredients in a large glass jar with a tight-fitting lid. Secure the lid and shake to blend. This rub will keep in the cupboard for several months.

Dukka

Adapted from a recipe by the late Laurie Colwin (see box on page 63), this Egyptian nut and spice powder is addictive. We've kicked up the heat by adding red pepper flakes to the original recipe. Sprinkle it on food before slow smoking, or sprinkle it on simply grilled food after cooking. We love it on grilled vegetables, grilled or smoked chicken, or grilled flatbreads that have been brushed with olive oil. MAKES ABOUT ³/₄ CUP

¹/₂ cup walnut pieces

¹/₄ cup sesame seeds

2 tablespoons coriander seeds

1¹/₂ tablespoons cumin seeds

1¹/₂ teaspoons black peppercorns

1¹/₂ teaspoons coarse kosher or sea salt

1 teaspoon ground cinnamon

1 teaspoon ground allspice

¹/₂ teaspoon red pepper flakes

1. In a small skillet over medium-high heat, toast all the ingredients, stirring constantly, until the walnuts have turned a deeper brown, about 5 minutes. Let cool slightly.

2. In a food processor or blender, or by hand in a mortar with a pestle, grind the mixture into a fine powder. Spoon into a small glass jar with a tight-fitting lid. Secure the lid and shake to blend. This powder will keep in the cupboard for several months.

Tricolored Peppercorn Rub

You'll need a mortar and pestle to crack but not completely grind the toasted peppercorns. But once you taste this rub on a grilled filet mignon, strip steak, or tuna steak, or on a smoked brisket or rib roast, you'll be glad for the effort. For an even greater hit of peppercorn, serve grilled beef, salmon, or tuna steaks with this rub, accompanied by Peppercorn Beurre Blanc (page 102). Wow! **MAKES ABOUT ¹/₃ CUP**

> 2 tablespoons Szechuan or white peppercorns
> 2 tablespoons black peppercorns
> 1 tablespoon dried green peppercorns
> 1 tablespoon coarse kosher or sea salt

1. Place all the ingredients in a small cast-iron skillet over medium-high heat and toast, stirring frequently, until the spices become aromatic, about 2 minutes.

2. Scrape the mixture into a mortar and grind them with a pestle until crushed and still somewhat coarse. Use right away.

Rosemary Pesto

Bold, gutsy, and Ethel Merman–like, this version of pesto has a "nothing like a dame" flavor. We like to slather it on pork tenderloin or pork chops, lamb steaks or rack of lamb, or beef tenderloin before grilling over a medium-hot fire (so the pesto doesn't char too much) on a well-oiled grill rack. Turn the meat only once and very carefully, using two grill spatulas. Rosemary pesto is also great on grilled bread or tossed with grilled zucchini and summer squash coins. **MAKES ABOUT 1 CUP**

> ¹/₂ cup fresh rosemary leaves
> 8 cloves garlic, peeled
> ¹/₂ cup pine nuts
> ¹/₂ cup olive oil
> 1 tablespoon fine kosher or sea salt
> 1 teaspoon freshly ground black pepper

In a food processor, process the rosemary, garlic, and pine nuts together until you have a smooth paste. With the processor running, drizzle in the olive oil in a slow, steady stream until the pesto solidifies. Add the salt and pepper and pulse to combine. Use immediately or spoon into a small jar with a tight-fitting lid. This pesto will keep in the refrigerator for up to 3 days or in the freezer for up to 6 months.

In Laurie Colwin's Pantry

In *More Home Cooking: A Writer Returns to the Kitchen* (HarperCollins, 1993), Laurie Colwin waxes rhapsodic on her favorite condiments. They're some of our favorites, too.

"I myself am hipped on a number of condiments without which I would not dream of cooking," Colwin wrote. "This shows me to be a politically correct and multicultural person. After all, to cook without stepping out of your own country is boring, the sort of culinary equivalent of reading only what are now called DWEMs—dead white European males."

Here's a sampling of Colwin's favorite condiments—and how we use them.

- *Lime pickle* (Colwin favored Bedekar's Lime Chilli Pickle) mixed with yogurt to accompany grilled chicken

- *Fermented black beans* sprinkled over olive-oil-and-garlic-marinated grilled vegetables or on top of grilled focaccia

- *Capers* in browned butter served with simply grilled fish

- *Thai red curry paste* mixed with canned unsweetened coconut milk as a dipping sauce for grilled shrimp

- *Gomashio*, a Japanese condiment of toasted sesame seeds and salt, sprinkled over simply grilled foods

- *Dukka*, an Egyptian spice powder (page 61), sprinkled over anything

Chive Pesto

Karen's vegetable and herb garden consists of four raised beds. One of the beds is bordered with onion chives and another with garlic chives. "That's a lot of chives!" Judith wisecracked, until Karen made this pesto at a class they taught at KitchenArt in West Lafayette, Indiana. "Put this in our BBQ Queen book, please," Judith urged. "It would be a fabulous condiment on a great grilled burger or chicken breast." 'Nuf said. MAKES ABOUT 1 CUP

> **2 cups chopped fresh garlic or onion chives**
>
> **¹/₂ cup pine nuts**
>
> **1 clove garlic, crushed or roughly chopped**
>
> **³/₄ cup regular or extra virgin olive oil**
>
> **¹/₂ cup freshly grated Parmesan or Romano cheese**
>
> **Kosher or sea salt and freshly ground black pepper to taste**

In a food processor, process the chives, pine nuts, and garlic until they form a smooth paste. With the processor running, drizzle in the olive oil in a slow, steady stream until the pesto solidifies. Add the Parmesan, season with salt and pepper, and pulse just to combine. Use immediately or spoon into a small jar with a tight-fitting lid. This pesto will keep in the refrigerator for 4 to 5 days or in the freezer for up to 6 months.

Five-Spice Asian Paste

Spread this paste over duck before grilling or smoking for a fusion feast of Asian barbecue. We also love it on salmon fillets, pork tenderloin, or even oysters before grilling or smoking. Five-spice powder, with its hit of anise, is available at better grocery stores and Asian markets. MAKES ABOUT 1¹/₄ CUPS

> **1 cup firmly packed light brown sugar**
>
> **2 tablespoons soy sauce**

2 tablespoons vegetable oil

1 tablespoon five-spice powder

2 cloves garlic, minced

In a small bowl, combine all the ingredients until you have a paste. Use immediately or spoon into a small jar with a tight-fitting lid. This paste will keep in the refrigerator for up to 1 week.

Porcini Paste

Dried porcini mushrooms, available in the produce section of better grocery stores, can make a very savory addition to the spice cupboard. Simply grind them into a powder in a clean coffee grinder or blender, then use them in delicious concoctions like this one. Slather this paste on a big, thick steak, on smaller filets mignons, on a pork tenderloin, or on a whole chicken destined for the rotisserie. Let marinate for at least 30 minutes, then cook. This paste gives foods a deep, complex, somewhat garlicky, decidedly luscious flavor. We adapted this recipe from one by our barbecue buddy Paul Kirk. MAKES ABOUT 3/4 CUP

2 tablespoons sugar

1 tablespoon kosher salt

5 large cloves garlic, minced

1 tablespoon red pepper flakes

1 tablespoon freshly ground black pepper

1/4 cup dried porcini mushrooms, ground to a powder in a coffee grinder

1/4 cup extra virgin olive oil

In a small bowl, combine all the ingredients until you have a paste. Use immediately or spoon into a small jar with a tight-fitting lid. This paste will keep in the refrigerator for up to 1 week.

Mustard-Mayo Slather

Short of buying a jar of Hellmann's Dijonnaise, this couldn't get any easier. Use a brush to slather it over ribs, pork loin roast, pork tenderloin, a whole chicken, chicken breasts, or a leg of lamb before smoking, or on salmon, char, trout, catfish, or halibut fillets before planking. **MAKES ABOUT 1 CUP**

> ¹/₂ cup Dijon mustard
>
> ¹/₂ cup mayonnaise (lowfat is okay)

Whisk the ingredients together in a bowl. Use immediately.

Mustard-Mayo-Dill Slather: Add 1 teaspoon dillweed, 1 teaspoon granulated garlic, and the juice of ¹/₂ lemon. This is especially good on fish or chicken. **MAKES ABOUT 1 CUP**

Mustard-Mayo-Orange Slather: Add 1 tablespoon Spicy Orange Rub (page 51). Primo on chicken and pork. **MAKES ABOUT 1 CUP**

Mustard-Mayo-Tarragon Slather: Add 2 teaspoons dried tarragon, 1 teaspoon ground white pepper, and the juice of ¹/₂ lemon. A winner on chicken, pork, and fish. **MAKES ABOUT 1 CUP**

Soak or Drizzle: Marinades Versus Vinaigrettes

What's the difference between a marinade and a vinaigrette? Both usually have similar ingredients—a vegetable oil, either acidic lemon juice or vinegar, and seasonings. If you know the difference between a facial toner (higher in alcohol or acid) and a moisturizer (higher in oil), this will be a snap. The crucial difference is in the ratio of vegetable oil to vinegar. In marinades, the ratio is in favor of vinegar, sometimes as much as three parts vinegar to one part oil. That's why more acidic marinades are used to imbue foods with flavor before cooking. A vinaigrette has more oil, sometimes half vinegar and half oil, sometimes two or three parts oil to one part vinegar. Vinaigrettes are more often used as a "crowning glory"—as a finishing "sauce" poured over a salad or drizzled on grilled foods—because there's not as much of an acidic punch and the higher oil content helps them coat better. You *can* use a vinaigrette as a marinade (and a lot of Grill Gals use bottled Italian-style vinaigrette as an easy marinade), but it's a good idea to pat the food dry before grilling to avoid flare-ups.

The trick with marinades is to know when and how long to use them. A marinade is used to flavor, not tenderize, but it does help leaner meats and poultry, such as flank steak and turkey, stay moist during grilling or smoking and perks up their somewhat bland flavor. If you keep meat, fish, or vegetables in a marinade too long, they will become mushy, as the higher acidic content will start to break down the proteins.

Most fish and shellfish should marinate for only 30 minutes. The acid in a marinade could cook the fish, and you'll end with ceviche, not grilled or smoked fish.

Sturdy vegetables such as onions, carrots, and bell peppers can marinate for several hours. Tomatoes, zucchini, eggplant, and mushrooms are delicate and need only an hour or so. They will become waterlogged if marinated too long.

Cuts of beef, pork, chicken, and lamb can marinate for 8 to 12 hours or overnight, as long as the marinade is not too acidic or intensely flavored.

For the best flavor, make the marinade right before you want to use it. Most marinades will keep in the refrigerator for up to a week, but they will deteriorate in flavor.

In every recipe here, the BBQ Queens decree how each marinade or vinaigrette is best used and for what foods.

Rosemary, Garlic, and Lemon Baste

Looser than a paste, this is a wonderfully aromatic baste to use on beef steaks, pork chops, pork tenderloin, chicken breasts, or leg of lamb before and during grilling. We also love this brushed on the cut sides of Italian bread sliced lengthwise, then wrapped in foil and put on the grill to warm. Or try brushing it on pizza dough, then sprinkle the dough with shredded mozzarella and grill. Or slather it on fish, chicken, pork, or lamb cubes threaded on skewers. For the best texture, use a mortar and pestle. You also may use a food processor. MAKES ABOUT 1/2 CUP

> 1 tablespoon finely chopped fresh rosemary
> 1/2 teaspoon fine kosher or sea salt
> 2 cloves garlic, minced
> 1/2 cup olive oil
> Juice of 1 lemon
> Freshly ground black pepper to taste

1. If using a mortar and pestle, combine the rosemary, salt, and garlic in the mortar and grind into a fine paste with the pestle. Drizzle in the olive oil and grind again. Add the lemon juice, grind, and taste. Add more salt, if desired, and season with pepper.

   If using a food processor, follow the directions above while pulsing the processor on and off to avoid overprocessing.

2. The baste will keep in the refrigerator for up to 1 week.

Aromatic Lemon-Herb Marinade

Fresh herbs, lemon juice, and garlic combine to make this fabulously aromatic marinade. It's great on everything from vegetables to duck, lamb, fish, and shellfish. We also love it as a marinade for rotisserie chicken or pork. MAKES ABOUT 3 CUPS

> 1 cup olive oil
> 1/2 cup fresh lemon juice (3 to 4 lemons)
> 1/2 cup dry white wine

5 cloves garlic, minced

2 tablespoons chopped fresh basil

2 tablespoons chopped fresh mint

2 tablespoons chopped fresh oregano

2 tablespoons chopped fresh rosemary

2 tablespoons chopped fresh Italian parsley

2 teaspoons celery salt

Whisk together all the ingredients in a medium-size bowl. Use immediately or pour into a large jar with a tight-fitting lid. This marinade will keep in the refrigerator for up to 3 days. Let come to room temperature before using.

Homemade Teriyaki Marinade

Teriyaki is one of those formerly "foreign" dishes—like salsa and bruschetta—that have now gone mainstream in American cuisine. We think we know what it is. After all, you can find bottled teriyaki sauce at the grocery store and teriyaki-grilled foods on just about every casual restaurant menu. But we've only scratched the surface. The word "teriyaki" is a combination of the Japanese words *teri*, meaning "glaze," and *yaki*, meaning "to broil." In a teriyaki dish, ingredients are cooked over high heat after being marinated in or basted with teriyaki sauce, which gives luster or shine to the food. The key ingredient in teriyaki sauce is mirin, a pale gold, sweet Japanese wine made from fermented rice (look for the Takara Shuzo brand). Mirin is very good at masking any slight fishy smell, so it's a wonderful ingredient in fish marinades (see Japanese-Style Grilled Fish, page 258). Use this as a marinade, baste, or sauce for just about anything you want to grill. MAKES ABOUT 1 CUP

¹/₂ cup soy sauce

¹/₂ cup mirin (see headnote)

2 tablespoons sugar

Combine all the ingredients in a small saucepan over medium heat and bring to a simmer. Cook, stirring, until the sugar has completely dissolved and the flavors have blended. Let cool. Use immediately or pour into a small jar with a tight-fitting lid. This marinade will keep in the refrigerator indefinitely.

Garlic-Citrus Marinade

This is a delicious way to marinate skirt, sirloin, or flank steak, but it's also good with chicken, pork, lamb, fish, or vegetables. Guess we like this with everything! **MAKES ABOUT ³/₄ CUP**

¼ cup fresh lime juice (4 to 5 limes)

¼ cup fresh orange juice (1 to 2 oranges)

2 cloves garlic, minced

2 tablespoons olive oil

2 tablespoons red wine vinegar

2 tablespoons chopped fresh Italian parsley

1 teaspoon dried oregano

Place all the ingredients in a small jar with a tight-fitting lid. Cover and shake to blend. This marinade will keep in the refrigerator for up to 1 week.

Provençal Red Wine Marinade

Use this heady blend as a marinade for lamb, beef, or chicken destined for the rotisserie or the grill. It's also good as a finishing touch to grilled vegetables, especially portobello mushrooms. If you want to transform this into a vinaigrette—wonderful over any of our seafood salads—whisk in ³/₄ cup more olive oil and add a squeeze of lemon juice. **MAKES ABOUT 1¹/₂ CUPS**

1 cup dry red wine

¼ cup olive oil

4 cloves garlic, minced

1 tablespoon dried herbes de Provence

2 teaspoons fine kosher or sea salt

1 teaspoon freshly ground black pepper

Combine all the ingredients in a medium-size jar with a tight-fitting lid. Cover and shake to blend. This marinade will keep in the refrigerator for up to 1 week.

Rosemary-Mustard Marinade

This marinade is fabulous as a pretreatment for grilled butterflied leg of lamb, lamb chops, lamb shanks, lamb anything. We also like it with pork tenderloin and pork chops. If you want to transform it into a vinaigrette (great over grilled vegetables or smoked goat cheese), whisk in ¹/₂ cup more olive oil and add a squeeze of lemon juice. **MAKES ABOUT 2 CUPS**

³/₄ cup dry red wine
¹/₂ cup olive oil
¹/₃ cup Dijon mustard
¹/₄ cup red wine vinegar
¹/₄ cup fresh rosemary leaves
2 tablespoons green peppercorns in brine, drained
1 tablespoon dried oregano
2 large cloves garlic, minced

Place all the ingredients in a food processor and process until the rosemary leaves are completely ground. Use the day you make it.

Amogio

Amogio is a Sicilian marinade composed of lemon juice and/or white wine, olive oil, garlic, and herbs—the exact recipe varies from household to household. It's used as both a soak and a drizzle, so remember to keep about ¹/₂ cup reserved for drizzling on food that has been grilled or smoked. Marinate chicken, pork, lamb, or beef for up to 24 hours. Amogio is especially good on grilled chicken skewers. MAKES ABOUT 1³/₄ CUPS

> 3 tablespoons minced garlic
> ¹/₂ cup olive oil
> ¹/₂ cup dry white wine
> ¹/₂ cup fresh lemon juice (3 to 4 lemons)
> ¹/₄ cup chopped fresh Italian parsley
> 1 tablespoon chopped fresh mint
> ¹/₄ teaspoon red pepper flakes

1. Combine all the ingredients in a medium-size bowl.

2. To use, reserve ¹/₂ cup of the marinade in the refrigerator and use the rest to marinate the food for at least 1 hour or overnight. Grill or smoke the food, then drizzle with the reserved marinade right before serving.

Fennel and Orange Marinade

Sweet and fragrant, this marinade is great with pork, chicken, or lamb. We especially like it with rotisserie or slow-smoked pork loin. MAKES ABOUT 3 CUPS

> 1 cup cider vinegar
> ¹/₂ cup olive oil
> ¹/₄ cup clover or other medium-colored honey
> ¹/₂ cup dry white wine

Juice and grated zest of 2 oranges

3 large cloves garlic, minced

2 shallots, minced

3 tablespoons fennel seeds

1 teaspoon freshly ground black pepper

$^1/_2$ teaspoon fine kosher or sea salt

In a medium-size bowl, whisk together all the ingredients. Use the same day.

Fennel and Orange Drizzling Sauce: To make this into a drizzling sauce, use half the recipe to marinate the food and reserve the other half in the refrigerator. Bring to room temperature right before serving and whisk in an additional $^1/_2$ cup olive oil. **MAKES ABOUT 3$^1/_2$ CUPS TOTAL**

Tequila-Lime Marinade

Sort of like a margarita, but more savory. We love this as a marinade for grilled fish or shellfish, chicken, zucchini or yellow summer squash, and ears of fresh corn. After grilling or smoking fish or shellfish—especially shrimp or scallops—drizzle some of this on top. MAKES ABOUT $^3/_4$ CUP

$^1/_4$ cup tequila

$^1/_4$ cup fresh lime juice (4 to 5 limes)

$^1/_4$ cup olive oil

2 cloves garlic, minced

1 tablespoon minced shallot

$^1/_2$ teaspoon kosher salt

$^1/_2$ teaspoon red pepper flakes

Combine all the ingredients in a small jar with a tight-fitting lid. Cover and shake to blend. The marinade will keep in the refrigerator for up to 1 week.

Lemongrass Marinade

A little bit of this flavorful and aromatic marinade goes a surprisingly long way. Use it to flavor fish, chicken, or vegetables before grilling. This contemporary take on a marinade is somewhere between a traditional liquid marinade and a paste. **MAKES ABOUT ²/₃ CUP**

1 tablespoon thinly sliced fresh lemongrass (available at Asian markets)

1 clove garlic, minced

1 tablespoon grated fresh ginger (if using a microplane, you don't need to peel)

1 small red Thai chile, trimmed, seeded, and finely chopped

1 teaspoon Asian fish sauce

1 teaspoon rice vinegar

2 teaspoons cornstarch

1 tablespoon peanut oil or other vegetable oil

¹/₂ cup chicken or vegetable broth

1 teaspoon soy sauce

1 teaspoon toasted sesame oil

Kosher or sea salt and freshly ground white pepper to taste

In a medium-size bowl, mix all the ingredients together. This marinade will keep, covered, in the refrigerator for up to 3 days.

Tandoori Marinade

Cooling with yogurt and warm with spices, this marinade helps keep foods such as chicken, lamb, fish, and vegetables moist during indirect grilling and rotisserie cooking at a medium temperature (tandoori marinade is not meant for high-heat grilling). Traditionally a technique from northern India, "tandoori" refers to cooking over coals in a clay vessel, or tandoor. A covered grill works about the same way, as Grill Gal and cookbook author Smita Chandra points out in *Indian Grill: The Art of Tandoori Cooking at Home* (Ecco Press, 1999). In this recipe, adapted from one by Chandra, the saffron turns the marinade—and the food—a wonderful pale gold. Marinate food for up to 24 hours in the refrigerator before grilling. There is no need to baste, as tandoori food self-bastes. **MAKES ABOUT 1¹/₄ CUPS**

1 cup plain yogurt (don't use reduced fat)

¹/₄ teaspoon saffron threads

Juice of ¹/₂ lemon

4 cloves garlic, minced

One 1-inch piece fresh ginger, grated (if using a microplane, you don't need to peel)

1 tablespoon finely chopped fresh cilantro

1 tablespoon vegetable oil

1 teaspoon ground coriander

1 teaspoon ground cumin

In a medium-size bowl, whisk the yogurt until smooth. Whisk in the saffron, then the remaining ingredients. Use the day you make it.

Lemon-Tarragon Vinaigrette

The BBQ Queens love the combination of lemon and tarragon. So when we saw this recipe created by California wine country chef and cookbook author John Ash, we knew we had to adapt it for our book. Fresh tarragon has a pronounced anise flavor, compared to dried tarragon, which tastes and smells more like new-mown hay. Ash uses fresh, but we prefer dried in our version, which can also serve as a marinade. (If you want to use fresh, substitute 2 tablespoons finely minced fresh tarragon for the dried.) This is dynamite with chicken, fish, or shellfish. We also recommend using it to dress grilled vegetables. **MAKES ABOUT 2 CUPS**

¹/₂ cup fresh lemon juice (3 to 4 lemons)

1 teaspoon grated lemon zest

2 tablespoons tarragon vinegar

1 tablespoon finely minced shallot

2 teaspoons dried tarragon

2 teaspoons honey, or to taste

¹/₂ cup olive oil

¹/₄ cup chicken broth

Fine kosher or sea salt and ground white pepper to taste

In a medium-size bowl, combine the lemon juice, zest, vinegar, shallot, tarragon, and honey and mix with a hand blender. Whisk in the olive oil and broth and season with salt and white pepper. The vinaigrette will not emulsify. Use immediately or pour into a medium-size jar with a tight-fitting lid. It will keep in the refrigerator for up to 3 days.

Saffron Vinaigrette

We prefer this gorgeously sunny dressing as a finishing sauce for grilled fish, shellfish, chicken, or vegetables. It's wonderful over still-warm new potatoes that have been steamed or grilled, or as the dressing for a grilled fish or shellfish salad. In our view, saffron is too expensive to be relegated to a mere marinade. It needs to be shown off after cooking, not before. In this recipe, you first infuse the olive oil with the saffron, then whisk the oil into the remaining ingredients for the vinaigrette. MAKES ABOUT 1 1/2 CUPS

1 cup olive oil

1/4 teaspoon saffron threads

1/2 cup white wine vinegar or sherry vinegar

2 teaspoons Dijon mustard

Fine kosher or sea salt and freshly ground black pepper to taste

1.　Pour the olive oil into a small saucepan over low heat. Stir in the saffron and heat until warm, about 10 minutes. Remove from the heat and let the mixture infuse for 10 to 15 minutes.

2.　In a small bowl, whisk the vinegar and mustard together. Slowly pour in the warm saffron oil and whisk to blend. Season with salt and pepper and whisk again. Use immediately.

Wheat Beer Vinaigrette

On the days before Carry Nation, Kansas—where "prairie girl" Judith lives—had more than 80 mom-and-pop breweries. Outdoor beer gardens shaded by hop vines provided a cool place to sip a frothy mug on a hot day. Today, microbreweries dot the Great Plains. And what better beer to drink than a wheat beer—made from wheat grown and harvested a few miles down the road—brightened with a little lemon? Wheat beer gives this vinaigrette a mellow flavor that is delicious as a salad dressing or a marinade for grilled asparagus or meat, especially flank steak. You could also simmer this vinaigrette, whisk in 2 tablespoons of unsalted butter just before taking it off the heat, and have a delicious sauce for steak. **MAKES ABOUT 1 1/2 CUPS**

1 cup wheat beer

1/3 cup olive oil

Juice of 1 lemon

2 cloves garlic, minced

1 tablespoon wildflower, clover, or other medium-colored honey

1 tablespoon Dijon mustard

1 teaspoon ground white pepper

Whisk all the ingredients together in a medium-size bowl. Use the day you make it.

They Dubbed It . . . Coleslaw

Go to any casual restaurant or barbecue joint, and coleslaw will be on the menu, usually as part of a "platter" offering of a sandwich or entrée with French fries. From the Dutch *kool* for cabbage and *sla* for salad, coleslaw existed in our culinary melting pot long before the term was finally attached to the basic recipe. Cabbage, though not native to the Americas, arrived in seed form with the first Pilgrims and Puritans. Greens such as cabbage, raw or cooked and simply dressed with vinegar and oil, were so common that few seventeenth-century recipes exist. Why write it down when it was easy enough to remember?

Other European immigrants with a fondness for pickled or sweet-and-sour cabbage paved the way for the many varieties of coleslaw that we enjoy today. Compilers of the 1875 *Presbyterian Cook Book* from Dayton, Ohio, were very fond of coleslaw. They included three recipes and actually called the dish "cole-slaw." One is made with chopped celery and hard-boiled eggs, another with celery seeds, and all three with a boiled dressing. When North Carolinians got together for a pig-pickin' in the lean days after the Civil War, they had to have vinegar-dressed slaw as an accompaniment.

As BBQ Queens, we love all kinds of slaws because they do double duty as vegetable and salad, can be made ahead before you go out to the grill or smoker, and give you lots of bang for your culinary buck.

Blue Cheese Coleslaw

This has become Judith's family's favorite coleslaw, great with grilled burgers and steaks or slow-smoked ribs. She prefers to use Maytag blue cheese from Iowa for its mellow, creamy blue cheese bite. **SERVES 8**

SLAW

2 pounds Napa cabbage, cored and shredded

8 ounces blue cheese, crumbled

¹/₄ cup chopped green onions

DRESSING

³/₄ cup vegetable oil

¹/₃ cup cider vinegar

2 tablespoons sugar

1 teaspoon celery seeds

¹/₂ teaspoon kosher or sea salt

¹/₂ teaspoon ground white pepper

¹/₄ teaspoon dry mustard

2 cloves garlic, minced

1. To make the slaw, toss the cabbage, blue cheese, and green onions together in a large salad bowl. Set aside or keep covered and refrigerated for up to 24 hours.

2. To make the dressing, right before serving whisk all the ingredients together in a small bowl. Pour over the slaw and toss to coat evenly. The slaw will wilt after it is tossed with the dressing, so serve right away.

Crunchy Broccoli Slaw with Thai Chile-Peanut Dressing

This is a great way to get kids to eat their broccoli. We could make a meal of this alone—and sometimes do. SERVES 8

SLAW

One 16-ounce package broccoli slaw (shredded raw broccoli with red cabbage and carrot)

One 8-ounce can sliced water chestnuts, drained

1 large red bell pepper, seeded and very thinly sliced

THAI CHILE-PEANUT DRESSING

One 12-ounce bottle Thai sweet chili sauce

1/2 cup salted roasted peanuts (dry-roasted is fine)

2 tablespoons toasted sesame oil

1/2 cup water

1. To make the slaw, combine the broccoli slaw, water chestnuts, and bell pepper in a large bowl and set aside.

2. To make the dressing, in a food processor, process the chili sauce, peanuts, and sesame oil together until the peanuts are chopped fine. Add the water and pulse several times to combine. Pour the dressing over the slaw and toss to blend. Serve right away.

Layered Vinegar Slaw

Traditionally served with barbecued pork of all kinds, this slaw is best made the night before, then stirred together right before serving. There's nothing better on a pulled pork sandwich. SERVES 8

SLAW

1 medium-size head cabbage, cored and shredded

1 cup shredded carrot

1 large onion, diced

3/4 cup sugar

DRESSING

³/₄ cup vegetable oil

1 cup distilled white vinegar or cider vinegar

1 tablespoon dry mustard

1 tablespoon celery seeds

1 tablespoon fine sea salt

1.   To make the slaw, in a large serving bowl, layer, in order, the cabbage, carrot, onion, and sugar.

2.   To make the dressing, combine all the ingredients in a medium-size saucepan and bring to a boil. Immediately pour over the cabbage mixture but do not stir. Allow to cool, then cover and refrigerate overnight.

3.   Stir together right before serving.

Mediterranean Summer Squash Slaw

Adapted from a recipe by cookbook author Janet Hazen, this "slaw"—heady with the flavor of fresh basil—will keep for up to 3 days, covered, in the refrigerator (without the basil), and it's great with grilled foods of all kinds. We use a mandoline to cut the squash. SERVES 6

6 small zucchini, ends trimmed and cut into matchstick-size pieces

6 small yellow summer squash, ends trimmed and cut into matchstick-size pieces

6 medium-size ripe tomatoes, finely chopped

1 clove garlic, minced

2 tablespoons extra virgin olive oil

Kosher or sea salt and freshly ground black pepper to taste

1 cup finely chopped fresh basil

1.   In a large serving bowl, combine the squash, tomatoes, and garlic. Drizzle with the olive oil, then season with salt and pepper.

2.   Just before serving, stir in the basil.

Frozen Asset Slaw

This unusual slaw is crisp when defrosted. The large amount of sugar keeps it that way, but the vinegar cuts the sweetness. This is not for the low-carb crowd, but it is a great make-ahead side dish for everyone else. **SERVES 10**

1 medium-size head cabbage, cored and chopped

1 teaspoon fine sea salt

4 stalks celery, thinly sliced

1/2 large green bell pepper, seeded and chopped

1/2 large red bell pepper, seeded and chopped

1 cup distilled white vinegar

2 cups sugar

1 teaspoon celery seeds

1 teaspoon mustard seeds

1. Place the cabbage in a large bowl and sprinkle with the salt. Let stand for 1 hour.

2. Combine the celery and peppers in another large bowl and set aside.

3. In a medium-size saucepan, combine the vinegar, sugar, celery seeds, and mustard seeds. Bring to a boil, let boil for 1 minute, and let cool to lukewarm, about 15 minutes.

4. Squeeze and drain the cabbage. Add the cabbage to the celery and peppers and mix well. Pour the cooled vinegar mixture over the salad and stir to combine. Transfer the slaw to a freezer container and freeze for at least 24 hours or up to 3 months.

5. Before serving, defrost the slaw for 10 to 20 minutes at room temperature (the amount of time will vary depending on the size of the container). When you can stir the slaw with a fork, it's ready to serve.

Red Cabbage and Apple Slaw

To make this slaw up to a day ahead, combine the dressing ingredients and store in the refrigerator. If you wish, you can also shred the cabbage and place in a plastic bag in the refrigerator. Then all you have to do is prepare the apples before serving and assemble everything else instantly. The pretty green and red colors of this slaw are perfect for a holiday buffet. **SERVES 4 TO 6**

SLAW

2 Granny Smith apples, cored and diced

4 cups cored and coarsely shredded red cabbage

DRESSING

¹⁄₄ cup cider vinegar

¹⁄₄ cup vegetable oil

2 tablespoons sugar

¹⁄₂ teaspoon ground cumin

¹⁄₂ teaspoon fine sea salt

Freshly ground black pepper to taste

1. To make the slaw, combine the apples and cabbage in a large serving bowl.

2. To make the dressing, combine all the ingredients in a measuring cup. Taste for salt and pepper. Pour over the cabbage mixture and stir to blend. Refrigerate for up to 1 hour before serving.

Citrus Caesar Vinaigrette

This has more citrus and less garlic than the traditional Caesar dressing and is wonderful on salads or on vegetables, fish, shellfish, chicken, or pork—before or after grilling. Anchovy paste is available in metal tubes at better grocery stores and gourmet shops. Or buy canned anchovies and mash them with a fork. MAKES ABOUT 1 CUP

2/3 cup extra virgin olive oil

3 tablespoons fresh lemon juice

2 tablespoons anchovy paste

1 tablespoon white wine vinegar

1 tablespoon grated lemon zest

1 clove garlic, minced

Combine all the ingredients in a small jar with a tight-fitting lid. Cover and shake to blend. Store in the refrigerator for up to 1 week.

Balsamic-Thyme Vinaigrette

Hearty, savory, and delicious on grilled vegetables—especially mushrooms and eggplant—or a goat cheese salad, this vinaigrette is also great for marinating flank steak or pork. MAKES ABOUT 1 CUP

1/4 cup balsamic vinegar

3/4 cup extra virgin olive oil

2 teaspoons fresh thyme leaves

Fine kosher or sea salt and freshly ground black pepper to taste

Combine all the ingredients in a small jar with a tight-fitting lid. Cover and shake to blend. This vinaigrette will keep in the refrigerator for up to 1 week.

Fresh Basil Vinaigrette

When fresh basil is luxuriant and aromatic in your garden (the BBQ Queens grow their own) or at the farmers' market, use it to make this addictive vinaigrette. You'll need a very large bunch (or three to four packages from the grocery store) to make 1 cup chopped basil, but this luscious vinaigrette is worth it. Because basil can discolor quickly, make this right before serving. MAKES ABOUT 2 CUPS

1½ cups extra virgin olive oil

½ cup fresh lemon juice (3 to 4 lemons)

2 cloves garlic, minced

1 tablespoon Dijon mustard

1 cup finely chopped fresh basil

Fine kosher or sea salt and freshly ground black pepper to taste

Combine all the ingredients in a medium-size jar with a tight-fitting lid. Cover and shake to blend. Use as soon as you make it.

Hot Shallot Vinaigrette

Drizzle this vinaigrette over grilled fish fillets, fish steaks, or oysters for a fabulous finish. It's also good over grilled vegetables or a finely shredded cabbage salad. MAKES ABOUT 1 CUP

8 shallots, minced

½ cup minced fresh Italian parsley

½ cup olive oil

¼ cup fresh lemon juice (about 2 lemons)

2 tablespoons balsamic vinegar

Kosher or sea salt and freshly ground black pepper to taste

1. Whisk together the shallots, parsley, olive oil, lemon juice, and vinegar in a medium-size saucepan. Season with salt and pepper.

2. Right before serving, bring to a boil over high heat. Reduce the heat to low and simmer until the shallots are translucent, about 4 minutes. Use immediately.

Chipotle Vinaigrette

We demonstrated this vinaigrette for the editors at Meredith Corporation (the home of *Better Homes and Gardens, Country Home, Traditional Home, Ladies' Home Journal, Midwest Living,* and *More* magazines) to rave reviews. It can go on just about anything, from salads to grilled or smoked foods. We adapted the recipe from one by the late, great food writer Michael McLaughlin and used it in our book *Fish & Shellfish, Grilled & Smoked* (The Harvard Common Press, 2002). But it's too good to limit to seafood alone, so here it is again. **MAKES ABOUT 1 CUP**

3 tablespoons sherry vinegar

1 tablespoon balsamic vinegar

2 cloves garlic, peeled

2 canned chipotle chiles in adobo sauce (or more to taste), chopped, plus 2 tablespoons adobo sauce

¹/₂ teaspoon fine kosher or sea salt

²/₃ cup olive oil

Freshly ground black pepper to taste

In a food processor or blender, combine the vinegars, garlic, chipotles, adobo sauce, and salt and process until smooth. With the motor running, add the olive oil in a slow, steady stream through the feed tube until incorporated. Season with pepper and pulse to blend. Use immediately or pour into a small jar with a tight-fitting lid. This vinaigrette will keep in the refrigerator for up to 3 days.

Lemon Butter Drizzle

When you want a very easy yet ingenious baste, marinade, or finishing sauce, this is it. We love it on everything from steak to asparagus, salmon to tomatoes, shellfish to mushrooms, chicken to eggplant. MAKES ABOUT 1/2 CUP

1/2 cup (1 stick) unsalted butter, melted

Juice and grated zest of 1 lemon

2 tablespoons chopped fresh herbs, such as Italian parsley, chives, tarragon, and/or basil

In a small bowl, combine the melted butter and lemon juice and zest. Add the herbs right before basting or serving. Keep warm so the butter stays melted.

Vietnamese Drizzle

There is lots of aromatic, sour pizzazz in this recipe, adapted from one by food writer Nigella Lawson. It's wonderful on grilled foods of all kinds, especially shrimp or asparagus, or on Rotisserie Chicken (page 217). It's perfect for Atkins or South Beach Diet aficionados—just use sugar substitute. Bottled fish sauce is available in the Asian section of most supermarkets. And if you want to sneak in a few drops of toasted sesame oil, who are we to argue? MAKES ABOUT 3/4 CUP

One 1-inch piece fresh ginger, grated (if using a microplane, you don't need to peel)

2 cloves garlic, minced

2 small red serrano or Thai chiles, finely chopped (with or without seeds)

1/4 cup Asian fish sauce

2 tablespoons fresh lime juice

1/4 cup water

2 tablespoons sugar

In a small bowl, whisk together all the ingredients. Use the day you make it.

Honey-Almond Grilling Glaze

Aglaze usually has a higher concentration of sugar than does a drizzle, marinade, or vinaigrette. The sugar is what provides the sheen when you brush the glaze on food during the last minutes of grilling. This sweetly aromatic glaze is excellent on grilled seafood, chicken, or pork. Brush it on 1 minute before your food is ready to come off the grill. Don't brush it on too soon, or the sugar will char. Don't turn or glaze the other side—just let the heat of the grill set the glaze on top. This is also yummy as a finishing sauce. **MAKES ABOUT 2¹/₂ CUPS**

¹/₂ cup (1 stick) plus 3 tablespoons unsalted butter

2 tablespoons all-purpose flour

1 cup slivered almonds

2 tablespoons Cajun Steak Rub (page 58) or Cajun seasoning

1 cup chopped celery

1 cup clover or other medium-colored honey

1 cup chicken broth

1 teaspoon grated lemon zest

¹/₈ teaspoon freshly grated nutmeg

1. In a small saucepan over medium heat, melt 3 tablespoons of the butter. Whisk in the flour until smooth and cook until the mixture smells slightly nutty, 1 to 2 minutes; set aside.

2. In a 10-inch skillet over medium-high heat, melt the remaining ¹/₂ cup butter. When it begins to sizzle, add the almonds, Cajun rub, and celery and cook, stirring frequently, until the almonds are browned. Stir in the honey, broth, lemon zest, and nutmeg and cook, stirring occasionally, to let the flavors blend, about 3 minutes. Whisk in the flour and butter mixture until the sauce has slightly thickened, 30 to 60 seconds. Remove from the heat.

3. Brush the glaze on top of the grilled food about 1 minute before it's done. Reserve any unused glaze. Close the grill lid so the glaze can set. Pass the reserved glaze at the table. The glaze will keep in the refrigerator for up to 1 week.

BBQ Queens' Love Potion for the Swine

This is our version of the luscious, thick sauce that our barbecue team has used to win the Battle of the Sexes Barbecue Contest and also has sold for charity. We always tell people that this sauce has aphrodisiac properties so we sell more bottles! You can judge for yourself whether any of these ingredients have romantic potential. If you are a chile head, add 1 to 2 tablespoons more dry mustard and red pepper flakes. If you like to use barbecue sauce as a mop when you're slow smoking, add an extra $1/4$ to $1/2$ cup vinegar to thin it. This all-purpose sauce tastes great on barbecued chicken or brisket, but it's really kickin' with ribs. Give a bottle of homemade sauce to family and friends—or that special someone. **MAKES ABOUT 6 CUPS**

One 24-ounce bottle ketchup

One 12-ounce bottle chili sauce

$1/2$ cup firmly packed dark brown sugar

$1/2$ cup honey

$1/2$ cup cider vinegar

$1/2$ cup molasses

$1/4$ cup dry mustard

2 tablespoons red pepper flakes

1 tablespoon celery seeds

1 tablespoon garlic salt

1 tablespoon Worcestershire sauce

1 tablespoon liquid smoke flavoring

1 teaspoon onion salt

$1/4$ cup water

In a large saucepan, combine all the ingredients and simmer over medium-low heat for 45 to 60 minutes. After you pour the ketchup and chili sauce into the saucepan, turn the almost-empty bottles upside down and add the rest to the mixture. Use immediately, or store, covered, in the refrigerator for several months.

The Doctor Is In
Apricot-Bourbon Barbecue Sauce

Some people doctor up cake mixes. The BBQ Queens doctor up barbecue sauce. That's because it's hard, at home, to duplicate the silky smoothness of the manufactured products when you make barbecue sauce from scratch. So find a tomato-based barbecue sauce you like and experiment. This version is great with lamb, pork, or chicken on the grill, rotisserie, or smoker. **MAKES ABOUT 2 CUPS**

1 cup tomato-based barbecue sauce of your choice

³/₄ cup apricot nectar

¹/₄ cup bourbon

Fresh lemon juice to taste, if needed

In a medium-size bowl, whisk together the barbecue sauce, nectar, and bourbon. Taste, then add lemon juice, if necessary, to sharpen the flavor. Use immediately, or pour into a covered container and store in the refrigerator indefinitely.

Tiara-Worthy Variations: To your favorite 14-ounce bottle of tomato-based barbecue sauce, add one of the following:

- 2 tablespoons of your favorite rub mixture to make **Spicy Barbecue Sauce**

- 2 teaspoons liquid smoke flavoring to make **Smoky Barbecue Sauce**

- 1 cup seedless raspberry jam and 3 tablespoons seeded and finely chopped jalapeños for **Raspberry-Jalapeño Barbecue Sauce**

- ¹/₂ cup clover or other medium-colored honey for **Honeyed Barbecue Sauce** (especially good with a mustard-based barbecue sauce)

- 2 tablespoons soy sauce and 2 teaspoons toasted sesame oil for **Asian Barbecue Sauce**

- 1 chopped canned chipotle chile in adobo sauce, plus 1 tablespoon adobo sauce, for **Chipotle Barbecue Sauce**

Simply Delicious Bordelaise Sauce

It doesn't get much easier or more delicious than this shortcut sauce. (The classic French recipe uses homemade beef stock that has reduced for hours.) We love this sauce with everything from gourmet grilled hamburgers to rib-eye and filet mignon steaks. Bordelaise is best with beef, although it can be mighty tasty on grilled pork or lamb chops—or a leg of lamb, for that matter. **MAKES ABOUT 2¹/₂ CUPS**

One 10.5-ounce can beef broth

1 beef broth can dry red wine

1 bay leaf

1 teaspoon dried thyme

2 cloves garlic, minced

2 green onions

¹/₄ cup (¹/₂ stick) unsalted butter, cubed

Juice of ¹/₂ lemon, or to taste

Freshly ground black pepper to taste

1. In a small saucepan over medium-high heat, bring the beef broth, wine, bay leaf, thyme, garlic, and green onions to a boil. Reduce the heat to medium-low and simmer until reduced by half, about 12 minutes.

2. Strain the solids out of the mixture and return the liquid to the pan over medium-low heat. Whisk in the butter, one cube at a time, until the butter is suspended in the mixture. Remove from the heat and stir in the lemon juice. Season with pepper. Keep warm in the top of a double boiler or transfer to a stainless steel bowl and set over a pan of hot, not boiling, water until ready to serve.

Mango-Lemon Sauce

Sublimely simple and superbly delicious, this sauce is especially fabulous with grilled or smoked shellfish. If you can't find mango puree (look in the freezer section), buy a ripe mango and peel, seed, chop, and puree it in a food processor. Lime juice is also delicious in place of the lemon. MAKES ABOUT 1 CUP

     1 cup mango puree
     1 tablespoon fresh lemon juice
     $1/2$ teaspoon ground cumin
     $1/4$ teaspoon cayenne pepper
     Kosher salt to taste

In a small bowl, whisk all the ingredients together. Use the day you make it.

Raspberry and Blood Orange Sauce

We love this on grilled chicken breasts, fish fillets or steaks, lamb chops, or pork tenderloin. Blood orange juice is sometimes available bottled at health food stores. MAKES ABOUT $1/2$ CUP

     $2/3$ cup fresh blood orange juice (10 to 12 blood oranges) or a combination of fresh orange juice and fresh lemon juice (6 to 7 oranges and 2 lemons)
     $1/3$ cup raspberry vinegar
     $1/4$ cup ($1/2$ stick) unsalted butter, cut into small pieces
     Fine kosher or sea salt and ground white pepper to taste

1. In a small, heavy saucepan over high heat, bring the orange juice and vinegar to a boil. Continue to boil until reduced to a syrupy liquid, about 8 minutes.

2. Quickly whisk in the butter until melted. Remove from the heat and season with salt and white pepper. Use immediately.

Poblano Cream Sauce

This fabulously easy sauce is great with grilled skirt steak, chicken, or pork tenderloin. If you can't find a fresh poblano, substitute a jalapeño. **MAKES ABOUT 1 1/2 CUPS**

   1 poblano chile, smoked (see page 140)
   2 cups heavy cream or evaporated milk
   1/2 cup (1 stick) unsalted butter, cut into pieces
   Kosher or sea salt and freshly ground black pepper to taste

1.   Combine the poblano and cream in a medium-size, heavy saucepan and simmer over medium heat until reduced to 1 cup, about 15 minutes.

2.   Strain the mixture, discard the chile, and return the cream to the pan over low heat. Whisk in the butter, one piece at a time, until you have a smooth sauce. Season with salt and pepper and serve immediately.

Smoked Garlic and Cilantro Cream Sauce

Just reading that recipe title makes our mouths water! We adapted this fabulous sauce from one by fellow Grill Gal Blanca Aldaco, a chef in San Antonio, Texas. Aldaco likes to serve it over grilled chicken breast, pork tenderloin, or shellfish that has been marinated for an hour in a combination of 6 tablespoons olive oil, 3 tablespoons fresh lime juice, and garlic salt to taste. This is enough sauce for six grilled boneless, skinless chicken breasts. If you don't want to use smoked garlic, substitute two minced garlic cloves for a sharper but still delicious flavor. **MAKES ABOUT 2 1/2 CUPS**

   2 cups heavy cream
   1/2 cup fresh cilantro leaves, plus more for garnish
   3 tablespoons fresh lime juice
   1/2 teaspoon kosher or sea salt
   6 cloves garlic, smoked (see page 140) and peeled

1. In a blender or food processor, combine all the ingredients and process until smooth.

2. Transfer the puree to a medium-size saucepan over medium-high heat and cook until the sauce begins to bubble. Serve immediately.

Roasted Red Pepper Sauce

We love grill-roasted or smoked red bell peppers, but we also know that not everybody has them on hand all the time. The BBQ Queens' cupboards always contain jars of roasted red peppers that we can use as a high-flavor convenience food to add snap to any sauce or dressing. We love this sauce on anything grilled, and it goes exceptionally well with foods that have been slathered with Rosemary Pesto (page 62) before grilling. **MAKES ABOUT 2 CUPS**

2 grill-roasted large red bell peppers (see page 145) or one 12-ounce jar roasted red peppers, drained

20 oil- or brine-cured Kalamata or Niçoise olives, pitted

$1/2$ cup fresh lemon juice (3 to 4 lemons)

2 tablespoons balsamic vinegar

2 teaspoons capers, drained

2 teaspoons anchovy paste

3 tablespoons olive oil

Fine kosher or sea salt and freshly ground black pepper to taste

Combine the red peppers, olives, lemon juice, vinegar, capers, and anchovy paste in a food processor and process until fairly smooth. With the machine running, drizzle the olive oil through the feed tube in a steady stream until the sauce solidifies. Season with salt and pepper. Use immediately or spoon into a medium-size jar with a tight-fitting lid. This sauce will keep in the refrigerator for up to 3 days or in the freezer for up to 6 months.

Tomato-Fennel Sauce

The sunny flavors in this colorful, chunky sauce go well with grilled fish, chicken, shellfish, eggplant, or lamb. Fennel looks somewhat like celery, but with a broader base and delicate frond-like leaves. It has a mild, sweet, licorice-like flavor that blends well with sharp, sassy tomato. Use vegetable broth in place of chicken for a vegetarian sauce. **MAKES ABOUT 4 CUPS**

5 tablespoons olive oil

1 shallot, finely chopped

1 clove garlic, minced

1/4 cup roughly chopped carrot

1/4 cup roughly chopped celery

1/2 cup roughly chopped fennel stalks

1/2 cup Pernod, anisette, ouzo, or other anise-flavored liqueur

One 28-ounce can chopped tomatoes (we prefer Muir Glen fire-roasted tomatoes), with their juice

1 cup chicken broth

Kosher or sea salt and freshly ground black pepper to taste

1.   In a medium-size saucepan, heat 2 tablespoons of the oil over medium-high heat. Add the shallot, garlic, carrot, celery, and fennel and cook, stirring, until tender, about 5 minutes. Stir in the Pernod and cook until it is almost evaporated, 5 to 7 minutes. Stir in the tomatoes and broth and cook, stirring occasionally, until thickened, about 30 minutes.

2.   When ready to serve, season with salt and pepper and stir in the remaining 3 tablespoons olive oil.

Pistachio-Pomegranate Sauce

We wish we could reach out from the pages of this book and give you a taste of this sauce, but you'll have to make it yourself (or come to one of our cooking classes) to sample it. We *loooooooove* this on grilled, rotisserie, or smoked lamb—especially rack of lamb. It's also good with grilled pork, duck, or chicken. In the Kansas City area, we find pomegranate molasses at Asian and Indian markets, bottled pomegranate juice at Whole Foods Market or health food stores, and grenadine at the liquor store. MAKES ABOUT 2 CUPS

1 cup shelled unsalted pistachios

¹/₄ cup water

¹/₄ cup (¹/₂ stick) unsalted butter

1¹/₂ teaspoons firmly packed light brown sugar

1 teaspoon honey

2 tablespoons port or dry sherry

¹/₄ cup pomegranate molasses

¹/₄ cup pomegranate juice

Juice of ¹/₂ lemon

Grenadine

Fine kosher or sea salt and freshly ground black pepper to taste

Chopped unsalted pistachios for garnish

1. Divide the shelled pistachios in half. Grind half in a food processor and set aside. Combine the remaining whole pistachios and the water in a small saucepan and bring to a boil. Remove from the heat, cover, and set aside.

2. Melt the butter in a medium-size saucepan over medium-high heat and stir in the brown sugar, honey, port, pomegranate molasses, and pomegranate juice. Cook for 2 minutes, stirring, then add the lemon juice and blend in the ground pistachios. Drain the whole pistachios and stir into the sauce. Add a few drops of grenadine until you have a pleasing rosy color. Season with salt and pepper.

3. To serve, nap the food with the sauce and garnish with chopped pistachios.

Food Processor or Blender Hollandaise

Serve this wonderful all-purpose sauce on grilled vegetables, fish, chicken, or that breakfast classic—eggs Benedict. MAKES ABOUT 1 1/2 CUPS

6 large egg yolks

2 tablespoons fresh lemon juice

1 teaspoon dry mustard

1 cup (2 sticks) unsalted butter, melted and still hot

1/4 teaspoon cayenne pepper, or to taste

Fine kosher or sea salt to taste

Place the egg yolks, lemon juice, and mustard in a food processor or blender and process until smooth. Drizzle in the hot melted butter, pulsing the food processor or with the blender on low speed, until the sauce thickens. Add the cayenne and season with salt. Keep warm in the top of a double boiler or transfer to a stainless steel bowl and set over a pan of hot, not boiling, water until ready to serve.

Emulsion Sauces

As we developed more as cooks, we began to experiment with emulsion sauces—those sauces made with an acidic base of white wine, vinegar, or lemon juice to which egg yolks and/or butter are added to make a sauce similar to a thin but still rich mayonnaise. Emulsion sauces such as hollandaise, Béarnaise, and *beurre blanc* are fantastic with grilled foods of all kinds. If you've never attempted them, now's the time to start.

Our suggestion is to begin with Food Processor or Blender Hollandaise (above), then move on to Rustic Béarnaise Sauce (page 98) and the *beurre blanc* recipes (pages 99–102). You do have to stay close by when you make these sauces—not talk on the phone or put in a load of laundry. Emulsion sauces require your undivided attention.

If—*quelle horreur!*—your emulsion sauce breaks (that is, the butter begins to leach out of the sauce instead of staying suspended), no problem. Just whisk an ice cube or two into the broken sauce to bring it back to its beauteous emulsified state. If your sauce does break, it's because you've kept it on the heat too long, so be mindful next time.

Rustic Béarnaise Sauce

This sauce is a staple at Judith's house, an accompaniment she has been making since the 1970s (when she was a very precocious elementary school student). Chunkier and zippier than the classic smooth and mild Béarnaise, this version goes with anything grilled. **MAKES ABOUT 1 CUP**

$^1/_3$ **cup dry white wine**

$^1/_4$ **cup tarragon vinegar**

1 tablespoon finely chopped shallot

1 teaspoon dried tarragon

$^1/_4$ **teaspoon fine kosher or sea salt**

$^1/_2$ **cup (1 stick) plus 3 tablespoons unsalted butter, cubed**

3 large egg yolks, lightly beaten

Cayenne pepper to taste

In a small saucepan, bring the wine, vinegar, shallot, tarragon, and salt to a boil. Continue to boil until reduced to 2 tablespoons, about 8 minutes. Reduce the heat to low and whisk in the butter, one cube at a time. When the butter has almost melted, whisk in the egg yolks and keep whisking to blend the yolks and butter. Remove from the heat when slightly thickened, 4 to 5 minutes. Taste for tarragon and season with cayenne. Serve immediately.

Smoked Chile Beurre Blanc

hen we saw this recipe on the Cookshack Web site, we knew we had to have it in our book. So we fooled around with it and came up with the BBQ Queens' version. If you smoke food ahead for leftovers, as we're always preaching, and have smoked bell peppers, jalapeños or other chiles, and garlic already frozen (see page 140), making this sauce is a snap. We love it on anything. **MAKES ABOUT 4 CUPS**

2 cups dry white wine

$1/2$ cup white wine vinegar

$1/4$ cup finely chopped green onions

2 tablespoons heavy cream

1 red bell pepper, smoked, seeded, and chopped (about $3/4$ cup)

1 yellow bell pepper, smoked, seeded, and chopped (about $3/4$ cup)

1 green bell pepper, smoked, seeded, and chopped (about $3/4$ cup)

2 jalapeños, smoked, seeded, and chopped (about $1/4$ cup)

2 shallots, smoked, peeled, and chopped (about 2 tablespoons)

2 large cloves garlic, smoked and peeled (about 2 teaspoons)

$3/4$ cup ($1 1/2$ sticks) unsalted butter, at room temperature, cubed

Coarse kosher or sea salt and freshly ground black pepper to taste

1. In a large saucepan, combine the wine, vinegar, and green onions and bring to a boil. Continue to boil until reduced by half, about 10 minutes. Whisk in the cream and smoked vegetables and cook until the vegetables are warm, about 5 minutes. Remove from the heat.

2. Whisk in the butter, one cube at a time, until melted into the sauce but not separated. Season with salt and pepper and serve immediately.

Mustard-Cornichon Beurre Blanc

Somewhere between the classic, piquant *sauce Gribiche* and the mellower Béarnaise, this easy sauce offers a jolt of flavor that is perfect with grilled steak, lamb, or fish. Cornichons, small 2-inch-long pickles usually served with pâtés, are available in small jars at better grocery stores. They add wonderful texture and taste. This is adapted from a recipe by Stuart Cameron, chef at the Napa Valley Grille in Providence, Rhode Island. **MAKES ABOUT 1 1/2 CUPS**

> 1/2 cup (1 stick) unsalted butter, softened
>
> 1/3 cup Dijon mustard
>
> 1 cup dry white wine
>
> 1/3 cup tarragon vinegar or white wine vinegar
>
> 1 shallot, minced
>
> 2 tablespoons minced fresh tarragon or 2 teaspoons dried tarragon
>
> 12 cornichons, finely chopped
>
> 1/3 cup heavy cream
>
> Fine kosher or sea salt and freshly ground black pepper to taste

1. In a small bowl, mix the softened butter and mustard together. Cover and refrigerate for 15 minutes.

2. Combine the wine, vinegar, and shallot in a small saucepan and bring to a boil. Continue to boil until reduced to 1/2 cup, about 10 minutes.

3. Reduce the heat to low and whisk in the butter mixture, 1 tablespoon at a time. Continue whisking until the butter has been incorporated into the sauce. Whisk in the tarragon, cornichons, and heavy cream. Season with salt and pepper and serve immediately.

Raspberry Beurre Blanc

The BBQ Queens love raspberries in general, but in this sauce, they're divine. Serve it with grilled zucchini or yellow summer squash, duck or turkey breast, chicken, pork tenderloin, salmon, or scallops. **MAKES ABOUT 1 1/2 CUPS**

1 tablespoon minced shallot

1/4 cup fresh lemon juice (about 2 lemons)

1 cup dry white wine

1 cup fresh or individually frozen raspberries (no need to defrost)

1 small clove garlic, minced

1/4 cup sugar

1 cup heavy cream

1/4 cup (1/2 stick) cold unsalted butter, cubed

1. In a small saucepan over medium-high heat, combine the shallot, lemon juice, wine, raspberries, garlic, and sugar and bring to a boil. Continue to boil until reduced to about 1/4 cup, about 5 minutes. (If you don't want raspberry seeds in your sauce, strain the mixture, discard the solids, and return the liquid to the pan.)

2. Pour in the cream, return to a boil, and continue to boil until reduced by half, about 5 minutes.

3. Remove from the heat and whisk in the butter, one cube at a time, until the sauce glistens and thickens. Keep warm in the top of a double boiler or transfer to a stainless steel bowl and set over a pan of hot, not boiling, water until ready to serve.

Peppercorn Beurre Blanc

Sprinkle foods destined for the grill or smoker with Tricolored Peppercorn Rub (page 62), then serve this sauce as an accompaniment for a welcome culinary hot flash. **MAKES ABOUT 1 CUP**

2 teaspoons Szechuan or white peppercorns

1 teaspoon black peppercorns

1 teaspoon dried green peppercorns

3/4 cup dry white wine

1 tablespoon minced shallot

1 cup (2 sticks) cold unsalted butter, cubed

1/4 teaspoon fine kosher or sea salt

1. Place all the peppercorns in a small cast-iron skillet over medium-high heat and toast, stirring frequently, until aromatic, about 2 minutes. Scrape into a mortar and grind with a pestle until crushed but still somewhat coarse.

2. In a small saucepan, bring the crushed peppercorns, wine, and shallot to a boil. Continue to boil until reduced to 2 tablespoons, 10 to 15 minutes. Remove the pan from the heat and turn the heat to low. Whisk in 2 cubes of butter, then return the pan to the heat. Whisk until the butter has almost melted into the liquid. Continue whisking in the butter, one cube at a time, until all the butter has been emulsified into the sauce and the sauce has thickened. Remove from the heat immediately and whisk in the salt. Keep warm in the top of a double boiler or transfer to a stainless steel bowl and set over a pan of hot, not boiling, water until ready to serve.

Kimizu

This Japanese-style emulsion sauce uses cornstarch instead of butter as an extra thickening agent. Watch this sauce carefully, as it cooks over low heat. If it begins to boil, it will curdle (and an ice cube whisked in won't help, because the sauce contains no butter). This delicately flavored sauce, adapted from a recipe by Mary Evely at Simi Winery in California, goes very well with any grilled mild-flavored fish, such as tilapia, John Dory, farm-raised catfish, halibut, haddock, walleye, or Alaskan cod. It's also great with lightly smoked shrimp or scallops. **MAKES ABOUT ³/₄ CUP**

> **3 large egg yolks**
> **³/₄ cup water**
> **3 tablespoons rice vinegar**
> **1 tablespoon sugar**
> **1 tablespoon cornstarch**
> **1 teaspoon wasabi paste or powder (available at Asian markets)**

1. Place all the ingredients in a food processor or blender and process until smooth.

2. Transfer to a small saucepan over low heat. Cook, stirring constantly, until the sauce thickens, about 15 minutes. Keep warm in the top of a double boiler or transfer to a stainless steel bowl and set over a pan of hot, not boiling, water until ready to serve.

Lemon-Garlic Mayonnaise

Spoon this creamy mayonnaise over your favorite grilled fish, shellfish, vegetables, or poultry. It has the flavor of aioli, without the preparation. **MAKES ABOUT 1 CUP**

> **1 cup mayonnaise (lowfat is okay)**
> **Juice of 2 lemons**
> **1 clove garlic, minced**
> **1 teaspoon ground white pepper**

Combine all the ingredients in a small bowl, whisking to blend. This mayonnaise will keep, covered, in the refrigerator for up to 2 weeks.

Rustic Aioli

Traditional aioli, a garlicky emulsion sauce from the south of France, is made with a mortar and pestle or a bowl and whisk. Arguments fly as to whether traditional aioli can really be made in the food processor. We've tried making aioli by hand and with a machine, and believe it or not, both take the same amount of time. The texture is more emulsified in the processor version, however. Here is the handmade version, made even zestier by the judicious addition of anchovies and basil. For the food processor technique, see White Truffle Aioli (recipe follows). We love aioli as an accompaniment to grilled foods of all kinds. **MAKES ABOUT 1 CUP**

2 large egg yolks, preferably organic

2 anchovy fillets, minced, or 1 tablespoon anchovy paste

2 cloves garlic, minced

2 tablespoons chopped fresh basil or 1 teaspoon dried basil

$1/2$ teaspoon Worcestershire sauce

$1/2$ teaspoon red wine vinegar

1 tablespoon fresh lemon juice

1 cup olive oil

Fine kosher or sea salt and hot pepper sauce to taste

Place the egg yolks in a medium-size glass bowl and microwave for 15 to 20 seconds on high. Whisk them together and add the anchovies, garlic, basil, Worcestershire, vinegar, and lemon juice. Slowly whisk in the olive oil. If the mixture gets too thick, thin with a little warm water. Season with salt and hot sauce. Mix thoroughly, cover, and refrigerate until ready to serve. This sauce will keep, covered, in the refrigerator for up to 3 days.

White Truffle Aioli

The BBQ Queens are quite fond of aioli, that mayonnaise-like sauce that can take on many different flavorings. This version takes on the heady, earthy perfume of the white truffle, its essence captured in vegetable oil. Our suggestion is to add just half of the white truffle oil at first, taste and see whether you like it, and then add the rest, if desired. White truffle oil can be overpowering if you use too much. You can buy small bottles of white truffle oil at gourmet shops or order it online. (Try adding a few drops to mashed potatoes or risotto. Delicious!) We love this aioli with grilled or smoked beef tenderloin, grilled potatoes, or grilled tuna. It's dynamite on grilled chicken or steak sandwiches, too. We adapted this from a recipe by Richard Chamberlain of the restaurant at the Little Nell in Aspen, Colorado. MAKES ABOUT 1¹/₂ CUPS

2 large egg yolks

1 teaspoon fresh lemon juice

1 large clove garlic, minced

¹/₄ teaspoon kosher or sea salt

¹/₄ teaspoon ground white pepper

1 cup olive oil

2 tablespoons white truffle oil, or to taste

Place the egg yolks in a medium-size bowl and microwave for 15 to 20 seconds on high. Whisk them together and add the lemon juice, garlic, salt, and white pepper. Whisk until smooth. Slowly whisk in the olive oil and truffle oil until the sauce thickens. Use immediately, or spoon into a small jar with a tight-fitting lid and store in the refrigerator for up to 3 days.

Baked or Barbecued Beans

Anyone who has ever gnawed on a rib bone knows that the three real, true American side dishes for a slow-smokin' barbecue are barbecued or baked beans, coleslaw, and potato salad. That being said, the recipes vary as much as the topography of the land and the style of barbecue practiced on it.

For beans, the differences are in the variety of beans used and whether they're in a spicy or sweet sauce, cooked with or without meat, and cooked indoors or out on the smoker. We prefer to put these right on the smoker along with whatever else we're smoking—ribs, pork butt, brisket—or rotisserie cooking. Here are some recipes that any BBQ Babe would be proud to serve.

Texas-Style Pinto Beans

We adapted this recipe from Paris Permenter and John Bigley's *Texas Barbecue* (Pig Out Publications, 1994). They're delicious with Texas-style barbecued brisket, chicken, ribs, or pork butt. Pinto beans have a creamy, velvety texture when they're done. **SERVES 12**

> 1 pound dried pinto beans
>
> Three 10-ounce cans Ro-Tel diced tomatoes with green chiles, with their juice
>
> 8 ounces sliced bacon, chopped
>
> 1 medium-size white onion, chopped
>
> 2 jalapeños, seeded and chopped
>
> $1/2$ teaspoon ground cumin
>
> $1/2$ teaspoon cayenne pepper
>
> $1/2$ teaspoon chili powder
>
> $1/2$ teaspoon fine kosher or sea salt
>
> $1/2$ teaspoon freshly ground black pepper
>
> Chopped green onions for garnish (optional)

1. Pick over the beans, rinse, place in a large bowl, and add enough cold water to cover. Let stand at room temperature for several hours or overnight.

2.   Drain the beans, rinse well, and transfer to a large pot. Add the remaining ingredients and enough hot water to cover.

3.   To cook outdoors, prepare an indirect fire in a smoker. Smoke the beans, with the lid closed, until tender, 5 to 6 hours. To cook indoors, bring the beans to a boil, cover, and simmer on the stovetop until tender, 3 to 4 hours.

BBQ Queens' Barbecued Beans

Here's a Kansas City–style barbecued bean recipe. Most competition barbecuers use canned pork and beans, but you can use 3 cups dried navy beans if you want to be a purist. Simply soak them in water overnight, then drain and cook them in a pot with enough water to cover until tender, about 40 minutes. We recommend BBQ Queens' Love Potion for the Swine (page 89) barbecue sauce for this recipe. SERVES 12

> 8 cups canned pork and beans
> 1 cup firmly packed light or dark brown sugar
> 1 large onion, finely chopped
> 1/2 cup ketchup
> 2 cups smoky, spicy barbecue sauce of your choice
> 1/4 cup Dijon mustard
> 2 cups chopped smoked meats, such as beef, pork, sausage, or turkey
> Kosher or sea salt and freshly ground black pepper to taste

1.   Combine all the ingredients in a large, heavy casserole dish or disposable aluminum pan.

2.   To cook outdoors, prepare an indirect fire in a smoker. Smoke the beans, with the lid closed, at 225 to 250°F until smoky and bubbling, about 3 hours. To cook indoors, preheat the oven to 350°F and bake, uncovered, until thickened, browned, and bubbling, about 1 1/2 hours.

Jazzy Java Baked Beans

A traditional baked bean recipe enlivened with a jolt of java! Coffee is sometimes used as a mop or basting mixture for slow-smoked brisket and pork butt, so it's a natural in any bean dish you would serve with them. SERVES 12

1 pound dried navy beans

8 ounces sliced bacon, diced

1 medium-size onion, diced

4 cloves garlic, minced

1/4 cup lightly packed dark brown sugar

1 tablespoon molasses

2 tablespoons brown mustard

2 cups water

1 cup strong black coffee

1 cup barbecue sauce of your choice

1 teaspoon hot pepper sauce

Fine kosher or sea salt and freshly ground black pepper to taste

1.   Pick over the beans, rinse, and place in a large bowl. Cover with water and let stand for several hours or overnight.

2.   Drain the beans, rinse well, and transfer to a large Dutch oven. Add the remaining ingredients and stir to combine.

3.   To cook indoors, preheat the oven to 300°F. Bake, stirring once an hour, until the beans are soft and the liquid syrupy, about 4 hours. To cook outdoors, prepare an indirect fire in a smoker and smoke the beans with the lid closed at 225 to 250°F until smoky and bubbling, 4 to 5 hours.

Easy Southern-Style Baked Beans

Here's a sweeter-style baked bean recipe that bakes lower and slower. These beans could also be put in the smoker to smoke-cook for 3 hours. SERVES 8

> Three 15-ounce cans pork and beans
>
> 1 cup firmly packed light brown sugar
>
> ³/₄ cup ketchup
>
> ³/₄ cup cola
>
> 1 medium-size onion, diced
>
> 2 teaspoons dry mustard
>
> 6 to 8 slices bacon

1. Preheat the oven to 300°F.

2. In a large bowl, combine the beans, brown sugar, ketchup, cola, onion, and mustard. Spread the beans in a 13 x 9-inch baking dish and lay the bacon slices over the top. Bake until the beans are bubbling and the bacon is thoroughly cooked, about 1¹/₂ hours.

The Doctor Is In Easy Aioli

The BBQ Queens like big flavor, and aioli fits the ticket. Shortcut aioli can be pretty good when you use a good-quality store-bought mayonnaise. We are particularly fond of a canola-based mayonnaise that is the house brand at Whole Foods Market. The product is creamy and makes for a more authentic "doctored" aioli. However, any good-quality mayonnaise you like will taste fine—just don't use salad dressing. **MAKES ABOUT 1 CUP**

1 cup good-quality mayonnaise

2 tablespoons fresh lemon juice

2 teaspoons grated lemon zest

2 cloves garlic, minced

Fine kosher or sea salt to taste

In a medium-size bowl, whisk all the ingredients together. This sauce will keep, covered, in the refrigerator for 7 to 10 days.

Tiara-Worthy Variations: Here are more easy ways to doctor up aioli, whether it's a shortcut or entirely homemade. To 1 cup The Doctor Is In Easy Aioli, add one of the following:

- **2 tablespoons prepared horseradish to make Horseradish Aioli (great on steak or smoked or rotisserie beef sandwiches)**

- **1/2 cup finely chopped roasted red peppers (homemade, see page 145, or from a jar) to make Roasted Red Pepper Aioli**

- **1 smoked tomato (see page 161), peeled, seeded, and chopped, to make Smoked Tomato Aioli**

- **1/2 cup finely chopped fresh herbs to make Fresh Herb Aioli**

- **2 tablespoons homemade or prepared pesto to make Pesto Aioli**

Creamy Blue Cheese Dressing

This wonderfully pungent blue cheese dressing from Judith's *Prairie Home Cooking* (The Harvard Common Press, 1999) makes a great dipping sauce for chicken wings or raw or grilled vegetables. It's also superb served over a crisp wedge of iceberg lettuce. If you like a thinner consistency, add 2 to 3 more tablespoons of vinegar. **MAKES ABOUT 4 CUPS**

2 cups sour cream

8 ounces good-quality blue cheese, such as Maytag, crumbled

$^2/_3$ cup mayonnaise

3 tablespoons cider vinegar

1 teaspoon red pepper flakes

Onion salt, celery salt, and Worcestershire sauce to taste

Combine all the ingredients in a medium-size bowl, whisking to blend. For the best results, cover and let the flavors develop in the refrigerator for 24 hours before serving chilled. This dressing will keep, covered, in the refrigerator for up to 2 weeks.

Tzatziki

Fresh pita bread, brushed with olive oil and grilled, or grilled or rotisserie lamb, tastes even more fabulous when served with this Greek yogurt sauce, enlivened with garlic, cucumber, and dillweed. It's easy to make, but allow enough time to drain the yogurt. Do this by lining a colander with cheesecloth, a double thickness of sturdy paper towels, or a very thin tea towel. Place the colander in a bowl and spoon the yogurt into the colander. Wait for the excess liquid to drain away, which takes about 2 hours at room temperature. You'll end up with about 1 cup of drained liquid to discard. If you can find real Greek yogurt, you can skip the draining. MAKES 3 GENEROUS CUPS

> 4 cups plain yogurt (don't use reduced fat), drained (see headnote)
>
> 1 medium-size cucumber, peeled, seeded, and finely shredded
>
> 4 large cloves garlic, minced
>
> 2 tablespoons olive oil
>
> 1/2 teaspoon dillweed
>
> Fine kosher or sea salt and freshly ground black pepper to taste

Transfer the drained yogurt to a medium-size bowl. Blot the shredded cucumber with paper towels to remove as much moisture as possible. Stir the cucumber, garlic, olive oil, and dillweed into the yogurt. Season with salt and pepper. Use immediately, or spoon into a covered container and store in the refrigerator for up to 3 days.

An A to Z of Grilled and Smoked Veggies, Cheeses, and Pizza

Charred or smoked vegetables fresh from the grocer, farmers' market, or your own backyard get an extra depth of flavor from fire and smoke. ♕ Cheese is served well by a kiss of smoke, whether through traditional smoking or sitting atop an aromatic wood plank. We like pizza on the grill, charred crisp on one side, then flipped and layered with thinly sliced vegetables and charred crisp again. Even a loaf of bread, slathered with something good, then tightly wrapped in foil and placed above the flames, gets a crusty burnish that is yummy. ♕ Fresh thick or thin spears of asparagus or slices of zucchini are drizzled with a bit of olive oil and grilled until charred a caramel brown or smoked with aromatic woods that make the freshest vegetables taste incredible. And oh my, what you can do with those charred and smoked veggies—from Grilled Gazpacho (page 155) to Smoked Tomato and Basil Butter (page 177).

Say cheese, please, and make mine smoked—from a wheel of Brie to a crock of goat cheese. Pizza and bread on the grill put their indoor oven counterparts to absolute shame. And best yet, all this outdoor cooking keeps the kitchen cool in the summer and neat and tidy in the winter.

Grilled Asparagus 117

Grilled Asparagus
with Shaved
Parmigiano-Reggiano 118

Asian-Style Asparagus
with Peanut Butter
Dipping Sauce 118

Grilled Asparagus Frittata 118

Grilled Corn 119

Southwestern-Style
Grilled Corn Relish 120

Grilled Corn and Smoked
Vegetable Pudding 120

Grilled Corn Layered Salad 120

Smoked Corn in the Husks 121

Smoked Corn, Sliced Tomato,
and Slivered Red Onion
Salad 122

Smoky Chipotle
Corn Pudding 122

Smoked Corn, Ham,
and Hominy Casserole 123

Grilled Eggplant 123

Grilled Eggplant, Peppers,
and Goat Cheese
with Balsamic-Thyme
Vinaigrette 124

Sonoma Farmers' Market
Eggplant Spread 124

Warm Asian
Eggplant Salad 125

Grilled Eggplant Roll-Ups
with Feta-Olive-Lemon
Filling 126

Fettuccine with Grilled
Eggplant–Garlic Sauce 126

Grilled Greens 126

Grilled Radicchio and
Red Cabbage with
Herbed Caesar Dressing 127

Grilled Romaine
Caesar Salad 127

Grilled Romaine and
Green Onions with
Lemon and Olives 127

Fennel and Feta Salad 128

Grilled Cheese in a Sarong 128

GRILLED VEGETABLES ON PARADE

Grilled Vegetable Platter with
Fresh Basil Vinaigrette 129

Grilled Vegetable and
Goat Cheese Terrine 130

Grilled Mushrooms 132

Grilled Portobellos with
Garlic, Pine Nuts, Basil,
and Goat Cheese 133

Grilled Portobello
Mushroom "Burgers" 133

Smoked Mushrooms 134

Smoked Stuffed
Mushrooms 135

Smoked PLT 136

Smoked Mushroom Bisque 136

Grilled Onions 137

Grilled Green Onions
and Red Onion Slices 138

Grilled Onion Soufflé 138

Grilled Onions with
Thyme and Garlic Cream 138

Smoked Onions 139

Honey-Basted
Smoked Onions 141

Smoked (or Grilled)
Onion Marmalade 141

Smoked Onion Tart 141

Pickled Brewpub
Smoked Onions 142

Grilled Peppers 142

Cheesy Grilled
Pepper Boats 143

Grilled Chiles Rellenos
with Baby Shrimp 143

BBQ QUEENS' GRILLED
ANTIPASTO PLATTER

Queen-Size Spiced Olives 145

Grill-Roasted Peppers 145

Pick a Peck of
Grilled Peppers Sauce 145

Grilled Potatoes 147

Grilled Whole Potatoes 148

Rustic Grill-Roasted
Potato Salad 148

Grilled Red Potato and
Fennel Salad 148

Grilled Vegetable Tart 149

Skewered Potatoes
(and Other Vegetables) 149

THE UNGRILLED POTATO SALAD

Creamy Dijon Potato Salad
for a Crowd 151

Grilled Antipasto Skewers 151

Grilled Sweet Potato and
Red Onion Skewers 151

Smoked Potatoes 152

Smoked Potato and
Aioli Gratin 152

BBQ Queens' Smoked
Potato Casserole 153

Smoked Potato Soup 153

Smoked New or
Fingerling Potato Platter 154

Grilled Summer Squash 154

Grilled Gazpacho 155

Char-Grilled Baby Summer
Squash 155

GRILLED VEGETABLES ON PARADE

Vegetable Ribbon Skewers 156

Smoked Squash   157

Smoked Vegetable Confit   158

Smoked Vegetable Confit
on Country Bread
with Tapenade and
Goat Cheese   158

Linguine with Smoked
Butternut Squash,
Fresh Sage, and
Morel Cream Sauce   158

Smoked Spicy
Acorn Squash   159

Grilled Tomatoes   159

Grilled Tomato
"Burgers" with
Herbed Cream Cheese   160

Grilled Goat Cheese
Tomatoes   160

Grilled Roma Tomatoes
with Anchovy, Garlic,
and Parsley   160

Grilled Tomatoes Provençal   160

Indoor Grilled Tomatoes
Provençal   161

Smoked Tomatoes   161

TWO SMOKIN' SALSAS

Charred Tomato-Chipotle
Salsa   162

Grilled Tomatillo Salsa   163

Smoked Tomato Grits   164

Smoked Greek Stuffed
Tomatoes   164

Fettuccine with Smoked
Garlic and Tomatoes   165

Smoked Tomato with
Tuna, Lemon, and Herbs   165

Stir-Grilled Vegetables   166

Thai-Style Stir-Grilled
Vegetables in
Lemongrass Marinade   167

Stir-Grilled Balsamic-Thyme
Vegetables   167

Stir-Grilled Summer Squash
with Fresh Herbs   167

Mediterranean-Style
Stir-Grilled Mushrooms
and Olives   168

Stir-Grilled Red Bell Peppers
with Garlic and Thyme   168

Stir-Grilled Asian
Lettuce Wraps   168

Smoked Soft Cheese   169

Crunchy Smoked
Cheese Dip   170

Smoked Goat
Cheese Salad   170

Smoked Cheesy
Smashed Potatoes   170

Homemade Vegetable
Crisps with Smoky
Cheese Dip   170

Smoky Beef and
Asparagus Saddlebags   171

Smoked Semisoft Cheese   172

Smoky Grilled Cheese
Sandwich   173

Smoked Mozzarella,
Tomato, and
Fresh Basil Salad   173

Smoked Gouda and
Tomato Pasta Salad   173

Planked Semisoft Cheese   174

Maple-Planked Cheese
with Tricolored Peppers   175

Hickory-Planked Cheese
with Dried Cranberry
Relish   175

SAVORY BREADS ON THE GRILL

Wood-Grilled Flatbreads   176

Cheesy Italian Pesto Bread   177

Rustic Bread with Smoked
Tomato and Basil Butter   177

Fiesta Bread   178

Grilled Pizza   179

Garlic-Herb Pizza Dough   180

Grilled Pizza with
Fire-Roasted Tomato
and Olive Topping   180

Grilled Pizza with
Caramelized Onions
and Brie   180

Grilled Leaf-Wrapped
Bread Sticks   181

Bolani (Afghani Flatbreads
with Fresh Herb Filling)   182

GRILL GALS: SHE GRILLS FAST
AND FABULOUS ONE-DISH
MEALS MENU

Super Sicilian Sandwich   184

Grilled Artichoke Pizza on
Parmesan-Herb Crust   185

Grilled Asparagus

Asparagus on the grill is as good as it gets. In Kansas City, our outlying pick-your-own asparagus farms gear up for business as early as late April and go into June. Anything you do to fresh-picked asparagus tastes delicious. But grilled asparagus aficionados fall into two camps—those who prefer the very slender baby stalks and those who like the fatter more mature spears.

Obviously, it's easier to grill the fatter stalks, as they take the heat better and are less likely to fall through the grill grate. Look for the freshest asparagus with tight buds and avoid those with woody stalks. If your asparagus is a bit old (you can tell by looking at the bottom, or cut part, of the stalk—if it looks old, it is), we recommend blanching it in boiling water for 2 minutes, plunging it into a bowl of ice water, patting it dry, and brushing it with olive oil. Then grill for about 6 minutes over a hot fire.

If you prefer the skinniest asparagus spears you can find, a grill wok or grill rack is your best friend. Toss the spears with a little olive oil and grill over a hot fire.

To avoid losing medium or large spears through the grill grate, you can either skewer the spears together using the double-skewer approach (see page 32) or place the spears on a grill rack. On a gas grill, it is easiest to place the spears perpendicular to the openings in the grill grate.

Oh, and the easiest way to trim the woody bottoms off asparagus is to simply hold an end of a spear in each hand and snap. The asparagus will automatically snap off at the best place, leaving the tough end to discard and the tender end to eat.

Grill asparagus right alongside chicken breasts, pork tenderloin, steaks, or burgers. Leftovers will keep in a covered container in the refrigerator for 3 to 4 days. SERVES 6 TO 8

>   **2 pounds fresh asparagus, bottoms trimmed**
>   **Olive oil**
>   **Fine kosher or sea salt to taste**

1.   Prepare a hot fire in a grill.

2.   Lay the asparagus spears in a deep baking dish and drizzle with olive oil to coat lightly. Sprinkle with salt.

3.   Place the spears perpendicular to the openings in the grill grate so they don't fall through. Grill until crisp-tender and slightly charred, 8 to 10 minutes for thick stalks and 6 to 7 minutes for thin ones. Serve hot or at room temperature.

Grilled Asparagus with Shaved Parmigiano-Reggiano: Top your grilled asparagus with shavings of Parmigiano-Reggiano (or Pecorino Romano) cheese. Other crumbled cheeses of choice would be feta cheese, goat cheese, blue cheese, or *ricotta salata*. **SERVES 6 TO 8**

Asian-Style Asparagus with Peanut Butter Dipping Sauce: Serve this as an appetizer or side dish. The marinade used here is great with other vegetables, pork, chicken, fish, and even beef. We always have a large quantity of it on hand because it keeps in the refrigerator for a couple of weeks. Also, it is the base for the peanut butter dipping sauce, which is very addictive and also excellent served with grilled lamb or pork or as a dressing for Asian noodles. In a medium-size bowl, combine 1/2 cup soy sauce, 1/2 cup rice vinegar, 2 tablespoons toasted sesame oil, 2 tablespoons clover or other medium-colored honey, 1 teaspoon minced fresh ginger (if using a microplane, you don't need to peel), 2 minced garlic cloves and 1/2 teaspoon lemon pepper seasoning and use to marinate the asparagus for 30 to 60 minutes before grilling as instructed above. Reserve the marinade. For the dipping sauce, in a small bowl whisk together 1/2 cup smooth or crunchy peanut butter and 2 to 4 tablespoons of the reserved marinade. Add more marinade if you want the dipping sauce to be thinner. Serve on the side with the asparagus. **SERVES 6 TO 8**

Grilled Asparagus Frittata: Use this recipe as a blueprint frittata recipe for any leftover grilled or smoked vegetables you may have in the fridge. Leftover grilled or smoked meat would make a tasty addition, too. Turn on the oven broiler. Grate about 3/4 cup Parmesan or Pecorino Romano cheese and set aside. In a large 10- to 12-inch ovenproof sauté pan, heat 1 tablespoon olive oil. Add 1/2 sliced medium-size onion and cook, stirring, until tender. Add 2 cups chopped grilled asparagus and cook, stirring a few times, until hot, 3 to 4 minutes. Turn off the heat and let the pan sit. In a medium-size bowl, beat 6 large eggs with about half the cheese, then season with fine kosher or sea salt to taste and 1/2 teaspoon red pepper flakes. Pour into the sauté pan on top of the veggies. Do not stir. Sprinkle the remaining cheese over the top. Place the pan under the broiler until the frittata is light and puffy and just beginning to brown, 3 to 4 minutes. Remove from the oven and cut into wedges. **SERVES 4 TO 6**

Grilled Corn

Really good fresh sweet corn is in season for so short a time that we've all learned to gorge on it while the gorgin' is good. After you've had it boiled and served with a smear of unsalted butter, it's time to branch out a bit.

Sweet corn varieties such as Silver Queen, Purdue Super Sweet, Country Gentleman, and Peaches and Cream are mighty fine on the grill. Fresh picked is best, so go to your farmers' market in the morning or pick from your own garden, then keep the corn cool until you're ready to grill the same day; that will deter the natural sugars from converting to starch.

We think it's a great idea to grill a lot of corn at one time. Invite friends and family over for a cookout, allowing extra ears for those who will eat more than one, or grill for leftovers. If you do have leftovers, cut the kernels off the cob and refrigerate them in a covered container for 3 to 4 days.

Our grilled corn is great just as it comes off the grill, but if you're feeling decadent, by all means slather on the butter or drizzle on a flavored oil. **SERVES 8 TO 10**

12 ears corn, in the husks

¹/₂ cup olive oil

Fine kosher or sea salt and freshly ground black pepper to taste

1. Pull back the husks from each ear and remove the corn silk. Pull the husks back over the corn, put in a large bucket of cold water, and soak for 30 minutes while you prepare your fire.

2. Prepare a hot fire in a grill.

3. When ready to grill, remove the corn from the water and drain. Pull a long piece of husk off each ear of corn, then pull back the husks and tie them together with the long piece. Drizzle the kernels on each ear with olive oil and sprinkle with salt and pepper. Place the corn on the grill, with the husk "handles" off the fire. Grill for 2 to 4 minutes total, turning by hand with the husk handles or with grill tongs every 30 seconds or so. You want a slight browning or charring of the kernels, not blackened corn. Serve hot.

It Keeps Going and Going and . . .

You can recycle a marinade that has been used only for vegetables. If the marinade has been used for fish, meat, or poultry, however, dispose of it.

 **Crowning Glories**

Grilled corn is delicious all by itself or slathered with:

Smoked Tomato and Basil Butter *(page 177)*

Chive Pesto *(page 64)*

Southwestern-Style Grilled Corn Relish:
Make this when you have 2 leftover ears of grilled corn, then serve it with grilled fish or chicken and Poblano Cream Sauce (page 93) or Smoked Garlic and Cilantro Cream Sauce (page 93) for a fabulous meal in minutes. It's also good in a grilled chicken burrito. Cut the kernels off the corn. In a medium-size bowl, combine the corn; 1 peeled, seeded, and diced medium-size ripe tomato; 1 seeded and finely chopped jalapeño; the juice of 1 lime; 1/2 teaspoon kosher or sea salt; and 1 tablespoon olive oil. Cover and refrigerate until ready to serve. Stir before serving.
MAKES ABOUT 2 CUPS

Grilled Corn and Smoked Vegetable Pudding:
Here's the classic updated with a bit of char and a kiss of smoke. Preheat the oven to 350°F. In a greased baking dish, combine 2 cups grilled corn kernels (about 4 ears) and 2 cups mixed smoked vegetables, such as tomatoes, bell peppers, onions, and garlic (see page 140). Top with 1 minced garlic clove and 8 ounces finely shredded sharp cheddar cheese. In a medium-size bowl, whisk together 2 cups milk, 4 large eggs, 1 teaspoon kosher or sea salt, and 1/4 teaspoon cayenne pepper, then pour over the corn mixture. Bake until bubbling and set, 50 to 60 minutes. Serve hot.
SERVES 6 TO 8

Grilled Corn Layered Salad:
Our first encounters with layered salads came in the early 1970s, when we started attending and giving wedding showers and needed luncheon dishes that required minimal expense and culinary skill. The layered salad filled the bill. Here is one adapted from many that gets rave reviews. Prepare it in a glass bowl to show off the layers. In a large 3-quart salad bowl, spread 3 cups chopped fresh spinach. Sprinkle with 1/4 teaspoon kosher or sea salt, 1/4 teaspoon freshly ground black pepper, and 1 teaspoon sugar. Have ready 1 pound crumbled crisp-cooked sliced bacon, 6 peeled and sliced hard-boiled large eggs, 1 cup thinly sliced celery, 2 cups grilled corn kernels (about 4 ears), and 1/2 cup sliced green onions. Layer beginning with the crumbled bacon, then the eggs, celery, corn, and green onions. In a small bowl, combine 1 package dry ranch dressing, 1 cup lowfat sour cream, and 1 cup mayonnaise. Spread over the salad to seal. Sprinkle 1 1/2 cups freshly grated Parmesan or Romano cheese over that. Cover tightly with plastic wrap and refrigerate overnight. Toss just before serving. **SERVES 8 TO 12**

Smoked Corn in the Husks

Many people have read the works of Garrison Keillor (of *A Prairie Home Companion* fame and as Mr. Blue, the former advice columnist on Salon.com) or have heard him on National Public Radio. But he's also a fresh corn fanatic. The proof? Our favorite Keillor quote from his book *Leaving Home* (Penguin, 1987): "Sweet corn was so delicious, what could have produced it except sex? . . . People have wanted sex to be as good as sweet corn and have worked hard to improve it, and afterward they lay together in the dark and said . . . 'That was so wonderful . . . but it wasn't as good as fresh sweet corn.'"

Here in Kansas City, where the climate can be really dry in the summer, we usually get the Peaches and Cream variety of sweet corn. But Judith still longs for the tender and sweet Silver Queen variety she used to enjoy in Ohio. Silver Queen corn is so good that it has inspired another kind of royalty—the Silver Queen Corn Queens in Raleigh, North Carolina. Fellow Harvard Common Press author Debbie Moose (*Deviled Eggs: 50 Recipes from Simple to Sassy*, 2004) is one of them, and she says that because her group of Silver Queen Corn Queens is so fine, you have to say "queen" twice. They *are* mighty fine.

And sweet corn is mighty fine, too. Fresh-picked, pale yellow corn in season is the best, of course, for the following recipes. Smoked corn stays moist but takes on a smoky aroma. As always, we like to smoke with leftovers in mind—in this case, for use in soups and salads, or to make a smoked corn relish.

You can also smoke frozen shoepeg corn that has been defrosted. Place it in a disposable aluminum pan, anoint it with oil and seasonings, and smoke it for 30 to 45 minutes. **SERVES 12**

SUGGESTED WOOD: Apple, cherry, oak, or pecan;
avoid mesquite or even hickory, which can be too heavy

12 ears corn, in the husks
¹/₂ cup olive oil
Kosher salt and freshly ground black pepper to taste

1. Pull back the husks from each ear and remove the corn silk. Pull the husks back over the corn and put it in a large bowl or bucket of cold water. Soak for 1 to 2 hours.

2. Prepare a fire in a smoker.

3.   When ready to smoke, remove the corn from the water and drain. Pull back half of the husks and drizzle each ear with olive oil and sprinkle with salt and pepper. Smoke over indirect heat at 225 to 250°F for 1 to 1¹/₂ hours, until the corn is tender.

4.   To serve, pull a long piece of husk off each ear of corn, then pull back the husks and tie them together with the long piece.

Crowning Glories

**Smoked corn is delicious with similar finger-lickin' dishes, such as
Smoked Pork Butt (page 409) and Smoked Wings and Things (page 212).
Also try it slathered or sprinkled with:**

Lemon Butter Drizzle (page 87)

Chive Pesto (page 64)

Spicy Red-Hot Lemon Pepper Rub (page 53)

Smoked Corn, Sliced Tomato, and Slivered Red Onion Salad:

Consider this a basic blueprint for a tasty summer salad, or enhance it with myriad other ingredients, such as grilled peppers, squash, or green onions; olives and artichoke hearts; or smoked peppers and onions. Jazz up the dressing with additional herbs and a bit of spicy mustard, if you like. Arrange 2 or 3 peeled and sliced garden-ripe tomatoes on a large platter and scatter 12 slivered fresh basil leaves over them. Cut the kernels from 4 ears smoked corn. Combine with ¹/₂ cup slivered red onion, drizzle with ¹/₄ cup extra virgin olive oil and 2 tablespoons balsamic vinegar, and season with coarse kosher or sea salt and freshly ground black pepper to taste. Toss gently, then spoon over the tomato slices and serve.
SERVES 4

Smoky Chipotle Corn Pudding:

Leftover smoked corn never tasted so good as in this piquant corn pudding. This is a delicious side dish to serve at Thanksgiving, too. Turn up the heat by adding more chipotles, but be careful. The remaining chipotles can be stored in individual sealable plastic bags. Label, date, and place in the freezer, where they will keep for several months. Preheat the oven to 350°F. Grease a 1-quart baking dish. In a large bowl, combine 2 cups smoked corn kernels (about 4 ears), 1 chopped canned chipotle chile in adobo sauce plus 1 tablespoon adobo sauce, ¹/₄ cup chopped green onions, 1¹/₂ tablespoons all-purpose flour, 2 teaspoons sugar, ¹/₄ teaspoon kosher salt, and ¹/₄ teaspoon cornstarch. In a small bowl, beat 2 large eggs and stir in 1 cup heavy cream. Pour into the corn mixture and mix well, then spoon into the prepared baking dish. Place the dish in a larger, shallow pan and add water to a depth of 1 inch. Place both pans in the oven and bake until a knife inserted in the center comes out clean, about 1 hour. **SERVES 6 TO 8**

Smoked Corn, Ham, and Hominy Casserole: Use either white or yellow hominy for this unique casserole, which can be made with or without the ham. By all means, use leftover Double-Smoked Ham (page 411) if you have it. Preheat the oven to 350°F. Grease a large baking dish. In a large bowl, combine 2 cups smoked corn kernels (about 4 ears); 2 cups canned hominy, drained well on paper towels; 1 cup cubed or shredded smoked ham; 2 minced garlic cloves; and 1 cup finely shredded sharp cheddar cheese. In a small bowl, beat 2 cups whole milk and 4 large eggs together. Whisk in 1 teaspoon kosher or sea salt, 1/4 teaspoon cayenne pepper, and 1/4 teaspoon ground cumin and pour over the corn mixture. Bake until set and the top is bubbling, 50 to 60 minutes. Remove from the oven and let rest for 5 to 10 minutes before serving. **SERVES 6 TO 8**

Grilled Eggplant

The BBQ Queens love the regal purplish hue of eggplant, but eggplant, quite frankly, is a very bland-tasting vegetable—kind of a vegetable version of tofu. The upside to this blandness is that eggplant is the perfect vehicle for rubs, bastes, slathers, marinades, and sauces. So get thee to the rubs and marinades chapter to liven up thy eggplant.

When you grill eggplant, you get a smoky char that adds a deeper, richer flavor to this hot-weather Mediterranean vegetable—without the extra fat of the traditional fried or roasted eggplant common in Italian cuisine. Use any kind of eggplant you want—the large, elongated purple (Agora), the more slender Japanese (Asian Bride or Farmer's Long), the small, oval white (Easter Egg), or the Italian heirlooms (Violette di Firenze or Rosa Bianca) with their rosy lavender and white globe fruits. White varieties of eggplant have a milder, fuller flavor than those of purple varieties, but we encourage you to try many different varieties from your farmers' market or grocery store.

Whether sliced into long, thin pieces or cut into rounds, eggplant doesn't need to be salted or peeled before grilling. Either a charcoal or a gas grill works well. You can also use a grill pan indoors on the stovetop. Eggplant slices are sturdy enough to be placed directly on the grill grate, but if you're nervous, use an oiled perforated grill rack. Grill eggplant at the same time you're grilling a leg of lamb or lamb chops for a Middle Eastern–inspired meal. **SERVES 4**

2¹⁄₂ pounds eggplants, ends trimmed and cut lengthwise into ¹⁄₂-inch-thick slices

Olive oil

Fine kosher or sea salt and freshly ground black pepper to taste

1. Prepare a hot fire in a grill.

2. Brush or spray the eggplant slices on both sides with a light coating of olive oil. Grill for 3 to 4 minutes per side, turning once (or three times if you want good grill marks). Season with salt and pepper. Serve hot.

Crowning Glories

Grilled eggplant is delicious dressed with:

Citrus Caesar Vinaigrette *(page 84)*

Roasted Red Pepper Aioli *(page 110)*

Tzatziki *(page 112)*

Grilled Eggplant, Peppers, and Goat Cheese with Balsamic-Thyme Vinaigrette:
Greet your vegetarian pals with this entrée, and they'll love you to death. As a side dish, it goes well with grilled steak or fish. While you're grilling the eggplant, also put a whole medium-size red and a whole medium-size yellow bell pepper on to char on all sides. Remove the peppers from the grill and place them, hot, in a plastic bag to steam for a few minutes. Let cool slightly, then remove the skin and seeds with a paring knife and discard. Slice the peppers into long, thin strips. Slice a small red onion into thin rings. Arrange the grilled eggplant on a rectangular platter and top with the roasted pepper strips, then layer on the onion rings. Scatter about 4 ounces crumbled fresh goat cheese on top, drizzle everything with ¹⁄₂ cup Balsamic-Thyme Vinaigrette (page 84), and garnish with chopped fresh Italian parsley. **SERVES 6**

Sonoma Farmers' Market Eggplant Spread:
A graphic designer friend of Judith's, Mary Carroll, created this recipe when she lived in California. No matter where you live, this will have you California dreamin'. Grill the eggplant so it is well browned on both sides. Place the entire recipe of hot-off-the-grill slices in a food processor and add 1 tablespoon sea salt, 4 minced garlic cloves, 1 teaspoon dried tarragon, ¹⁄₄ teaspoon freshly ground

black pepper, and 1 teaspoon sugar. Process until smooth and well blended. With the machine running, drizzle in ¹/₂ cup olive oil through the feed tube to make a smooth spread. Serve on flatbread or crackers. This will keep, covered, in the refrigerator for up to 2 days. **SERVES 8**

Warm Asian Eggplant Salad: Here's a different twist on grilled eggplant. Arrange the grilled eggplant slices on a platter. In a small bowl, whisk together 2 tablespoons warm water, 2 tablespoons mirin (a sweet Japanese wine), 1 tablespoon soy sauce, ¹/₄ teaspoon toasted sesame oil, 3 finely chopped green onions, and freshly ground black pepper to taste. Drizzle over the eggplant, then sprinkle with 2 tablespoons each chopped fresh mint and cilantro. The Asian drizzle is also good on other grilled vegetables, fish, chicken, or pork. **SERVES 4**

An Obento Box Lunch

The BBQ Queens attended the James Beard Foundation Awards ceremony in New York City when Judith's cookbook *Prairie Home Cooking* (The Harvard Common Press, 1999) was nominated. They had a terrific time taking part in all the festivities. They even splashed out on an obento box lunch at Takashimaya, that minimalist luxury goods store on Fifth Avenue. An obento box is a tray with compartments containing small portions of several dishes, each with a different flavor, color, and texture. In its simplest form, an obento box is basically a sack lunch, Japanese style, but one prepared with great artistry. This isn't something you could do for a crowd, but if you're grilling for up to four people, you can give each person a tray with little dishes serving the following courses. Accompany with the best green tea you can find.

Warm Asian Eggplant Salad *(above)*
Chopstix Chicken with Gingered Teriyaki Glaze *(page 196)*
Batayaki Beef *(page 312)*
Steamed rice

Grilled Eggplant Roll-Ups with Feta-Olive-Lemon Filling: Pretend that you can see us doing the four queen waves to Nigella Lawson, our favorite Grill Gal. This is our take on an appetizer recipe in her wonderful cookbook *Forever Summer* (Hyperion, 2003). Before you go out to the grill, make the filling. In a medium-size bowl, mix together 8 ounces crumbled feta cheese; 1 tablespoon olive oil; 1/2 cup pitted, drained, and finely chopped oil- or brine-cured Kalamata or Niçoise olives; 2 tablespoons finely chopped green onions; and 1 teaspoon grated lemon zest. Get good grill marks on the eggplant slices. While they're still warm from the grill, place about 2 teaspoons of the feta filling on the end third of a grilled eggplant slice and roll it up. If you're nervous, secure each roll with a toothpick. Arrange the roll-ups on a platter. Serve warm or at room temperature. **SERVES 4 TO 6**

Fettuccine with Grilled Eggplant–Garlic Sauce: Fabulous! This sauce is also good over grilled vegetables of any kind, as well as grilled chicken, salmon, or pork tenderloin. Puree the entire recipe of grilled eggplant slices in a food processor along with 4 garlic cloves, 1/2 cup whole-grain or Dijon mustard, 1 cup heavy cream, and 1/2 cup chicken broth. Transfer to a medium-size saucepan and bring to a boil. Reduce the heat to medium-low and simmer until thickened, about 10 minutes. Season with kosher or sea salt and freshly ground black pepper to taste. **MAKES ENOUGH FOR 1 POUND COOKED FETTUCCINE**

Grilled Greens

Why not grill salad greens? As with any other food, grilling adds a touch of caramelization, which means *flavor*. You get some char on the outside leaves, while the inside leaves remain tender and crisp. The BBQ Queens choose sturdy greens for the grill: quartered heads of romaine, radicchio, red or green cabbage, or quartered fennel bulbs. We also like to wrap small rounds of cheese in "sarongs" of Swiss chard or spinach leaves that have been blanched, then brush the packets with vinaigrette and grill until the cheese softens and melts.

The trick to grilling and not burning the greens is a medium temperature and vigilance. Most greens take only 8 to 10 minutes to grill, but it's best to watch them carefully so they don't burn. Grill greens before or after you grill chicken breasts or steaks. You can slice the cooked chicken or steak and toss it with the greens for a grilled salad. **SERVES 6 TO 8**

1 small head radicchio, quartered lengthwise

1 small head red cabbage, quartered lengthwise and cored

2 large heads romaine lettuce, quartered lengthwise

Olive oil

Fine kosher or sea salt and freshly ground black pepper to taste

1. Prepare a medium-hot fire in a grill.

2. Brush the radicchio, cabbage, and romaine with olive oil and season with salt and pepper. Grill on the flat cut sides, turning once, until browned and sizzled on the outside and warm in the middle, 8 to 10 minutes total. Serve warm or at room temperature, as is or cut up as you prefer.

Crowning Glories

Grilled greens are delicious topped with:

Crumbled crisp-cooked bacon, finely chopped red or Spanish onion, and

Creamy Blue Cheese Dressing (page 111)

Garlic-Citrus Marinade (page 70)

Chipotle Vinaigrette (page 86)

Grilled Radicchio and Red Cabbage with Herbed Caesar Dressing: In a small bowl, whisk together 1 teaspoon anchovy paste or mashed anchovies, 1 tablespoon Dijon mustard, the juice of 1/2 lemon, 1 minced garlic clove, 1 teaspoon chopped fresh rosemary, 1 tablespoon minced fresh Italian parsley, and 6 tablespoons olive oil. Grill 1 small head radicchio and 1 small head red cabbage, both quartered lengthwise, as directed above. Drizzle the dressing over the grilled greens and serve. **SERVES 4**

Grilled Romaine Caesar Salad: Grill 2 large heads romaine lettuce, quartered lengthwise, as directed above. Place each grilled wedge on a salad plate and drizzle with Herbed Caesar Dressing (above), Citrus Caesar Vinaigrette (page 84), or your own favorite Caesar dressing. With a vegetable peeler, shave some Parmigiano-Reggiano cheese over each salad and serve. **SERVES 8**

Grilled Romaine and Green Onions with Lemon and Olives: Think old-fashioned wilted lettuce salad, but with a new, light twist. You can also try this using Belgian endive or Napa cabbage; double the grill time. Improvise and add grilled shrimp or scallops to make a complete meal. Grill 2 large heads romaine lettuce, quartered lengthwise, as directed above. Also throw 16 green onions onto the grill, cooking them until charred on all sides. In a small bowl, combine 1 tablespoon drained capers, 2 tablespoons chopped red bell pepper, the juice and grated zest of 1 lemon, 1/4 cup extra virgin olive oil, 1/4 teaspoon kosher or sea salt, and 1/4 teaspoon freshly ground black pepper. Plate each wedge of romaine and divide equally 1/4 cup pitted and drained oil- or brine-cured black olives and the green onions among the plates. Drizzle with the dressing and serve warm. **SERVES 8**

Fennel and Feta Salad: If you want to serve 1/4 fennel bulb to each guest, trim them of their fronds and grill as directed above until tender, 12 to 15 minutes. If your company grows, chop the fennel after it is grilled. In a large bowl, combine 2 to 3 tablespoons olive oil and 1 tablespoon fresh lemon juice. Season with kosher or sea salt and freshly ground black pepper to taste. Add 4 cups mixed greens, such as spinach and arugula, and toss to coat. Divide the greens among 4 serving plates. Top with the grilled fennel and sprinkle with 1/4 cup crumbled feta cheese. Serve immediately. **SERVES 4**

Grilled Cheese in a Sarong: Grilled cheese a new way! You know how helpful a good sarong wrap is for the dreaded bathing suit parade to the beach or pool. Swiss chard does the job here. Choose large, sturdy Swiss chard or spinach leaves to wrap any semisoft cheese you like, such as fontina, mozzarella, goat cheese, or Camembert. To blanch the leaves, bring a pot of water to a boil and plunge in 8 leaves until they wilt, about 1 minute. Transfer to a bowl of ice water to cool. Pat dry with paper towels and lay each leaf on a flat surface. Place a 1-inch-thick round or square of cheese in the center of each leaf, wrapping the ends to enclose the filling. Secure with a toothpick. Place each packet on a baking sheet and take to the grill. Coat a perforated grill rack with nonstick cooking spray and place on the hot grill. Brush each packet with Citrus Caesar Vinaigrette (page 84) and grill, turning once and basting with the vinaigrette, for 8 to 10 minutes total. Serve at the table, drizzled with the remaining vinaigrette. **SERVES 4**

Grilled Vegetables on Parade

Fresh vegetables are so naturally colorful and delicious, they don't need tiaras or beauty queen sashes to stand out. (Ouch, that hurts!)

We love these two grilled vegetable dishes because they taste wonderful, they're good for you, and they have a definite wow factor. There's also a distinct likelihood—for all of us—that at least one of our friends or relatives has become a vegetarian. Why discreetly slip a veggie burger onto someone's plate when you can please all your diners with one of these dazzling dishes?

Grilled Vegetable Platter with Fresh Basil Vinaigrette

Easy to prepare and assemble, this vegetarian appetizer, salad, or main dish platter has a rustic appearance and a vibrant flavor. It can be prepared hours ahead and kept at room temperature. It can also be doubled or tripled easily. Accompaniments include crusty bread and fresh goat cheese. **SERVES 8 TO 10**

> **2 pounds fresh asparagus**
> **8 baby eggplants**
> **4 large red bell peppers**
> **2 pounds baby yellow pattypan squash**
> **Olive oil**
> **Fine kosher or sea salt and freshly ground black pepper to taste**
> **2 pints cherry tomatoes**
> **Fresh basil sprigs for garnish**
> **Fresh Basil Vinaigrette (page 85)**

1. Prepare a hot fire in a grill. Coat two perforated grill racks or hinged grill baskets and a grill wok with nonstick cooking spray and set aside.

2. Prepare the vegetables. Snap off the tough ends of the asparagus. Trim the ends of the eggplants and cut each lengthwise into ¹/₂-inch-thick slices. Seed the red bell peppers and cut each lengthwise into ¹/₂-inch strips. Place the asparagus, eggplant slices, and bell

pepper strips on the prepared grill racks. Place the squash in the prepared grill wok. Spray the vegetables with olive oil and season with salt and pepper.

3.   Have a large bowl ready near the grill. Toss the squash in the grill wok, using wooden grill paddles or a grill spatula, until tender, about 10 minutes. Meanwhile, grill the vegetables on the grill racks, turning with grill tongs, until tender and slightly charred, 4 to 5 minutes per side. When the squash are done, transfer to the bowl and add the cherry tomatoes to the grill wok. Grill until the skins just begin to crack, about 5 minutes. When the asparagus, eggplant, and bell peppers are done, transfer to the bowl. Add the tomatoes and set aside to cool slightly.

4.   Arrange the vegetables on a large platter in a pleasing pattern or just a jumble, your preference. Garnish with the basil. Drizzle the vinaigrette over everything. Serve immediately, or cover with plastic wrap and let sit at room temperature for up to 2 hours.

Grilled Vegetable and Goat Cheese Terrine

We like this as the main dish for a fancy-schmancy ladies lunch or as a drop-dead-gorgeous dish you can bring to a gathering. Another redeeming feature is that it can be made up to 2 days ahead and kept covered in the refrigerator. Serve as is, drizzled with a little vinaigrette, or with crusty bread. **SERVES 8**

> 2 large red bell peppers
>
> 1 large eggplant, ends trimmed and cut lengthwise into $1/2$-inch-thick slices
>
> 2 large zucchini, ends trimmed and cut lengthwise into $1/4$-inch-thick slices
>
> Olive oil
>
> Fine kosher or sea salt and freshly ground black pepper to taste
>
> FILLING
>
> One 11-ounce package soft, mild goat cheese, such as Montrachet, at room temperature
>
> 3 tablespoons olive oil
>
> 2 tablespoons chopped fresh thyme
>
> Fine kosher or sea salt and freshly ground black pepper to taste

½ cup pitted oil- or brine-cured olives, such as Kalamata or Niçoise, drained and chopped

1 large bunch arugula, chopped

1 cup fresh arugula or other salad or herb leaves for garnish

1.   Prepare a hot fire in a grill.

2.   Brush or spray the peppers, eggplant, and zucchini slices with olive oil and season with salt and pepper.

3.   Have a baking sheet and a paper bag ready near the grill. Grill the vegetables, turning with grill tongs, until tender and slightly charred, 4 to 5 minutes per side. Transfer the peppers to the bag, close, and let steam for 15 minutes. Transfer the eggplant and zucchini to the baking sheet and let cool.

4.   With a paring knife, remove the charred skin, membranes, and seeds from the grilled peppers.

5.   To make the filling, place the goat cheese in a food processor and puree. With the machine running, drizzle the olive oil through the feed tube. Add the grilled peppers and pulse until the peppers are coarsely chopped and the cheese mixture begins to color. Pulse in the thyme. Season with salt and pepper.

6.   To make the terrine, line a 9 x 5-inch loaf pan with plastic wrap, leaving a 4-inch overhang all around. Place a single layer of grilled zucchini in the bottom, completely covering the bottom and trimming the slices to fit. Spread one-third of the cheese filling on top of the zucchini. Sprinkle with one-third of the chopped olives and arugula. Cover with a single layer of eggplant, trimming the slices to fit. Spread half of the remaining cheese mixture over the eggplant and sprinkle with half of the chopped olives and arugula. Finish with a single layer of eggplant, trimming to fit. Spread the remaining cheese mixture on top and sprinkle with the remaining chopped olives and arugula. Completely cover with the plastic wrap and refrigerate until firm, at least 6 hours or up to 24 hours.

7.   Remove the terrine from the refrigerator 30 minutes before you plan to serve it. To serve, arrange arugula leaves on a platter. Open the plastic wrap on top of the terrine. Unmold the terrine onto the platter, removing and discarding the plastic. Cut into slices and serve.

Grilled Mushrooms

Now that more and more mushroom varieties are hitting our grocery store shelves and farmers' market stalls, it's more fun than ever to grill these goodies. From the regular button mushrooms, you can branch out to sample cremini, chanterelle, shiitake, oyster, or portobello mushrooms. Look for fresh mushrooms that are firm and plump, with no discoloration around the edges and a fresh clean smell.

Mushrooms like a little drizzle of butter or olive oil and a sprinkling of salt when you grill them over a hot fire alongside whatever you're cooking for dinner. That way, they sizzle and brown instead of steam. Small mushrooms that may fall through the grill grate may be grilled on skewers or stir-grilled in an oiled and preheated grill wok. SERVES 4

1 ½ pounds fresh mushrooms

3 to 4 tablespoons olive oil, as needed

Fine kosher or sea salt to taste

2 tablespoons balsamic vinegar (optional)

2 tablespoons chopped fresh herbs, such as Italian parsley, chives, rosemary, thyme, and/or oregano (optional)

1 loaf crusty bread (optional), sliced

1. Prepare a hot fire in a grill. Place an oiled grill wok, iron skillet, or grill rack directly over the fire. Heat the cooking vessel until very hot.

2. Brush any dirt off the mushrooms with a paper towel. Trim off any dry or ragged ends. Remove the stems from portobello or shiitake mushrooms. If necessary, cut the mushrooms so that they are a uniform size, place in a large bowl, add the olive oil, and toss to coat. Season with salt.

3. Transfer the mushrooms to the cooking vessel over the hot fire. Cook for about 8 minutes, tossing them several times so they do not burn. Remove from the grill. If you wish, toss them with the vinegar and herbs, then serve hot and sizzling with the sliced bread, if using.

 **Crowning Glories**

Grilled mushrooms are delicious alone or topped or tossed with:

Simply Delicious Bordelaise Sauce *(page 91)*

Pesto Aioli *(page 110)*

Grated Parmesan cheese and chopped fresh herbs

Citrus Caesar Vinaigrette *(page 84)*

Grilled Portobellos with Garlic, Pine Nuts, Basil, and Goat Cheese:

Often the BBQ Queens disagree on how to prepare something. We guess it's our way of "dueling" without the swords. Bottom line is that the disagreements are simply personal preferences about how to prepare something. For this dish, Judith likes to grill the gill side of the mushrooms with the grill lid open, then turn them, add the goodies, and finish grilling with the lid closed. Karen likes to fill the caps with all the goodies and grill the bottom side only with the grill lid closed. So pick your favorite way. Remove the stems from 4 large portobello mushrooms, then brush both sides with 1/4 cup extra virgin olive oil. In a small bowl, combine 4 minced garlic cloves; 8 ounces crumbled or cubed goat cheese (or feta cheese, Boursin, Gorgonzola, or Brie); 2 tablespoons toasted pine nuts; and 8 to 10 chopped fresh basil leaves. *Karen's version:* Place one-fourth of the mixture inside each mushroom cap. Season with kosher or sea salt to taste. Place the mushroom caps directly over the hot fire and grill with the lid down until the mushrooms are soft, 8 to 10 minutes. *Judith's version:* Grill the mushrooms gill side down for about 4 minutes with the grill lid open. Turn the mushrooms, fill them with the goodies, and season with salt. Close the lid and grill for another 4 minutes. Serve hot. **SERVES 4 AS A MAIN DISH**

Grilled Portobello Mushroom "Burgers":

We love these vegetarian burgers, especially with melted mozzarella and pizza sauce as a condiment. Blend 2 tablespoons olive oil and 1 minced garlic clove together in a small bowl. Remove the stems from 4 large portobello mushrooms and brush with the garlic oil. Grill over a hot fire for about 4 minutes per side, until the mushrooms are soft. Place on French bread or sesame seed hamburger buns and serve with mayonnaise, lettuce, and tomato slices, if desired. **SERVES 4**

Smoked Mushrooms

From button mushrooms to portobellos, smoking enhances this earthy vegetable as nothing else can. The simplest way to smoke is to leave the mushrooms whole, but they may be sliced, if you like.

When we embellish the mushrooms—or get decked out in our gaudy costume jewelry for a royal culinary appearance—it's hard to stop. Mushrooms can take on any number of flavors, from savory cheese and garlic to sweet bell pepper and herbs to mellow cream. They're also wonderful as "burgers" or as a burger topping, pickled, sliced on a salad, in a soup or sauce, on a pizza, with pasta, or stuffed.

But sometimes the BBQ Queens disagree on their preparation. Judith likes to remove the gills of the portobellos before smoking them for a cleaner presentation when they are sliced. If the mushrooms are very fresh, Karen prefers to leave the gills on—one less chore for this royal gal. You decide which method you prefer.

Experiment with the smoke flavor by adding water-soaked ground pecan shells, corncobs, grapevine, or woody herb stalks to the fire. **SERVES 4**

SUGGESTED WOOD: Fruitwood, hickory, maple, mesquite, or oak

1 pound button, cremini, or portobello mushrooms
2 tablespoons olive oil
Coarse kosher or sea salt to taste

1. Prepare an indirect fire in a smoker.

2. Trim the mushroom stems, removing them completely if using portobellos. Place the mushrooms in a disposable aluminum pan. Drizzle with the olive oil and toss to coat. Place in the smoker, cover, and smoke at 225 to 250°F until the mushrooms are supple to the touch, golden brown, and fragrant. The smaller button-size mushrooms will take 30 to 40 minutes, portobellos about 1 hour.

3. Remove from the smoker and season with salt. If there are juices in the pan, you may drizzle them over the mushrooms or reserve for another use. Serve immediately.

👑 Crowning Glories 👑

Smoked mushrooms pair well with smoked or rotisserie main dishes and sauces such as:

Simply Delicious Bordelaise Sauce *(page 91)*

Chile–Ginger–Green Onion Sauce *(page 318)*

Fresh Basil Vinaigrette *(page 85)*

An Aioli Platter

Presenting beautifully grilled food on a large platter is a great way to entertain. Whenever we do this dish for our cooking classes, people rave. The aioli platter is an updated version of the French classic dish of boiled salt cod with a garlicky mayonnaise, which was usually served as part of the Christmas festivities. But who wants boiled salt cod when you can have a succulent grilled salmon fillet? We love to surround the salmon with seasonal vegetables chosen for their color as well as flavor, although really good oil- or brine-cured black olives and artichokes hearts are always welcome.

In summer, we might place mounds of steamed *haricots verts* or freshly grated carrot tossed with a dressing around the salmon. In winter, we use roasted fingerling potatoes and steamed baby carrots. Anything, of course, tastes good with aioli.

Grilled salmon fillets *(page 257)*

Rustic Aioli *(page 104)*

Haricots Verts Salad with Mustard-Shallot Vinaigrette *(page 327)*

Bistro Grated Carrot Salad *(page 329)*

Celery Root Rémoulade *(page 328)*

Grilled Mushrooms *(page 132)*

Grilled Potatoes *(page 147)*

Oil- or brine-cured Kalamata or Gaeta olives

Artichoke hearts

Smoked Stuffed Mushrooms: Whether these treats are served with dinner or passed as an appetizer, they are divine. Everyone will proclaim you a BBQ Babe! Clean and stem 24 large mushrooms; chop the stems finely. Heat 2 tablespoons olive oil in a medium-size skillet over medium heat. Add the mushroom stems and 1 chopped medium-size onion. Cook, stirring, until the onion is transparent, about 5 minutes. Set aside. In a food processor, combine one 8-ounce package softened cream cheese, $1/2$ cup grated Pecorino Romano cheese, 2 teaspoons snipped fresh chives, 2 tablespoons chopped fresh Italian parsley, the sautéed onion and mushrooms, and fine kosher or sea salt and freshly ground black pepper to taste. Blend until smooth. Stuff the mushroom caps evenly with the cheese mixture. Arrange the mushrooms on a perforated grill rack or in a disposable aluminum pan and place in the smoker. Cover and smoke at 225 to 250°F for 1 hour. **SERVES 12 AS AN APPETIZER OR 8 AS A SIDE DISH**

Smoked PLT: Portobello mushroom, lettuce, and tomato on rustic Asiago bread or a bun is a delight whether you're vegetarian or not. The flavorful heft of the mushroom makes meat unnecessary, but if you'd like to add a slice or two of crisp-cooked apple-smoked bacon, be our guest. If you're serving a crowd, make this sandwich on a split loaf of Italian bread and, depending on the size of the loaf, triple or quadruple the ingredients. Slice into 6 to 8 sandwiches and serve the gang. For 1 sandwich, begin with a bun slathered with aioli (see pages 104–105 and 110) or store-bought mayonnaise. Place a smoked portobello mushroom on the bun and add a slice of beefsteak tomato and a crunchy lettuce leaf. Season with coarse kosher or sea salt and freshly ground black pepper to taste and enjoy.

Smoked Mushroom Bisque: Rich, creamy bisques are elegant, yet homey and comfortable, too. This simple from-scratch soup forbids you to think of the canned version. Melt 2 tablespoons unsalted butter in a large saucepan over medium heat. Add $1/2$ cup chopped onion (use grilled or smoked onion if you have it) and cook, stirring, until softened, about 5 minutes. Stir in 2 tablespoons all-purpose flour to make a roux and cook for 2 minutes. Add 2 tablespoons sun-dried tomato paste or finely chopped oil-packed sun-dried tomatoes and blend. Slowly add $1^{1}/2$ cups heavy cream or evaporated milk and stir until thickened. Add $1/4$ cup brandy and 1 pound fresh mushrooms that have been smoked as described above and chopped, plus any mushroom juice from the pan. Heat to warm through. Season with kosher salt and freshly ground black pepper. If the soup is too thick (remember that a bisque usually is creamy and thick), thin it by adding $1/4$ to $1/2$ cup beef or vegetable broth. **SERVES 4**

Grilled Onions

Grilling onions is a snap. It's so simple, in fact, that you might have some resident doubters try to steer you toward a more complex method. But don't listen to them!

The first time Karen tried to grill her garden onions (bulbs, green stems, and all), her husband, Dick, thought she was nuts. Karen harvested her first cultivated onion crop (it was all of three onions), brushed off the dirt, and put the unpeeled onions directly over the hot fire in their charcoal grill. Dick, of course, told her they wouldn't be any good this way. He wanted to remove the skins, but Karen insisted that they stay on the grill until charred well on the outside. The outer skins were charred enough that it was easy to remove them. The finished onions were lightly caramelized and so, so sweet.

Use any kind of onion you want—paper-skinned keeping onions such as yellow, white, Spanish, or red; sweet varieties such as Walla Walla, Maui, or Vidalia; or bulb onions with green shoots such as torpedoes or garden onions. We don't recommend grilling other members of the onion family—shallots and garlic—because they're fiddly to grill and taste better slow smoked. If you're determined to grill shallots and garlic, then thread whole shallots and individual garlic cloves onto a skewer, brush them with olive oil, and grill over a hot fire, turning frequently, for about 5 minutes, until browned and softened.

This is a great campfire recipe, too. Simply place the whole onions with their skins into the embers of the fire and roast until the skins are charred and the onions are tender when pierced with a fork.

You don't need to brush the onions with olive oil if you leave the skins on during grilling. That means lower fat, and we like that! Just remember to be gentle when rubbing the skins off after they're done. Grilled onions are a knockout side dish with steak or burgers. **SERVES 3 TO 6**

> **3 medium-size white, yellow, or red onions (about 1^1/$_2$ pounds), or 12 bulb or green onions (the white bulbs are larger—2 to 3 inches in diameter—than the smaller green onions)**

1. Prepare a hot fire in a grill.

2. Place the onions, with the skins on, directly over the fire. Grill, turning so that the entire outside gets well charred, at least 25 minutes.

3. When cool enough to handle, gently rub the charred outer skin off the onions. Serve whole or cut in half.

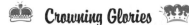

Grilled onions are delicious alone or topped with:

Smoked Hickory Salt *(page 57)*

Kimizu *(page 103)*

BBQ Queens' Love Potion for the Swine *(page 89)*

Grilled Green Onions and Red Onion Slices:
Even easier and faster, try grilling green onions to serve as a side dish or garnish. They are especially pretty served on a platter of mixed vegetables or an aioli platter. The green onions may be skewered with either toothpicks or wooden skewers so they don't fall through the grill grates. This makes them easier to turn, too. Slice the red onions ³/₄ to 1 inch thick. You can also try this with sweet white or yellow onions. Clean and rinse 2 bunches of green onions (about 20 onions). Trim the tops and bottoms and pat dry. Lightly coat the green onions and 2 sliced red onions with 2 tablespoons olive oil. Using a hot fire, place the green onions directly over the fire and perpendicular to the openings in the grill grate so they will not fall through. Set the red onion slices directly over the fire or stick a skewer through them to keep the rings intact. Grill the green onions for 6 to 7 minutes, turning to char evenly. Grill the onion slices for 10 to 12 minutes (or more), turning once halfway through the cooking time. Serve hot or at room temperature. **SERVES 6 TO 8**

Grilled Onion Soufflé:
If the title is too fancy for you, just call this onion pie. It is an upscale way to use onions, whether you grill them fresh or use leftovers from the grill or sauté pan. Preheat the oven to 350°F. Coat a large soufflé dish with nonstick cooking spray. In a large bowl, combine 3 pounds peeled and chopped grilled onions (about 6 large), ¹/₂ cup freshly grated Parmesan or Pecorino Romano cheese, ¹/₂ cup finely shredded Gruyère or sharp cheddar cheese, 3 lightly beaten large eggs, 1 tablespoon Dijon mustard, 1 teaspoon Worcestershire sauce, and ¹/₄ teaspoon red pepper flakes. Blend well. Pour into the prepared dish and bake until puffed and golden brown, about 45 minutes. Serve hot. **SERVES 6**

Grilled Onions with Thyme and Garlic Cream:
We changed our grilling method a bit to accommodate this recipe, which is fabulous. We love these sumptuous guy-in-your-life-pleasing grilled onions served with grilled steaks or pork tenderloin. You'll want a hot fire to grill the steaks, but more of a medium heat to do the onions. The trick is to find a place on your grill where the heat is not as intense. Just feel around with your hand to find a relatively cool spot. We've found that placing the onions along the edge of the grill grate or even up on a rack several inches above the grate will work. In a small bowl, whisk to-

gether 2 minced garlic cloves, $1/2$ teaspoon dried thyme, $1/2$ teaspoon freshly ground black pepper, $1/2$ teaspoon coarse kosher or sea salt, and 1 cup heavy cream. Slice about $1/2$ inch off the top and bottom of 6 to 8 small peeled yellow onions (about 3 inches in diameter). Brush the bottom of each with olive oil. With a grapefruit spoon or paring knife, cut out a small, 1-inch-deep core from the top of each onion. Spoon in about 1 tablespoon of the garlic cream, letting some drizzle down the sides. Place the onions around the perimeter of a hot fire in your grill. Cover and grill for about 20 minutes without turning (although you should twirl the onions around if they get scorched on one side), until the onions have browned and softened (you can grill the steaks at the same time over the hot fire). Serve with the remaining cream spooned over the top. **SERVES 4 TO 6**

Smoked Onions

Big girls do cry when onions are in the picture. But we cry for joy because the flavor is so luscious when this most common of root vegetables is kissed with smoke. Once smoked, they can be placed in labeled and dated sealable plastic bags and frozen for a couple of months—but only if you don't have time to put them to good use right then and there.

We like to smoke onions for a couple of hours, until they are very soft. The extra time allows for more caramelization, too—remember, brown is the color of taste. We smoke with wood for the first hour, then let them cook for another hour without adding more wood. Three chunks of water-soaked wood is our mantra if you're using an electric smoker. For a charcoal smoker, if you're using hardwood lump charcoal, three chunks will do as well.

Smoked onions may be pickled; put into soup, sauce, or pasta; placed on a pizza or tart; or stuffed. **SERVES 4**

SUGGESTED WOOD: Alder, fruitwood, mesquite, oak, or pecan

1 pound onions of your choice

2 tablespoons olive oil

Coarse kosher or sea salt and freshly ground black pepper to taste

1. Prepare an indirect fire in a smoker.

2. Remove the outer papery skins of the onions and cut off the tops and bottoms. The onions may be sliced or left whole. Place in a disposable aluminum pan, drizzle with the

Smoking for Compliments, er, We Mean Condiments

Like most women, we prefer to do two or three things at once, so while we're smoking ribs or chicken, we also smoke bell peppers, garlic, shallots, and/or chiles.

Smoking softens and bronzes, but doesn't char, these vegetables. They take on a smoky aroma and flavor that is luscious in sauces, soups, stews, casseroles—you name it.

Preparing these vegetables can be as easy as drizzling them with olive oil and placing them whole in disposable aluminum pans. Or you can prepare them in the following ways:

Bell peppers: We like to smoke red, green, and yellow bell peppers for color and flavor. Simply remove the stems, then cut the peppers in half and remove the seeds. Place the halves in a disposable aluminum pan and drizzle with olive oil.

Chiles: You can smoke any fresh chile, such as Anaheim, jalapeño, serrano, or even Hatch chiles from New Mexico (we especially love those!). Remove the stems and seeds, then place in a disposable aluminum pan and drizzle with olive oil.

Garlic: To smoke a whole head of garlic, use a paring knife to slice off about 1/2 inch of the pointed top to reveal the individual cloves. Trim the bottom of the bulb, if necessary, so that it sits evenly. Set the head in a special garlic smoker or disposable aluminum pan and drizzle with olive oil. To smoke individual cloves of garlic, choose the biggest ones. Peel, then thread onto wooden skewers (no need to soak first) and drizzle with olive oil. Place the skewers right on the smoker grate over indirect heat.

Shallots: To smoke a whole shallot bulb, use a paring knife to slice off about 1/2 inch of the pointed top. Trim the bottom of the bulb so that it sits evenly. Set the shallot in a garlic smoker or disposable aluminum pan and drizzle with olive oil.

SUGGESTED WOOD: Hickory, maple, mesquite, or oak

Smoke the vegetables at 225 to 250°F until soft and aromatic, 1 to 1 1/2 hours. Obviously, a whole bulb of garlic will take longer to smoke and soften than individual cloves, so keep checking after 1 hour in the smoker. Don't smoke these veggies for more than 1 1/2 hours. Too much smoke can result in a bitter flavor.

Let the vegetables cool, roughly chop, and place in labeled sealable plastic bags. They will keep in the freezer for up to 6 months. Then it's time to do another batch.

olive oil, and toss to coat. Season with salt and pepper and place in the smoker. Cover and smoke at 225 to 250°F until supple to the touch, golden brown, and fragrant. Sliced onions will take 30 to 40 minutes, whole onions about 1 hour (or more).

3.   Remove from the smoker. If there are juices in the pan, drizzle them over the onions or reserve for another use. Serve immediately.

Crowning Glories

Smoked onions pair well with:
Smoked Pork Loin *(page 404)*
Smoked Leg of Lamb *(page 438)*
Smoked Brisket *(page 356)*

Honey-Basted Smoked Onions: This steps up the caramelization process of the onions and is very pretty. Cut 4 sweet onions in half. Remove the outer papery skins and trim off the tops and bottoms. Place the onions cut side up in a disposable aluminum pan and smoke as directed above. Meanwhile, in a small saucepan, combine 2 tablespoons each honey, unsalted butter, and balsamic vinegar and cook over low heat until the butter melts and everything is blended together. Begin liberally basting the onions with the mixture every 15 minutes. Smoke for about 1 hour total. When done, the onions will be a burnished color and perfect to serve on a platter with the main dish of your choice. **SERVES 8**

Smoked (or Grilled) Onion Marmalade: In a word, divine! This simple marmalade is a must to make if you plan on smoking or grilling onions. Spread it over a butterflied pork loin roast, roll up the pork, and then roast in the oven, rotisserie cook, or smoke for a signature dish. The marmalade is also good spooned over a block of cream cheese for an easy, but again signature, appetizer to serve with crackers. Roughly chop 2 smoked or grilled medium-size onions and place in a medium-size bowl. Add 2 tablespoons each balsamic vinegar and honey. Season with coarse kosher or sea salt and freshly ground black pepper to taste. **MAKES ABOUT 2 CUPS**

Smoked Onion Tart: Let's make this so easy that your 10-year-old princess-in-training could make it. Begin with a base crust, which can be defrosted frozen puff pastry placed on a cookie sheet or a store-bought Boboli. Spread 4 ounces softened Boursin or crumbled goat cheese over the crust. Thinly slice 2 grilled or smoked medium-size onions and scatter over the cheese. Bake in a preheated 350°F oven until the crust is crisp, 20 to 25 minutes. Then decide whether you want to invite three people to share this with you or not. **SERVES 1 TO 4**

Pickled Brewpub Smoked Onions: Great with a pub lunch of crusty bread, sweet butter, aged cheddar cheese, and a glass of microbrewed beer, this recipe works with either grilled or smoked onions, but they need to be very small. Peel (which is the hardest part) about 2 pounds small white boiling or creamer onions about 1 inch in diameter. Place in a disposable aluminum pan and toss or spray with 2 tablespoons olive oil. Smoke as directed above until tender. While the onions are smoking, combine 5 cups malt vinegar, 1/2 cup sugar, 2 tablespoons pickling spices, 5 whole cloves, and 10 to 12 black peppercorns in a large saucepan. Bring to a boil, then continue to boil for 5 minutes. Set aside to cool. Combine the smoked onions and pickling liquid in a plastic tub or a large glass jar with a tight-fitting lid. Let steep in the refrigerator for at least 3 weeks before using. These onions will keep in the refrigerator for up to 6 months. **SERVES 4 TO 6**

Grilled Peppers

During the 1980s, the world of peppers exploded for many Americans. Most of us had grown up thinking a pepper meant green bell pepper, the immature vegetable that, if left on the plant, would mature and turn red, yellow, or orange. All of a sudden, there were jalapeños and even hotter poblano, serrano, and Thai chiles. What a revelation. People were having hot flashes all over the place and loving it.

Both sweet bell peppers and hot chiles taste great on the grill. However, bell peppers are treated more as a vegetable dish, while chiles are used more as a flavoring or part of a dish. Both are easy to grill.

To grill the smaller chiles, pierce them lengthwise with a double set of skewers to keep them from spinning as you turn them. **SERVES 6**

> 2 red bell peppers, seeded and cut lengthwise into 1-inch wedges
>
> 2 green bell peppers, seeded and cut lengthwise into 1-inch wedges
>
> 2 yellow or orange bell peppers, seeded and cut lengthwise into 1-inch wedges
>
> 1/4 cup olive oil
>
> Fine kosher or sea salt and freshly ground black pepper to taste

1. Prepare a hot fire in a grill. Place an oiled perforated rack directly over the fire.

2. In a large bowl, combine all the ingredients and toss well to coat the peppers. Place the peppers on the grill rack and grill until scorched and blackened underneath, about 5 minutes. Turn and grill for another 3 to 4 minutes, until blackened.

3. Transfer to a platter, taste for salt and pepper, and serve hot or at room temperature.

Crowning Glories

Grilled peppers can be tossed into hot pasta with more olive oil and minced garlic or served with:

Rustic Aioli (page 104)

Bacon-Wrapped Turkey Fillets (page 223)

Grilled Italian sausage (page 365)

Cheesy Grilled Pepper Boats: This fanciful recipe is a great vegetarian appetizer to make when you can find good-quality fresh bell peppers in different colors. (If you grow your own, experiment with what you have on hand.) Stem, seed, and quarter 4 bell peppers. Place the pepper "boats" skin side down on a baking sheet. In a medium-size bowl, combine one and a half 8-ounce packages softened cream cheese; 1/2 cup chopped fresh basil; 1/2 cup chopped fresh Italian parsley; 1/2 cup pitted, drained, and chopped oil- or brine-cured Kalamata olives; and freshly ground black pepper to taste. Dollop a big spoonful of the cream cheese mixture into each boat. Sprinkle 1 tablespoon freshly grated Parmesan or Pecorino Romano cheese on top. Transfer the boats to an oiled grill grate, cover, and grill until the bottoms are scorched and the cheese has melted, 4 to 5 minutes. Serve hot. **SERVES 8**

Grilled Chiles Rellenos with Baby Shrimp: We love these grilled with a kiss of smoke (see page 13), but they're delicious just simply grilled. Cut a slit lengthwise in each of 6 poblano chiles. Remove the seeds and ribs, taking care not to tear the peppers. In a medium-size bowl, combine one 15-ounce can drained and rinsed Great Northern or cannellini beans, 1 pound peeled and deveined baby shrimp, one 8-ounce package cubed Boursin or other herb and garlic cream cheese, 1/4 cup salsa, 1 teaspoon chili powder, and 1 teaspoon ground cumin. Gently spoon the filling into the peppers. Use toothpicks across the opening of each pepper so they don't gape open during cooking. Place the stuffed peppers on an oiled perforated grill rack and brush with olive oil. Place the rack

BBQ Queens' Grilled Antipasto Platter

For a big backyard do, nothing beats a platter of antipasto. Let color and shape be your guide in selecting a variety of our grilled vegetables. One of the timesaving benefits to this kind of appetizer is that some of the foods can be from the pantry. We particularly like artichoke hearts, an assortment of oil- or brine-cured olives, capers, sardines, anchovies, tapenade (black olive paste), and pickled vegetables.

For even more effortless entertaining—so you don't chip a nail or frizz or flatten your hairdo as your guests are arriving—grill everything the day before, let the foods bathe in the olive oil overnight in the refrigerator, and assemble everything right before your party. For presentation, a rectangular platter is very pretty with rows of each item. An oval or round platter looks great with the items arranged in wedge shapes. **SERVES 10 TO 12**

3 cups Queen-Size Spiced Olives (right)
3 cups grill-roasted red bell peppers cut into strips (3 or 4 peppers; see right)
3 cups canned fire-roasted whole tomatoes (we like the Muir Glen brand), drained
3 cups mixed grilled seasonal vegetables
Extra virgin olive oil
4 ounces Pecorino Romano cheese
Crusty bread, sliced

On a large platter, arrange a row of each vegetable. Drizzle lightly with olive oil, then shave the cheese evenly over the top. Serve with the bread.

in the grill, cover, and cook over a hot fire for 2 minutes. Turn, using grill tongs, grill for another 2 minutes, and turn again. Keep turning and cooking until the peppers are soft and slightly charred on all sides. Serve hot, passing extra salsa at the table. **SERVES 6 AS AN APPETIZER OR LIGHT LUNCH**

Queen-Size Spiced Olives

Of course we use queen-size olives for a royal antipasto platter. "The olives are dandy in martinis or Manhattans, too," says Karen's King Richard. MAKES ABOUT 5 CUPS

One 42-ounce jar pimento-stuffed queen-size green olives, undrained
40 whole cloves
16 large cloves garlic, sliced
3 tablespoons distilled white vinegar
4 teaspoons red pepper flakes
4 teaspoons dillweed

In a large saucepan, combine all the ingredients and bring just to a boil. Remove from the heat. Using a canning funnel, divvy up the olives, juice, and flavorings into clean sterile jars or return to the original jar. Let cool, then tighten the lid(s). Refrigerate for at least 2 weeks to let the flavors blend. They will keep in the refrigerator for 2 to 3 months.

Grill-Roasted Peppers

To grill-roast peppers, place them on an oiled perforated grill rack. Set the rack directly over a hot fire, turning the peppers until they blister and burn on all sides, 15 to 20 minutes. Place the peppers in a paper bag to steam. When cool, remove the skins, seeds, and membranes with a paring knife.

Pick a Peck of Grilled Peppers Sauce: When garden-fresh peppers of all varieties dominate your garden or farmers' market, turn them into this satisfying sauce. Grilling and caramelizing the peppers and onions deepens and enriches their natural sweetness. Use 1/2 to 3/4 cup of this sauce over 1 pound cooked penne and garnish with chopped fresh

Italian parsley and freshly grated Parmesan cheese, spread it over a wheel of warm Brie for an appetizer, or enjoy it on a grilled chicken sandwich. Brush with olive oil 6 seeded and sliced bell peppers, 6 seeded and sliced chiles (any variety), and 3 sliced onions. Grill as directed above until scorched and softened. Process together in a food processor, in batches if necessary, until roughly chopped. Heat $1/2$ cup olive oil in a large saucepan over medium-high heat. Add $1/4$ cup chopped garlic and cook, stirring, for 1 minute. Add the chopped grilled vegetables and cook, stirring, until much of the liquid from the vegetables has cooked away and they are just beginning to brown, about 10 minutes. Serve hot or let cool, then transfer to a covered container and refrigerate until ready to serve. This sauce will keep in the refrigerator for up to 2 weeks and in the freezer for up to 6 months. **MAKES ABOUT 2 CUPS**

Grilled Potatoes

It's amazing now to think that people had to be persuaded even to try the lowly potato. Indigenous to South America, the earliest potatoes were very small and multicolored: purple, yellow, orange, red, russet, and brown. Like other plant varieties from the New World, the potato was brought back to Europe by the 1550s but didn't really catch on at first. It took the efforts of an ill-fated queen to make it happen.

In the mid-1700s, Antoine-Auguste Parmentier, courtier to Marie Antoinette, decided that the potato was the plant that would ease the famine that still plagued rural France. However, the wily Parmentier didn't start an educational campaign to promote the potato. He didn't tell people the potato was good for them. Instead, he posted guards around his potato fields, which encouraged people to steal this apparently precious vegetables and try cooking them at home. He encouraged Marie Antoinette to wear potato flowers in her hair, the "milk mustache" ploy of the eighteenth century.

So we're taking a tip from Parmentier and we're telling you not to try any of these recipes. No matter which varieties you *don't* try—russet, red, sweet, Yukon Gold, fingerling, or new—potatoes are superb grilled.

Use small new or fingerling potatoes, or cut larger potatoes into wedges, for faster grilling. Just make sure the wedges or whole potatoes are uniform in size. If not, you'll need to adjust the cooking time to accommodate the different sizes. Crusty charred potato wedges taste wonderful unadorned, or you can fancy them up with a dipping sauce on the side. SERVES 6

2 large russet potatoes, scrubbed and cut lengthwise into $1/2$-inch wedges
2 large red potatoes, scrubbed and cut lengthwise into $1/2$-inch wedges
2 large sweet potatoes, scrubbed and cut lengthwise into $1/2$-inch wedges
$1/4$ cup olive oil
1 tablespoon seasoned salt
1 tablespoon seasoned pepper

1. Prepare a hot fire in a grill. Place an oiled grill rack directly over the fire.

2. In a large bowl, combine all the ingredients and toss well to coat the potatoes. Place the potatoes on the grill rack. Because of the olive oil, there may be flare-ups, so close the grill lid quickly. After a minute or so, open the lid. Cook for about 40 minutes total, turning the potatoes with long-handled spatulas about every 10 minutes so they brown evenly. Serve hot or at room temperature.

 **Crowning Glories**

Grilled potatoes are delicious alone or dolloped with:
Rustic Aioli (*page 104*)
Ranch dressing, sour cream, or caviar
Smoked Tomato and Basil Butter (*page 177*)

Grilled Whole Potatoes:
Scrub 6 potatoes, rub each with $1/2$ teaspoon olive oil, and sprinkle lightly with garlic salt. Place the potatoes directly over a medium-hot fire, close the lid, and grill-roast for about 45 minutes, turning halfway through the cooking time. The potatoes should be browned and fork tender. If your fire is too hot and the potatoes are burning instead of browning, move them to the indirect side of the grill and close the lid. Continue cooking until done. Serve like a baked potato. **SERVES 6**

Rustic Grill-Roasted Potato Salad:
Here we offer a potato salad that may be served hot or at room temperature. Add ingredients such as roasted red peppers, chopped celery, hard-boiled eggs, capers, or artichoke hearts, and it goes from simple and satisfying to sublime. Place 6 whole grill-roasted potatoes, sliced or chunked, skins on or off, in a large bowl. Sprinkle with 3 tablespoons tarragon vinegar. Add 1 sliced small red onion, 1 minced garlic clove, $1/4$ cup chopped fresh Italian parsley or chervil, and 3 tablespoons olive oil. Season with kosher or sea salt and freshly ground black pepper to taste. Lightly toss to blend. Serve hot. If refrigerated, let the salad come to room temperature before serving.
SERVES 8 TO 10

Grilled Red Potato and Fennel Salad:
Slightly charred from the grill, sweet from the fennel, and salty from the olives, this potato salad is great to take on a tailgate picnic—or snarf down as a one-dish meal. In a large bowl, toss together 2 pounds quartered small red potatoes; 2 trimmed, quartered, cored, and thinly sliced medium-size fennel bulbs; and $1/4$ cup olive oil. Season lightly with kosher or sea salt and freshly ground black pepper. Grill as directed above, turning often, until blistered, slightly blackened, and tender, about 15 minutes. Transfer to a bowl and toss with another $1/4$ cup olive oil; $1/4$ cup red wine vinegar; $1/3$ cup pitted, drained, and chopped oil- or brine-cured Niçoise olives; and $1/3$ cup chopped green onions. Taste for salt and pepper. This salad can be made several hours ahead and kept at room temperature or a day ahead and refrigerated, tightly covered. Let come to room temperature before serving. **SERVES 4 TO 6**

Grilled Vegetable Tart: This is an elegant yet easy dish to make for company. Serve it with your favorite green salad for lunch or a light supper. No one will suspect that you've used leftovers. This tart can be made ahead and frozen, then rebaked at 350°F for 30 to 45 minutes. Preheat the oven to 400°F. Unfold 1 defrosted sheet frozen puff pastry and roll out to a 15 x 12-inch rectangle on a sheet of waxed paper. Transfer to an 11 x 8-inch tart pan with a removable bottom, allowing the excess pastry to flop over the edges. Fold the excess pastry inside so that it is even with the rim of the pan. Press the pastry against the side of the pan, then, using a sharp knife, trim the pastry even with the edge of the pan except at the corners. Pinch the pastry at the corners so that it extends ¼ inch above the pan. Spread 6 cups mixed grilled or smoked vegetables (such as 2 cups each chopped or sliced potatoes, onions, and mushrooms) over the pastry. Drizzle 1 tablespoon olive oil over the vegetables. Season with kosher salt and freshly ground black pepper to taste. Bake for 15 minutes. Remove from the oven and top with 6 crumbled slices crisp-cooked bacon and 1 cup shredded Gouda cheese. Return to the oven and bake until the top is browned and the pastry is cooked through, 15 to 20 minutes more. Cut the tart into 6 or 8 pieces and serve hot or warm. **SERVES 6 TO 8**

Skewered Potatoes (and Other Vegetables)

This is the BBQ Queens' take on the classic Italian dish of roasted potatoes with olive oil and rosemary. Use sturdy, fresh rosemary branches (from the produce section of the grocery store, a nursery, or your own garden) as skewers for small new potatoes. This recipe also works with coins of zucchini and yellow summer squash; peeled and deveined large shrimp; or chunks of chicken, beef, lamb, or pork (all uncooked before grilling). **SERVES 4 TO 6**

> **12 fresh rosemary branches, about 8 inches long**
> **12 small new potatoes, cooked in boiling water for 5 minutes and drained**
> **Rosemary, Garlic, and Lemon Baste (page 68)**

I.   With your fingers or a paring knife, remove the leaves from the bottom two-thirds of each rosemary branch. Save some of the leaves to make the baste. Thread 3 potatoes on each branch. Brush with the baste and place each skewer on a tray to rest for 30 minutes. Reserve the remaining baste.

The Ungrilled Potato Salad

As accompaniments to grilled or smoked foods, potatoes add a mellow note—a transition from the smoky, caramelized, carbon flavors of meats to the sharp, bitter flavors of vegetables and the sour taste of vinaigrette on salads. Atkins diet or no, potatoes give the palate a little rest—comfort food for the overwhelmed.

One of our favorite ways to eat potatoes with grilled or smoked foods is in potato salad, and one of our *favorite* favorites is Tapas-Style Potato Salad from our book *Fish & Shellfish, Grilled & Smoked* (The Harvard Common Press, 2002). It's just potatoes, mayonnaise, minced garlic, and chopped Italian parsley, but oh how good! You also can't go wrong with the simple combination of cooked russet or Idaho potatoes, mayonnaise, chopped green onions, salt, and ground white pepper.

We like to dress our salads while the potatoes are still warm, making them absorb more of the dressing. We agree with food writer Laurie Colwin's comment that, "It is always wise to make too much potato salad. Even if you are cooking for two, make enough for five."

Here's one of our *new* favorite potato salads.

2. Prepare a hot fire in a grill.

3. Grill the skewers for 4 to 5 minutes per side, brushing a few times with the baste, until the potatoes get grill marks and are tender all the way through. Serve hot or at room temperature.

 Crowning Glories

These potatoes are delicious dipped into:

Food Processor or Blender Hollandaise (page 97)

Roasted Red Pepper Aioli (page 110)

Extra virgin olive oil

Creamy Dijon Potato Salad for a Crowd

When you have lots of hungry folks to feed, this is the potato salad to do it. With just a slight mustard flavor, it is rich and oh so satisfying. **SERVES 14 TO 16**

> 9 medium-size russet potatoes
> 4 hard-boiled large eggs, peeled and roughly chopped
> 1/2 cup thinly sliced celery
> 1/3 cup chopped onion
> 2 cups mayonnaise
> 1/4 cup Dijon mustard
> 2 teaspoons fine kosher or sea salt
> 2 teaspoons freshly ground black pepper
> 1 teaspoon sweet Hungarian paprika

1. In a large pot with enough water to cover, boil the potatoes until tender, about 30 minutes. Drain and let cool slightly. When cool enough to handle, peel and cube to yield 9 cups. Place in a large bowl and stir in the eggs, celery, and onion.

2. In a medium-size bowl, whisk the mayonnaise, mustard, salt, pepper, and paprika together until smooth. Add to the potato mixture, tossing gently. Serve slightly warm, or cover and refrigerate until ready to serve. It will keep in the refrigerator for up to 1 week.

Grilled Antipasto Skewers: Alternate parboiled new potatoes with chunks of haloumi or fontina cheese, pitted and drained oil- or brine-cured Kalamata or Niçoise olives, and wedges of roasted red peppers from a jar on rosemary skewers. Brush with the baste and grill for 4 to 5 minutes per side. Serve hot or at room temperature, on a platter. **SERVES 4 TO 6**

Grilled Sweet Potato and Red Onion Skewers: This is a colorful appetizer. Peel 2 medium-size sweet potatoes and cut into 1 1/2- to 2-inch chunks. Parboil for 7 to 8 minutes, until just able to pierce with a fork. Cut 2 medium-size red onions into wedges. Alternate sweet potato chunks and onion wedges on the rosemary skewers. Brush with the baste and grill for 4 to 5 minutes per side. Serve hot or at room temperature, on a platter. **SERVES 4**

Smoked Potatoes

Ⓦhen our working tiaras get a little dingy from barbecue smoke, sometimes we think about getting away from all that fire and becoming one of those outrageous and sexy Sweet Potato Queens. That's when we throw a couple of sweet potatoes on the smoker.

But don't limit yourself to sweet potatoes. You can also smoke new, red, russet, Idaho, fingerling, or Yukon Gold potatoes as a stand-alone side dish or in place of boiled or baked potatoes in all kinds of salads, casseroles, and soups. SERVES 4

SUGGESTED WOOD: Apple, cherry, hickory, or pecan

1 pound potatoes of your choice, scrubbed

Olive oil

Coarse kosher salt and freshly ground black pepper to taste

1. Prepare an indirect fire in a smoker.

2. Prick the potatoes all over with a fork or paring knife. Rub with olive oil and season with salt and pepper. Smoke the potatoes until tender, about 1 hour for fingerling potatoes, 1¹/₂ hours for medium-size potatoes, and 2 hours for large potatoes. Serve just like baked or roasted potatoes.

Crowning Glories

Smoked potatoes pair well with smoked or rotisserie main dishes such as:

Smoked turkey (page 226 or 230)

French Tarragon Rotisserie Chicken (page 218)

Rotisserie Leg of Lamb (page 431)

Smoked Potato and Aioli Gratin: We used to get weak in the knees when we thought about Harrison Ford (Judith) or Sean Connery (Karen). Now we feel a sinking spell coming on when we taste this dish in our imaginations—or even better, in real life. Whoooeee! If you love smoke and you love garlic, this is just the thing to serve with a grilled, smoked, or rotisserie leg of lamb. Smoke 6 medium-size potatoes until almost tender, about 1¹/₂ hours. Peel, slice as thinly as you can, and place in a bowl. Gently fold in Rustic Aioli (page 104) if you're feeling gutsy or White Truffle Aioli (page 105) if you're feeling flush until well blended. Transfer to a greased casserole dish and bake at 400°F until golden, about 15 minutes. **SERVES 6 TO 8**

BBQ Queens' Smoked Potato Casserole: We made up this recipe after we had traveled to do a cooking class and discovered we had forgotten to bring shredded hash browns for our Absolutely Decadent Potatoes (which cookbook author and food scientist Shirley Corriher loves). We did have leftover potatoes we had smoked for the previous class, so voilà!—a new recipe was born. And it's durn good. We think Shirley, the Queen of Culinary Questions, will approve. Preheat the oven to 300°F. Coat a 2-quart baking dish with nonstick cooking spray. Slice 1 1/2 pounds smoked potatoes (you can peel them if you wish, but it's not necessary) and place half in the prepared dish. Drizzle with 2 table-spoons melted unsalted butter and 1/3 cup heavy cream. Sprinkle with 1 tablespoon minced fresh chives, 1/2 teaspoon garlic powder and fine kosher or sea salt and freshly ground black pepper to taste. Repeat the layering one more time. Bake until browned and bubbling, about 2 hours. Ahhh. **SERVES 6 TO 8**

Smoked Potato Soup: Comfort food from the hearth. Smoke 4 large russet or Idaho potatoes. Cut in half and scoop out the flesh; discard the skins. In a medium-size saucepan, melt 1/2 cup (1 stick) unsalted butter over medium-high heat. Add 1/2 cup finely chopped onion and 1/2 cup all-purpose flour and cook until the onion is transparent, about 3 minutes. Whisk in 4 cups whole milk and cook until smooth and thickened. Add the potato pulp and season with kosher salt and freshly ground black pepper to taste. Stir in 6 slices crumbled crisp-cooked bacon, 4 chopped green onions, and 1 cup finely shredded sharp cheddar cheese. Cook over medium heat until heated through, 6 to 8 minutes. Stir in one 8-ounce container sour cream (lowfat is okay) and heat for 1 minute. Serve garnished with more crumbled bacon, chopped green onions, and shredded cheese, if desired. **SERVES 8 TO 10**

Smoked New or Fingerling Potato Platter: This is a great no-brainer appetizer. You can smoke the potatoes ahead of time, then warm them up in the oven before serving. For tailgating, put the hot potatoes in an empty beverage cooler to keep them warm. Smoke 2 to 3 pounds small new or fingerling potatoes as directed above and arrange them on a platter. Accompany with bowls of sour cream, tapenade (black olive paste), chopped red or green onions, crumbled crisp-cooked bacon, or whatever tickles your fancy. Guests pick up a small potato and dip. **SERVES 8 TO 12**

Grilled Summer Squash

A hot fire, a brush of olive oil, a sprinkling of fresh herbs, a bit of salt, and careful attention add up to great grilled summer squash. Zucchini or yellow summer squash are a great choice when you're in a hurry because they cook so fast and can take on many different flavorings almost instantly. If you have squash in your garden, this is a handy recipe to have on hand. One day you have tiny baby squash in your garden, and the next day they're big old torpedoes. If you garden, pick 'em when they're little. If you're buying them, get the smallest ones you can find.

Don't be afraid to get a good char on summer squash, similar to caramelizing in a sauté pan, but don't cook them so long that they get mushy. If you want to cut the squash into rounds or large chunks, you may want to use a grill wok instead. **SERVES 4**

> **4 small to medium-size zucchini or yellow summer squash**
> **¹⁄₄ cup olive oil**
> **¹⁄₂ cup chopped fresh herbs, such as Italian parsley, chives, and/or tarragon**
> **Fine kosher or sea salt and freshly ground black pepper to taste**

1. Prepare a hot grill.

2. Trim the tops and bottoms of the squash. Slice about 1 inch thick on the diagonal or lengthwise. Place in a bowl or sealable plastic bag, add the oil, and toss until well coated.

3. Place on the grill (or a perforated grill rack) and cook for 7 to 10 minutes, turning every 2 to 3 minutes. The squash are done when they're charred and slightly soft but not mushy.

4. Transfer to a bowl and toss with the fresh herbs. Season with salt and pepper and serve.

 *Crowning Glories*

Grilled summer squash is delicious all by itself or topped with or added to:

Smoked Tomato and Basil Butter *(page 177)*

Grilled Asparagus Frittata *(page 118)*

Grilled Pizza with Caramelized Onions and Brie *(page 180)*

Grilled Gazpacho: This is the ultimate gazpacho, with flavors to hit every one of your taste buds. Use leftover grilled vegetables or grill everything fresh. Smoked vegetables will fare well in this soup, too. Place 2 large onions cut into 1/2-inch-thick slices, 2 medium-size zucchini trimmed and cut lengthwise into 1/4-inch-thick strips, and 1 large red and 1 large green bell pepper cut in half and seeded on an oiled perforated grill rack, skin side down. Brush the vegetables with a little olive oil on both sides. Grill over a hot fire, turning once, until slightly charred and caramelized, about 5 minutes per side. Remove from the grill and set aside to cool. When cool enough to handle, peel most of the blistered skins from the peppers. Place the grilled onions, zucchini, and peppers in a food processor and pulse several times until coarsely chopped. Transfer to a large bowl and add 8 seeded and diced large ripe tomatoes; 3 peeled, seeded, and diced medium-size cucumbers; 8 minced garlic cloves; 1/2 cup fresh sourdough bread crumbs; 1/2 cup red wine vinegar; and 2 cups tomato juice. Stir with a wooden spoon. Add 2/3 cup olive oil, stir, and season with fine kosher or sea salt and freshly ground black pepper to taste. Cover and refrigerate for 4 to 5 hours. To serve, ladle into 6 shallow soup bowls and garnish with 1/2 cup lowfat sour cream and a mixture of 1/4 cup chopped green onions; 2 tablespoons finely diced red onion; and 1/4 cup peeled, seeded, and chopped cucumber. **SERVES 6**

Char-Grilled Baby Summer Squash: Judi and Bill Walker are great friends of the Adlers. Karen was introduced to this simple and scrumptious platter of grilled baby squash while vacationing at the Walkers' Michigan summerhouse. Oil a perforated grill rack and set aside. In a large bowl, place 2 pounds mixed baby summer squash (pattypan, zucchini, yellow, or whatever is small and fresh from the market). Drizzle with 2 to 3 tablespoons olive oil and season with 1 teaspoon coarse kosher or sea salt and 1 teaspoon lemon pepper seasoning. Place the vegetables on the rack and grill, turning several times, until they are softened and have grill marks, 15 to 20 minutes. **SERVES 6 TO 8**

Vegetable Ribbon Skewers

This is really a girly-girl recipe, with ruffles and ribbons and the need for a gentle touch. If you have a mandoline, this is the time to get it out. If not, slice the veggies as thinly as humanly possible; otherwise, the slices will crack as you try to thread them onto the skewers. Try carrot, zucchini, and yellow squash ribbons for a wow-y effect on a platter. Use medium to large, evenly shaped vegetables to get the best-looking slices. These veggies are very appealing to kids, but you might have to help them slide the veggies off the skewers. SERVES 4

> 2 large, thick carrots, peeled
> 1 medium-size zucchini, ends trimmed
> 1 medium-size yellow summer squash, ends trimmed
> 12 wooden skewers, soaked in water for at least 30 minutes before grilling
> 1 recipe Lemon Butter Drizzle (page 87)
> Chopped fresh herbs, such as basil, Italian parsley, and/or cilantro, for garnish

1. Using a very sharp knife or mandoline, cut the vegetables lengthwise into paper-thin slices. Immediately (so the slices don't dry out and crack), gently gather each slice into a large ruffle and thread it onto a skewer, 3 slices per skewer. Place carrots on one, zucchini on another, and so on, so that every person will have three different vegetable skewers. Place the skewers on a baking sheet and brush with the drizzle.

2. Prepare a hot fire in a grill.

3. Grill the skewers for 3 to 4 minutes per side, turning once, until grill marks appear. Brush with more of the drizzle, garnish with the chopped herbs, and serve hot or at room temperature.

Smoked Squash

Both winter and summer squash get the royal treatment from slow smoking. Winter squash taste great in its own right from the smoker, but summer squash is better combined with onions, eggplants, and tomatoes.

We prefer to par-cook winter squash until it's almost tender before throwing it in the smoker. We leave small acorn squash whole but cut larger squash such as butternut into big pieces. Then we place the squash cut side down on a baking sheet lined with aluminum foil or parchment paper and bake in a preheated 350°F oven for 30 to 45 minutes before putting it in the smoker. Alternatively, you can microwave it, cut side down, in a glass baking dish for about 10 minutes on high before smoking.

Summer squash can just be cut into rounds or cut in half lengthwise before going in the smoker.

Sometimes we like to sprinkle a rub on squash—BBQ Queens' All-Purpose Rub (page 49), Spicy Orange Rub (page 51), and Zesty Sugar and Spice Rub (page 52) are good—before smoking. And as we keep saying, we like to smoke with leftovers in mind. **SERVES 4**

SUGGESTED WOOD: Apple, cherry, hickory, or pecan

> **4 medium-size zucchini or yellow summer squash, ends trimmed and sliced into rounds or cut in half lengthwise; 1 large butternut, hubbard, delicata, or sweet dumpling squash, peeled, seeded, cut into pieces, and par-cooked (see headnote); or 4 small acorn squash, left whole and par-cooked**
>
> **Olive oil or other vegetable oil**
>
> **Kosher or sea salt and freshly ground black pepper to taste**

1. Prepare an indirect fire in a smoker.

2. Arrange the squash cut side up in a disposable aluminum pan. Drizzle with oil and season with salt and pepper. Cover and smoke at 225 to 250°F until tender, about 1 hour. Serve hot.

 Crowning Glories

Smoked squash pairs well with smoked or rotisserie main dishes such as:

Smoked turkey *(page 226 or 230)*

Rosemary-Scented Grilled Butterflied Chicken *(page 205)*

Smoked Leg of Lamb *(page 438)*

Smoked Vegetable Confit: Also called a *bayaldi* of vegetables, this is a casserole of sliced summer squash, tomatoes, and onions that is slow smoked to perfection. It's a great dish to put on with something else you're smoking. Or make two confits, one to serve, the other to make wonderful sandwiches (see below). In a square disposable aluminum pan, arrange 1 thinly sliced red or Spanish onion on the bottom and scatter 2 chopped garlic cloves and 1 teaspoon each chopped fresh thyme and rosemary over the onion. Slice the following vegetables 1/4 inch thick, then alternate them in the pan in rows, so that the slices are standing up: 2 small yellow summer squash, 2 small zucchini, 4 yellow pear tomatoes, 4 Roma tomatoes, and 2 Japanese eggplants. Drizzle with olive oil, then sprinkle with coarse kosher or sea salt and ground white pepper to taste. Cover and smoke at 225 to 250°F, basting with olive oil every 30 minutes, until the vegetables are tender, 2 1/2 to 3 hours. **SERVES 6**

Smoked Vegetable Confit on Country Bread with Tapenade and Goat Cheese: This open-faced sandwich is the biggest reason we make Smoked Vegetable Confit (above). If you're a low-carb person, you can skip the country bread and just enjoy the confit topped with a slice of goat cheese and a dollop of tapenade (black olive paste). On a slice of toasted artisanal or country bread, spread 1 tablespoon tapenade. Top with confit and a 1/4-inch-thick slice fresh goat cheese. Place on a baking sheet and toast in a preheated 450°F oven until the cheese begins to melt, 3 to 4 minutes. Eat with a knife and fork. **SERVES 1**

Linguine with Smoked Butternut Squash, Fresh Sage, and Morel Cream Sauce: Smoke an extra butternut squash to use in this recipe. With its autumnal colors and hint of wood smoke, this is one great dish. Dried morels are much more readily available in the produce section of grocery stores than ever before. Soak 1/4 cup dried morels in warmed brandy to cover for 15 minutes. Cook 1 pound linguine according to the package directions. While the pasta is cooking, melt 2 tablespoons unsalted butter in a large skillet over medium-high heat and cook 12 fresh sage leaves for 1 minute. Remove from the pan and set aside. Add 4 green onions cut on the diagonal into 1-inch pieces to the pan. Cook, stirring, until tender, about 3 minutes. Stir in the morels and brandy and cook for 1 minute, then stir in 1 cup heavy cream. Cut the smoked squash into bite-size pieces and stir into the cream sauce. When the linguine is done, drain the pasta and add it to the skillet, tossing to blend the pasta and sauce. Serve garnished with sage leaves. **SERVES 6 TO 8**

Smoked Spicy Acorn Squash: Here's a great side dish to serve with smoked turkey for Thanksgiving. Cut 3 medium-size acorn squash in half horizontally and remove the seeds. Brush the cut sides with vegetable oil, then cover with aluminum foil. Poke a few holes in the foil to let the smoke permeate the flesh. Place cut side (foil side) down on the smoker rack and smoke at 225 to 250°F until tender, about 2 hours. When ready to serve, melt 6 tablespoons (¾ stick) unsalted butter in a small skillet and stir in 1 teaspoon ground cinnamon, ¼ cup firmly packed dark brown sugar, and ½ teaspoon chili powder. Drizzle over the cut surfaces of the squash and serve. (Alternatively, remove the squash flesh from the skin and place in a large bowl. Combine the butter mixture with the squash. Place in a shallow baking dish and bake at 350°F until heated through, about 30 minutes.) **SERVES 6**

Grilled Tomatoes

Summer and tomatoes are synonymous. In Missouri and Kansas, we keep our fingers crossed that a couple of our garden tomatoes are ripe by the Fourth of July. To grill the first tomatoes of the season would be sacrilegious. The peasant comes out in us, and we want plain and simple sliced tomatoes, sprinkled only with a bit of kosher or sea salt and freshly ground black pepper. However, by the time August rolls around and the vines are laden with the bright red love fruit, we are ready to give tomatoes the royal barbecue treatment.

Hearty beefsteak, Better Boy, Better Girl (our favorite!), and other meaty tomato varieties are best for the heat of the grill. Overripe tomatoes will get too mushy, so stay with ripe but firm tomatoes for the best results. **SERVES 4**

> **2 large ripe but firm beefsteak tomatoes**
> **Extra virgin olive oil**
> **Fine kosher or sea salt and freshly ground pepper to taste**

1. Prepare a hot grill.

2. Remove the stemmed cap from the tomatoes. Cut them into ¾-inch-thick slices and lightly coat with olive oil to keep them from sticking to the grill grate. Place directly over the heat and cook for 2 to 3 minutes per side. Transfer to a platter and season with salt and pepper. Serve immediately.

Crowning Glories

Grilled tomatoes are delicious served with:

Citrus Caesar Vinaigrette *(page 84)*

Roasted Red Pepper Aioli *(page 110)*

Grilled Green Onions and Red Onion Slices *(page 138)*

Grilled Tomato "Burgers" with Herbed Cream Cheese: Here's a creative take on the common burger. Combine one 8-ounce package softened cream cheese, 1 minced garlic clove, 2 tablespoons chopped fresh basil, and 1 tablespoon snipped fresh chives in a small bowl. Slice open 4 kaiser rolls and grill until warm. Spread the inside of each roll with the herbed cream cheese mixture. Place 2 grilled tomato slices on each bun and serve. **SERVES 4**

Grilled Goat Cheese Tomatoes: This recipe is in our book *Fish & Shellfish, Grilled & Smoked* (The Harvard Common Press, 2002). It is simply divine and must be included again. Because you don't flip the tomatoes to grill on both sides, a thinner slice works well here. Drizzle eight 1/2-inch-thick slices beefsteak tomatoes with olive oil and seasoned with kosher or sea salt and freshly ground black pepper to taste. Top each tomato with 1 ounce crumbled fresh goat cheese. (You may also use crumbled feta cheese or blue cheese or cubed Boursin, herbed cream cheese, or mozzarella.) Sprinkle with chopped fresh herbs, if you like. Grill directly over a hot fire or on a grill rack until the tomatoes are warmed through and the cheese has melted, 6 to 8 minutes. Serve hot. **SERVES 4**

Grilled Roma Tomatoes with Anchovy, Garlic, and Parsley: This is an easy appetizer served with grilled country bread or as part of an antipasto platter. You need 1 1/2 pounds Roma tomatoes. Cut each tomato lengthwise into 6 wedges and arrange in a disposable aluminum pan. In a small bowl, whisk together 1 tablespoon anchovy paste, 2 minced garlic cloves, 1/4 teaspoon red pepper flakes, 1/4 cup chopped fresh Italian parsley, and 1/2 cup olive oil. Drizzle over the tomatoes and toss to blend. Place the pan on the grill, cover, and cook, turning once, until the tomatoes are tender, wrinkled, and slightly browned, 20 to 30 minutes. Serve warm or at room temperature. **SERVES 6**

Grilled Tomatoes Provençal: This is a terrific recipe for tomatoes that are not quite at their peak. If using vine-ripened fruits, make sure they are not too ripe. Core 4 large tomatoes, then cut in half lengthwise. Lightly coat the cut sides with olive oil and set aside. Combine 4 to 6 minced garlic cloves, 1/2 cup fresh bread crumbs, 1/4 cup chopped fresh

Italian parsley, and 2 to 3 tablespoons freshly grated Pecorino Romano cheese in a small bowl. Set aside. Grill the tomatoes as directed above, cut side down, for 2 to 3 minutes. Transfer to a serving platter. Sprinkle with the crumb mixture and drizzle with olive oil. Serve warm or at room temperature. **SERVES 4**

Indoor Grilled Tomatoes Provençal: Heat 1 tablespoon olive oil in a large skillet over high heat. Place the tomatoes cut side down in the skillet and cook for 2 to 3 minutes. Sprinkle with the crumb mixture and drizzle with olive oil. **SERVES 4**

Smoked Tomatoes

Smoking fresh tomatoes is simplicity itself. It's one of those fairly effortless ways to ratchet up the flavor in your food—without fat grams or carbs. And we love that! Smoking tomatoes leaves you plenty of time for other important tasks—such as retouching your makeup, getting a pedicure, or making a hair appointment (or, let's get real here, baking the dessert, setting the table, cleaning the house, carpooling, etc.).

The BBQ Queens love to smoke several tomatoes at once, then peel, seed, and dice them for immediate use, as in the addictive Smoked Tomato and Basil Butter (page 177), and for later on. Because they're already cooked, they freeze well for up to 3 months. You can eat them plain with just a drizzle of olive oil and a sprinkling of sea salt, stuff and smoke them, or smoke and chop them for use in other recipes. If you have vegetarian guests, this is a great barbecue dish that you can serve in place of smoked meat, as in Smoked Greek Stuffed Tomatoes (page 164).

We don't recommend smoking smaller cherry-type tomatoes, because they smoke to mush and are fiddly to eat. We also don't recommend heirloom tomatoes, whose different and delicate flavors, colors, and textures would be overpowered by the smoke. **SERVES 4**

SUGGESTED WOOD: Apple, hickory, pecan, or a combination

4 large beefsteak tomatoes, cored, or 12 Roma tomatoes, cut in half lengthwise

I. Prepare an indirect fire in a smoker.

2. Place the tomatoes cut side up in a disposable aluminum pan. Cover and smoke at 225 to 250°F until the tomatoes have softened and the skins begin to crack, 1 to 1¹/₂ hours. Serve immediately.

Two Smokin' Salsas

Salsa is the number-one-selling condiment in the United States. Why? Because it tastes so good! It's best when chunky and more like a relish. The BBQ Queens offer two of their favorites here: a southwestern-flavored salsa and an authentic Mexican one.

Charred Tomato-Chipotle Salsa

Adapted from a recipe by Paul Kirk, author of *Paul Kirk's Championship Barbecue* (The Harvard Common Press, 2004), this is big-flavor, lowfat, low-carb cooking at its finest. We love it with grilled fish steaks, such as salmon, swordfish, tuna, or halibut. **MAKES ABOUT 1 1/2 CUPS**

- 1 cup wood chips or chunks, mesquite or flavor of your choice
- 3 dried arbol or cayenne chiles
- 1 cup boiling water
- 1 large ripe tomato
- 1/2 medium-size onion, peeled
- 1 large clove garlic, peeled
- 2 canned chipotle chiles in adobo sauce, plus 2 teaspoons adobo sauce
- 2 tablespoons chopped fresh cilantro
- 2 teaspoons fresh lime juice
- Fine kosher or sea salt and freshly ground black pepper to taste

1. Soak the wood chips or chunks in water for at least 30 minutes. (If you're using chunks, soak for at least 1 hour.) Place the dried chiles in a heatproof bowl, pour the boiling water over them, and let stand for 30 minutes. Drain the chiles. Discard the stems and seeds and finely chop the chiles.

2. Prepare a medium-hot fire in a grill. Lightly brush the grill grate with vegetable oil. When the coals have ashed over, add the wood chips. Place the tomato stem side down in the center of the grill. Cover and cook, turning occasionally, until softened and charred all over, about 10 minutes. Meanwhile, thread the onion and garlic clove onto a skewer.

Place the skewer at the edge of the fire, where it is cooler. Cook, turning occasionally, until lightly browned and just softened, about 8 minutes.

3.   Core, peel, and seed the tomato. In a blender or food processor, combine the tomato pulp with the chopped chiles, smoked garlic and onion, chipotles and adobo sauce, cilantro, and lime juice. Process until just a little chunky. Season with salt and pepper. Serve immediately, or cover and refrigerate for up to 1 week.

Grilled Tomatillo Salsa

Complex and smoky, this green salsa goes well with grilled fish and chicken. You can also use it as a dip for tortilla chips or a chunky dressing for a taco salad. MAKES ABOUT 1 1/2 CUPS

> **8 tomatillos**
> **1 small onion, peeled**
> **4 cloves garlic**
> **2 Anaheim chiles**
> **1/2 bunch fresh cilantro**
> **1/4 teaspoon sugar**
> **2 tablespoons olive oil**

1.   Prepare a medium-hot fire in a grill.

2.   On an oiled perforated grill rack, grill the tomatillos, onion, garlic, and chiles, turning occasionally, until softened and charred in places, 8 to 10 minutes. Let cool briefly. When cool enough to handle, husk the tomatillos and peel the garlic. Stem and seed the chiles.

3.   Place the grilled vegetables in a food processor along with the cilantro, sugar, and olive oil and process until just a little chunky. Use immediately or spoon into a small jar with a tight-fitting lid. This salsa will keep in the refrigerator for up to 3 days.

Smoked Tomato Grits:
When we saw this recipe from Atlanta chef Doug Turbush in the *Atlanta Journal-Constitution*, we knew we had to try it. These are grits to the max! And their wonderful flavor comes from pureed hickory-smoked tomatoes, jalapeños, onion, and garlic. Turbush uses a stovetop smoker (see page 34). We've adapted his recipe as follows. Using hickory, smoke as directed above 4 ripe Roma tomatoes cut in half lengthwise, 4 peeled garlic cloves, 1 thickly sliced white onion, and 2 stemmed jalapeños. Puree the vegetables in a blender or food processor. In a large pot, whisk together 1 cup half-and-half, 1 cup heavy cream, 3 tablespoons tomato paste, and the smoked puree and bring to a boil. Wearing oven mitts, gradually whisk in $3/4$ cup yellow stone-ground grits, reduce the heat to low, and simmer, stirring frequently with a wooden spoon, until the mixture thickens, about 10 minutes. Season with kosher salt and freshly ground black pepper to taste. If you like, divide the grits among 4 plates and top with grilled scallops (see page 289). **SERVES 4**

Smoked Greek Stuffed Tomatoes:
This is a great main dish for a hot summer day. Use textured vegetable protein (TVP) or crumbled firm tofu in place of ground lamb or beef for a vegetarian entrée. Core 8 large beefsteak tomatoes, scoop out most of the pulp with a grapefruit spoon, transfer the pulp to a food processor, and puree. Heat 2 tablespoons olive oil in a large skillet over medium-high heat. Add 2 minced garlic cloves, 1 pound ground lamb or beef, and the tomato puree and cook until the meat is no longer pink, 8 to 10 minutes. Transfer to a bowl and stir in $1/4$ cup dry white wine, $1/4$ cup dry bread crumbs, 1 lightly beaten large egg, 2 teaspoons dried oregano, $1/2$ cup crumbled feta cheese, and 2 tablespoons finely chopped fresh Italian parsley. Place the tomato shells in a disposable aluminum pan and spoon in the filling. Cover and smoke at 225 to 250°F until warmed through, about 1 hour. Drizzle with a little olive oil and serve warm or at room temperature. Or cover and refrigerate and serve cold. **SERVES 8**

Fettuccine with Smoked Garlic and Tomatoes: Here's another great way to use smoked tomatoes and 1 whole smoked garlic clove. Cook 1 pound fettuccine according to the package directions. Peel, seed, and chop 4 large smoked tomatoes and place in a large bowl. Squeeze the softened smoked garlic clove out of its skin into the bowl. Add ¼ cup extra virgin olive oil. When the pasta is done, drain and toss with the garlic and tomato mixture. Sprinkle ¼ cup shredded fresh basil leaves on top, toss again, and season with coarse kosher or sea salt and freshly ground black pepper to taste. **SERVES 4 TO 6**

Smoked Tomato with Tuna, Lemon, and Herbs: Smoke for leftovers, we always say. With a tomato you've already smoked, make the best tuna salad you've ever had. Combine 1 peeled, seeded, and chopped smoked tomato and one 6.5-ounce can drained water-packed tuna in a medium-size bowl. Stir in the grated zest of 1 lemon, 2 tablespoons fresh lemon juice, ½ teaspoon dried oregano, 1 minced garlic clove, and ¼ cup extra virgin olive oil and gently combine. Spread on toasted slices of baguette or use to make a yummy tuna salad sandwich. **MAKES ABOUT 1 CUP**

If You Can't Grill with the Equipment You Love, Love the Equipment You Grill With

I have grilled under just about every circumstance imaginable, including a fancy country inn where there was no kitchen, only a fireplace in the room. I went down to the local grocery, bought all the foods I could find that could be cooked on a grill-type arrangement, hurried back to my room to put papers down in front of the fireplace, and cooked right there. It was wonderful to have something delicious to eat when the dining accommodations could not provide it: grilled tortillas; tomatoes, sliced and grilled; red peppers, red onions, and chicken pieces, all cooked over the aromatic open fire.

—Alice Waters, *Chez Panisse Menu Cookbook* (Random House, 1982)

Stir-Grilled Vegetables

Stir-grilling vegetables is simplicity itself. You need veggies cut into small pieces, a sealable plastic bag, a marinade of some kind, a grill wok, wooden stir-grilling paddles or grill spatulas, and a grill.

Basically, you marinate the veggies in the bag, then pour the contents of the bag into the grill wok, which is placed over the sink or in the grass outside (no mess). Then you cook the veggies on the grill, stirring with the paddles or spatulas, until the food is done to your liking. For more information on this technique, see Stir-Grilling 101 (page 32).

You'll be amazed at the extra flavor stir-grilling can impart to the most basic of foods. Once you've tried this recipe, get creative and try other tender vegetables, such as zucchini, yellow summer squash, cherry or grape tomatoes, onions of all kinds, sugar snap peas, and more.

Do not slice the vegetables too thinly, or they may fall through the holes in the grill wok. The only other mistake is to put too much in the wok. Fill it only halfway so you have room to stir and turn the vegetables with the paddles. You don't want any of those delicious veggies to escape, now, do you?

Serve stir-grilled veggies with any grilled food, such as chicken breasts, Italian sausage, fish fillets or steaks, lamb or pork chops, beefsteaks, fajitas, or pork tenderloin. **SERVES 4**

> 1 large red bell pepper, seeded and sliced
> 1 large green bell pepper, seeded and sliced
> 1 large red onion, sliced
> 1/4 cup olive oil
> Garlic salt and freshly ground black pepper to taste

1. Place the vegetables in a large sealable plastic bag and drizzle with the olive oil. Seal the bag and turn to blend. (This recipe can be prepared to this point up to 24 hours ahead and refrigerated.)

2. Prepare a hot fire in a grill and spray a grill wok lightly with olive oil.

3. Turn the bag of marinated vegetables into the prepared grill wok so the extra oil drains away. Place the wok on a baking sheet and take it out to the grill. Place the wok over direct heat and stir-grill, tossing the mixture with wooden paddles or grill spatulas, until all the vegetables have browned and the onions are tender and caramelized, 10 to 15 minutes. Transfer to a bowl, season with salt and pepper, and bring to the table to serve with other grilled fare.

Stir-grilled veggies are delicious topped with:
Freshly grated Parmesan or Asiago cheese
Chopped fresh herbs
Crumbled feta or fresh goat cheese

Thai-Style Stir-Grilled Vegetables in Lemongrass Marinade:
It's amazing how much flavor you get from the very lowfat, aromatic Lemongrass Marinade (page 74). The tofu takes on the flavor of the marinade and adds body to this dish, so don't leave it out. Serve this with Texas pecan rice or the more fragrant jasmine rice. As a finishing touch, use Vietnamese Drizzle (page 87) over all. In a sealable plastic bag, place 8 ounces firm tofu cut into 1-inch pieces, 4 ounces sliced fresh mushrooms, 1 pint grape or cherry tomatoes, one 8-ounce can drained sliced water chestnuts, 1/2 cup green onions cut on the diagonal into 1-inch pieces, and 1 cup cored and chopped Napa cabbage. Pour the marinade over everything, seal the bag, and toss to coat. Marinate in the refrigerator for 30 minutes, then drain and stir-grill as directed above until everything is lightly browned, about 15 minutes. Serve over rice, garnished with toasted sesame seeds. **SERVES 4**

Stir-Grilled Balsamic-Thyme Vegetables:
This is a wonderful side dish to serve with steak for a hearty meal or with an omelet for a light supper. Place 1 pint cherry tomatoes, 2 sliced small zucchini, 2 sliced small yellow summer squash, 1 cup sliced red onion, and 1 cup seeded and sliced red bell pepper in a sealable plastic bag. Pour 1 recipe Balsamic-Thyme Vinaigrette (page 84) or 1 cup bottled balsamic vinaigrette over everything. Seal the bag and toss to cost. Marinate at room temperature or in the refrigerator for at least 30 minutes or up to 2 hours. Drain and stir-grill as directed above until everything is lightly browned, about 15 minutes. Serve hot as a side dish or tossed with hot pasta, then sprinkled with freshly grated Parmesan cheese or crumbled feta cheese. **SERVES 6**

Stir-Grilled Summer Squash with Fresh Herbs:
This stir-grilled dish is as delicately flavored as it is colored, with the pale yellows and greens of fresh summer squash and zucchini. The BBQ Queens love it with grilled, rotisserie, or smoked chicken or fish during the dog days of summer. Place 4 sliced small zucchini, 4 sliced small yellow summer squash, 1 bunch green onions cut on the diagonal into 1-inch pieces, and 1/2 cup olive oil in a sealable plastic bag. Seal the bag and toss to coat. Refrigerate, if you wish, until ready to grill, up to 12 hours. Drain and stir-grill as directed above until everything is lightly browned, about 15 minutes. Transfer the vegetables to a large serving bowl and toss with 1/2 cup

mixed chopped fresh herbs, such as tarragon, chives, and basil. Season with fine kosher or sea salt and freshly ground black pepper to taste. Serve hot or at room temperature. **SERVES 6**

Mediterranean-Style Stir-Grilled Mushrooms and Olives:

Mushrooms are made for vegetable medleys. Use this recipe as a blueprint for adding your favorite Mediterranean flavors, such as lemon zest, artichoke hearts, red bell peppers, and even a bit of anchovy. Scent it with your favorite herbs. If you have any leftovers, use them as a topping for pizza. In a large bowl, combine 1 pound trimmed fresh mushrooms (such as cremini or portobellos), 1 slivered red onion, 3 minced garlic cloves, 1/2 cup pitted and drained oil- or brine-cured olives (such as Kalamata), 2 tablespoons chopped fresh Italian parsley, 1 teaspoon chopped fresh rosemary, 2 tablespoons olive oil, 1 tablespoon fresh lemon juice, and coarse kosher or sea salt and freshly ground black pepper to taste. Toss to blend evenly. Drain (reserving any remaining liquid) and stir-grill as directed above for about 10 minutes, tossing the vegetables two or three times during the grilling. Just as the vegetables are almost done, close the grill lid for a minute or two to heat thoroughly. Transfer to a platter, drizzle with the reserved liquid, and serve hot or at room temperature. This is also wonderful with 1 to 2 cups grilled shrimp (see page 289) or shredded grilled chicken (see page 191) added and served over pasta or rice. **SERVES 4 TO 6**

Stir-Grilled Red Bell Peppers with Garlic and Thyme:

This dish is adapted from a recipe by famed Parisian chef Joël Robuchon, who has so many shining Michelin stars he has to wear shades. We love it paired with smoked goat cheese. Combine 4 seeded and sliced red bell peppers, 5 minced large garlic cloves, 2 teaspoons chopped fresh thyme, 3 tablespoons olive oil, and 1 tablespoon sherry vinegar in a sealable plastic bag and marinate in the refrigerator for 30 minutes or up to 24 hours. Drain and stir-grill as directed above until the peppers are tender and caramelized, 15 to 20 minutes. Serve hot, at room temperature, or cold. **SERVES 4**

Stir-Grilled Asian Lettuce Wraps:

Once you get the hang of stir-grilling, you can really get creative. In this update of a sophisticated Chinese, Thai, or Vietnamese restaurant classic, most of the filling is grilled, then wrapped in lettuce leaves. These are "tacos" for a new generation! This recipe is adapted from one by Rebecca Miller, marketing director for our beloved Whole Foods Market in Overland Park, Kansas. In a large bowl, mix together 1 pound firm tofu cut into pieces or 1 pound ground turkey or chicken, 1 tablespoon toasted sesame oil, 4 minced garlic cloves, 2 tablespoons finely minced fresh ginger (if using a microplane, you don't need to peel), 2/3 cup teriyaki sauce, and 1 bunch green onions cut on the diagonal into $^1/_2$-inch pieces. Cover and refrigerate until ready to cook, up to 8 hours. Arrange Boston lettuce leaves on a platter. Place 1 cup shredded carrot, 1 cup peeled and seeded cucumber cut into matchsticks, and 1 cup daikon (Oriental radish) cut into matchsticks on the platter. Drain the tofu mixture and stir-grill as directed above for 15 to 20 minutes, until the tofu is browned (or the ground meat is cooked through) and the green onions are tender and caramelized. Transfer to a serving bowl and serve with the platter of toppings and a small bowl of hoisin sauce. To make a wrap, spoon some of the cooked filling into the center of a lettuce leaf, sprinkle on the toppings of your choice, and dip the wrap in hoisin sauce. **SERVES 4**

Smoked Soft Cheese

Smoked soft cheese—such as fresh goat cheese, Boursin, or cow's milk cream cheese—is a revelation. The first time we tried smoking cheese was for a cooking class in St. Louis. Our smoked goat cheese was such a hit that we've been making it ever since.

At first we worried that the soft cheese might melt in the process, but we were wrong! At 225 to 250°F, even a soft cheese stays firm and gets deliciously smoky. From trial and error, we have found that it's essential to spray or brush the cheese with olive oil before smoking; if you don't, an unappetizingly dry brown skin will form on the cheese. And you want sort of a blank-slate mild cheese, not one that's assertively flavored. After all, the smoky flavor will dominate.

We recommend cutting either fresh goat cheese or full-fat or lowfat cream cheese into smaller pieces before smoking: the more surface area, the more smoke flavor.

And let us nag you yet again: smoke for leftovers! Use smoked soft cheese as a sandwich spread or dip, or as the basis for unique pasta dishes or green salads. Try blending a combination of cheeses together, such as feta and cream cheese, or grated Romano and cream cheese—get the picture? **SERVES 8**

SUGGESTED WOOD: Hickory or pecan

$^1/_4$ **cup olive oil**

$^1/_4$ **cup seasoned dry bread crumbs**

$^1/_4$ **teaspoon kosher salt**

$^1/_4$ **teaspoon freshly ground black pepper**

8 ounces fresh goat cheese or cream cheese, cut into 8 pieces

1.   Prepare an indirect fire in a smoker.

2.   Pour the olive oil into a small shallow bowl. Combine the bread crumbs, salt, and pepper in another shallow bowl. Dip each piece of cheese into the olive oil, then into the crumb mixture to coat completely. Place the cheese in a disposable aluminum pan, put the pan in the smoker, and close the lid. Smoke at 225 to 250°F for 1 hour. Serve warm. Smoked soft cheese will keep in the refrigerator for up to 1 week.

👑 Crowning Glories 👑

Smoked soft cheese is delicious served atop a vinaigrette-dressed salad or as a topping for or part of:

Grilled Pizza (page 179)

Savory Breads on the Grill (pages 176–178)

Grilled Vegetable Platter with Fresh Basil Vinaigrette (page 129)

Crunchy Smoked Cheese Dip: Spread the cheese evenly in an 8-inch square disposable aluminum pan. Drizzle with olive oil to cover. Combine $1/4$ cup seasoned dry bread crumbs, $1/4$ teaspoon kosher salt, and $1/4$ teaspoon freshly ground black pepper and sprinkle over the cheese. Smoke for 1 hour, then serve in a bowl, with pita chips for dipping. **MAKES ABOUT 1 CUP**

Smoked Goat Cheese Salad: This is our favorite way to enjoy smoked goat cheese. Rinse and pat dry 4 cups salad greens and place in a large bowl. Whisk together 1 tablespoon Dijon mustard, 1 minced garlic clove, $1/4$ cup white wine vinegar, $1/2$ cup olive oil, and coarse kosher or sea salt and freshly ground pepper to taste. Drizzle over the greens and toss. Arrange the greens on 4 salad plates and top each salad with a round of smoked cheese. **SERVES 4**

Smoked Cheesy Smashed Potatoes: See why we say to smoke for leftovers? In a medium-size saucepan, bring 4 peeled and diced large baking potatoes and enough water to cover to a boil. Continue to boil until the potatoes are tender, about 15 minutes. Drain and transfer to a serving bowl. With a potato masher or fork, smash the potatoes with 6 to 8 ounces smoked cream cheese. Add some finely chopped green onions if you wish. Season with sea salt and freshly ground black pepper to taste. Serve hot. **SERVES 4 TO 6**

Homemade Vegetable Crisps with Smoky Cheese Dip: Technicolor chips and a smoky cheese dip will banish the thought of regular chip-and-dip offerings. Use a mandoline to slice these vegetables paper-thin: 1 peeled large baking potato, 1 peeled large sweet potato, 1 peeled large beet. Place on paper towels and pat dry. Heat about 2 inches of vegetable oil in a high-sided skillet, electric skillet, or deep fryer to 350°F. Fry the vegetables in batches until golden. Remove from the oil with a slotted spoon and drain on paper towels. Immediately season with coarse kosher or sea salt and freshly ground black pepper to taste. Make the dip by mashing together 8 ounces smoked goat or cream cheese, 1 cup sour cream, and fine kosher or sea salt and freshly ground black pepper to taste. Serve the crisps on a platter, nestled around a bowl of the dip. **SERVES 4**

Smoky Beef and Asparagus Saddlebags: Here's a great make-ahead appetizer for when the check really is in the mail. In a medium-size bowl, mix together 8 ounces softened

There Is Nothing Like a Dame Royal Feast

On a fall night in a Chicago suburb, the BBQ Queens were summoned to provide a sumptuous grilled and smoked dinner for 50 members and guests of the Windy City's chapter of Les Dames d'Escoffier. We had been invited to do our BBQ Queen gig—complete with the four queen waves—at the behest of our good friend Dame Rose Kallas, who always thinks BIG. Dame Betty Hughes from Weber-Stephen provided a couple of charcoal water smokers for the smoking, and Rose had a huge outdoor grill—as well as a large lower-level catering kitchen. We arrived in Chicago a day ahead to get started. We knew we better be good because the partygoers included top chefs, cookbook authors, and culinary corporate gurus. We were up to the challenge and received rave reviews for our dinner. Rose hired a kicky bluegrass band, and everyone enjoyed the evening in her wonderful garden, twinkling with votives.

Grilled Pizza with Caramelized Onions and Brie (page 180)
Smoked Goat Cheese Salad (page 170)
Apple-Smoked Turkey (page 233)
Smoked Pork Ribs (page 384)
Blue Cheese Coleslaw (page 79)
A Platter of Fresh Tomatoes (page 206)
Dessert bar

smoked cream cheese, 2 tablespoons prepared horseradish, ¹/₄ cup crumbled crisp-cooked bacon, and 2 tablespoons finely chopped fresh Italian parsley. Plunge 24 long chive stems into boiling water to blanch for 10 seconds, then remove with a slotted spoon and let cool on paper towels. Cook 24 thin asparagus spears in the boiling water just until crisp-tender, drain, and set aside. Slice a cooled 2-pound Grilled Beef Tenderloin (page 336) into 24 thin slices. Lay the slices out on a sheet of waxed or parchment paper. Spread each slice with about 1 tablespoon of the cream cheese mixture. Place an asparagus spear in the center of each slice and roll up. Tie each roll together with a chive stem. Place on a tray, cover, and refrigerate until ready to serve, up to 24 hours. **SERVES 6 TO 8**

Smoked Semisoft Cheese

Once you've got the hang of Smoked Soft Cheese (page 169), it's time to spread your wings a bit. There's a whole semisoft cheese world of mozzarella, Edam, Gouda, Brie, Monterey Jack, and even pepper Jack out there waiting to be smoked.

Serve one of your home-smoked cheeses as part of a cheese platter, use it to make incredible grilled cheese sandwiches, or blend it into a gourmet pasta salad. And notice how smoked mozzarella really jazzes up that classic salad of tomato, mozzarella, and fresh basil.

Don't worry about the cheese melting in the smoker. At 225 to 250°F, even a soft cheese stays firm and gets deliciously smoky. Just make sure you spray or brush the cheese with olive oil before smoking; if you don't, an unappetizingly dry brown skin will form. And again, go for a cheese with a milder flavor. There's no point in overpowering the rich nuttiness of a wonderful Gruyère by laying on the smoke, but bring on those shy, self-effacing Goudas and Edams for a smoky makeover.

We recommend using small rounds or blocks of semisoft cheese. Cut larger portions of cheese into smaller wedges before smoking. The more surface area that's exposed, the more smoke flavor the cheese will have. **SERVES 4**

SUGGESTED WOOD: Hickory or pecan

¹/₄ cup olive oil

Four 3-ounce wedges semisoft cheese, such as mozzarella, Gouda, Edam, or Monterey Jack

1. Prepare an indirect fire in a smoker.

2. Pour the olive oil into a small bowl. Dip each cheese wedge into the olive oil to coat completely. Place in a disposable aluminum pan and smoke at 225 to 250°F for 1 hour.

Crowning Glories

Smoked semisoft cheese is delicious served atop a baked potato,

stirred into a vegetable soup, or served with:

Grilled Onions (*page 137*)

Grilled Tomatoes (*page 159*)

Grilled Boneless, Skinless Chicken Breasts (*page 191*)

Smoky Grilled Cheese Sandwich: Let your smoked cheese cool, then thinly slice or shred it to use in grilled cheese sandwiches like this one. Butter one side of each of 2 slices of good-quality rustic bread. Place 1 slice buttered side down in a skillet. Add the smoked semisoft cheese and 1 tablespoon each smoked shallot, bell pepper, and garlic (see page 140) or jarred roasted red peppers and pitted, drained, and sliced oil- or brine-cured Kalamata olives. Place the remaining bread slice on top, buttered side up. Cook over medium-high heat for 3 to 4 minutes per side, turning when the bread is a deep golden brown. **SERVES 1**

Smoked Mozzarella, Tomato, and Fresh Basil Salad: *Insalata Caprese*, look out! Here comes the new kid on the block. Slice 2 large ripe tomatoes and 2 small rounds of smoked mozzarella. Alternate the tomato and mozzarella slices on a small platter or 2 individual salad plates. Drizzle with your favorite vinaigrette and garnish with chopped fresh basil. **SERVES 2**

Smoked Gouda and Tomato Pasta Salad: We love a salad similar to this that you can get at Whole Foods Market. Have ready 8 ounces finely shredded smoked Gouda and 2 chopped smoked tomatoes (see page 161). Cook 1 pound penne pasta according to the package directions. Drain, saving some of the pasta water, and return to the pot. Drizzle with about 2 tablespoons olive oil and quickly toss. Sprinkle on the shredded Gouda and toss again until the cheese melts into the pasta. Stir in the tomatoes and 1 teaspoon dried basil. Season with coarse kosher or sea salt and freshly ground black pepper to taste. If the pasta is too dry, add about ¼ cup of the reserved pasta water to the mixture to moisten it. Serve immediately. **SERVES 6 TO 8**

Planked Semisoft Cheese

Besides 8-minute shrimp from the stovetop smoker (see page 37), this is our other favorite appetizer. First of all, it has a colorful, rustic appeal. Second, it's easy to do. And third, the gently aromatic flavor breathes a little life into that somewhat tired (but still yummy) appetizer of baked Brie.

You can use any semisoft cheese you like, from Brie to Camembert to Gouda. But we don't recommend giving this treatment to a really fine cheese, which is best savored in its natural state.

You can use any type of untreated wood plank. Because we live in Kansas City, a grilling and smoking mecca, we can get all kinds of planks, including alder, cedar, pecan, hickory, and maple. The aromatic flavor you get from a plank is mild, so be assured that whatever kind of wood you use, you will get very tasty results.

There are two tricks to planking. The first is to make sure you soak your plank in water for at least 1 hour before using. The second trick is to use a dual-heat fire—a hot fire on one side of the grill and a medium fire on the other. See Planking 101 (page 42) for the whole process. You also have to be able to close the lid for your food to cook, so a grill without a lid is not an option. (You can plank in the oven, however.)

We love to accompany this appetizer with cocktail crackers of all kinds, sliced baguettes, or sliced artisanal breads. **SERVES 12**

One 12 x 10 x 1-inch plank, maple or wood of your choice, soaked in water for at least 1 hour before grilling

One 1-pound wheel of Brie, about 8 inches in diameter

¹/₂ cup lingonberry preserves or chutney

1. Prepare a dual-heat fire in a grill (see headnote).

2. Place the plank on the grill rack over the hot fire until it begins to char and pop. Turn the plank over and move to the medium fire. Carefully place the Brie on the charred side of the plank. Cover and cook until the Brie begins to soften and melt, about 10 minutes.

3. Serve on the plank, with lingonberry preserves spooned on top of the cheese.

Crowning Glories

This is also delicious topped with:

Smoked Tomato and Grilled Red Onion Relish *(page 324)*

Charred Tomato-Chipotle Salsa *(page 162)*

Southwestern-Style Grilled Corn Relish *(page 120)*

Maple-Planked Cheese with Tricolored Peppers: This is a colorful and flavorful appetizer, perfect for casual entertaining. In a large sealable plastic bag, toss 1 cup each yellow, green, and red bell pepper strips with 1/4 cup olive oil. Transfer to a large grill wok or disposable aluminum pan. Prepare a dual-heat fire (see headnote). Grill the pepper strips on the hot side of the grill, turning, until softened and slightly charred, about 10 minutes. Set aside. Using a maple plank, plank a 1-pound wheel of Brie, Camembert, or Gouda as directed above. Arrange the peppers over and around the cheese and serve hot with assorted crackers and breads. **SERVES 12**

Hickory-Planked Cheese with Dried Cranberry Relish: This is great cold-weather fare to nibble when you're sitting by the fire. Serve as an accompaniment to a simmering soup or stew, or serve during the holidays with oven-toasted slices of *panettone*, the Italian holiday sweet bread. Make up a batch of relish by combining 1/3 cup chopped onion, 1/3 cup seeded and chopped jalapeños, 1/3 cup seeded and chopped green bell peppers, 1/3 cup sweetened dried cranberries, and 1/3 cup canned cranberry relish. Add fresh lemon juice to taste. Using a hickory plank, plank a 1-pound wheel of Brie, Camembert, or Gouda as directed above. Spoon the relish on top of the cheese and serve hot with assorted breads and crackers. **SERVES 12**

As an accompaniment to any grilled or smoked food, a savory bread satisfies like nothing else. A loaf-type sandwich cooked on the grill puts a fresh and delicious new spin on a casual dinner—with minimal cleanup and no hot oven to heat up your kitchen. Wrap these breads in aluminum foil and place on the grill (or in the oven) while your other food is cooking. If you have a hot fire, place the breads as far away from the heat source as possible (off to the side away from the coals in a charcoal grill or on a shelf in a gas grill) or turn them frequently to prevent scorching.

Wood-Grilled Flatbreads

Even packaged pita bread tastes better when you grill it with a kiss of smoke. You want a heavier smoke from hickory, pecan, or mesquite, because these breads hit the grill for only a few minutes. **SERVES 8**

> **8 pita breads, 1 long loaf Afghan bread, 8 flour tortillas, or other wheat-based flatbreads**
> **Olive oil**

1. Prepare a hot fire in a grill and set up for grilling with a kiss of smoke (see page 13), using hickory, pecan, or mesquite.

2. Brush the breads on both sides with olive oil and place on a baking sheet to take outside. Have a sheet of aluminum foil ready to cover the baking tray full of warm breads.

3. Grill each flatbread until grill marks appear on both sides, about 2 minutes per side, turning with grill tongs. Place the grilled breads on the baking sheet and cover with foil to keep warm. Serve warm.

Cheesy Italian Pesto Bread

This is a delicious alternative to garlic bread and wonderful served with any kind of salad topped with grilled chicken, beef, or seafood. **SERVES 8**

> **1 large loaf Italian or French bread**
> **Olive oil**
> **Two 4-ounce jars prepared pesto**
> **1 cup freshly grated Parmesan or Asiago cheese**

1. Prepare a medium-hot fire in a grill or preheat the oven to 350°F.

2. Slice the bread in half lengthwise. Brush olive oil on the cut surfaces. Spread the pesto on the bottom half of the loaf and sprinkle the cheese over the pesto. Replace the top half of the loaf and brush the top with olive oil. Wrap in aluminum foil and grill or bake until warmed through, 10 to 15 minutes.

Rustic Bread with Smoked Tomato and Basil Butter

We love this flavored butter on just about anything, but slathered on a crusty loaf of bread and warmed on the grill is the best. **SERVES 4 TO 6**

> **1 large loaf Italian or French bread**
>
> **SMOKED TOMATO AND BASIL BUTTER**
> **2 large smoked tomatoes (see page 161), peeled, seeded, and chopped**
> **1 cup (2 sticks) unsalted butter, softened**
> **1/2 cup chopped fresh basil**
> **Kosher or sea salt and freshly ground black pepper to taste**
>
> **Olive oil**

1. Prepare a medium-hot fire in a grill or preheat the oven to 350°F.

2. Slice the loaf in half lengthwise.

3. To make the butter, mash together the tomatoes, butter, and basil in a medium-size bowl. Season with salt and pepper. Spread the butter on the cut surfaces of the bread and reform into a loaf. Brush the top with olive oil. Wrap in aluminum foil and grill or bake until warmed through, 10 to 15 minutes.

Fiesta Bread

Grill Gal Judi Walker says people go crazy over this bread, so you might want to make a double batch. We agree! SERVES 6 TO 8

> ³/₄ cup (1¹/₂ sticks) unsalted butter, softened
>
> 2 teaspoons Dijon mustard
>
> 2 teaspoons onion flakes
>
> 2 teaspoons fresh lemon juice
>
> 1 teaspoon beau monde seasoning
>
> 1 tablespoon poppy seeds
>
> 1 large loaf Italian or French bread
>
> 12 to 16 slices Swiss, Monterey Jack, pepper Jack, or provolone cheese

1. Prepare a medium-hot fire in a grill or preheat the oven to 350°F.

2. In a small bowl, combine all the ingredients except the bread and cheese. Cut the bread into 1-inch-thick slices, but do not cut all the way through. Spread the butter mixture on the cut sides of the bread. Place a slice of cheese in each slit. Wrap in aluminum foil and grill or bake until warmed through and the cheese has melted, about 25 minutes.

Grilled Pizza

When the moon in the sky's like a big pizza pie, that's *amore* (or something like that). Yes, the BBQ Queens love pizza on the grill.

Although you get a better smoke flavor by using hardwood charcoal in a kettle grill, this recipe also works with a gas grill. The technique is to grill one side of the pizza first over direct heat, flip it over onto a baking sheet and add the toppings, and then carefully slide the pizza onto the grill over indirect heat to finish cooking. With a frosty glass of wheat beer served up with a wedge of lemon and a fresh fruit dessert, you can beat the heat in style. **MAKES TWO 12- TO 15-INCH PIZZAS OR FOUR 8-INCH PIZZAS**

FOOD PROCESSOR PIZZA DOUGH

3$^1/_4$ cups all-purpose flour

$^1/_4$ cup semolina or cornmeal

2 tablespoons instant yeast

1 cup warm water (about 110°F)

3 tablespoons olive oil, plus more for brushing

1 tablespoon honey

$^1/_2$ teaspoon kosher or sea salt

Toppings of your choice

1. To make the dough, combine the flour, semolina, and yeast in a food processor. Combine the water, olive oil, honey, and salt in a measuring cup and stir to blend. With the machine running, pour the liquid mixture through the feed tube in a steady stream. Process until the dough forms a mass and pulls away from the side of the bowl.

2. Turn the dough out onto a floured work surface and knead by hand until smooth and elastic, about 5 minutes. Place in a large oiled bowl, turn to coat, and cover with plastic wrap. (The dough can be refrigerated for up to 3 days at this point. After that, it will taste bitter. Let the dough come to room temperature, then let it rise the final time before continuing.) Let rise in a warm place until doubled in bulk, 1 to 1$^1/_2$ hours.

3. Divide the dough in half and press or roll each half into the desired size pizza.

4. Prepare an indirect fire in a grill (a medium-hot fire on one side and no fire on the other).

5. To grill using a pizza stone, place the pizza stone on a grill rack over medium-high heat, cover, and let preheat for 10 minutes. Sprinkle cornmeal on 2 large baking sheets and place a round of dough on each sheet. Have olive oil for brushing and the toppings ready and bring everything out to the grill. Slide a round of pizza dough onto the preheated stone. Brush with olive oil and arrange the toppings on the dough. Cover and grill until the dough is golden brown and the toppings are hot, 10 to 15 minutes.

To grill directly on the grill grate, sprinkle cornmeal on 2 large baking sheets and place a round of dough on each sheet. Have olive oil and the toppings ready and bring everything out to the grill. Brush one side of the pizza dough with olive oil and place, oiled side down, on the grill grate. Grill for 1 to 2 minutes, until you see the dough start to bubble. Brush the top side with olive oil and flip the dough, using tongs, back onto the baking sheet. Arrange the toppings on the pizza. Use a grill spatula to place it on the indirect side of the grill. Cover and grill until the toppings are hot, about 5 minutes.

Garlic-Herb Pizza Dough: Heat 2 tablespoons olive oil in a small skillet over medium heat. Add 1 tablespoon minced garlic, 1/4 teaspoon dried oregano, 1/4 teaspoon dried basil, and 1 teaspoon freshly ground black pepper. Cook, stirring, until the garlic softens, about 2 minutes. Remove from the heat, let cool, and add to the flour along with the honey mixture in step 1 above. **MAKES TWO 12- TO 15-INCH PIZZAS OR FOUR 8-INCH PIZZAS**

Grilled Pizza with Fire-Roasted Tomato and Olive Topping: This zesty, savory topping is well suited to the smoky flavor of the pizza. Chop 1 recipe Grilled Tomatoes (page 159) or one 28-ounce can drained Muir Glen fire-roasted tomatoes. Transfer to a bowl and add 1 large grill-roasted red bell pepper (see page 145) or 1/2 cup jarred roasted red peppers cut into strips; 2 tablespoons drained capers; 12 chopped small green olives; and 12 drained, pitted, and chopped oil- or brine-cured Kalamata olives. Have 1 cup finely shredded fontina cheese ready. Prepare the pizza dough as described above. Spoon the topping over the dough, spreading it evenly, then sprinkle evenly with the cheese. Grill as described above. **MAKES TWO 12- TO 15-INCH PIZZAS OR FOUR 8-INCH PIZZAS**

Grilled Pizza with Caramelized Onions and Brie: This sophisticated pizza is wonderful served as an appetizer. While the pizza dough is rising, melt 2 tablespoons unsalted butter in a large skillet over medium-low heat. Add 2 thinly sliced large onions and cook until translucent and very soft, about 15 minutes. Sprinkle with 1/2 teaspoon sugar and drizzle with 2 tablespoons port. Turn the heat to medium-high and cook, stirring, until the onions turn golden brown all over. Remove from the heat and set aside to cool. (You can make the caramelized onions up to 1 week in advance. Store them, covered, in the re-

frigerator.) When you're ready to grill, have 8 ounces Brie cut into small pieces ready. When the pizzas are ready for topping, use a fork to spread the caramelized onions over the dough and top with the Brie. Grill as described above. **MAKES TWO 12- TO 15-INCH PIZZAS OR FOUR 8-INCH PIZZAS**

Grilled Leaf-Wrapped Bread Sticks:
Judith created a similar recipe in *Prairie Home Breads* (The Harvard Common Press, 2001) and for *Cooking Light* magazine. Somehow the combination of bread dough, beet leaf, and coarse salt tastes like black olives. Serve the bread sticks on a large earthenware platter surrounding a bowl of sour cream or extra virgin olive oil for dipping. While the pizza dough is rising, oil a perforated grill rack and set

Pizza Party with Pizzazz

Kids of all ages—and that includes our adult cooking school students—love making their own pizzas. Talk about fun! This party offers a personalized pizza for each guest. Set up a table with mounds of pizza dough and plenty of flour and allow your guests to have a hands-on cooking experience.

The pizza toppings can come from the pantry—jarred roasted red pepper strips, artichoke hearts, black beans, salsa, fire-roasted tomatoes, capers, anchovies, chutney, and tapenade (black olive paste)—and the grocery store deli or salad bar—pregrilled or smoked meats, olives, and assorted veggies. Of course, you can try some of our recipes if you'd like to offer grilled sausage, smoked onions, or even smoked mozzarella. Start with our homemade pizza dough, fire up the grill, and go from there.

Food Processor Pizza Dough *(page 179)*
Grilled Peppers *(page 145)*
Grilled Summer Squash *(page 154)*
Grilled or smoked sausage *(page 365–368)*
Fire-Roasted Tomato and Olive Topping *(page 180)*
Caramelized Onions and Brie *(page 180)*
Smoked Onions *(page 139)*
Smoked mozzarella *(page 172)*

aside. Rinse and pat dry 24 fresh beet or chard leaves, 6 to 8 inches long. After the dough has gone through its first rise, roll it out on a floured work surface to make a 12-inch square. With a serrated knife or pizza wheel, cut into twelve 1-inch-wide strips. Cut each strip in half horizontally and place each strip on the prepared grill rack. Carefully wrap a beet leaf around the middle of each strip, tucking the ends underneath the dough. Brush the strips with olive oil and sprinkle with coarse kosher or sea salt to taste. Cover with plastic wrap and let rise in a warm place until doubled in bulk, about 45 minutes. Remove the plastic wrap. Place the grill rack over a medium-hot fire, cover, and grill for 5 minutes. Brush with olive oil again and carefully turn the bread sticks if the bottoms are getting too browned. Grill for another 5 minutes, until the bread sticks are puffed and browned. Serve warm. **MAKES TWENTY-FOUR 6-INCH-LONG BREAD STICKS**

Bolani (Afghani Flatbreads with Fresh Herb Filling): These savory flatbreads, from a recipe by Latifa Raoufi (see page 332), are usually served on a platter. Instead of making the dough, Raoufi says that you can also use prepared pizza dough or defrosted frozen bread dough. While the pizza dough is rising, make the filling. In a medium-size bowl, combine 1 cup finely chopped green onions, 1 cup finely chopped fresh cilantro, 1 seeded and finely chopped small hot green chile (such as Thai or jalapeño), and 1/4 teaspoon fine kosher or sea salt. Transfer to a sieve placed over a small bowl and let drain for about 15 minutes. Discard the liquid and return the herb mixture to the bowl. Stir in 1 table-spoon vegetable oil and set aside. Punch down the dough and turn out onto a floured work surface. Using a serrated knife, cut the dough into four pieces. Roll each piece into a 12 x 8-inch oval. Place one-quarter of the filling on the top half of each oval, leaving a 1-inch border. Brush water along the border and fold the bottom half of the oval over the filling. Press the edges of the dough together. Brush each bolani with vegetable oil and grill over a hot fire until grill marks appear, 2 to 3 minutes per side. Cut each bolani in half and serve warm or at room temperature. **SERVES 4**

Grill Gals

She Grills Fast and Fabulous One-Dish Meals Menu

Super Sicilian Sandwich

Grilled Artichoke Pizza on Parmesan-Herb Crust

Blond and trim thirty-something Rozane Miceli Prather jokes that she "doesn't eat in order to run, but runs in order to eat." During the week, Rozane limits herself to short runs of just a few miles. On weekends, she tries to get in a long run of at least 10 miles. When training for a race or a marathon, she runs 25 to 30 miles a week. Rozane's teenage children, Paul and Jenna, and her husband, Dean, sometimes run along with her.

Because Rozane works from her Kansas City home as a freelance writer of travel guidebooks, she can usually start something for dinner in the afternoon. And she loves to grill. "I like to do the whole meal on the grill, if I can," she says. "The flavor is so wonderful, and you don't have to have a lot of fat to get the flavor." Her Super Sicilian Sandwich and Grilled Artichoke Pizza on Parmesan-Herb Crust are good examples of delicious foods that are low in fat, high in flavor, and easy to do. And no guilt, whether you run or not!

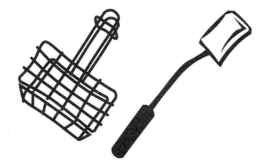

Super Sicilian Sandwich

You can assemble the sandwich hours ahead, wrap it in aluminum foil or plastic wrap, and refrigerate it so you're ready to put it on the grill as soon as you get home from a busy day. Rozane likes to serve this with potato salad and fresh fruit. **SERVES 4 TO 6**

1 loaf Italian or French bread
1/3 cup chopped fresh basil
2 tablespoons olive oil
1 tablespoon balsamic vinegar
6 ounces mozzarella, thinly sliced
8 ounces thinly sliced lean deli roast beef
2 Roma tomatoes, thinly sliced lengthwise
1/2 cup seeded mild banana peppers cut into rings or thin strips
Freshly ground black pepper to taste

1. Cut the bread in half lengthwise. With your fingers or a fork, hollow out about a third of the top half of the loaf.

2. In a small bowl, combine the basil, oil, and vinegar. Layer half the cheese, and all of the meat, tomatoes, and banana peppers on the bottom half of the loaf. Drizzle with the basil mixture and season with black pepper. Top with the remaining cheese and the hollowed-out top. Wrap well in heavy-duty aluminum foil.

3. When ready to serve, prepare a medium fire in a grill.

4. Grill the foil-wrapped sandwich, turning once, until heated through, 20 to 25 minutes. Slice and serve hot.

Grilled Artichoke Pizza on Parmesan-Herb Crust

Here's a good reason to make pizza at home—fabulous flavor. Get your kids or grand-kids involved in making the dough, putting on the toppings, and grilling the pizza. This is great as a main dish or appetizer. **MAKES ONE 14-INCH PIZZA OR FOUR 7-INCH PIZZAS**

CRUST

3 to 3½ cups all-purpose flour

1 package instant or bread machine yeast

¾ teaspoon kosher or sea salt

2 cloves garlic, minced

½ cup freshly grated Parmesan cheese

½ teaspoon cracked black peppercorns

2 teaspoons dried basil, oregano, or rosemary

1 cup warm water (about 110°F)

2 tablespoons extra virgin olive oil

TOPPINGS

One 14-ounce can artichoke hearts, drained and thinly sliced

1 cup red onions sliced into thin wedges

1½ cups sliced fresh mushrooms

8 ounces mozzarella, shredded

2 tablespoons extra virgin olive oil

1. To make the crust, combine 2 cups of the flour, the yeast, salt, garlic, Parmesan, peppercorns, and basil in a large bowl. Stir in the water, olive oil, and enough of the remaining flour to make a soft dough. Knead lightly on a floured work surface until smooth, about 5 minutes. Cover and let rest for 10 minutes.

2.   Prepare a medium-hot fire in a grill. Lightly oil a heavy-duty baking sheet or a perforated grill rack.

3.   Roll out the dough to fit the pan and transfer to the pan.

4.   To top the pizza, arrange the artichokes, onions, and mushrooms on the dough. Place the baking sheet on the grill, close the lid, and grill for 20 to 30 minutes, sprinkling on the shredded mozzarella during the last 10 minutes of grilling. The pizza is done when the crust has browned on the edges and the cheese has melted. Just before serving, drizzle with the olive oil.

Taking Wing: Poultry and Game Birds

f you take an informal poll of what people like best to grill, hamburgers and hot dogs would probably be first, followed by steak. But running a close third is chicken. If you also take a similar poll of what people like best to slow smoke, brisket and ribs would be first, followed by chicken or turkey. 👑 Happily, you're in good hands with the BBQ Queens, because we can do it all and are delighted to show you how. 👑 If you've tried to grill a boneless, skinless chicken breast and it ended up either like chicken sushi or dry shoe leather, we have an easy new technique that guarantees moist, tasty results every time. Plus, if you've ever thought "chicken—again?" we have lots of new ways for you to give it a lick of flame or a kiss of smoke—skewered, stir-grilled, planked, rotisserie cooked, or smoked on the stovetop. For those on a low-carb or high-protein diet, these new ways with chicken add big flavor without extra calories.

When chicken goes on sale, buy it in quantity, then grill or smoke for leftovers, as the BBQ Queens are always saying to do. That way, you'll have time another day to give yourself a pedicure for those strappy summer sandals.

Turkey is fast becoming the new "in" thing to grill or smoke, because it's moist, delicious, economical, and high in protein. Because turkey tenderloins and breasts are bigger than those from chicken, we offer special grilling techniques for them. And if you've ever considered slow smoking or rotisserie cooking a whole turkey, now's your chance.

Domestic duck and Cornish game hens are also fabulous on the grill or in the smoker, and we have lots of yummy recipes for them. We find that serving grilled duck or Cornish game hens makes a meal seem more festive. We're also including game birds (see more about them on page 245), because these are more available than they used to be and because Karen is such an expert at cooking them—grilling, smoking, and every other way imaginable. (That's what happens when your husband is an avid hunter.) Judith benefits by being the beneficiary of the Adlers' wild bounty.

Grilled Boneless, Skinless Chicken Breasts 191

Grilled Chicken Lemonata 192

Cubano Grilled Chicken with Picadillo Olive Salsa 192

Grilled Chicken with Thousand-Herb Sauce 192

One-Dish-Meal Grilled Chicken Sicilian 192

Chicken Breasts Grilled Indoors 192

Planked Boneless, Skinless Chicken Breasts 193

Planked Chicken Breasts with Pecorino Romano–Artichoke Glaze 194

Planked Balsamic-Thyme Chicken with Peppers and Onions 194

Grilled Chicken Skewers 195

Chopstix Chicken with Gingered Teriyaki Glaze 196

Grilled Chicken Satay 196

Curlicue Chicken Caesar Salad 196

Stir-Grilled Chicken and Vegetables 198

Stir-Grilled Chicken with Asparagus and Shaved Parmigiano-Reggiano 199

Stir-Grilled Chicken and Summer Vegetable Pasta with Fresh Basil Vinaigrette 199

Stir-Grilled Tequila-Lime Chicken 199

Grilled Bone-In, Skin-On Chicken Breasts 199

Grilled Cheese-Stuffed Bone-In Chicken Breasts 200

Pesto Chicken Sandwich with Cranberry Preserves 201

Fresh Greens and Grilled Chicken Salad 201

Grilled Half a Chicken 201

GRILL GALS: THE SILVER QUEEN CORN QUEEN GRILLS MENU

Fresh Corn and Tomato Salad 203

Beelzebub's Bloody Marys 204

Rosemary-Scented Grilled Butterflied Chicken 205

YOU SAY TO-MAH-TO, THE BBQ QUEENS SAY TOMATO

A Platter of Fresh Tomatoes 206

Italian Roma Tomato Salad 207

Roasted Cherry Tomatoes with Frizzled Herbs 208

Late-Harvest Tomato Tart 209

Grilled Wings and Things 210

Sizzling Wings and Things with Sage Butter and Romano Cheese 211

Grilled Chicken Wings Amogio 211

Grilled Drumsticks or Thighs Stuffed with Herbed Goat Cheese or Boursin 211

Smoked Wings and Things 212

Chopped Smoked Chicken Salad 213

Pulled Smoked Chicken Salad with Basil Mayonnaise 213

Barbecued Chicken on Fire 213

BBQ BABES: SHE'LL SMOKE FOR SOUP MENU

Smoked Chicken Breasts with Southwest Heat 215

Green Chile and Smoked Chicken Soup 216

Rotisserie Chicken 217

French Tarragon Rotisserie Chicken 218

Puerto Rican–Style Rotisserie Chicken 218

Karen's Famous Rotisserie Chicken Sandwich 218

Smoked Whole Chicken 219

Italian Barbecued Chicken 220

Rosemary-Garlic Smoked Chicken 220

Smoked Sesame-Soy Marinated Chicken 221

Smoked Chicken and Vegetable Lasagna 221

Grilled Turkey Breast Tenderloin Steaks 222

Tarragon Grilled Turkey Breast 223

Turkey Steaks with Spicy Horseradish Sauce 223

Bacon-Wrapped Turkey Fillets 223

Smoked Boneless Turkey Breast 226

Smoked Turkey with Cranberry-Orange Salsa 227

Penne with Smoked Turkey, Goat Cheese Cream Sauce, and Sun-Dried Tomatoes 227

Brie and Basil–Stuffed Turkey Breast 227

Rotisserie Turkey 228

Traditional Rotisserie Turkey Gravy 229

Day-After Rotisserie Turkey Sandwich 229

Smoked Whole Turkey   230

Smoked Turkey and
Monterey Jack Club
Sandwiches   231

Smoked Turkey Hash   231

BBQ BABES: SHE'S SMOKIN' AND
TALKIN' TURKEY MENU

Apple-Smoked Turkey   233

Rosemary-Apple Salsa   234

Grilled Duck Paillards   235

Grilled Duck Paillards
with Dried Sweet
Cherry–Port Sauce   237

Grilled Duck Breast Salad   237

Smoked Whole Duck   238

Smoked Duck and
Wild Rice Soup   239

Smoked Duck Breasts   239

Smoked Duckling with
Five-Spice Asian Paste   239

Duck on a Beer Can   239

BBQ BABES: SHE'S WILD FOR
SMOKE MENU

*Apricot and Cognac–Glazed
Duck*   241

Drunk Elk or Venison   242

Durn Good Rice   243

Grilled Stuffed Apples   244

Grilled Game Birds   245

Cornish Game Hens with
Orange-Honey Baste   246

Grilled Cornish Game Hens
à la Chez Panisse   246

Warm Grilled Quail Salad
with Spiced Pears and
Mushrooms   246

Smoked Small Game Birds 247

Bacon-Wrapped Smoked
Quail and Pheasant   248

Smoked Game Bird Salad   248

Smoked Game Birds
and Pasta   249

Smoked Pheasant Breasts   249

Sangria!   250

Grilled Boneless, Skinless Chicken Breasts

Sometimes the seemingly simplest things to grill can be the most difficult. Take the boneless, skinless chicken breast, for example. Julia Child popularized this cut during the late 1960s and early 1970s on her groundbreaking PBS cooking program *The French Chef*. In those days, you had to bone and skin the chicken breast yourself. Now you can pick up a package of boneless, skinless breasts in any grocery store.

When you look at a chicken breast, you'll see that it's very thin at the ends and thick in the middle. How do you grill it so that every part stays tender and juicy? By turning it into a *paillard*, a French term for a boneless piece of meat that has been flattened to an equal thickness. The easiest way we've found to do this with chicken is to use the rim of a saucer. Simply pound the chicken breast, starting in the middle and working your way out to the sides, until the chicken is of an even $1/4$- to $1/2$-inch thickness. This technique—and these recipes—also works for veal paillards (also known as scallops, or *scaloppine* in Italian), usually cut from the leg and pounded thin.

On a hot grill or in a grill pan over high heat, a chicken or veal paillard will take a total cooking time of 10 minutes per inch of thickness. Grill a $1/2$-inch-thick paillard for $2^1/2$ minutes per side, or 5 minutes total. A $1/4$-inch-thick paillard will take about only $1^1/4$ minutes per side, so it makes sense to serve it with equally fast side dishes, such as Haricots Verts with Lemon, Garlic, and Parsley (page 274).

SERVES 4

> **4 boneless, skinless chicken breast halves, pounded to a $1/2$-inch thickness**
> **Olive oil**
> **Fine kosher or sea salt and freshly ground black pepper to taste**

1. Prepare a hot fire in a grill.

2. Brush or spray the paillards on both sides with olive oil. Grill for $2^1/2$ minutes per side, turning once. Season with salt and pepper and serve.

 *Crowning Glories*

Try serving your grilled chicken breasts with a baked potato, a green salad, and lemon wedges or a splash or dollop of:

Citrus Caesar Vinaigrette *(page 84)*
Roasted Red Pepper Aioli *(page 110)*

Grilled Chicken Lemonata: Usually served with veal scaloppine, this easy sauce is a wonderful last-minute glaze for grilled chicken paillards as well. In a small saucepan over medium-high heat, warm 2 tablespoons fresh lemon juice for about 30 seconds, then swirl in 2 tablespoons cut-up unsalted butter and 2 tablespoons finely chopped fresh Italian parsley until the butter has melted. Grill the chicken as described above. Spoon a little sauce over each grilled paillard and serve. **SERVES 4**

Cubano Grilled Chicken with Picadillo Olive Salsa: After applying the olive oil to each paillard, dust or sprinkle both sides with your favorite Caribbean or jerk seasoning, then grill as directed above. For the salsa, in a medium-size bowl combine 1 chopped medium-size onion, 1 seeded and chopped large red bell pepper, one 10-ounce can Ro-Tel diced tomatoes with green chiles (with their juice), $3/4$ cup drained and chopped pimento-stuffed green olives, $1/2$ cup golden raisins, 1 tablespoon drained capers, and 1 tablespoon Worcestershire sauce. Grill the chicken as described above. Serve each grilled paillard with a topping of salsa. **SERVES 4**

Grilled Chicken with Thousand-Herb Sauce: Okay, so there really aren't a thousand herbs in this sauce. The fresh flavor only *suggests* a thousand. The sauce brings out the best in the chicken breasts, as well as grilled vegetables such as asparagus or zucchini. Like Chimichurri Sauce (page 346), this sauce is more like a vinaigrette. In a small bowl, combine 3 tablespoons extra virgin olive oil, 1 cup finely minced mixed fresh herbs (we like tarragon, Italian parsley, basil, and chives), and 2 tablespoons tarragon vinegar. Season with fine kosher or sea salt and freshly ground black pepper to taste. Grill the chicken as described above. Spoon a little sauce over each grilled paillard and serve. **SERVES 4**

One-Dish-Meal Grilled Chicken Sicilian: When the summer vegetable and herb gardens are at their peak, this is a delicious and healthy recipe to prepare. If you like, you can substitute grilled polenta for the linguine, or steamed white rice seasoned with additional rub. Drizzle the paillards with 2 tablespoons olive oil and sprinkle with $1/4$ cup Spicy Red-Hot Lemon Pepper Rub (page 53), then grill as directed above. Transfer to a plate. Heat $1/4$ cup olive oil in a large skillet over medium heat. Add 2 chopped large garlic cloves, 1 slivered

red onion, and 2 red bell and 2 green bell peppers seeded and cut into matchsticks. Cook, stirring, until crisp-tender. Add 2 to 3 chopped Roma tomatoes, 1 cup pitted and drained oil- or brine-cured Kalamata or Niçoise olives, and 2 tablespoons each chopped fresh thyme and basil. Cook, stirring a few times, until hot. Pour into a bowl and set aside until ready to serve. In the same pan, pour in 1 cup chicken broth and add 1 pound cooked linguine. Heat thoroughly over medium-high heat. Divide the linguine equally among 4 plates. Place a paillard on top of the pasta in each plate. Divide the vegetables equally over the paillards and serve. **SERVES 4**

Planked Boneless, Skinless Chicken Breasts

Planking boneless, skinless chicken breasts is yet another way to do something deliciously different with a common ingredient. Cooking on a plank produces chicken that is tender and juicy, with the slight woodsy aroma of the plank. With a dual-heat fire, one side hot and the other side at medium heat, you can plank cook more quickly. (See page 42 for complete directions on how to plank.) Just make sure you soak your plank for at least 1 hour before you put it on the grill.

The BBQ Queens' way is to start simple, then get fancy, so we begin with a plainer version of planked chicken, then jazz it up below. Feel free to use whatever planks are available in your area—alder, cedar, hickory, maple, even pecan. Each wood imparts a different yet gentle aroma to the food as it cooks.

One caveat: Keep a spray bottle of water by the grill just in case your plank catches fire and you need to douse the flames. That has never happened to us, but if you have a gas grill with a grate very near the heat source, it's best to be prepared.

For a side dish, you could plank asparagus, sliced bell peppers and onions, or thinly sliced zucchini. Use the same treatment as in the master recipe and cook it along with the chicken until done to your liking. Of course, a yummy potato salad never goes amiss, either. **SERVES 4**

> **4 boneless, skinless chicken breasts**
>
> **Olive oil**
>
> **Lemon pepper seasoning to taste**
>
> **One 16 x 6 x ¹/₂-inch cedar or oak plank, soaked in water for at least 1 hour before grilling**

1. Prepare a dual-heat fire, with a hot fire on one side and a medium fire on the other.

2. Place the chicken on a baking sheet, brush or spray with olive oil, and season with lemon pepper seasoning. Bring the chicken and plank outside.

3. Place the plank over the hot fire until it begins to smoke and pop, 4 to 5 minutes. Turn the plank over and move to the medium-heat side. Carefully place the chicken breasts on the charred side of the plank. Cover and cook until an instant-read meat thermometer inserted in the thickest part of the meat registers 160 to 165°F, 12 to 15 minutes. Serve hot.

👑 Crowning Glories 👑👑
Planked chicken is delicious topped with:
Chive Pesto *(page 64)*
Rustic Aioli *(page 104)*
Tomato-Fennel Sauce *(page 95)*

Planked Chicken Breasts with Pecorino Romano–Artichoke Glaze:
A simple topping—in this case, a version of the tried-and-true artichoke dip—complements the aromatic wood flavor of the chicken. Make the topping from scratch or use a jar of prepared artichoke pesto. For other topping variations, try tapenade (black olive paste), Rosemary Pesto (page 62), Rosemary, Garlic, and Lemon Baste (page 68), or Mustard-Mayo-Dill Slather (page 66). Make the glaze by placing one 8-ounce can drained artichoke hearts in a food processor and pulse to chop roughly. Add 8 ounces freshly grated Pecorino Romano (or Asiago) cheese and 1 cup mayonnaise (lowfat is okay). Pulse to blend. (Use immediately or spoon into a glass jar with a tight-fitting lid. The glaze will keep, covered, in the refrigerator for up to 3 days.) Season the chicken breasts with lemon pepper seasoning, spread with the artichoke glaze, and plank as directed above. **SERVES 4**

Planked Balsamic-Thyme Chicken with Peppers and Onions:
In this recipe, we soak 2 planks and cook chicken and vegetables on each. Make 1 recipe Balsamic-Thyme Vinaigrette (page 84). Cut 1 seeded medium-size green bell pepper into strips and 1 medium-size red onion into slivers. Place the chicken breasts and vegetables in a sealable plastic bag and pour in half the vinaigrette. Let marinate in the refrigerator for 30 minutes or up to overnight. Remove the chicken and vegetables from the marinade, place on a baking sheet, and take outside. Prepare the planks as described above. Arrange 2 chicken breasts and half the vegetable mixture on each plank. Cook as directed above. Serve the chicken and vegetables drizzled with the remaining vinaigrette. **SERVES 4**

Grilled Chicken Skewers

When you want to add a little creativity to plain old chicken on the grill, think skewer (see **The Art of the Skewer, page 29**).

If you're using wooden skewers, make sure you soak them in water for at least 30 minutes before grilling to keep them from singeing. You could also expand your idea of "skewer" to include fresh rosemary branches from your garden, the new metal spiral skewers that you can serve right on a dinner plate, or even fresh spikes of sugar cane (available at Hispanic markets).

The BBQ Queens don't recommend combining chicken with vegetables or fruits on the same skewer. The different ingredients have different cooking times, and you'll end up with either overdone vegetables or underdone chicken. But it is fun to serve grilled new potatoes on rosemary branches or grilled vegetable kabobs as an easy side dish that you can cook before, after, or while you're grilling the chicken.

We like to bring all the chicken skewers out to the grill on two baking sheets, one stacked on top of the other. The top one is for the raw chicken, the bottom one is for the cooked chicken, and never the twain shall meet for food safety reasons. **SERVES 4 TO 6**

> **2 pounds boneless, skinless chicken breasts or thighs, cut into 36 pieces or 18 strips**
> **1 cup bottled Italian-style vinaigrette**
> **2 tablespoons soy sauce**
> **Juice and grated zest of 1 lemon**

1. Rinse the chicken and place in a large sealable plastic bag. Pour the vinaigrette over the chicken and add the soy sauce and lemon juice and zest. Seal the bag and turn several times to coat the chicken. Marinate in the refrigerator at least 20 minutes or up to 2 hours.

2. Prepare a hot fire in a grill.

3. Remove the chicken from the bag and thread 3 pieces or a strip of chicken on each skewer. Grill until the chicken is firm and opaque all the way through, 2 to 3 minutes per side. Serve hot.

Skewered chicken is delicious served with dipping sauces such as:

Picadillo Olive Salsa (page 192)

Ancho Mayonnaise (page 311)

Thai Green Curry Sauce (page 290)

Chopstix Chicken with Gingered Teriyaki Glaze:
Ho-hum chicken gets an Asian-style makeover, skewered on fresh bamboo shoots, which you can cut off a bamboo plant (making sure, of course, that it hasn't been treated with anything). Or use traditional wooden skewers, also cut from bamboo. Bamboo is the new darling of kitchenware aficionados for cutting boards and serving pieces, because it is a renewable resource and looks great, too. The teriyaki glaze adds flavor and a burnished sheen to this dish. Make the glaze by combining 1 teaspoon peeled and finely minced fresh ginger, 1/4 cup home-made (see page 69) or prepared teriyaki sauce, and 2 tablespoons vegetable oil in a small bowl. Have ready 12 fresh bamboo shoots or 12 wooden skewers, about 8 inches long, soaked in water for at least 30 minutes before grilling. Cut the chicken into 36 pieces and thread 3 pieces onto each bamboo shoot, piercing the chicken first with a wooden skewer if necessary. Brush the chicken with the glaze, place the skewers on a baking sheet, and refrigerate for 30 minutes. Reserve the remaining glaze. Grill the skewers, brushing with the glaze, as directed above. Serve hot. **SERVES 4 TO 6**

Grilled Chicken Satay:
For more of a satay look and taste to your chicken skewers, cut the meat into 12 to 18 strips. Place them in a sealable plastic bag. Prepare 1 recipe Cilantro-Peanut Dipping Sauce (page 389) and pour half of it over the chicken. Seal the bag and refrigerate for 30 minutes. Reserve the remaining sauce in a small bowl. Have ready 12 to 18 wooden skewers or fresh sugar cane spikes, about 8 inches long, soaked in water for at least 30 minutes before grilling. Thread 1 chicken strip onto each skewer. Grill the skewers as described above. Serve hot with the remaining dipping sauce. **SERVES 4 TO 6**

Curlicue Chicken Caesar Salad:
Have fun grilling and serving chicken pieces on spiral metal skewers in this new take on grilled chicken Caesar salad. Make 1 recipe Citrus Caesar Vinaigrette (page 84). Cut the chicken into 36 pieces. Place the chicken and half the vinaigrette in a sealable plastic bag and refrigerate for 1 hour, turning several times. Right before you're ready to grill, divide one 8-ounce package Caesar salad greens among 6 plates. Have ready 6 spiral metal skewers (or 12 wooden skewers, about 8 inches long, soaked in water for at least 30 minutes before grilling). Thread 6 pieces of chicken on

each metal skewer (3 on each wooden skewer). Grill the skewers as described above. Serve each curlicue skewer (or 2 wooden skewers) on a plate of greens, drizzled with the remaining vinaigrette. **SERVES 6**

An (Almost) All-Female Barbecue Team

Before the 'Que Queens barbecue team (to which Karen and Judith, the BBQ Queens, belong), there was Boss Hawg, a Memphis-based team of four women—Linda Thomason, Mabel Thomason (Linda's mother), Judy Braswell, and Virginia Smith—and one man, Virginia's husband, Randy. (Head cook Linda's only complaint about Randy is that he won't shave his legs, but because Virginia doesn't seem to mind, Linda doesn't make an issue of it.)

Hairy legs or not, Boss Hawg has been competing in barbecue contests since 1981 and has come away with top honors in many. In 1987, the team placed third in Ribs in the prestigious Memphis in May contest.

Breaking into a traditionally all-male realm was not too difficult, Linda says. "At first, the male teams were stunned at an 'all-female' cooking team on the barbecue circuit. We have turned around the perception a bit. Barbecuers are not a sexist bunch and kinda look out for us."

Karen and Judith's competition barbecue team, the 'Que Queens, had a similar experience in a Battle of the Sexes Barbecue Contest, a fun for-charity contest that pits a women's team against a men's team. The guys have looked out for the 'Que Queens, too. Sorta. "I got to the cooking site at 6:30 A.M. before the rest of our team," Karen recalls. "The guys offered me coffee, so I took a sip and almost fell over from all the booze in it. Next they offered me a bloody mary. By 9:00 A.M., they were on to beer."

By the time the judges were assembled to taste barbecued ribs from the men's and women's teams at 11:00 A.M., guess which team was well on its way to losing?

Stir-Grilled Chicken and Vegetables

How easy is this for a weeknight meal? Cut boneless, skinless chicken breasts or thighs into small pieces along with the vegetables of your choice, marinate everything in a sealable plastic bag, and stir-grill it all together in a grill wok. As you toss the food over the hot fire with wooden paddles or grill spatulas, you can look forward to minimal kitchen cleanup.

For instructions on how to stir-grill, see page 32. Serve stir-grilled dishes as is or accompany them with steamed rice, soba noodles, or pasta. **SERVES 4**

1½ pounds boneless, skinless chicken breasts, cut into 2-inch pieces

2 cups fresh or defrosted frozen snow peas or 2 cups zucchini cut into small pieces

1 bunch green onions, cut on the diagonal into 1-inch pieces

1 pint yellow teardrop tomatoes or 2 cups chunked yellow (or other color) tomatoes

¾ cup bottled balsamic vinaigrette

1 clove garlic, minced

1. Place the chicken and vegetables in a sealable plastic bag and add the balsamic vinaigrette and garlic. Seal the bag and toss to coat the chicken and vegetables with the marinade. Let marinate in the refrigerator for 30 minutes.

2. Prepare a hot fire in a grill. When ready to grill, add fruitwood such as cherry, apple, or pear for a kiss of smoke (see page 13).

3. Coat a grill wok with nonstick cooking spray and place over the sink or outside on the grass. Pour the marinated chicken and vegetables into the wok, allowing the excess marinade to drain away. Place the grill wok over direct heat and stir-grill, tossing the food with wooden paddles or grill spatulas, until everything is lightly browned, 12 to 15 minutes. Close the lid for 2 to 3 minutes to heat thoroughly, then serve.

 **Crowning Glories**

Stir-grilled chicken is delicious topped with a garnish of:

Chopped fresh herbs

Gremolata *(page 274)*

Crumbled smoked goat cheese *(page 169)*

Stir-Grilled Chicken with Asparagus and Shaved Parmigiano-Reggiano: For a different flavor, marinate the chicken and 1 pound trimmed asparagus cut on the diagonal into 2-inch pieces in your favorite Italian-style vinaigrette or Amogio (page 72). Grill as directed above. Shave Parmigiano-Reggiano cheese over each serving. **SERVES 4**

Stir-Grilled Chicken and Summer Vegetable Pasta with Fresh Basil Vinaigrette: So many ways to stir-grill chicken, so little time! Make 1 recipe Fresh Basil Vinaigrette (page 85). Marinate the chicken along with 1 small zucchini cut into rounds, 1 small yellow summer squash cut into rounds, and 1 cup grape or cherry tomatoes in half of the vinaigrette. Grill as directed above. Serve over 1 pound cooked pasta, drizzled with the remaining vinaigrette. **SERVES 4**

Stir-Grilled Tequila-Lime Chicken: This is definitely a recipe for margarita lovers (count us in). Make 1 recipe Tequila-Lime Marinade (page 73). Marinate the chicken along with 1 small zucchini cut into rounds, 1 small yellow summer squash cut into rounds, and 1 cup grape or cherry tomatoes in the marinade. Grill as directed above and serve with lime wedges. **SERVES 4**

Grilled Bone-In, Skin-On Chicken Breasts

Many people prefer bone-in chicken, claiming that it has more flavor than boneless, skinless breasts. We like chicken any way you grill it. Here's how to tackle the breast of the bird with the bone in. To start with, bone-in chicken breasts take longer to grill (all meat takes longer with the bone in). So the trick is to cook them longer without drying them out. To do this, you must have the skin on and turn them several times (every 5 to 10 minutes for about 30 minutes) over a medium-hot fire. For this, long-handled hinged tongs are a necessity, and you may want to wear long heat-resistant gloves as well. *Important:* The chicken breasts should be set out at room temperature for 20 to 30 minutes before grilling. This allows the seasoning to impart more flavor and results in a breast that is hot and juicy all the way through.

Is the extra effort worth it? You bet! The skin gets charred and caramelized and is delicious. The skin also gives you a little "pouch" that can be stuffed with cheese, pesto, flavored butter, herbs, prosciutto, or anything else that sounds appealing to you. And having the bone in and skin on keeps the meat juicier and hotter for a longer period of time after it comes off the grill. Such a deal!

The BBQ Queens offer a very simple treatment for the master recipe. Once you get the hang of that, sprinkle on Spicy Red-Hot Lemon Pepper Rub (page 53) or BBQ Queens' Photo Op Barbecue Rub (page 58), or soak the chicken in Fennel and Orange Marinade (page 72), before grilling.

While you're grilling the chicken, why not grill some vegetables, too? We like Grilled Asparagus (page 117) or Grilled Romaine and Green Onions with Lemon and Olives (page 127). Or serve the chicken with sliced fresh tomatoes and warmed rustic bread. SERVES 4

> 4 bone-in, skin-on chicken breast halves
> Olive oil
> Kosher or sea salt and seasoned pepper of your choice to taste
> 2 lemons, cut in half

1. Prepare a medium-hot fire in a grill.

2. Brush the chicken on both sides with olive oil and sprinkle with salt and seasoned pepper. Lightly brush the cut sides of the lemons with oil, too.

3. Place the chicken skin side down over the fire. Grill with the lid open for about 30 minutes, turning the chicken every 5 to 10 minutes. Baste with olive oil, if you wish. Grill the lemons cut side down for 5 to 7 minutes during the last 10 minutes of cooking. The chicken is done when an instant-read meat thermometer inserted in the thickest part of the breast registers 170 to 175°F. Serve with the grilled lemons on the side.

Crowning Glories

Grilled chicken breasts are delicious anointed with:

Pesto Aioli (page 110)

Mango-Lemon Sauce (page 92)

Poblano Cream Sauce (page 93)

Grilled Cheese-Stuffed Bone-In Chicken Breasts: Stuffing is an extra step that can be done several hours ahead or even the day before. Gently loosen part of the skin without tearing it. Stuff each breast with a 1/4-inch-thick slice of pepper Jack cheese or 1 tablespoon pimento cream cheese. Lightly coat the chicken with olive oil and season with kosher

or sea salt and freshly ground black pepper to taste. Grill as directed above and serve. **SERVES 4**

Pesto Chicken Sandwich with Cranberry Preserves: Slice any leftover chicken for a sandwich. Spread 1 tablespoon Chive Pesto (page 64) on a slice of bread. Spread another slice of bread with cranberry preserves (or chutney). Pile on the chicken, close the sandwich, and eat. **SERVES 1**

Fresh Greens and Grilled Chicken Salad: Arrange 1 cup greens on each of 4 salad plates. Top each plate of greens with 3 or 4 oil- or brine-cured olives, 2 tablespoons crumbled feta cheese, 4 or 5 halved cherry tomatoes, and several strips of grilled chicken breast. Drizzle with Lemon-Tarragon Vinaigrette (page 75) and serve. **SERVES 4**

Grilled Half a Chicken

Once you master grilling bone-in, skin-on chicken breasts (see page 199), grilling half a chicken is a snap. Half a chicken is a handsome piece of meat, and this is about as large a piece of chicken as you'll want to grill over direct heat. (For a whole chicken, it's best to smoke it slow or grill it on the indirect side of a medium-hot grill. Slow smoking at 225 to 250°F will take about 30 minutes per pound of chicken, or 2 to 2¹/₂ hours for a 4-pound bird. Indirect grilling at a higher temperature of 350°F will take about 1¹/₂ hours for the same size bird.)

Place 2 chicken halves that weigh about 2 pounds each in a sealable plastic bag. Place the bags upright in the sink. Pour 1 cup of your favorite marinade—try Homemade Teriyaki Marinade (page 69) or Hot Shallot Vinaigrette (page 85)—over each half and close the bag. Reserve ¹/₂ cup marinade for basting. Marinate in the refrigerator for at least 1 hour or up to 12 hours.

When ready to grill, take the chicken out of the refrigerator and let sit at room temperature for about 30 minutes. Prepare a medium-hot fire in a grill. Grill the chicken for 35 to 40 minutes over direct heat, turning every 5 to 10 minutes and basting with the reserved marinade. The chicken is done when an instant-read meat thermometer inserted in the thigh registers 170 to 175°F. **SERVES 4**

Grill Gals

The Silver Queen Corn Queen Grills Menu

Fresh Corn and Tomato Salad
Beelzebub's Bloody Marys
Rosemary-Scented Grilled Butterflied Chicken

Judith met Debbie Moose, a Silver Queen Corn Queen, when Judith was giving cooking classes at A Southern Season in Chapel Hill, North Carolina. Debbie was easy to spot because she was the only person—other than Judith—wearing a tiara, and a very dainty one at that.

Now an award-winning freelance food writer, Debbie used to be the food editor for the *News & Observer* in nearby Raleigh. Along the way, she has cooked up some pretty good stuff—and become a Silver Queen Corn Queen, part of a group of women who get together for coffee every Saturday and for regular margarita gatherings at one member's pool during warm weather. "We are registered with the Sweet Potato Queens as a bona fide chapter—or one member was supposed to make us legal, and I assume she did," Debbie says. "We picked the name out of our love of summer sweet corn, and because we're so queenly, we had to say it twice!"

Debbie believes that "charcoal is The One True Grilling Method." Her variations on the classic deviled egg are collected in her first cookbook, *Deviled Eggs: 50 Recipes from Simple to Sassy* (The Harvard Common Press, 2004). She is a cook after our own hearts—someone who is inspired to throw things together first, then figure out just what she did later.

Fresh Corn and Tomato Salad

"I tossed this together to use up a summer bounty of fresh vegetables from my local farmers' market," Debbie says. "The dressing will soften the corn somewhat, but because it isn't cooked, be sure to use only the freshest, most tender summer corn for this salad. You could turn this from a side dish to a main dish by adding a cup of cooked black beans." **SERVES 6**

$^1/_2$ cup white wine vinegar

1 cup olive oil

Kosher or sea salt and freshly ground black pepper to taste

1 clove garlic, crushed

3 cups fresh sweet corn kernels, such as Silver Queen, Peaches and Cream, or Country Gentleman (about 6 ears)

2 medium-size ripe tomatoes, peeled, seeded, and chopped

1 medium-size green bell pepper, seeded and chopped

1 medium-size Vidalia or other sweet onion, chopped

1. In a small bowl, combine the vinegar and olive oil. Season with salt and pepper, add the garlic, and set aside for a few minutes.

2. In a large bowl, stir together all the remaining ingredients. Remove the garlic from the vinaigrette and pour over the vegetables. Stir to combine. Taste for salt and pepper. Cover with plastic wrap and refrigerate for 4 to 6 hours before serving.

Beelzebub's Bloody Marys

This one is adapted from Debbie's book, *Deviled Eggs.* "Add as much Tabasco as you can stand," she says. Puree the sun-dried tomatoes in the food processor for the best texture. One of her tasters called these "the naughtiest deviled eggs ever." MAKES 6

3 hard-boiled large eggs, peeled and cut in half lengthwise

2 tablespoons mayonnaise

1³/₄ teaspoons pureed oil-packed sun-dried tomatoes

1¹/₂ teaspoons prepared horseradish

¹/₄ teaspoon Tabasco sauce, or more to taste

¹/₄ teaspoon vodka (optional)

¹/₂ teaspoon Worcestershire sauce

1¹/₂ teaspoons finely chopped celery with leaves, plus more for garnish

¹/₄ teaspoon Dijon mustard

¹/₄ teaspoon celery seeds

Kosher or sea salt and freshly ground black pepper to taste

1.   In a small bowl, mash the egg yolks. Add the mayonnaise and combine. Stir in the tomato puree, horseradish, Tabasco, vodka (if using), Worcestershire, celery, mustard, and celery seeds. Season with salt and pepper.

2.   Fill the egg whites with the mixture and garnish with chopped celery. Refrigerate for several hours or overnight for the flavors to blend. Serve cold.

Rosemary-Scented Grilled Butterflied Chicken

Debbie adapted this recipe from one by Jeanne Voltz, the late great Grill Gal, in *Barbecued Ribs, Smoked Butts and Other Great Feeds* **(Alfred A. Knopf, 1996). SERVES 4**

One 3¹/₂- to 4-pound chicken

Olive oil

2 lemons, cut in half

2 cloves garlic, cut into slivers

Kosher or sea salt and freshly ground black pepper to taste

5 or 6 fresh rosemary branches, 6 to 8 inches long

1. Butterfly the chicken by cutting vertically through the backbone with a pair of kitchen shears. Press the chicken firmly to flatten it out as much as possible. Place the chicken in a large bowl and rub it all over with olive oil. Squeeze both lemons over the chicken, rubbing in the juice. Sprinkle with the garlic and season with salt and pepper. Marinate in the refrigerator for 2 to 3 hours.

2. Soak the rosemary branches in water to cover for at least 10 minutes (a little longer won't hurt). Weight them down with a saucer, if necessary, to keep the herbs submerged. Meanwhile, prepare a hot fire in a covered charcoal or gas grill.

3. When ready to grill, remove the chicken from the marinade. Remove the rosemary branches from the water and shake off the excess water. Place the branches on the hot grill in such a way that they won't fall through. Brush the underside of the chicken with a bit of olive oil and place skin side up on top of the branches. Cover and cook for 10 to 15 minutes. Brush the chicken with olive oil and turn over so the skin side is against the rosemary. Cover and cook for another 10 to 15 minutes. If the chicken begins to turn too dark, pull it to the side of the grill briefly. If the rosemary begins to flame, remove it or spritz lightly with water. Continue to check and turn the chicken, brushing with more oil, if necessary, every 10 minutes or so until an instant-read meat thermometer inserted in the thickest part registers 170 to 175°F, about 40 minutes total. Serve hot.

You Say To-mah-to, the BBQ Queens Say Tomato

You may be familiar with the late Duchess of Windsor and her famous alleged remark, "One can never be too rich or too thin." Because she was from the United States, we think she might have wanted to add, "And one can never have too many tomatoes!" (even though the duchess banished any chef who had the audacity to serve tomatoes with their seeds).

We also sympathize with Imelda Marcos (a dethroned "queen," sort of) who *almost* said, "One can never have too many shoes—or too many tomatoes."

Karen and her husband, Dick, always grow tomatoes in their backyard garden. Dick's favorites are the beefsteak-style tomatoes that are perfect for slicing. Karen likes to grow cherry, Roma, teardrop, and heirloom varieties. Karen never refrigerates her tomatoes. If she has too many, she shares them with friends (such as Judith!).

Fresh tomatoes add a bit of acidity to a grilled meal, which rounds out the slight bitterness from the exterior char and the sweet interior of grilled foods. They add color and pop to a platter or table, and they're easy to prepare. What more could you want?

A Platter of Fresh Tomatoes

When making a platter of tomatoes, think color and shape. Slice some of the tomatoes and quarter others; keep some of the cherry or grape tomatoes whole and cut others in half. Then add any of the following items:

Cheese: Crumbled blue cheese, goat cheese, or feta cheese, or sliced fresh mozzarella

Onions: Slivers of red onion or rings of Maui or Vidalia onions

Peppers: Rings of green, yellow, or red bell peppers; diced or sliced chiles such as banana or jalapeño chiles

Olives: Green or black

Savories: **Anchovy fillets, capers, sliced hearts of palm, or quartered artichoke hearts**

Mayonnaise: **Doctor up 1 cup mayonnaise with 1 tablespoon fresh citrus juice of your choice, 1 chopped garlic clove, and 1 1/2 teaspoons of your favorite chopped fresh herb**

Vinegar or vinaigrette: **Drizzle with balsamic vinegar or other vinegar or vinaigrette, bottled or homemade**

Italian Roma Tomato Salad

In our book, "rustic" means easy to prepare, tasty, and pretty—in a rough-and-ready kind of way. **SERVES 6**

> **9 Roma tomatoes, cut in half**
>
> **1/2 cup pitted oil- or brine-cured olives, such as Kalamata or Niçoise, drained**
>
> **2 ounces fresh mozzarella, cubed**
>
> **2 ounces feta cheese, crumbled**
>
> **1/4 cup packed fresh basil leaves, torn**
>
> **2 tablespoons extra virgin olive oil**
>
> **Sea salt and freshly ground black pepper to taste**

Place the tomatoes, olives, cheeses, and basil in a large bowl. Drizzle with the olive oil, season with salt and pepper, toss lightly, and serve right away.

Roasted Cherry Tomatoes with Frizzled Herbs

Karen's friend Maureen Hasseltine first served this while Karen was visiting her in Cabo San Lucas, Mexico. Maureen loves to use fresh basil from her garden, and lots of it, with a shaved hard cheese such as Parmesan. When Karen returned home to her winter garden in Kansas City, she had only fresh oregano available. It worked like a charm, too. So now we say experiment and use what is fresh from your garden. **SERVES 6 TO 8**

2 pints cherry or grape tomatoes

10 to 12 fresh herb sprigs, such as basil, oregano, and/or dill, to your taste

1/2 cup shaved hard goat cheese

1 tablespoon olive oil

Fine kosher or sea salt and freshly ground black pepper to taste (optional)

1. Preheat the oven to 350°F.

2. Place the tomatoes in a shallow 1-quart baking dish and bake until some of them have burst their skins, about 15 minutes.

3. Remove from the oven and quickly tuck the herbs around the tomatoes. Sprinkle with the cheese and drizzle with the olive oil. Return to the oven for 10 minutes. The herbs will be very crisp and the cheese will have melted. Season with salt and pepper, if you like, but the flavor is quite luscious without them. Serve hot.

Late-Harvest Tomato Tart

Inspired by Susan Herrmann Loomis's tomato tart recipe in her *Farmhouse Cookbook* (Workman, 1991), this dish is great when you have a big bowl of assorted cherry-type tomatoes. MAKES ONE 9-INCH TART; SERVES 6 TO 8

1 sheet frozen puff pastry, defrosted

1 cup heavy cream

2 large eggs

1 tablespoon chopped fresh thyme or tarragon or 1 teaspoon dried thyme or tarragon

2 small cloves garlic, minced

Fine kosher or sea salt and freshly ground black pepper to taste

12 ounces Swiss cheese, cubed

5 pounds mixed ripe tomatoes, such as cherry, grape, and teardrop

1. Preheat the oven to 425°F.

2. Roll out the puff pastry to an 11-inch square. Line a 9-inch tart pan with the pastry, trim the edges, and prick with a fork. Place in the freezer for 5 minutes, then bake until golden, about 10 minutes. Remove from the oven.

3. In a large bowl, whisk together the cream and eggs. Blend in the thyme and garlic, then season with salt and pepper.

4. Arrange the cheese cubes evenly in the crust. Cut the larger tomatoes in half and leave the smaller ones whole. Scatter the tomatoes over the cheese. They will mound slightly in the center of the pan, which is fine.

5. Pour the cream mixture into the crust. Place the tart on a baking sheet and bake for 10 minutes, then reduce the oven temperature to 350°F and continue to bake until the custard is set and the pie is golden on top, 45 to 55 minutes. Let cool for at least 10 minutes before serving warm or at room temperature.

Grilled Wings and Things

I❋❋❋❋**I**

If your royal budget is a concern, get thee to the market and buy chicken wings. Buy legs and thighs, too, which are sometimes sold very cheaply as chicken quarters. Make no bones about it, chicken wings, legs, and thighs are some of the tastiest parts of the bird. The flavor comes from the rich, succulent meat close to the bone. Invite your family and friends over to eat, drink, and be merry. You might be on a budget, but they'll never know.

You can add flavor in two ways. Brush the parts with olive oil, then sprinkle on a rub, such as the Middle Eastern za'atar (sumac, sesame, salt, and dried thyme) or another herb and spice mixture, and grill. Or flavor dem bones by marinating or basting with a hot vinegar sauce, an Asian-style sauce with soy sauce as a component, Amogio (page 72), or good old American barbecue sauce. Just remember that anything with sugar in it will burn faster than other marinades, so be prepared to move the chicken to the indirect side of the fire to quell any flare-ups (or have a spray bottle handy to douse them with water).

Grilling with a kiss of smoke (see page 13) makes wings and things fit for a queen (or king). For a smoky flavor, add a handful of water-soaked wood chips to a hot charcoal fire or make up an aluminum foil package of water-soaked wood chips or dry wood pellets for a gas grill. We especially like apple, cherry, hickory, and pecan with chicken.

Leaving the chicken wings whole is the simplest and fastest way to prepare them. If you like to serve them as drummies, place the wings on a cutting board and split them at the joints with a sharp knife, then discard the tips. Also use a chef's knife to split the drumsticks from the thighs for easier eating and smaller portions. **SERVES 4**

> **2 pounds chicken wings, drumsticks, and/or thighs**
> **1 cup bottled Italian-style vinaigrette**
> **Juice and grated zest of 1 lemon**

1. Rinse the chicken and place in a large sealable plastic bag. Pour in the vinaigrette and add the lemon juice and zest. Seal the bag and mix by turning it several times. Marinate in the refrigerator for at least 20 minutes or up to 2 hours.

2. Prepare a hot fire in a grill.

3. Remove the chicken from the bag and place directly over the fire. Pour the marinade into a container and use to baste the chicken every 5 minutes for the first 15 minutes, then discard. Continue to grill, turning, until nicely browned and crisp all over and

the meat begins to shrink at the base of the bone. Total cooking time is about 20 minutes for wings, 30 minutes for thighs or drumsticks. Serve hot.

Crowning Glories

Wings and things are great served with a dipping sauce such as:

Creamy Blue Cheese Dressing (page 111)

Spicy Lemon-Soy Sauce (page 312)

Peanut Butter Dipping Sauce (page 118)

Season or marinate the chicken pieces with any of these:

Spicy Orange Rub (page 51)

BBQ Queens' All-Purpose Rub (page 49)

Vietnamese Drizzle (page 87)

Sizzling Wings and Things with Sage Butter and Romano Cheese:

This one goes together quick—the hot crispy chicken being topped with the butter and cheese as soon as it comes off the grill. Cook the chicken as described above. Meanwhile, in a small saucepan over medium heat, melt 1/2 cup (1 stick) unsalted butter and add 3 or 4 fresh sage leaves. Cook until the butter browns and is infused with the sage flavor, about 20 minutes. When the chicken is done, transfer to a platter, drizzle with the hot sage butter, sprinkle with 1/3 cup freshly grated Romano cheese, and serve. Yum! **SERVES 4**

Grilled Chicken Wings Amogio:

Judith prepared these for a cooking class she did at A Southern Season in Chapel Hill, North Carolina. Arrange the wings on a brightly colored platter for instant pizzazz as a finger-lickin'-good appetizer or casual main dish. If the bars on your grill grate are far apart, place the wings on a perforated grill rack and grill them in batches. Make 1 recipe of Amogio (page 72), reserving 1/2 cup for drizzling. Place 3 pounds chicken wings in a large sealable plastic bag. Pour in the remaining amogio, seal the bag, and marinate in the refrigerator for at least 1 hour or overnight. Remove the chicken, discarding the marinade. Grill as instructed above. Drizzle a little of the reserved amogio over each wing and serve. **SERVES 4**

Grilled Drumsticks or Thighs Stuffed with Herbed Goat Cheese or Boursin:

When we were kids, our dads told us that wings were scrawny and not very good. So that left the drumsticks to vie for. Now you can buy packages of just drumsticks, wings, or thighs, making family life a bit more civilized. Prepare 2 legs or thighs for each person. (On second thought, you may want to double this recipe for leftovers.) Begin with 8 chicken drumsticks or thighs that have been rinsed and patted dry. Loosen the skin from each chicken piece and stuff 1¹/₂ teaspoons herbed fresh goat cheese or Boursin under the skin (¹/₄ cup total). Smear ¹/₂ teaspoon Dijon mustard (4 teaspoons total) over each chicken piece, then season with a spice rub or kosher or sea salt and freshly ground black pepper to taste. Finish with 8 slices hickory-smoked bacon, 1 slice wrapped around each chicken piece and secured with a toothpick. Grill over a medium-hot fire for about 30 minutes, turning to brown all over. Now go eat—and no fighting allowed! **SERVES 4**

Smoked Wings and Things

By now we think you've caught on to the fact that smoking time depends on how much food is in the smoker—it's a per pound thing, for the most part. So let's have fun with all these chicken pieces, and remember that you can use these recipes with different chicken parts as well. Mix and match your favorite marinades, rubs, pastes, and drizzles to have slightly different smoked wings and things every time you go out to the smoker. Try Tequila-Lime Marinade (page 73) or Tricolored Pepper-corn Rub (page 62) for something a little different, or even bottled Italian-style vinaigrette if that's what you have on hand. **SERVES 8 TO 10**

SUGGESTED WOOD: Apple, oak, maple, mesquite, or hickory

Two 3-pound fryers, cut into serving-size pieces, or about 5 pounds chicken parts

2 cups Tandoori Marinade (page 74)

1. Rinse the chicken and place in a shallow dish. Pour 1 cup of the marinade over the chicken. Let sit at room temperature in a cool kitchen for about 30 minutes, turning the pieces to coat well and flavor.

2. Prepare an indirect fire in a smoker.

3. Place the chicken on the smoker, cover, and smoke at 225 to 250°F. After 2 hours, start basting with the remaining 1 cup marinade every 30 minutes for another 1 to 2 hours. The chicken is done when an instant-read meat thermometer inserted in the thickest part of the meat registers 170 to 175°F. The wings and breasts will get done sooner than the thighs and legs. Serve hot.

 **Crowning Glories**

Smoked chicken parts are delicious served with potato or pasta salad,
baked beans, or A Platter of Fresh Tomatoes (page 206), along with your
favorite barbecue sauce or a dipping sauces, such as:
Creamy Blue Cheese Dressing (page 111)
Chipotle Barbecue Sauce (page 90)

Chopped Smoked Chicken Salad: A fave that gets raves! Chop 1 head iceberg lettuce and arrange on a platter. In columns, place 3 peeled and chopped hard-boiled large eggs; 1 cup chopped artichoke hearts; 1 cup pitted, drained, and sliced oil- or brine-cured black olives; 2 cups chopped smoked (or grilled or rotisserie) chicken down the center of the plate; 1 cup chopped red tomatoes; 8 slices crumbled crisp-cooked bacon; and 4 ounces crumbled blue cheese or feta cheese. Drizzle with your favorite dressing and serve. **SERVES 6 TO 8**

Pulled Smoked Chicken Salad with Basil Mayonnaise: Using the meat from 4 smoked (or grilled) chicken breast halves, pull the meat off the bones into strips. To make the mayonnaise, in a small bowl whisk together 2 cups good-quality mayonnaise, $1/2$ teaspoon dry mustard, the juice and grated zest of 1 lemon, and $1/4$ cup chopped fresh basil. Wash 1 medium-size head butter lettuce and arrange the leaves on a large platter. Place a bowl in the center of the platter and transfer the mayonnaise to it. Arrange the pulled chicken around the bowl. Crumble 4 ounces feta cheese over the chicken. Place cherry or grape tomatoes and assorted olives around the rim of the platter and serve. **SERVES 6**

Barbecued Chicken on Fire: This smoked chicken is a little faster to cook because you use more heat and boneless, skinless chicken breasts. Combine 1 cup spicy barbecue sauce, $2/3$ cup orange marmalade, 1 tablespoon Worcestershire sauce, and 2 teaspoons prepared horseradish in a medium-size bowl. Reserve 1 cup of the sauce in a small bowl for serving on the side. The remaining sauce is for basting. Rinse and pat dry 6 pounds boneless, skinless chicken breast halves (about 12), then season with kosher salt and freshly ground black pepper to taste. Grill over a hot fire for about 2 minutes per side to sear and mark, basting with the sauce. Move the chicken to the indirect side of the grill and add 1 cup wood chips soaked in water for at least 30 minutes. Cover and maintain a medium-hot fire. Baste the chicken every 10 minutes until done, about 45 minutes. An instant-read meat thermometer inserted in the thickest part of the meat should register 160 to 165°F. Serve with the reserved sauce. **SERVES 10 TO 12**

BBQ Babes

She'll Smoke for Soup Menu

Smoked Chicken Breasts with Southwest Heat
Green Chile and Smoked Chicken Soup

The Jamisons, Bill and Cheryl, blazed the barbecue trail with their phenomenally successful *Smoke & Spice* (The Harvard Common Press, 1994 and 2003), which won both International Association of Culinary Professionals (IACP) and James Beard Foundation awards. Cheryl sent us these terrific recipes, which we adapted.

Like the BBQ Queens, Cheryl often makes extra smoked foods to have leftovers for other dishes at her home in Santa Fe, New Mexico. She likes to smoke even lower and slower than we do, at about 200 to 220°F (we like to keep it at 225 to 250°F). Try chicken smoked at both temperatures and see which you prefer.

The soulful Green Chile and Smoked Chicken Soup is one of the couple's favorite leftover chicken treats. It's so good you'll be tempted to fire up your smoker and make it from scratch. You can easily cook the chicken a day or two ahead of when you want to prepare the soup.

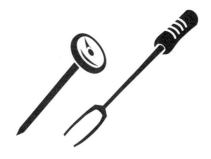

Smoked Chicken Breasts with Southwest Heat

Earthy and pungent with heat hitting the back of your throat is what you get with this delicious smoked chicken. Serve it with a side of Rustic Bread with Smoked Tomato and Basil Butter (page 177). SERVES 4

SUGGESTED WOOD: Apple or a combination of apple and hickory

SOUTHWEST HEAT

2 tablespoons ground Hatch chile (see page 140)

2 tablespoons ground ancho chile (see page 59)

2 teaspoons coarse kosher or sea salt

2 teaspoons ground cumin

1/4 teaspoon dried oregano, preferably Mexican

4 or 5 bone-in, skin-on chicken breast halves (7 to 8 ounces each)

1.   At least 2 hours before you plan to barbecue, or up to the night before, make the heat by combining all the ingredients in a small bowl. With your fingers, loosen the skin of the breasts and massage the chicken with the spice mixture, rubbing over and under the skin. Place the breasts in a sealable plastic bag and refrigerate for at least 1 1/2 hours or up to 12 hours.

2.   Prepare an indirect fire in a smoker. Remove the chicken from the refrigerator and let sit at room temperature for about 20 minutes.

3.   Transfer the chicken pieces to the smoker, skin side up. Cover and cook at 200 to 220°F until cooked through and the juices run clear when a skewer is inserted in the thickest part, 50 to 60 minutes. Enjoy right away, or let cool for making the following soup.

Green Chile and Smoked Chicken Soup

This is spicy and addictive. If you can find Hatch chiles (from Hatch, New Mexico), use them. SERVES 8

2 tablespoons vegetable oil

1 medium-size onion, chopped

2 large carrots, chopped

2 to 3 cloves garlic, to your taste, minced

8 cups chicken broth

One 14-ounce can stewed tomatoes, preferably a Mexican-flavored variety, with their juice

1 cup chopped roasted mild green chiles, such as Hatch or poblano, preferably fresh or defrosted frozen chiles

2 cups grilled or smoked fresh corn kernels (about 2 ears) or defrosted frozen kernels

1¼ teaspoons dried oregano

Coarse kosher or sea salt to taste

1 recipe Smoked Chicken Breasts with Southwest Heat (page 215)

Minced fresh cilantro and finely shredded Monterey Jack cheese for garnish

1.   Warm the oil in a large pot over high heat. Stir in the onion, carrots, and garlic and cook, stirring, until the onion is softened and browned on the edges. Frequently scrape up the vegetables from the bottom of the pan. Pour in the broth and add the tomatoes, chiles, corn, oregano, and salt. Bring to a boil, then reduce the heat to a simmer and cook until all the vegetables are tender, 25 to 30 minutes. (The broth can be prepared a day or two ahead to this point and refrigerated. Bring back to a simmer before adding the chicken.)

2.   When the chicken is cool enough to handle, shred the meat into bite-size chunks, discarding the skin and bones or saving them to make smoky chicken stock later. Stir the chicken into the broth and continue to simmer for about 10 minutes. Ladle the soup into bowls, garnish with cilantro and cheese, and serve hot.

Rotisserie Chicken

On the last decade or so, rotisserie chicken has gone from a rare treat to a staple of weeknight family dinners. It seems as if every larger-scale grocery store, deli, or takeout restaurant offers rotisserie chicken in some way, shape, or form. But if you like rotisserie chicken that you buy, you'll *love* rotisserie chicken you make yourself.

You'll want a good-quality chicken to start with—preferably free-range, meaning the chicken was free to roam and search for its own food, not raised in close quarters in a huge chicken house. Because the flavor of the bird itself stands out when you rotisserie it, quality does matter. You'll want a younger chicken in the fryer range—3 to 4 pounds at the most. Remember to check both cavities of the bird for those little bundles of neck and giblets and remove them.

Check the maximum weight your rotisserie motor can handle, then buy your chicken. Rotisserie 2 or 3 chickens at a time and plan for delicious leftovers. (Karen makes the absolute best rotisserie chicken sandwiches; she packs them for when the BBQ Queens hit the road to give cooking classes or perform at other royal engagements.) This is our essential rotisserie chicken recipe. You could also marinate the chicken in Aromatic Lemon-Herb Marinade (page 68) or sprinkle on a rub after marinating the chicken; try Fair for Fowl Rub (page 51), Spicy Orange Rub (page 51), or Zesty Sugar and Spice Rub (page 52). The flavor of this chicken is so good and its texture so tender that we regard it as a standalone dish—no sauce needed. SERVES 6 TO 8

> 1/2 cup chopped fresh Italian parsley
> 6 cloves garlic, minced
> Juice of 2 lemons
> 1/4 cup olive oil
> Two 3- to 4-pound free-range chickens, giblets and necks removed
> Kosher or sea salt and freshly ground black pepper to taste

1. In a small bowl, stir the parsley, garlic, lemon juice, and olive oil together. With a brush, slather the mixture all over the chickens, inside and out. Cover the chickens with plastic wrap and refrigerate for at least 1 hour or overnight.

2. Set up your grill for rotisserie cooking (see page 33). Prepare a medium fire (around 350°F).

3. Season the chickens with salt and pepper inside and out. Tie the legs together with kitchen twine. Attach a clamp to one end of each chicken. Push the rotisserie rod

through one clamp and the center of the chicken so the bird is balanced. Place the other chicken, clamp side out, on the rod, then push the rod through the second clamp. Attach the clamps to the spit and place a drip pan under the chickens. Cover and cook until an instant-read meat thermometer inserted in the thigh registers 170 to 175°F and a skewer inserted in the thickest part of a leg produces clear juices, about 1½ hours.

4.   Transfer the chickens to serving platters and tent with aluminum foil to keep warm. Let rest for 15 minutes before carving and serving.

 **Crowning Glories**

Rotisserie chicken is delicious served family style with potato salad, sliced tomatoes, and other accompaniments that reflect the best of the farmers' market, such as:

Mediterranean Salad with Lemon-Sumac Vinaigrette *(page 279)*

Grilled Romaine Caesar Salad *(page 127)*

Grilled Corn *(page 119)*

French Tarragon Rotisserie Chicken: Instead of the herb and garlic slather, mix together ½ cup (1 stick) softened unsalted butter, 1 small bunch chopped fresh tarragon, and the juice of 1 lemon. Slather each chicken with this mixture inside and out, then sprinkle with kosher or sea salt and ground white pepper to taste. Marinate and cook as directed above. **SERVES 6 TO 8**

Puerto Rican–Style Rotisserie Chicken: Here's another intensely aromatic way of doing a whole chicken. Instead of the herb and garlic slather, in a mortar with a pestle crush together 8 black peppercorns, 1 tablespoon sea salt, and 4 garlic cloves until the peppercorns are at least cracked and you have a somewhat smooth paste. Using the pestle, stir in 1 tablespoon dried oregano, the juice of 2 limes, and 2 tablespoons olive oil until well blended. Slather each chicken with this mixture inside and out. Marinate and cook as directed above. **SERVES 6 TO 8**

Karen's Famous Rotisserie Chicken Sandwich: No boring airline food or typical burger fast food for the BBQ Queens when we travel! Karen packs two of these sandwiches in a cooler for the road. (They are so big, we eat only half at a time.) Even if we're driving in rain or get stuck driving around and around a country town (which we did once), these melt-in-your-mouth sandwiches sustain us. The surprising secret? Still-warm hard-boiled eggs that seem to vanish into the mayonnaise. Place 2 large eggs in a saucepan with water to cover, then bring to a boil over medium heat. Cook for 5 minutes, take off the heat to finish cooking gradually, then somewhat cool for about 8 minutes. Peel the eggs, then cut into very small pieces while still warm. Combine with 1 tablespoon chopped shallot, 1 tablespoon finely chopped celery, 1 cup chopped leftover rotisserie chicken, and $1/4$ to $1/2$ cup mayonnaise. Season with kosher or sea salt and freshly ground black pepper to taste. Spread the chicken salad between 2 slices of good-quality sourdough bread slathered with Dijon mustard. Add lettuce, if you like. **SERVES 1**

Smoked Whole Chicken

Smoked chicken is a versatile dish. You can never have too much of it on hand. Add it to salads, pasta dishes, chowders, or soups; use it to top a pizza; or combine it with crisp-cooked bacon for a club sandwich at lunch. If you love roast chicken, you'll also want to try it smoked. The difference is simply exchanging your hot oven for a slow smoker and allowing the extra time it takes for chicken to cook. It's sublime, queen's honor.

A whole chicken weighs anywhere from 3 to 6 pounds, with the 3- to 4-pound size being the most common. Use a good-quality bird, preferably free-range.

The smoking process is very similar to that for rotisserie cooking (see page 33). So if you don't have a rotisserie, you'll be smokin' your birds this way. The skin browns to a glistening mahogany color, and the meat is juicy and smoky. As with smoked pork butt, you can either slice or pull apart the meat of a slow-smoked chicken.

With all of the wonderful dishes you can make, the BBQ Queens recommend smoking two or three chickens at a time. (You can always throw one of the smoked chickens in the freezer for later—well wrapped, of course.) Smoking will take 45 to 60 minutes per pound of bird at 225 to 250°F. (Remember, the weather affects your smoking time, so allow more time for cold and windy weather and less time on a hot, still day.) Basically, a 4-pound chicken needs to smoke for about 3 hours, until the leg joint moves easily.

Don't forget to check the chicken's cavities for the giblets and neck, then anoint it with oil and season to taste. The fancier treatment is to sprinkle the bird with a rub (see pages 49–62), coat it with a slather (see page 66), or place it in a marinade (see pages 67–75) before smoking. Chicken is mild and adaptable to many different flavors, so we give you the royal okay to experiment. **SERVES 4 TO 6**

SUGGESTED WOOD: Fruitwood, grapevines, oak, mesquite, or hickory, or a combination

Two 3- to 4-pound chickens, giblets and necks removed

2 tablespoons olive oil

Fine kosher or sea salt and freshly ground black pepper to taste

I. Prepare an indirect fire in a smoker.

2. Rinse the birds thoroughly and pat dry. Rub 1 tablespoon olive oil over each and rub with salt and pepper. Place the birds in the smoker, close the lid, and smoke at 225 to 250°F. The chickens are done when a leg joint moves easily and the meat is no longer pink, about 2½ hours. An instant-read meat thermometer inserted in the thigh should register 170 to 175°F. Serve hot, or let cool to room temperature and place in the refrigerator. When cold, wrap in aluminum foil or plastic to keep for a couple of days chilled—perfect for raiding the icebox on a hot summer night.

Crowning Glories

Smoked whole chicken is delicious marinated in, prepared with, or served with:

Provençal Red Wine Marinade (page 70)

Fair for Fowl Rub (page 51)

Mustard-Mayo-Tarragon Slather (page 66)

Lemon Butter Drizzle (page 87)

Italian Barbecued Chicken: One of the members of the 'Que Queens, our competition barbecue team, owned her own barbecue restaurant. Jean Tamburello's Italian fusion barbecue at Marty's Bar-B-Que made the pages of *Saveur* magazine and was the toast of the town in Kansas City for years, until she retired and closed the restaurant. Her Italian fusion barbecue secret? Marinate a whole chicken in Amogio (page 72), smoke it, and then serve the smoked chicken with fresh amogio at the table. Simply delicious! **SERVES 4**

Rosemary-Garlic Smoked Chicken: This is from Karen's *Best Little Barbecue Cookbook* (Celestial Arts, 2000). It is as good as, if not better than, any store-bought rotisserie garlic chicken. Plus, when you prepare it yourself, you have braggin' rights. Coat each chicken with 1 tablespoon olive oil and sprinkle with 1 tablespoon chopped fresh rosemary. Cut about ½ inch off the top of 2 heads of garlic and place 1 head in the cavity of each chicken. Smoke as directed above and discard the garlic before serving. **SERVES 4 TO 6**

Smoked Sesame-Soy Marinated Chicken: A terrific marinade can make all the difference in the world. Combine ³/₄ cup soy sauce, 2 tablespoons toasted sesame oil, 2 tablespoons dark honey, and 2 minced garlic cloves in a small bowl. Place each chicken in a sealable plastic bag and pour half of the marinade into each bag. Seal the bags and marinate in the refrigerator for at least 2 hours or up to 12 hours. Remove the chickens, discarding the marinade, and smoke as directed above. This Asian-style recipe also turns the smoky chicken into a perfect shredded meat to serve on a salad drizzled with Citrus Caesar Vinaigrette (page 84) that you spike with an additional 1 to 2 tablespoons soy sauce. **SERVES 4 TO 6**

Smoked Chicken and Vegetable Lasagna: Sometimes making lasagna can be a real mess, and we don't like that. Here is a recipe you can prepare in make-ahead steps. Preheat the oven to 350°F. In a large bowl, combine one 16-ounce container ricotta cheese, 1 cup freshly grated Pecorino Romano cheese, 2 cups whole milk, and 1 teaspoon garlic salt. (The sauce can be made several days ahead and refrigerated.) Pour 1 cup of the sauce in a greased 13 x 9 x 2-inch baking pan. Lay 3 no-cook lasagna noodles over the sauce. Top with 1¹/₂ cups sliced grilled or smoked portobello mushrooms (see page 132 or 134) and 1 cup sauce. Lay 3 more lasagna noodles over the mushrooms. Top with 2 to 3 cups shredded smoked chicken (or duck) and 1 cup sauce. Repeat with the last layer of noodles, topped with more mushrooms or sliced grill-roasted bell peppers (see page 145) and the remaining 1 cup sauce. Sprinkle with 1 cup freshly grated Pecorino Romano cheese. (The lasagna can be refrigerated for up to 1 day.) Bake until browned and bubbling, 35 to 40 minutes. Remove from the oven and let sit for 15 minutes, then serve hot. **SERVES 10 TO 12**

Grilled Turkey Breast Tenderloin Steaks

Turkey is the real lean and mean deal for all of you high-protein, low-carb aficionados. Because turkey is mild, you can rub, slather, or sauce it any way you like. Haven't tried turkey on the grill yet? There is no trick, really, just common sense. The most difficult part is which cut to choose, because turkey comes in all sizes and shapes: whole, legs, turkey breast bone-in and boneless, cutlets, chops, tenderloin, tenderloin steaks, and ground.

Turkey makes for a light and easy summertime feast. Our Tarragon Grilled Turkey Breast (next page) comes out moist and delicious—fit for a queen! An easy chutney, store-bought or homemade (which is also good over cream cheese), is a delicious partner to turkey or chicken, hot or cold. Cool side dishes, such as coleslaw, pasta salad, or sliced tomatoes, complement the tasty bird and take you far from the roasted Thanksgiving turkey.

Let's focus on the easiest part to grill, turkey breast tenderloin steaks cut $^1/_2$ inch thick. Yeah, we know the grocery store has those thick-cut turkey steaks with bacon wrapped around them, but they're about $1^1/_2$ inches thick and take longer to cook, plus it takes time to get the bacon crisp (and they end up tasting like bacon). We prefer thinner steaks for our simple version here.

We recommend a medium to medium-hot fire for turkey, because you don't want the meat to dry out before it's cooked all the way through. For some of these recipes, you'll need to prepare an indirect fire, which means you'll have a medium-hot fire on one side and no fire on the other side. Cook boneless turkey cuts to an internal temperature of 160 to 165°F and bone-in cuts to 170 to 175°F. Serve your grilled turkey with Grilled Red Potato and Fennel Salad (page 148) or Warm Asian Eggplant Salad (page 125). **SERVES 4**

> **Four 4- to 6-ounce turkey breast tenderloin steaks, $^1/_2$ inch thick**
> **Olive oil**
> **Fine kosher or sea salt and freshly ground black pepper to taste**

1. Prepare a medium to medium-hot fire in a grill.

2. Rub the steaks with olive oil and season with salt and pepper. Place directly over the fire until no longer pink, turning once after the first 6 or 7 minutes, for a total of 12 to 15 minutes. Boneless turkey is done when an instant-read meat thermometer inserted in the meatiest part registers 160 to 165°F. Serve hot.

Crowning Glories

Grilled turkey is delicious served with:
Bourbon-Mustard Cream Sauce (page 377)
Chimichurri Sauce (page 346)
Grilled Tomatillo Salsa (page 163)

Tarragon Grilled Turkey Breast: This is a recipe for grilling half a bone-in turkey breast. It requires a much longer cooking time and needs to be constantly turned and basted while on the grill. The vinegar marinade gives the turkey a wonderful, tangy Carolina barbecue flavor. Rinse the split breast halves of 1 whole bone-in turkey breast and place in a sealable plastic bag. In a small bowl, combine 1/2 cup tarragon vinegar, 1/3 cup olive oil, 1 1/2 teaspoons poultry seasoning, 1 teaspoon dried tarragon, 2 minced garlic cloves, 1 1/2 teaspoons freshly ground black pepper, 2 teaspoons fine kosher or sea salt, 1 teaspoon hot pepper sauce, and 1 teaspoon fresh lemon or lime juice. Pour over the turkey, seal the bag, and marinate in the refrigerator for at least 1 hour or overnight. Remove from the marinade. Transfer the reserved marinade to a small saucepan, bring to a boil, and continue to boil for about 5 minutes. Cook the turkey directly over a medium-hot fire for about 1 hour, turning and basting with the reserved marinade every 5 minutes. The turkey is done when an instant-read meat thermometer inserted in the meatiest part registers 170 to 175°F. Serve hot. **SERVES 6 TO 8**

Turkey Steaks with Spicy Horseradish Sauce: The pungent flavors of this concoction complement plain meat, fish, and especially turkey. This is from Karen's *Best Little BBQ Sauces Cookbook* (Celestial Arts, 2000). In a small bowl, combine 1 cup lowfat sour cream, 1/4 cup prepared horseradish, 2 tablespoons chopped pimento, 1 tablespoon sweet Hungarian paprika, 1 teaspoon ground cumin, 1 teaspoon ground allspice, 1/2 teaspoon ground coriander, and 1/2 teaspoon red pepper flakes. Chill for at least 1 hour or up to 3 days before serving with the grilled turkey steaks. **SERVES 4**

Bacon-Wrapped Turkey Fillets: Yes, these are the grocery store treats that everyone buys. Lightly coat 4 turkey fillets with olive oil and season with kosher salt and freshly ground black pepper to taste. Roll each fillet into a cylinder. Wrap a slice of bacon around the middle of the cylinder, then wrap another slice around the cylinder lengthwise and secure with toothpicks. Grill the fillets for about 8 minutes, turning when the bacon begins to brown. Sear for 3 to 4 minutes, then move the fillets to the indirect side of the grill and close the lid. Cook until the center of a fillet registers 160 to 165°F on an instant-read meat thermometer, about 10 minutes. Serve with the condiments of your choice. **SERVES 4**

The Queen Waves

Whenever we do a cooking class or a demonstration, we always start out by teaching this important life skill.

Yes, knowing the four queen waves is a life skill. You never know when you're going to be homecoming queen, salesperson or employee of the year, mayor of your town, or the celebrity in a ticker-tape parade. That sort of thing can creep up on you unawares. It's best to be prepared for every eventuality. That's why most of us all have insurance. This is your celebrity insurance.

We have this information on good authority—from former Miss America Debbye Turner, who taught us these waves during a BBQ Queen television appearance in St. Louis.

It's hard to describe the waves in print; it's better to see them done in person. But we think you've probably seen enough beauty queen contests to get the general drift. So here are the four queen waves, from most rigorous (when your arm is fresh) to easier (when your arm is flagging, halfway through the parade) to the intimate wave when you're heading onstage to receive your award, your crown, your commendation, your key to the city, your accolade.

Screwing in the light bulb: With this wave, you just raise your arm so your upper arm is parallel to the ground, your elbow is bent, and your lower arm is straight up. Cup your hand and revolve your wrist a half turn and back, as if you were screwing in a light bulb. As Karen always says, this is Queen Elizabeth's favorite wave, although she does it differently because she's never had to screw in a light bulb.

Wiping the windshield: When your wrist starts to hurt, change to this wave. Again, raise your arm so your upper arm is parallel to the ground, your elbow is bent, and your lower arm is straight up. Open your hand so that your palm faces outward and wipe the windshield.

Fluttering the air: Okay, so now your wrist *really* hurts. Change to a wave that will take the kinks out. This is a limper wave, so be less rigid. Raise your arm so your upper arm is parallel to the ground, your elbow is bent, and your lower arm is straight up. Bend your wrist up and down as you flutter your fingers. Bend and flutter, bend and flutter. (This is also good for carpal tunnel prevention, so you could do this at your desk at work.)

The intimate wave: All right. You have walked onstage. You've won! Now it's time to thank all those little people, seated in the audience, who have helped you get where you are today. Look out at each one. Point your arm straight out at them and pat in the air. A squeal of glee (think boo-boo-be-doo—oooo!) usually accompanies this gesture. Do this as many times as necessary, but once is not enough.

Smoked Boneless Turkey Breast

■⟨⟨⟨⟨⟨■

Half a smoked boneless, skinless turkey breast makes four 6-ounce servings. (A turkey tenderloin, which is much smaller, serves only two.) If you want leftovers for sandwiches, you'd better smoke two halves. Because the turkey is skinless, it needs to be covered. You can wrap it in leaves, cornhusks (facing each other and tied together), or prosciutto or bacon. We like to think of it as a pretty package that keeps the turkey meat moist while it is being anointed with luscious smoke.

The turkey breast can be slathered with mustard, flavored mayonnaise, chutney, or preserves, then wrapped in its protective coat. Also, season the breast meat with the herbs and spices of your choice. Or get a little adventurous and try Spicy, Savory Seasoned Salt (page 56) or Porcini Paste (page 65).

Turkey breast (or tenderloin) can be butterflied and pounded thin to make beautiful roulades. Even easier than roulades is to make turkey pockets by slitting the turkey breast in half lengthwise, but not cutting it all the way through, then stuffing with herbs, cheese, bread or fruit stuffing, or vegetables before smoking.

In addition to smoking domestic turkey, you can also go wild. Karen's husband, Dick, hunts wild turkeys, and she's had good luck—and lots of practice—with cooking wild turkey breasts in the smoker. (The legs are too tough, and she usually cuts them off.) Prepare and smoke a wild turkey breast like its domestic long-lost cousin.

Turkey smokes best at 225 to 250°F. Cooking time is 30 to 40 minutes per pound, so 3 pounds of boneless turkey will take 1½ to 2 hours to smoke. **SERVES 4**

SUGGESTED WOOD: Fruitwood, grapevines, pecan, oak, or maple

> **2 boneless, skinless turkey breast halves (about 3 pounds)**
> **1 tablespoon olive oil**
> **4 ounces thinly sliced prosciutto**

1. Prepare an indirect fire in a smoker.

2. Rinse the turkey and pat dry. Lightly coat both breasts with the olive oil. Wrap each breast with half of the prosciutto. Place the turkey in the smoker, cover, and smoke at 225 to 250°F, until an instant-read meat thermometer inserted in the thickest part of the breast registers 160 to 165°F, 1½ to 2 hours. The turkey will have a hint of pink. Let rest for about 10 minutes before cutting into ³/₈-inch-thick slices. Serve warm or chilled.

Smoked turkey is delicious served with all the traditional Thanksgiving trimmings.
But why not try something new, such as:
Grilled Portobellos with Garlic, Pine Nuts, Basil, and Goat Cheese (page 133)
Grilled Vegetable Platter with Fresh Basil Vinaigrette (page 129)
Summer Tomato, Pine Nut, and Caper Relish (page 425)

Smoked Turkey with Cranberry-Orange Salsa:

Smoke the turkey breasts as described above, then make this salsa to serve with them. Over a medium-size bowl, grate the zest of 2 navel oranges. Peel the remaining white membrane from the oranges, discarding it. Chop the oranges and add to the bowl. Rinse and pick over 2½ cups fresh cranberries, place in a food processor, and coarsely chop. Add to the oranges along with 1 seeded and diced jalapeño and ¾ cup sugar. Toss to mix. (This salsa will keep in the refrigerator for several weeks or in the freezer for several months.) Serve with the smoked turkey. **SERVES 4**

Penne with Smoked Turkey, Goat Cheese Cream Sauce, and Sun-Dried Tomatoes:

Cook 1 pound penne according to the package directions. Drain (reserving 1 cup of the pasta water) and set aside. In a large skillet, heat 2 tablespoons olive oil over medium heat. Add 2 minced garlic cloves and cook, stirring, for 1 to 2 minutes. Add ¾ cup dry white wine and 1 bay leaf and bring to a boil, then reduce the heat to low and simmer for 10 minutes. Add 3 cups heavy cream and bring to a boil again. Reduce the heat to medium-low and simmer until thickened, about 4 minutes. Reduce the heat to low, whisk in 8 ounces crumbled fresh goat cheese, and simmer for about 5 minutes. (Be careful not to scorch.) Add the cooked pasta and gently warm, separating the penne. Stir in 1½ to 2 cups chopped smoked turkey. If the sauce is too thick, add 2 or 3 tablespoons of the reserved pasta water at a time until the sauce is a medium-thick consistency. Using kitchen shears, cut 8 oil-packed sun-dried tomatoes into thin slivers and stir into the pasta. Serve hot. **SERVES 6**

Brie and Basil–Stuffed Turkey Breast:

We were both awestruck looking at the oven- and grill-ready meats at the gourmet Dorothy Lane Markets in Dayton, Ohio. The Brie and basil–stuffed turkey breast was memorable, and we share our rendition here. Make a pocket slit in one 1½-pound boneless, skinless turkey breast. Place 3 or 4 thin slices of Brie evenly inside the slit. Tuck 4 or 5 fresh basil leaves evenly on top of the cheese. Wrap the breast with about 2 ounces thinly sliced prosciutto. Smoke as directed above, which will take about 1 hour. **SERVES 2**

Rotisserie Turkey

Every year, magazine and newspaper food editors ask the same question: what can we do differently with the holiday bird for our readers?

The BBQ Queens have the answer: rotisserie that turkey! You'll free up your oven, give a rambunctious or annoying relative something to do (keep an eye on the turkey outside), and serve a bronzed, delicious, juicy entrée worthy of being the centerpiece of your feast. Our only reservation is that most rotisserie units are not placed high enough above the grill grate to allow you to twirl around a big bird, although you can probably manage a 10- to 12-pound whole turkey or a turkey breast or two. Be sure to check the manufacturer's instructions before you head to the store.

Also check the maximum weight your rotisserie motor can handle *before* you buy your turkey. Our recipe gives directions for a traditional rotisserie setup with an electric motor over a gas grill. If you have a fancy-schmancy setup with infrared technology, refer to the manufacturer's instructions for cooking times, as your turkey will take less time.

Our essential rotisserie turkey recipe is similar to the one for chicken on page 217—slathered with a paste made from fresh tarragon, garlic, lemon juice, and olive oil, then grilled rotisserie style. (Remember to check both cavities of the turkey to remove the giblets and neck.)

Instead of gravy, try this with our scrumptious The Doctor Is In Apricot-Bourbon Barbecue Sauce (page 90). However, if you add water, the giblets and neck, a bay leaf, and an onion to the drip pan—and keep it full of hot water—you *can* make that traditional turkey gravy (see right).

Rotisserie turkey is wonderful served with Autumn Roasted Red Pepper and Cannellini Bean Relish (page 426) if you want to go contemporary, or with mashed potatoes, green bean casserole, cranberry relish, and all the traditional trimmings for a holiday meal. SERVES 8 TO 10

> 1 cup chopped fresh tarragon
>
> 6 cloves garlic, minced
>
> Juice of 4 lemons
>
> 1 cup olive oil
>
> One 10- to 12-pound turkey, giblets and neck removed
>
> Kosher and sea salt and freshly ground black pepper to taste

1. In a medium-size bowl, combine the tarragon, garlic, lemon juice, and olive oil. With a brush, slather the mixture all over the turkey, inside and out. Cover with plastic wrap and refrigerate for at least 1 hour or overnight.

2. Set up your grill for rotisserie cooking (see page 33). Prepare a medium fire (around 350°F).

3. Season the turkey with salt and pepper, inside and out. Tie the legs together with kitchen twine. Attach a clamp to each end of the turkey. Push the rotisserie rod through the clamps and the center of the turkey so the bird is balanced. Attach the clamps to the spit and place a drip pan under the turkey. Cover and cook until an instant-read meat thermometer inserted in the thickest part of a thigh registers 170 to 175°F or a skewer inserted in the thickest part of a leg produces clear juices, about 4 hours.

4. Transfer the turkey to a serving platter and tent with aluminum foil to keep warm. Let rest for 15 minutes before carving and serving.

Crowning Glories

**Rotisserie turkey is delicious anointed with one of these
during the last 1½ hours of cooking:**

Honeyed Barbecue Sauce *(page 90)*

Raspberry-Jalapeño Barbecue Sauce *(page 90)*

Pistachio-Pomegranate Sauce *(page 96)*

Traditional Rotisserie Turkey Gravy: When you set up your drip pan under the turkey, place 1 halved large onion, the giblets and neck, and a bay leaf in it. Add 2 cups water and keep replenishing the water during the time the turkey cooks. You want the onion and giblets to brown some but not dry out. When the turkey is done, bring the drip pan indoors and discard the giblets, neck, bay leaf, and onion. Transfer the liquid to a saucepan. Try to scrape as many of the browned bits into the pan as you can. You should have about 2 cups liquid. (If not, add canned chicken broth to make 2 cups.) In a jar with a tight-fitting lid, place 2 tablespoons all-purpose flour and 1 cup cold water. Secure the lid and shake to blend well. Place the saucepan over medium-high heat and bring to a boil. Slowly pour in the flour mixture, whisking constantly, until the gravy thickens. Season with kosher or sea salt and freshly ground black pepper to taste and serve hot. **MAKES ABOUT 3 CUPS**

Day-After Rotisserie Turkey Sandwich: The day after your rotisserie turkey feast, you can relax and enjoy this tasty sandwich made with leftovers. Between 2 slices of good-quality sourdough bread, pile slices of leftover turkey, a dollop of Roasted Red Pepper Aioli (page 110), and lettuce if you like. Ahhh. **SERVES 1**

Smoked Whole Turkey

raditionally, people smoke turkeys only for Thanksgiving. But when you fall in love with the exquisite kiss of smoke, how can you wait another year for moist and succulent smoked turkey?

When the Chicago chapter of Les Dames d'Escoffier invited us to do our BBQ Queen gig at a big party hosted by our good friend Dame Rose Kallas, three apple-smoked turkeys were on our menu (see page 171 for the rest). So the next time you need an entrée to serve a crowd, think smoked turkey!

Turkey smokes best at 225 to 250°F. The cooking time is about 30 minutes per pound, or until an instant-read meat thermometer inserted in the meatiest part of the thigh registers 175 to 180°F. Apply these guidelines whether you are smoking a whole turkey or a whole turkey breast with the bone in.

The turkey can be slathered with mustard, chutney, or preserves, or seasoned or marinated with Rosemary Salt (page 56) or Wheat Beer Vinaigrette (page 77). It adapts well to many flavors, so sprinkle with just about any rub you like. Our recipe is foolproof and produces a luscious and juicy bird. **SERVES 8 TO 10**

SUGGESTED WOOD: Apple, oak, maple, mesquite, or hickory

One 10- to 12-pound turkey, giblets and neck removed
2 to 3 tablespoons olive oil, as needed
3 tablespoons sweet Hungarian paprika
2 tablespoons fine sea salt
2 tablespoons lemon pepper seasoning

1. Rinse the bird and pat dry. Place in a disposable aluminum pan and coat lightly with oil.

2. In a glass jar with a tight-fitting lid, combine the paprika, salt, and lemon pepper. Shake to blend, then sprinkle on the turkey inside and out. Set the bird aside for about 20 minutes.

3. Prepare an indirect fire in a smoker.

4. Place the turkey in the smoker, cover, and smoke at 225 to 250°F until an instant-read meat thermometer inserted in the thigh registers 170 to 175°F, 4 to 5 hours. The smoked turkey will be golden brown on the outside and the meat will have a slightly pinkish color. Serve hot.

Crowning Glories

Smoked turkey is delicious served with all the traditional
Thanksgiving trimmings, or with oven-roasted potatoes and butternut
squash wedges seasoned with olive oil and fresh rosemary. In the
summer, serve it with your favorite barbecue side dishes, such as:

Smoked Tomato Grits (page 164)

Warm Asian Eggplant Salad (page 125)

Savory Breads on the Grill (pages 176–178)

Smoky Chipotle Corn Pudding (page 122)

Smoked Turkey and Monterey Jack Club Sandwiches: Don't you want one right now? Spread 4 slices of sourdough bread (toasted if you wish) with mayonnaise or Dijon mustard. For each sandwich, on 1 slice of bread layer a couple of slices of smoked turkey, 1 or 2 slices of Monterey Jack cheese, 2 or 3 slices of crisp-cooked bacon, and some sliced ripe avocado. Add a thin slice of tomato or slivers of oil-packed sun-dried tomatoes. Top with the other bread slice and feast. **SERVES 2**

Smoked Turkey Hash: You either like hash or you don't. Karen and Dick both love it, corned beef or turkey, made into a patty, sautéed until browned and crisp, and served with a soft fried or poached egg on top. This recipe makes it soufflé style in a lightly greased 13 x 9 x 2-inch pan. Preheat the oven to 375°F. In a food processor, coarsely chop enough smoked turkey to yield 3 cups and place in a large bowl. Add 1 finely chopped large onion, 3 cups chopped cooked potatoes or stuffing, 1 cup leftover or defrosted frozen corn (optional), 1/2 cup freshly grated Pecorino Romano cheese, 2 minced garlic cloves, and 2 tablespoons chopped fresh Italian parsley and mix well. Season with kosher salt and freshly ground black pepper to taste. In a medium-size bowl, beat together 3 large eggs and 1 cup half-and-half. Add to the turkey mixture, mix well, and spoon into the prepared pan. In a small bowl, combine 1/2 cup freshly grated Pecorino Romano cheese and 1/4 cup seasoned dry bread crumbs and sprinkle on top. Bake for 30 minutes, then turn on the broiler and brown the top. Serve with a mixed greens and frisée salad, with a poached egg atop either the hash or the salad. Very continental! **SERVES 10 TO 12**

BBQ Babes

She's Smokin' and Talkin' Turkey Menu

Apple-Smoked Turkey
Rosemary-Apple Salsa

BBQ Babe Carolyn Wells is the cofounder and executive director of the Kansas City Barbeque Society. During competition barbecue season from spring to fall, she's out and about every weekend, traveling all over the country as an ambassador for barbecue. She's at her busiest during the first weekend in October, when the gargantuan American Royal Barbecue Contest is in full swing in Kansas City.

Although she's a great judge of barbecue, Carolyn is also a pretty mean cook herself. She dished out this memorable smoked turkey and salsa to members of the food media in New York City at Tavern on the Green in the early 1990s to rave reviews. Try it as a fresh and delicious change of pace for Thanksgiving.

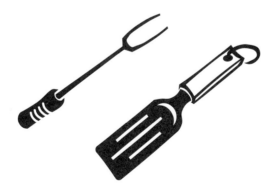

Apple-Smoked Turkey

The interior of a smoked turkey is a pinkish color, the exterior dark bronze. The best way to make sure it's done is to use an instant-read meat thermometer inserted in the thickest part of the thigh. When it registers 170 to 175°F, your bird is the word. You definitely won't mind these smoked turkey leftovers. They make terrific sandwiches.

SERVES 8

SUGGESTED WOOD: Apple or a combination of apple and hickory

One 10-pound turkey or 2 whole bone-in turkey breasts

1 cup balsamic vinegar

¼ cup water

3 tablespoons sweet Hungarian paprika

2 tablespoons coarse sea salt

2 tablespoons lemon pepper seasoning

¼ teaspoon dried marjoram

1. Remove the giblets and neck from the whole turkey, if using. Rinse the whole turkey or turkey breasts. Place in a large plastic bag and set in the kitchen sink.

2. Combine the vinegar, water, paprika, salt, lemon pepper, and marjoram in a glass jar with a tight-fitting lid. Cover and shake to blend. Pour the marinade into the bag and seal with a twist tie. Keeping the bag upright so it won't leak, let the turkey marinate in the refrigerator for at least 1 hour, preferably overnight. If the turkey is too large to fit in your refrigerator, put it in an iced cooler. Make sure it stays cold.

3. Prepare an indirect fire in a smoker.

4. Remove the turkey from the marinade and place in the smoker. Cover and smoke at 225 to 250°F until an instant-read meat thermometer inserted in the thickest part of the thigh registers 170 to 175°F, 4 to 5 hours. When the turkey is smoked, the meat will have a pale pink color. Serve hot.

Rosemary-Apple Salsa

The fresh crispness and tang of rosemary in this salsa pairs well with both poultry and pork. **MAKES ABOUT 4 CUPS**

- 1 large yellow bell pepper, seeded and chopped
- 1 Granny Smith apple, cored and chopped
- 1 large Jonathan apple, cored and chopped
- 8 green onions
- $1/3$ cup diced dried apricots
- 3 tablespoons fresh lemon juice
- 1 cup extra virgin olive oil
- 2 teaspoons finely chopped fresh rosemary
- $1/2$ teaspoon sea salt
- Freshly ground black pepper to taste

In a large bowl, combine all the ingredients. Cover and refrigerate for at least 1 hour before serving. This salsa will keep, covered, in the refrigerator for 3 to 4 days.

Grilled Duck Paillards

Karen and Dick like their wild mallard duck breast grilled or pan-seared to medium-rare (a medium temperature is also acceptable); medium-well to well done produces a dry, unappetizing dish. If that's the way you prefer your meat, perhaps duck is not for you. For a larger Muscovy duck breast, score the skin by using a sharp knife and cutting diagonal slashes through it (but do not cut into the duck meat). This allows the fat to cook off and the skin to crisp. Grill the larger breasts over medium-hot heat until an instant-read meat thermometer inserted in the thickest part registers 140 to 145°F for medium-rare, about 7 minutes.

Here's a lesson on making duck (or other wild game bird) breasts into a *paillard*, a French term for a boneless piece of meat that has been flattened to a uniform thickness. The easiest way we've found to do this is to use the rim of a saucer. Simply pound the breast, starting in the middle and working your way out to the sides, until the meat is an even ¹/₂ to 1 inch thick. In a hot grill or in a grill pan over high heat, cook the paillard for 10 minutes per inch of thickness. For example, grill a ¹/₂-inch-thick paillard for 2¹/₂ minutes per side, or 5 minutes total. If the skin is on the breast meat, cook the skin side an additional 1 to 2 minutes to get it nice and crispy.

While you're grilling duck, try these sides on the grill, too: Grilled Green Onions and Red Onion Slices (page 138), Char-Grilled Baby Summer Squash (page 155), and Grilled Tomatoes (page 159). **SERVES 4**

Four 4- to 5-ounce boneless, skinless wild or domestic duck breasts, flattened to about ¹/₂ inch thick (see headnote)

¹/₂ cup red wine

8 juniper berries

4 sprigs each fresh thyme and oregano

1 tablespoon olive oil

Kosher salt and freshly ground black pepper to taste

1. Place the duck breasts in a sealable plastic bag and add the wine, juniper berries, and herb sprigs. Seal the bag and marinate in the refrigerator for 1 to 2 hours.

2. Prepare a medium-hot fire in a grill.

3. Remove the duck from the bag and dispose of the marinade. Pat the duck dry, lightly coat with the olive oil, and season with salt and pepper. Place on the grill directly over the fire. Grill for 2¹/₂ to 3 minutes per side for medium-rare, or until an instant-read meat thermometer inserted in the thickest part registers 140 to 145°F.

Duck, Duck, Goose

Karen is the queen of game cooking. Her husband, Dick, is an avid hunter of upland game birds, waterfowl, and wild turkeys. Karen hunts a little, but her time is more successfully spent cooking the quarry. Upland game birds from the Midwest are plentiful and tasty, too, because the birds feed on the rich farmland crops and natural prairie grasses of the region. Elsewhere in the United States, ducks and other waterfowl may be referred to as gamy or fishy because their main food intake is fish.

Wild ducks and other game birds are very tasty when grilled. Sizes for dressed birds range from the smaller, 1-pound ducks such as teals and wood ducks, to midsize widgeons at 1½ pounds, to the prized mallards at about 2 pounds (farm-raised mallards are available, too). Canvasbacks and black ducks are a bit larger, at 3 pounds, and they are followed by geese, at 6 to 10 pounds. The differences between wild and farm-raised birds are the taste and the fat content, which is uniformly higher on farm-raised birds. The amount of fat on wild ducks and geese depends on what time of year they are killed. Early in the fall, the birds are leaner, and by winter, they are fattier.

The domestic ducks most readily available include the Pekin duck, also referred to as the Long Island duck, which is a big, plump white duck with a mild taste; the Muscovy duck, a flavorful and musky bird that is much larger than the Long Island duck; and Moulard duck, a cross of Muscovy and Pekin and prized for its delicious *foie gras*. Then there are upland game birds, which vary in size from the small quail (8 ounces) to the grouse, chukar, and prairie chicken (1 to 3 pounds) to the pheasant (4 to 6 pounds).

The point of all this for the cook is that when a recipe calls for duck or other game bird breasts, there are many variables: whether you are using wild or domestic, whether the skin is on or off, whether the breast is fatty or lean. The way we are going to address this huge variable is to prepare the breasts as paillards of a uniform thickness.

Grilling whole ducks or other birds is best over an indirect fire, which is more like smoking than grilling. The whole bird roasts in the closed grill over an indirect fire, with the temperature at 350°F. Domestic game birds will most likely have the skin on. Wild game birds are often field dressed by skinning them. Preparing these skinless birds on the grill requires care not to dry them out. One way to do this is by wrapping them in lettuce leaves, cornhusks, prosciutto, or bacon. Wild birds have little fat, so preparing them like a boneless, skinless chicken paillard (see page 191) is also an option.

 **Crowning Glories**

Grilled Duck Paillards with Dried Sweet Cherry–Port Sauce:

Score the skin of 4 boneless, skinless duck breasts pounded into 1-inch-thick paillards and sprinkle each with 1 tablespoon Spicy Red-Hot Lemon Pepper Rub (page 53). In a small saucepan, combine 1 cup beef broth, $1/4$ cup port, $1/2$ cup dried sweet cherries, 1 tablespoon soy sauce, and 2 tablespoons packed dark brown sugar. Bring to a boil and reduce by half, stirring often. Remove from the heat and add 1 tablespoon cornstarch dissolved in 2 tablespoons cold water. Whisk and return to medium heat to thicken slightly, continuing to stir, about 5 minutes. Set aside. Prepare a medium-hot fire in a grill. Grill the duck breasts skin side down until the skin is browned, about 7 minutes. Turn and grill for 5 minutes more. For medium-rare, the duck should register 140 to 145°F on an instant-read meat thermometer inserted in the thickest part of the breast. Slice on the diagonal, spoon the warm sauce over the meat, and serve. **SERVES 4**

Grilled Duck Breast Salad:

This is a favorite at the Adlers' house. In a large bowl, combine 1 cup shredded cooked duck, 1 cup fresh fruit (such as orange wedges or berries), $1/2$ cup crumbled Maytag blue cheese, 2 tablespoons slivered red onion, 3 cups lettuce, and 2 to 3 tablespoons of a sweet and tangy dressing such as Balsamic-Thyme Vinaigrette (page 84) or a homemade or bottled poppy seed dressing. Toss lightly to coat everything with the dressing. Serve with crusty bread (or a duck sandwich on the side). **SERVES 2**

Smoked Whole Duck

Karen is always tweaking her duck recipes and has found a couple of favorite ways to smoke duck. Shortcut versions of smoking include using store-bought spice blends. She says any kind of herb or pepper blend is quite nice. You can take the grocery store route and pick up a couple of McCormick spice blends (such as chipotle chile; see page 59) or buy an exotic blend online from Penzeys Spices or Vanns Spices (see Resource Guide, page 446). **SERVES 6**

SUGGESTED WOOD: Fruitwood, black walnut, pecan, or grapevines

3 wild or domestic ducks, such as mallards (about 6 pounds total)

1 tablespoon olive oil

3 tablespoons pepper blend

1 tablespoon fine kosher or sea salt

¹/₂ cup barbecue sauce of your choice, thinned with 2 tablespoons fresh lemon juice

1. Rinse the ducks well and make sure all the pinfeathers and shot have been removed. Singe the hairs off the birds. Pat dry. Place in a shallow disposable aluminum pan, rub with the olive oil, and sprinkle all over (including the cavities) with the pepper blend and salt.

2. Prepare a smoker for an indirect fire with a water pan filled with hot water. Add 3 or 4 chunks of water-soaked wood to the fire.

3. Smoke the ducks at 225°F for 20 to 30 minutes per pound, basting with the barbecue sauce 2 or 3 times during cooking. Three ducks weighing 6 pounds total will take 2 to 3 hours. The ducks are done when an instant-read meat thermometer inserted in a thigh registers 170 to 175°F. Serve hot.

 **Crowning Glories**

Serve your smoked duck with:

Classic Creamed Spinach *(page 319)*

Decadent Garlic Mashed Potatoes *(page 321)*

Smoked Tomato and Basil Butter *(page 177)*

Smoked Duck and Wild Rice Soup: This is a hearty soup fit for company. It works well if you have just a little leftover smoked duck or a lot. Heat 2 to 3 tablespoons olive oil in a large Dutch oven over medium-high heat. Add 1 chopped onion, 2 chopped carrots, and 2 chopped celery stalks and sauté for about 5 minutes, until softened. Turn the heat to medium-low, add 2 tablespoons all-purpose flour, and stir to make a roux. Increase the heat to medium and add two 10-ounce cans beef consommé. Cook, stirring, until thickened, about 10 minutes. Add 4 cups cooked wild rice and 1 to 2 cups chopped smoked duck meat. Add 1 to 2 cups water, enough just to cover all the food. Continue cooking until heated through. Serve hot, with 1 ounce feta cheese crumbled over each bowl. **SERVES 4 TO 6**

Smoked Duck Breasts: Wild duck breasts are usually skinless, but domestic duck breasts usually have the skin on. The skin and its layers of fat help keep the breasts from drying out. Lightly coat 4 duck breasts with olive oil and season with coarse kosher salt and freshly ground black pepper to taste. If using wild duck, wrap the breasts in bacon or prosciutto to keep the meat moist. Prepare a smoker as directed above. Place the breasts in the smoker and cook for 20 to 30 minutes per pound. Serve warm, or refrigerate and toss lightly with mayonnaise and chopped fresh herbs to make a simple duck salad. **SERVES 4**

Smoked Duckling with Five-Spice Asian Paste: This is Asian fusion cooking at its best. Rub the interior and exterior of a Long Island duck or two 8- to 10-ounce bone-in Muscovy duck breasts with Five-Spice Asian Paste (page 64). Place in a disposable aluminum pan, cover, and smoke as directed above. **SERVES 2**

Duck on a Beer Can: Try this one, my little ducky! Prepare a 3- to 4-pound duck by soaking it in a marinade or applying a dry rub of your choice. Place the duck cavity side down on a can of beer (or other liquid such as fruit juice or apple cider). Make an indirect fire in a smoker as described above. Close the lid and smoke at 300°F until an instant-read meat thermometer inserted in the thigh registers 160 to 170°F, about 1 hour. **SERVES 2**

BBQ Babes

She's Wild for Smoke Menu

Apricot and Cognac–Glazed Duck
Drunk Elk or Venison
Durn Good Rice
Grilled Stuffed Apples

BBQ Babe Candy Weaver's family-owned business BBQr's Delight manufactures flavored wood pellets for smoking. Yep, you got it, she makes her own smoke. And the flavors she creates are sublime, from the more unusual orange, mulberry, sassafras, black walnut, and savory herb to hickory, pecan, mesquite, oak, and more, totaling 12 flavors and growing. These all-natural wood pellets do not have to be presoaked, so they are ready to use at a moment's notice. You just wrap 1/3 cup of pellets in aluminum foil, poke holes in the packet, place it over the smoker's heat source, and get ready for some tasty eating. (See Resource Guide, page 447, for more information about this product.)

Candy is a country girl from Arkansas and proud of it. Here are some of her delectable recipes featuring game, which is plentiful in her neck of the woods. If game is not your thing, substitute chicken or turkey for the duck, and beef for the elk or venison. These recipes come from Candy's cookbook, *Smoking with Wood Pellets* (available from BBQr's Delight).

Apricot and Cognac–Glazed Duck

This glaze is also delicious on pork, ham, and other poultry. Two or three wild mallard ducks can be substituted for one larger duck. **SERVES 4**

APRICOT AND COGNAC GLAZE

8 ounces dried apricots, chopped, or ¼ cup apricot jam

1 cup cognac or brandy

1½ cups water

One 5-pound duck (or chicken, turkey, or goose)

1. To make the glaze, place the apricots and cognac in a small saucepan and cook over low heat until the apricots dissolve, 10 to 15 minutes. Add the water and simmer over medium heat until it just begins to boil. Turn the heat down and continue to simmer until the mixture is thick, about 10 minutes.

2. Prepare a medium-hot indirect fire in a grill. Put a mixture of pecan, black walnut, and sassafras pellets in an aluminum foil pouch or smoke box and set over the fire.

3. When the smoke starts, put the duck on the indirect side of the grill. If you have a rotisserie, you may use it (see page 33). Close the lid and cook the duck, turning every 20 minutes, for 1½ hours. Baste with the glaze for the last 20 to 30 minutes of cooking time. The duck is done when an instant-read meat thermometer inserted in the thigh and breast registers 180°F.

Drunk Elk or Venison

Because elk and venison are so lean, injecting the buttery cheese mixture is very important to keep the meat moist during cooking. **SERVES 6 TO 8**

One 3- to 4-pound elk or venison tenderloin or roast

INJECTION

2 cups beef broth

¹/₄ cup (¹/₂ stick) butter

8 ounces Merkts sharp cheddar cheese spread or other cheese spread

2 tablespoons granulated garlic

2 tablespoons Tiger Sauce or other hot pepper sauce

2 tablespoons soy sauce

2 tablespoons Worcestershire sauce

¹/₂ cup whiskey

MARINADE

¹/₂ cup olive oil

¹/₂ cup soy sauce

¹/₃ cup fresh lemon juice

2 tablespoons red wine vinegar

2 to 4 cloves garlic, to your taste, chopped

1. Bring the meat to room temperature.

2. To make the injection, combine all the ingredients in a small saucepan over low heat and stir until dissolved. Remove from the heat and let cool briefly, then pour into the injector and inject the meat in 8 to 10 places. Place the meat in a large sealable plastic bag.

3. To make the marinade, combine all the ingredients in a small bowl. Pour into the bag, seal, and refrigerate for 12 to 24 hours.

4. When ready to smoke, prepare an indirect fire in a grill. Place a packet of Jack Daniel's wood pellets (available from BBQr's Delight) over the fire.

5. When the fire reaches 250°F, remove the meat from the marinade and place it on the indirect side of the grill. Discard the marinade. Close the lid and cook until an instant-read meat thermometer inserted in the thickest part registers 130 to 140°F, 1 to 1½ hours.

Durn Good Rice

This recipe works with wild rice, too, which is a nice accompaniment to game. If you like, substitute 3 cups precooked wild rice for the raw rice. The beauty of this is that it's smoking right along with the meat. SERVES 4 TO 6

1 cup long-grain white or brown rice

1 small onion, finely chopped

¼ large red bell pepper, seeded and finely chopped

1 stalk celery, finely chopped

1 tablespoon unsalted butter

¼ teaspoon garlic powder

1 tablespoon Worcestershire sauce

2½ cups chicken broth or water

1 green onion, chopped, for garnish

2 tablespoons chopped fresh Italian parsley or cilantro for garnish (optional)

1. Place all the ingredients except the green onion and parsley in a heatproof baking dish or disposable aluminum pan and stir to combine. Cook on the indirect side of the grill (alongside the meat you are cooking) until all the liquid is evaporated and the rice is tender, 1 to 2 hours.

2. Remove the rice from the grill and garnish with the green onion and parsley before serving.

Grilled Stuffed Apples

Any flavor of smoke works well here. SERVES 4

> **4 Rome or Granny Smith apples**
>
> **1 teaspoon ground cinnamon**
>
> **4 teaspoons raisins**
>
> **4 teaspoons chopped nuts (optional)**
>
> **2 teaspoons honey**

Cut the top off each apple (looks like a cap) and save. Core the apples. Sprinkle the inside of each with 1/4 teaspoon cinnamon. Combine the raisins and nuts (if using) in a cup, then pack the center of each apple evenly with the mixture. Drizzle the stuffing with 1/2 teaspoon honey. Put the tops back on the apples. Place in a baking dish or disposable aluminum pan. Smoke for about 1 hour on the indirect side of the grill (alongside the meat you are cooking). Serve warm.

Grilled Game Birds

After the hazy heat of August on the prairie, the crisp blue skies of September herald the beginning of autumn and game bird hunting season. Pheasant, quail, ruffed and sharp-tailed grouse, and prairie chicken thrive in the tall prairie grasses, where they make their nests and raise their young. To stalk these upland game birds, hunters—including Karen's husband, Dick—walk through fields with their dogs, hoping to startle the birds into flight. Upland game birds—mainly quail and pheasant—are also farm-raised in Illinois and Indiana, supplying the restaurant trade as well as upscale butcher shops and gourmet markets (such as Whole Foods Market, Central Market, and Dean & Deluca).

Smaller birds, such as quail and woodcock, may be grilled, roasted, or baked. Cornish game hens, which are usually available frozen, are great substitutes for quail. Pheasant do better with lower, slower smoking. A marinade or baste containing butter or oil is used to keep the meat from drying out during hot and fast grilling.

Our basic recipe for grilled quail, woodcock, or Cornish game hens is based on one found in Karen's *Best Little Grilling Book* (Celestial Arts, 2000). Adding a handful of water-soaked apple, cherry, or grape wood chips to the fire will give these birds a pleasant, smoky flavor. To accompany grilled game birds, try Decadent Garlic Mashed Potatoes (page 321), Olive Oil Smashed Potatoes (page 320), or Crunchy Broccoli Slaw with Thai Chile-Peanut Dressing (page 80). SERVES 4

> 8 quail or woodcock, or 4 Cornish game hens, split in half
>
> Handful of apple, cherry, or grape wood chips (optional), soaked in water for at least 30 minutes before grilling
>
> 1 cup (2 sticks) unsalted butter, melted
>
> 2 teaspoons chopped fresh tarragon
>
> Fine kosher or sea salt and freshly ground black pepper to taste

1. Rinse the quail under cold running water, then pat dry.

2. Prepare a medium-hot fire in a grill. Add the wood chips, if desired.

3. In a medium-size bowl, stir together the melted butter and tarragon and take to the grill. Dip the quail in the mixture, then place on the grill. Grill for 3 to 4 minutes, turn, baste with the butter mixture, and grill for 3 to 4 minutes more. The quail breast meat will turn opaque and the underside will be pale pink. (The Cornish game hens will take 10 to 15 minutes per side. An instant-read meat thermometer inserted in the thickest part of the thigh should register 170 to 175°F. The meat should not be at all pink. Turn the hens every 5 minutes and baste while grilling.) Season with salt and pepper and serve hot.

Crowning Glories

Try slathering your game birds with:
Honeyed Barbecue Sauce *(page 90)*
Raspberry-Jalapeño Barbecue Sauce *(page 90)*
Asian Barbecue Sauce *(page 90)*

Cornish Game Hens with Orange-Honey Baste: You can slow smoke these game hens at 250°F for 1½ to 2 hours or grill them over a medium-hot fire (see above) for 25 to 30 minutes—it's your choice. A combination of mesquite and pecan wood chunks for smoking or wood chips for grilling adds another flavor component. (Soak the chunks in water for at least 1 hour before using. Soak the chips for at least 30 minutes.) Rinse and pat dry 4 Cornish game hens. Mix together 1 cup orange juice, 3 tablespoons Cointreau or other orange-flavored liqueur, ½ cup honey, and ¼ cup (½ stick) melted unsalted butter. Place the hens and marinade in an extra-large sealable plastic bag, seal, and marinate in the refrigerator for at least 4 hours or overnight, turning several times. Remove from the marinade and smoke or grill. **SERVES 4**

Grilled Cornish Game Hens à la Chez Panisse: This recipe is adapted from a grilled quail recipe by Alice Waters at Chez Panisse in Berkeley, California. In a small bowl, combine 1 cup dry white wine, ¾ cup olive oil, 3 sliced shallots, 6 minced garlic cloves, 10 juniper berries, and 3 bay leaves. Place 4 Cornish game hens (or woodcock or quail) in an extra-large sealable plastic bag, add the marinade, seal, and marinate in the refrigerator for several hours or overnight. Grill as directed above and serve simply garnished with Italian parsley sprigs and lemon wedges. **SERVES 4**

Warm Grilled Quail Salad with Spiced Pears and Mushrooms: Served in the fall or winter, this wonderful salad is both comforting and exotically aromatic. Use fresh shiitake mushrooms if you can find them; if not, sliced button mushrooms will do just fine. Arrange a handful of mixed greens (such as escarole, frisée, romaine lettuce, and baby spinach) on 4 salad plates. Right after you grill the quail (see above), tent them with aluminum foil to keep warm. Then peel, core, and slice 4 ripe but firm pears. Dust the slices with Zesty Sugar and Spice Rub (page 52). Melt 2 tablespoons unsalted butter in a large skillet over medium-high heat. Add the pear slices and cook, turning once, until tender, about 8 minutes. Remove from the pan and arrange over the salad greens. In the same pan over medium-high heat, cook 4 ounces stemmed and quartered shiitake mushrooms, stirring, until softened, about 5 minutes. Place on top of the pears. Place a grilled quail on top of each salad. Deglaze the pan over high heat with a mixture of 2 tablespoons cider vinegar, 1 tablespoon Dijon mustard, and 1 tablespoon olive oil, scraping up any browned bits from the pan. Boil for 30 seconds, stir, and drizzle over the salads. Serve warm. **SERVES 4**

Smoked Small Game Birds

Smoked game birds such as quail, chukar, and roughed grouse, all weighing in at 1 to 3 pounds, are perfect for the smoker. If you purchase the birds from a supplier, they will most likely be dressed out, with the skin on. If they come from a hunter, often they will be dressed without the skin. Skinless birds need to be wrapped with bacon or prosciutto so the meat doesn't dry out. Cornish game hens can be substituted in these recipes.

For other sizes of game birds, follow the directions for poultry weighing about the same. For instance, whole pheasant can be smoked using any of the poultry recipes. (Simply smoke for 20 to 30 minutes per pound.) Remember that game birds are often leaner than domestic birds and so tend to dry out faster, so shorten the cooking time.

When ready, the skin of smoked game birds is a glistening mahogany color and the meat is juicy and smoky. Just like smoked pork butt, you can either slice or pull apart the meat. Because these are smaller game birds, we recommend smoking four or more birds at a time. (One quail serves a dainty appetite. Two quail are a regular serving for dinner, but if you have more, smoke them—they will disappear quickly.) In place of the olive oil and salt and pepper, experiment with rubs (pages 49–62), slathers (page 66), or marinades (pages 67–75) prior to smoking. **SERVES 4**

SUGGESTED WOOD: Fruitwood, grapevines, oak, mesquite, or hickory, or a combination

8 quail or other small game birds (about 4 pounds total), skinned and cleaned
3 tablespoons olive oil
Fine kosher or sea salt and freshly ground black pepper to taste

1. Rinse the quail thoroughly and pat dry. Rub about 1 teaspoon olive oil over each quail, then rub with salt and pepper.

2. Prepare an indirect fire in a smoker.

3. Place the birds side by side in the smoker and close the lid. Smoke at 225°F. The quail are done when a leg joint moves easily and the meat is no longer pink, about 2 hours. An instant-read meat thermometer inserted in the meatiest portion of the bird but not touching the bone should register 170°F. Serve hot, or let cool to room temperature and refrigerate. When cold, wrap in aluminum foil or plastic and store in the refrigerator for up to 2 days.

Crowning Glories

Marinate, baste, or serve these birds up with:
Homemade Teriyaki Marinade *(page 69)*
Rosemary, Garlic, and Lemon Baste *(page 68)*
Hot Shallot Vinaigrette *(page 85)*

Bacon-Wrapped Smoked Quail and Pheasant: This recipe comes from Karen's *Best Little Barbecue Cookbook* (Celestial Arts, 2000). You need 8 skinned and cleaned quail, 1 skinned and cleaned pheasant cut in half, and 10 slices of bacon or prosciutto. In a large container, combine 1/2 cup soy sauce, 1/4 cup olive oil, 1/4 cup Marsala wine, the juice and grated zest of 1 orange, and 2 minced garlic cloves. Add the birds, cover, and refrigerate for 4 to 12 hours. Prepare a hot fire on one side of a grill. Remove the birds from the marinade and wrap each quail and pheasant half with a slice of bacon or prosciutto. Over the hot fire, sear the pheasant halves for about 3 minutes per side and quail for about 2 minutes per side. Place the pheasant halves bone side down on the indirect side of grill, then stack the quail on top of the pheasant. Close the lid and cook at 300°F for 30 to 45 minutes, until the leg joints move easily. (Wild pheasant legs can be very tough, sometimes even inedible, depending on the age of the bird.) The quail and pheasant should be done at the same time. If not, remove the quail and keep warm. Continue cooking the pheasant until an instant-read meat thermometer inserted in the thickest part of the breast registers 170°F. Serve immediately. **SERVES 8**

Smoked Game Bird Salad: This is the perfect way to use leftover poultry of any kind. Begin with 1 cup mixed greens or baby spinach. Garnish with pomegranate seeds; 1/2 teaspoon grated orange zest; 1/4 cup chopped fresh herbs; and 1 to 2 tablespoons toasted pine nuts, chopped pecans, or chopped walnuts. Drizzle with the vinaigrette of your choice. (Fresh Basil Vinaigrette, page 85, is nice.) **SERVES 1**

Smoked Game Birds and Pasta: This is a favorite summer recipe. Start with about 2 cups of game bird meat pulled off the bone. Place the meat and thinly sliced wedges of 2 or 3 ripe tomatoes in the bottom of a serving bowl. Cook 1/2 pound orzo according to the package directions in a pot of boiling water until *al dente*. Drain, then spoon over the meat and tomatoes. (The heat from the pasta will warm them.) Add 1 cup crumbled feta cheese and 1/4 cup snipped fresh chives. Toss, season with kosher salt and freshly ground black pepper to taste, and serve with grilled bread (see pages 176–178). **SERVES 4**

Smoked Pheasant Breasts

A boneless, skinless pheasant breast half weighs about 1 pound and has a lovely, sweet taste. Smoking a pheasant breast without having it dry out is a challenge. Try this easy recipe for 2 pheasant breast halves. Lightly oil the meat and sprinkle with Fair for Fowl Rub (page 51) or the seasoning of your choice. Wrap each breast with 2 or 3 thin slices of pancetta or prosciutto, securing the slices with a toothpick if necessary. Prepare a smoker with 3 or 4 cherry wood chunks (soaked in water for at least 1 hour before smoking). Place a water pan in the smoker and place the pheasant breasts on a rack above the pan. Smoke at 225°F until an instant-read meat thermometer inserted in the thickest part registers 155 to 160°F, 45 to 60 minutes. Let the meat sit for about 5 minutes, then slice and serve with Smoked Corn in the Husks (page 121) and a leafy green salad. **SERVES 4**

Sangria!

When Judith did a grilled and smoked tapas class at A Southern Season in Chapel Hill, North Carolina, the students slurped down a refreshing sangria with the little bites. Marilyn Markel, the director of the school, was gracious enough to let us have her recipe, which can be made with either red or white wine. **SERVES 4**

½ cup sugar
½ cup water
1 orange, washed and very thinly sliced
1 lemon, washed and very thinly sliced
1 lime, washed and very thinly sliced
One 750 ml bottle dry red or white wine
2 cups club soda or sparkling water

1. Make a simple syrup by combining the sugar and water in a small saucepan over high heat. Bring to a boil and cook until the sugar has completely dissolved, about 1 minute. Remove from the heat and let cool.

2. Place the sliced fruit in a 2-quart pitcher and pour the simple syrup over it. Using a stainless steel spoon, mash the fruit and syrup together. Allow to stand for 5 minutes, then mash it some more. Pour the wine over the fruit, stir, and refrigerate until cold, stirring occasionally.

3. To serve, pour the sparkling water into the pitcher, stir gently, and serve.

In the Swim: Fish and Shellfish

f there is one food that most people are afraid to cook, it's probably fish. In our book *Fish & Shellfish, Grilled & Smoked* (The Harvard Common Press, 2002), we took our readers step by step through the process of grilling and smoking the luscious and tender denizens of lakes, streams, and oceans. We've demonstrated how to grill, smoke, plank, stir-grill, skewer, and rotisserie cook fish and shellfish in countless classes around the country. So you can believe us when we tell you that cooking fish and shellfish is a lot easier than it seems. You'll want to use the freshest fish and shellfish you can find, and sometimes that might mean IQF (individually quick frozen) or FAS (frozen at sea). Go to a reputable fish-monger or market where there is a high turnover of product.

We're also including a fish substitution chart (see pages 254–255), so you can always be prepared to use the best fish possible. For example, if you want to grill bluefish but it's not available at the market, you can substitute a similar fish in flavor and texture. If you had your heart set on salmon but it's not available, you can use char or halibut. If all of the fresh fish looks past its prime, go with frozen from the freezer case, not frozen and thawed in the store (who knows how long the fish has been there?). As always, fresh fish and shellfish should smell briny, like the sea, not like ammonia, and be somewhat firm to the touch. Whole fish should have clear eyes.

Even when the skin has been removed from a fish fillet, you can still see where it used to be. So when you're grilling fish and we tell you to start with the flesh side down, you'll know which side that is (the interior side along the backbone, which never had skin on it). Grilling fish flesh side down first makes it easier for you to keep the fillet together after you turn it on the grill.

Grilled Fish Fillets 257

Herb-Grilled Fish 258

Grilled Fish Veracruzano 258

Grilled Fish with Basil Oil
Mashed Potatoes and
Warm Citrus Garnish 258

Japanese-Style
Grilled Fish 258

**Grilled Fish or Shellfish
Skewers** 259

Thai-Style Halibut on
Lemongrass Skewers 260

Caribbean Grouper on
Sugar Cane Skewers 260

Aussie Shrimp
on the Barbie with
Orange-Ginger Baste 261

Orange and
Tarragon–Glazed
Scallop Skewers 261

PASSING THE BAR

S'mores 262

*Chocolate-Coconut-
Macadamia Bars* 262

Pecan Pie Bars 263

Almond Cookie Brittle 264

Rice Krispies Treats 265

GRILL GALS: SHE SIZZLES
SEASHELLS BY THE SEASHORE MENU

*Oyster, Prosciutto, and
Bay Leaf Skewers* 267

*Grilled Clams with
Lemon Butter Drizzle* 268

*Tequila-Lime
Scallop Skewers* 269

*Zucchini-Stuffed Tomatoes
with Basil* 270

Grilled Fish Steaks 271

Down Under Grilled
Fish Steaks with
Lime-Ginger Marinade 271

Lime-Grilled Swordfish
with Charred Tomato-
Chipotle Salsa 272

Seared Rare Tuna Steaks
with Toasted Sesame Oil 272

GREAT VEGETABLE SIDE DISHES

*Haricots Verts with Lemon,
Garlic, and Parsley* 274

*Baby Carrots Braised in Late-
Harvest Riesling* 275

*Sautéed Baby Spinach with
Olive Oil and Garlic* 275

Smoked Fish Fillets 272

Smoked Fish with
Sauce Verte 273

Smoked Trout Benedict
with Confetti Hash 273

Smoked Fish Pâté with
Dill and Lemon 276

Planked Fish or Shellfish 277

Oak-Planked Peppercorn
Tuna Steaks with
Orange Mayonnaise 278

Cedar-Planked Shrimp
Chimichurri 278

SENSATIONAL SALADS

*Mediterranean Salad with
Lemon-Sumac Vinaigrette* 279

*Moroccan Orange, Fennel,
and Olive Salad* 280

Kath's Cucumbers 281

*Elaborate Yet Easy
Cucumbers in
Poppy Seed Dressing* 282

*Cauliflower, Roasted
Red Pepper, and
Cured Olive Salad* 282

Hearts of Palm Salad 283

Italian Bean Salad 284

Smoked Whole Fish 285

Happy, Happy,
Happy Hour Salmon 286

Happy, Happy, Happy
Hour Salmon Spread 286

Apple Cider–Smoked Trout
with Horseradish Cream 286

**Grilled Oysters, Clams,
or Mussels in the Shell** 287

Grilled Oysters in Pesto 288

Grilled Littleneck Clams
with Pernod Butter 288

Black Fettuccine with
Grilled Mussels,
Garlic, and Parsley 288

Italian-Style Grilled Lobster 288

**Grilled Shrimp, Scallops,
or Squid** 289

Grilled Shrimp or
Scallops in Thai
Green Curry Sauce 290

Grilled Shrimp with Nuevo
Latino Cocktail Sauce 290

Grilled Scallops with
Fennel, Red Pepper,
and Lemon-Tarragon
Vinaigrette 291

Grilled Stuffed Calamari with
Thousand-Herb Sauce 291

GRILL GALS: SHE SPENDS SUMMERS
OFF AT THE JERSEY SHORE MENU

*Grilled Prosciutto and
Basil–Wrapped Shrimp
with Garlic Dipping Sauce* 293

*Grilled Bruschetta with
Jersey Tomatoes* 294

Grilled Lobster 294

*Blueberry-Peach Tart
with Macaroon Crust* 295

Stir-Grilled Shellfish 297

"Wonton"-Wrapped
Stir-Grilled Shellfish 298

Grilled Squid Linguine
with Amogio 298

Stir-Grilled Scallop
Po'boy Sandwiches 298

FISH SUBSTITUTION GUIDE FOR THE GRILL

Use this guide to help you select the freshest fish at the market. If your fish choice is not available, substitute another fish from the same category, or one category over. Some recipes will work with almost any kind of fish, so experiment, if you like.

This guide will help you choose your fish by flavor—mild to pronounced—and by texture—firm to delicate. If you want to grill a delicate-texture fish, we recommend using a perforated grill rack, disposable aluminum pan, NordicWare fish boat, or heavy-duty aluminum foil. This is so the fish doesn't flake and fall through the grill grate onto the fire. Keep this in mind when choosing from the delicate texture category.

Names of fish can be confusing. There's the fish family name; the local or regional name; and possibly a Hawaiian, Spanish, or French name commonly used. The most common usage is included to aid you in your fish shopping.

FIRMNESS	MILD FLAVOR	MODERATE FLAVOR	FULL FLAVOR
FIRM TEXTURE	Blackfish	Black Drum	Bigeye Tuna/Ahi
	Halibut	Clams	Chilean Sea Bass
	John Dory/St. Peter's Fish	Cobia/Sargentfish	Cuttlefish
	Kinklip	Drum/White Sea Bass	Escolar
	Lingcod/Greenling	Moonfish/Opah	Garfish/Needlefish
	Lobster	Salmon	Marlin/A'u
	Monkfish	Shark	Mussels
	Oreo Dory	Shortbill Spearfish/Hebi	Octopus
	Prawns	Skate	Oysters
	Red Drum/Redfish	Striped Marlin/Nairagi	Sailfish
	Sea Bass/Loup de Mer	Sturgeon	Squid
	Sea Robin	Swordfish	Triggerfish
	Shrimp	Yellowfin Tuna	Tuna
	Soft-Shell Crab		

FIRMNESS	MILD FLAVOR	MODERATE FLAVOR	FULL FLAVOR
MODERATELY FIRM TEXTURE	Canary Rockfish/ Pacific Red Snapper	Arctic Char	Amberjack
	Catfish	Barracuda	Kingfish
	Grouper	Bonito	King Mackerel
	Haddock	Mahi-mahi/Dorado	Mackerel
	Ocean Perch/Rockfish/Redfish	Sablefish/Black Cod	Mullet
	Orange Roughy	Sea Bream/Daurade	Permit
	Pompano	Sea Trout/Weakfish	Yellowtail Jack/ Hamachi
	Porgy	Tilapia	Yellowtail Snap
	Scup/Porgy	Trout	Wahoo/Ono
	Sea Scallops		
	Sheepshead/Convictfish		
	Snapper		
	Striped Bass		
	Tilefish		
	Walleye		
	Whitefish		
	Wolffish		
DELICATE TEXTURE	Bass (Freshwater)	Butterfish	Anchovies
	Cod	Herring	Bluefish
	Crayfish	Pomfret/Dollar Fish	Buffalofish
	Flounder	Shad	Sardines
	Fluke	Smelts/Whitebait	
	Hake/Whiting		
	Hoki/Blue Hake		
	Pink Snapper/Opakapaka		
	Red Snapper		
	Sand Dab		
	Turbot		

Rules for Grilling and Smoking Fish and Shellfish

Preparing fish and shellfish for the grill or smoker is a snap: a brush of olive oil, a sprinkling of seasoning, or a marinade. Just don't marinate fish and shellfish for more than 30 minutes (as a general rule), or you could "cook" the delicate flesh into ceviche, which is delicious, but not what you want here. The only exception would be a very oily fish with a mildly acidic marinade, as in Japanese-Style Grilled Fish (page 258).

The rule of thumb for most fish is to grill it for 10 minutes per inch of thickness over a hot fire. That means if you have a typical 3/4-inch-thick fish fillet, measured at the thickest part, you should grill it for 3 1/2 to 4 minutes on the flesh side, turn the fillet, and grill it for 3 to 4 minutes more.

The exceptions to that rule are meaty fish such as tuna, swordfish, and shark, which many people like to eat rare to medium, and shellfish. These types of fish and shellfish will be well done over a hot fire in 6 to 7 minutes per inch of thickness. If you want a rare tuna steak, grill it for 1 to 2 minutes per side over a hot fire.

For smoking, which is done at 225 to 250°F, the timing is, of course, longer. As a rule, you want to smoke fish for 20 to 25 minutes per pound. A typical salmon fillet or steak will take 45 to 60 minutes to slow smoke, a whole fish 1 to 1 1/2 hours.

The general rules for grilling fish are:

1. Buy the freshest fish available, which sometimes will be frozen!
2. Marinate for only 30 minutes.
3. Grill for 10 minutes per inch of thickness.

The general rules for smoking fish are:

1. Buy the freshest fish available, which sometimes will be frozen!
2. Marinate for only 30 minutes.
3. Smoke for 20 to 25 minutes per pound.

Grilled Fish Fillets

Fish fillets are delicious, good for you, and quick to grill, yet many people still have qualms about cooking them.

In our book *Fish & Shellfish, Grilled & Smoked* (The Harvard Common Press, 2002), we began to spread the word that grilled fish is simple, easy, and fast. There are two key factors in grilling great fish fillets. The first is your choice of a fish fillet. If you're a beginner, start with farm-raised catfish because it's mild-flavored yet fairly firm in texture, so it stays together well on the grill. Then move on to salmon, halibut, and the whole big world of fish. When starting out, avoid very delicate and flat fish fillets, such as Dover sole or turbot. Once you get the hang of grilling fish, try these more delicate varieties. Just use an oiled perforated grill rack and two big fish spatulas to turn the fillets one time.

The second factor in grilling fish involves heat and timing. Grill fish fillets for 10 minutes per inch of thickness (judged by the thickest part of the fillet) over a hot fire. A catfish fillet, for example, is usually about 3/4 inch thick in the thickest part. That means you should grill the fillet for about 7 minutes total, turning once halfway through. A very thin Dover sole fillet, maybe 1/2 inch thick, will take 5 minutes total, turning once.

Marinate most fish for only 30 minutes maximum. Any longer, and an acidic marinade (one made with citrus juice, vinegar, or wine) could "cook" the fish into ceviche, which is delicious, but not what you want here. **SERVES 4**

> **4 fish fillets, skin removed, if necessary**
>
> **Olive oil**
>
> **Fine kosher or sea salt and freshly ground black pepper to taste**

1. Prepare a hot fire in a grill. Oil the grill grate or a perforated grill rack.

2. Brush or spray the fillets on both sides with olive oil. Place the fish flesh side down on the grill rack and grill for 10 minutes per inch of thickness, turning once halfway through. A fish fillet is done when it begins to flake when tested with a fork in the thickest part. Remove from the grill, season with salt and pepper, and serve hot.

 **Crowning Glories**

These fillets are scrumptious topped with a spoonful of:

Citrus Caesar Vinaigrette *(page 84)*

Roasted Red Pepper Aioli *(page 110)*

Poblano Cream Sauce *(page 93)*

Herb-Grilled Fish: Grilling fish over fresh herb leaves and woody stalks is an aromatic tradition from the south of France. The best "woody" herbs (meaning the plants develop woody stalks) for this are thyme, rosemary, and lavender. If you're using charcoal, prepare a hot fire and, right before grilling, place 6 large fresh or dried thyme, rosemary, or lavender branches on the fire. If you're using a gas grill, wrap the herbs in aluminum foil, poke holes in the top of the packet, and place on the coals. Brush 4 fish fillets with olive oil, season with one of our herb salts (see pages 55–57), and grill as directed above. **SERVES 4**

Grilled Fish Veracruzano: Before you grill your fish, make this zesty Spanish-inspired tomato sauce. We like to use fire-roasted canned tomatoes (Muir Glen brand) for a hit of smoky flavor. Heat 2 tablespoons olive oil in a medium-size saucepan over medium-high heat. Add 1 thinly sliced onion and 4 minced garlic cloves and cook, stirring a few times, until golden, about 5 minutes. Add 2 tablespoons chopped pickled jalapeño and one 28-ounce can fire-roasted tomatoes, undrained and chopped. (Use kitchen shears inserted in the open can to chop the tomatoes if they're not chopped already.) Cook, stirring, until almost all the liquid has evaporated, about 15 minutes. Stir in 1 tablespoon fresh oregano leaves or 1 teaspoon dried oregano and $1/2$ cup chopped green olives. Brush 4 fish fillets of your choice (we recommend fish from the Gulf of Mexico, such as red snapper, redfish, and grouper) with olive oil and grill as described above. Top with the sauce and serve with lime wedges. **SERVES 4**

Grilled Fish with Basil Oil Mashed Potatoes and Warm Citrus Garnish: Use a warm-water ocean fish such as red snapper, grouper, mahi-mahi, bonito, pompano, or tilapia for this aromatic and flavorful dish (see our fish substitution chart on pages 254–255). Peel and section 2 navel oranges and 2 limes. Heat 2 tablespoons olive oil in a large skillet over medium heat. Add the orange and lime sections and cook, stirring a few times, until lightly browned; keep warm. Bring $2^{1}/2$ pounds peeled and chopped red potatoes and water to cover to a boil and continue to boil until tender, about 15 minutes. Drain and keep covered. In a food processor, puree 30 fresh basil leaves and $3/4$ cup olive oil. Mash the potatoes with $1/2$ cup of the basil oil and season with kosher or sea salt and freshly ground black pepper to taste. Brush 4 fish fillets with the remaining basil oil, sprinkle with salt and pepper, and grill as directed above. Garnish each fillet with warm citrus and fresh basil leaves and serve with the potatoes. **SERVES 4**

Japanese-Style Grilled Fish: The marinade provides a robust flavor. To make sure it doesn't overpower the fish, we suggest using a strong-flavored, oily fish such as amberjack, bluefish, salmon, mackerel, marlin, mullet, or even our old standby, farm-raised catfish, which can take on any flavor. In a small saucepan, combine $1/4$ cup soy sauce, $1/4$ cup sake or dry white wine, $1/4$ cup mirin (a sweet Japanese wine), 2 tablespoons sugar, and 2 tablespoons peeled and finely chopped fresh ginger. Bring to a boil over medium-high heat, then immediately remove from the heat. Cover and let cool to room temperature. Arrange 4 fish fillets in a deep baking dish and pour the marinade over. Cover and refrigerate for 4 hours or overnight (this is okay with an oily fish and a mildly acidic marinade), turning the fish occasionally. Remove the fish from the marinade and pat dry. Brush with vegetable oil and grill as directed above. Serve each fillet garnished with paper-thin slices of lemon. **SERVES 4**

Grilled Fish or Shellfish Skewers

If you want to make sure your family is eating healthy food but they're getting tired of fish or shellfish, try grilling it on skewers.

Marinate the fish or shellfish while you start the grill, and have some helpers thread the pieces onto skewers. That's the only tricky part.

If you have bought fish steaks, just make sure all the skin is off, then cut the fish into cubes. If you have bought fish fillets, again make sure the skin is off. Cut the fish lengthwise into 2-inch-wide strips. If you have peeled and deveined shrimp or whole scallops, just rinse and pat them dry. When you thread the fish or shellfish onto skewers, make sure to leave a little breathing room between the pieces.

For skewers, we'll start you out with plain old wooden skewers, then get fancier as we go along with fresh stalks of lemongrass and spikes of sugar cane. Grill the skewers over a hot fire until the fish is opaque all the way through, a matter of minutes. Then serve with your favorite dipping sauce, maybe some of the reserved and unused marinade.

Grill some vegetables along with the fish skewers, serve a salad on the side, and you've got dinner!

If you're a beginner, we recommend that you start with farm-raised catfish. It's available year-round, is mild-flavored, can take any kind of seasoning or marinade, and is easy to work with. **SERVES 4**

> **4 farm-raised catfish fillets, skin removed**
> **$1/2$ cup bottled Italian-style vinaigrette**
> **16 wooden skewers, soaked in water for at least 30 minutes before grilling**

1. Prepare a hot fire in a grill.

2. Lay the fillets so the grain of the fish is horizontal. Using a pizza wheel or chef's knife, cut the fillets into 2-inch-wide strips. Place in a bowl and pour the vinaigrette over. Cover and refrigerate for 30 minutes.

3. Thread the fish pieces onto the skewers, leaving space between them. Grill for 2 to 3 minutes per side, turning once. Serve hot.

Crowning Glories

Top these beauties with:

More vinaigrette

Chopped fresh herbs

Finely chopped green onions, bell peppers, and tomatoes

Thai-Style Halibut on Lemongrass Skewers: Fresh lemongrass skewers add a fragrant citrus note to the halibut. If you use the packaged lemongrass stalks available in the produce section of most grocery stores, cut them lengthwise into 4 more slender stalks to use as skewers. You can also buy lemongrass plants at better plant nurseries. Green curry paste, fish sauce, and toasted sesame oil are available in the Asian section of grocery stores. Salmon would also taste wonderful prepared this way. Combine 1 tablespoon green curry paste, 1 minced garlic clove, 1 tablespoon grated fresh ginger (if using a microplane, you don't need to peel), 1 teaspoon Asian fish sauce, 1 tablespoon rice vinegar, 2 tablespoons vegetable oil, and 1 teaspoon toasted sesame oil in a small bowl. Spread the paste on 1¹/₂ pounds skinned halibut steaks, then cut into 1-inch pieces. Cover and refrigerate for 30 minutes. Have ready 12 fresh lemongrass stalks, about ¹/₄ inch in diameter and 6 inches long. Thread the halibut onto the stalks, 3 to 4 pieces per skewer. If necessary, pierce the fish with a wooden skewer first, then insert the lemongrass stalk. Do not crowd the pieces on the skewer. Grill as directed above, about 5 minutes per side. Serve hot or at room temperature. **SERVES 4**

Caribbean Grouper on Sugar Cane Skewers: If you love Caribbean rum drinks, you'll love this. You could substitute 18 sea scallops or large shrimp for the grouper. Cut 1¹/₂ pounds skinned grouper fillets into 2-inch-wide strips as directed above. Place the strips in a baking dish. Combine ¹/₄ cup light rum, ¹/₄ cup fresh lime juice (4 to 5 limes), ¹/₄ cup olive oil, 2 minced garlic cloves, and 1 tablespoon minced shallot in a bowl and pour half the marinade over the fish. Cover and refrigerate for 30 minutes. Reserve the remaining marinade in a small bowl. Have ready 6 slender spikes of sugar cane (at least 6 inches long; available at Hispanic markets, better grocery stores, and sometimes Target). Thread the fish onto the sugar cane, leaving space between the pieces. Place the reserved marinade by the grill. Set the skewers on the grill grate and brush each with a little marinade. Cover and grill for 2 to 3 minutes. When the fish is opaque on the bottom, turn the skewers and brush with the remaining marinade. Cover and cook for 2 to 3 minutes, until the fish is opaque all the way through. Serve hot. **SERVES 4**

Aussie Shrimp on the Barbie with Orange-Ginger Baste: The northern coast of Australia is replete with crustaceans of all kinds, including Moreton Bay "bugs," which are really large, crayfish-like shellfish. For this recipe, use the largest shrimp you can find—or even lobster tails out of the shell. Start with 12 to 24 peeled and deveined large shrimp. Soak 12 to 24 long wooden skewers in water for at least 30 minutes before grilling, then push the skewers through the shrimp lengthwise, from head to tail, with only 1 shrimp to a skewer. In a medium-size bowl, whisk together $1/4$ cup ($1/2$ stick) melted unsalted butter, 1 cup orange juice, 2 tablespoons sherry or rum, 1 teaspoon grated orange zest; 2 finely chopped green onions, and 1 teaspoon grated fresh ginger (if using a microplane, you don't need to peel). Reserve half of the sauce in a small serving bowl. Dip the skewered shrimp in the remaining sauce and place the skewers on an oiled perforated grill rack about 4 inches above the heat. Baste liberally with the sauce and grill for 2 to 4 minutes, turn, and grill for 2 to 4 minutes more, until pink and cooked through. Serve hot. Pass the reserved sauce at the table. **SERVES 6**

Orange and Tarragon–Glazed Scallop Skewers: A glaze, which has a higher sugar content than a marinade or baste, can both flavor and add a mouthwatering sheen to grilled foods. Orange and tarragon gently infuse these grilled scallops. This recipe also works well with shrimp. Make the glaze by mixing together 2 tablespoons olive oil, 1 teaspoon dried tarragon, 1 teaspoon grated orange zest, the juice of 1 orange, and 2 tablespoons clover or other medium-colored honey in a small bowl. Place 18 sea scallops, rinsed and patted dry, in a large sealable plastic bag and pour $1/2$ cup of the glaze over them. Seal the bag and refrigerate for 30 minutes. Reserve the remaining glaze in the bowl. Have ready 6 wooden skewers, soaked in water for at least 30 minutes before grilling. Thread 3 scallops on each skewer, leaving space between them. Place the reserved glaze by the grill. Set the skewers on the grill grate and use a spoon to drizzle each skewer with a little glaze. Cover and grill for 4 to 5 minutes, until the scallops are opaque on the bottom, then turn the skewers and brush with the remaining glaze. Cover and cook for 3 to 4 minutes, until the scallops are shiny yet opaque all the way through. Serve on a platter, over a bed of thinly sliced oranges and cucumbers. **SERVES 6**

Both Karen and Judith are dessert lovers. For barbecues, we're partial to bar cookies that can be made ahead and frozen. They're a perfect ending to a simple outdoor meal, and, like the biblical loaves and fishes, they can be portioned to feed any size crowd. We've chosen our easiest and very best to share with you.

S'mores

Kind of a stretch of the definition of bar cookies, but who cares when they're this good? If you've never shared this treat with your kids, it's time to get to it. For each s'more, you need 2 whole (double-section) graham crackers and a piece of milk chocolate about the same size. Place the chocolate on one cracker. Roast a marshmallow over the fire. When it is hot, place it on top of the chocolate and place the other cracker on top to make a sandwich. Let cool a little, then gobble it up.

Chocolate-Coconut-Macadamia Bars

Karen first came across a recipe similar to this while judging a holiday cooking contest. The saltines add just the right amount of salt to the recipe. **MAKES 24 LARGE OR 48 SMALL BARS**

 24 saltine crackers
 1 cup (2 sticks) unsalted butter
 1 cup firmly packed light or dark brown sugar
 1 cup sweetened flaked coconut
 1 1/2 cups semisweet chocolate chips
 1 cup roughly chopped macadamia nuts

1. Preheat the oven to 375°F. Line a 13 x 9 x 2-inch baking pan with aluminum foil, letting the ends of the foil extend over the sides of the pan.

2.   Place the crackers on the bottom of the foil-lined pan, 4 crackers wide by 6 crackers long.

3.   In a medium-size saucepan over medium heat, melt the butter. Add the brown sugar and, stirring gently, bring to a boil. Let boil for 2 minutes, then pour evenly over the crackers. Sprinkle the coconut, chocolate chips, and nuts in even layers on top. Place in the oven for 5 minutes.

4.   Remove from the oven and gently press the mixture down with the back of a spoon. Let cool for 15 to 20 minutes, then refrigerate for 10 to 15 minutes, until the chocolate is set.

5.   Remove from the refrigerator and lift the foil holding the bars onto a cutting board. Cut into 24 large or 48 small bars. To freeze, place 2 bars back to back and cover with plastic wrap. Put the wrapped bars in a freezer bag and freeze for up to 3 months.

Chocolate–Peanut Butter Bars: Omit the coconut and substitute ³/₄ cup peanut butter chips for an equal amount of the chocolate chips. **MAKES 24 LARGE OR 48 SMALL BARS**

Pecan Pie Bars

These bars are very sweet, like pecan pie. The little bit of salt helps balance the sugar. If you want a shot of chocolate, substitute chocolate graham crackers or sprinkle a cup of semisweet chocolate chips over the graham crackers before you pour the hot caramel sauce over them. **MAKES 24 LARGE OR 48 SMALL BARS**

9 whole graham crackers

1 cup (2 sticks) unsalted butter

1 cup firmly packed light or dark brown sugar

¹/₈ teaspoon kosher or sea salt

2¹/₂ cups pecan halves

1. Preheat the oven to 375°F. Line a 13 x 9 x 2-inch baking pan with heavy-duty aluminum foil, letting the ends of the foil extend over the sides of the pan.

2. Place the graham crackers in a single layer on the bottom of the foil-lined pan. Break 2 of the crackers into sections to fit; you should have 1 section left over (you have our permission to eat it).

3. In a medium-size saucepan over medium heat, melt the butter. Add the brown sugar and, stirring gently, bring to a boil. Let boil for 2 minutes, add the salt, and pour evenly over the crackers. Add the pecans in an even layer. Place in the oven for 5 minutes.

4. Remove from the oven and gently press the pecans down. Let cool for about 15 minutes, then refrigerate for another 15 minutes, until the mixture is set.

5. Remove from the refrigerator and lift the foil holding the bars onto a cutting board. Cut into 24 large or 48 small bars. To freeze, place 2 bars back to back and cover with plastic wrap. Put the wrapped bars in a freezer bag and freeze for up to 3 months.

Almond Cookie Brittle

Mix all the ingredients together in a bowl, pat the mixture into a baking sheet, bake, and then break into pieces—perfect for making with children or grandchildren. This one is from our book *Easy Grilling & Simple Smoking with the BBQ Queens* (Pig Out Publications, 1997). MAKES ABOUT 24 PIECES

> **1 cup (2 sticks) unsalted butter, very soft but not melted**
> **1 cup sugar**
> **1 teaspoon kosher or sea salt**
> **2 teaspoons almond extract**
> **2 cups all-purpose flour**
> **1 cup sliced almonds**

1. Preheat the oven to 350°F.

2. In a large bowl, beat the butter, sugar, salt, and almond extract together until creamy. Stir in the flour gradually, beating until just blended. Press the dough into a

16 x 10 x 1-inch baking sheet (or one with similar dimensions). Press the sliced almonds evenly on top of the dough. Bake for 20 minutes for chewier brittle or 25 minutes for crunchier brittle.

3.   Let cool in the pan. For more uniform pieces, score with a knife while still warm, then break into pieces when completely cooled. For more random pieces, let cool completely, invert onto a counter or cutting board, and break apart. Store in an airtight container.

Substitutions and Additions: For the almonds, you can substitute 1 cup white chocolate chips and 1 cup sweetened dried cranberries to make White Chocolate–Cranberry Brittle. Or top with 1/2 cup sweetened flaked coconut, 1/2 cup sliced almonds, and 1/2 cup semisweet chocolate chips to make Almond Joy Brittle. **MAKES 24 PIECES**

Rice Krispies Treats

This retro snack from Kellogg is a winner with both adults and children. Watch their happy faces when they munch on these treats. MAKES TWENTY-FOUR 2-INCH SQUARES

> **3 tablespoons unsalted butter**
> **4 cups miniature marshmallows**
> **6 cups Kellogg's Rice Krispies cereal**

1.   Melt the butter in a large saucepan over low heat. Add the marshmallows and stir until completely melted. Remove from the heat. Stir in the cereal and coat well.

2.   Coat a 13 x 9 x 2-inch baking pan with nonstick cooking spray. Evenly press the mixture into the pan using the back of a buttered spatula. The mixture will be sticky. Let cool on the counter or in the refrigerator.

3.   When completely cooled, cut into 2-inch squares. Serve immediately, or wrap individual squares in plastic, then place in a sealable plastic bag and keep in the refrigerator or freezer for 1 to 2 days. Remove when ready to serve.

Grill Gals

She Sizzles Seashells by the Seashore Menu

Oyster, Prosciutto, and Bay Leaf Skewers
Grilled Clams with Lemon Butter Drizzle
Tequila-Lime Scallop Skewers
Zucchini-Stuffed Tomatoes with Basil

Bonnie Tandy Leblang, registered dietitian, cookbook author, and syndicated food columnist, doesn't live too far from Long Island Sound in Connecticut. "No one can resist the aromas of sizzling kabobs or vegetables cooking on an outdoor grill," she says. "Patio cooking is the way to entertain friends on long summer evenings." Her menu reflects that, as she offers a sampling of three different kinds of shellfish, all of which cook very quickly on her charcoal grill, in recipes we have adapted.

The shellfish can be ready and waiting at the grill on ice as your guests arrive. If you use a charcoal grill, keep a charcoal chimney full of coals handy in case you linger too long with your guests, forget about cooking, and the coals die out. (Or use a gas grill. Or persuade one of your gentleman callers to "man" the grill for a while.) Serve the grilled shellfish with a side dish full of the best summer flavors and maybe some fruit that you grill as the coals are dying down. You could enjoy this menu tapas style—little bites of a progression of courses: grill the oysters first and enjoy them hot, then put the clams on the grill, followed by the scallop skewers.

Oyster, Prosciutto, and Bay Leaf Skewers

Fresh bay leaves are often available with other packaged herbs in the grocery store. Bay plants are available from nurseries—just pluck the leaves off the plant. If you can't find fresh bay, simmer 3 dried bay leaves in the basting mixture over low heat for about 5 minutes, remove from the heat, and infuse for 30 minutes. Remove the bay leaves and baste as directed. **SERVES 6 AS AN APPETIZER**

> 18 fresh shucked oysters
>
> 6 thin slices prosciutto, each cut lengthwise into thirds
>
> 6 wooden skewers, soaked in water for at least 30 minutes before grilling
>
> 18 fresh bay leaves (see headnote)
>
> **MUSTARD BASTING SAUCE**
>
> 1/2 cup Dijon mustard
>
> 1/4 cup rice vinegar or dry white wine
>
> 1/4 cup honey
>
> 1 tablespoon toasted sesame oil

1. Rinse the oysters under cold running water and pat dry. Wrap each oyster with a piece of prosciutto and arrange the oysters on a skewer, with a fresh bay leaf touching each one. Don't crowd the oysters on the skewer, or they will take longer to cook through. Remind your guests to remove the bay leaves before eating the oysters.

2. To make the basting sauce, mix all the ingredients together in a small bowl.

3. Prepare a hot fire in a grill.

4. Place the skewers on the grill grate and use a spoon to drizzle them with one-third of the basting mixture. Cover and grill for 4 to 5 minutes. When the oysters are opaque on the bottom, turn the skewers and baste with a brush. Cover and cook for 3 to 4 minutes, until the oysters are opaque all the way through. Brush again with the basting mixture and serve hot. (If you're grilling all three shellfish dishes, close the lid so the grill stays hot.)

Grilled Clams with Lemon Butter Drizzle

Hard-shell clams will pop open on a very hot grill, just like when you steam them. Use a perforated grill rack or two so you don't lose any in the coals. Discard any that have opened and won't close before cooking or that have not opened after cooking. You can scrub and rinse the clams about 1 hour before your guests arrive. Keep them in the refrigerator until 15 minutes before grilling. **SERVES 6 AS AN APPETIZER**

> **3 pounds hard-shell clams**
>
> **1 recipe Lemon Butter Drizzle (page 87)**
>
> **2 tablespoons chopped fresh herbs, such as Italian parsley, chives, tarragon, and/or basil, for garnish**

1. Scrub and rinse the clams under cold running water.

2. Prepare a hot fire in a grill.

3. Keep the drizzle warm in a metal container by the grill.

4. Place the clams on perforated grill racks. Cover and grill for 4 to 5 minutes, until they open.

5. Transfer the clams to a large platter and drizzle with the lemon butter. Garnish with the chopped herbs and serve. (If you're grilling all three shellfish dishes, place the cover back on the grill so it stays hot.)

Tequila-Lime Scallop Skewers

If you love margaritas, as we do, this is a great way to get that flavor on the grill.
SERVES 6 AS AN APPETIZER

18 large sea scallops

TEQUILA-LIME MARINADE

¹/₄ cup tequila

¹/₄ cup fresh lime juice (4 to 5 limes)

¹/₄ cup olive oil

2 cloves garlic, minced

1 tablespoon minced shallot

6 wooden skewers, soaked in water for at least 30 minutes before grilling

1.   Rinse the scallops under cold running water and pat dry.

2.   To make the marinade, combine all the ingredients in a small bowl. Place the scallops in a large sealable plastic bag and pour the marinade over. Seal the bag and refrigerate for 30 minutes.

3.   Prepare a hot fire in a grill.

4.   Remove the scallops, reserving the marinade. Thread 3 scallops lengthwise onto each skewer, leaving space between them. Place the remaining marinade in a small saucepan, bring to a boil, and continue to boil for 2 minutes. Transfer to a heatproof bowl and place by the grill.

5.   Place the skewers on the grill grate and use a spoon to drizzle them with one-third of the marinade mixture. Cover and grill for 4 to 5 minutes. When the scallops are opaque on the bottom, turn the skewers and baste with a brush. Cover and cook for 3 to 4 minutes, until the scallops are opaque all the way through. Brush again with the marinade and serve hot. (If you're grilling the vegetable dish next, place the cover back on the grill so it stays hot.)

Zucchini-Stuffed Tomatoes with Basil

This is an easy, delicious way to serve the best of summer. **SERVES 6 AS AN APPETIZER**

6 large ripe beefsteak (or other large) tomatoes, cored and hollowed out, leaving about a ¹/₂-inch wall of tomato pulp inside

2 or 3 small zucchini, finely diced

1 shallot, minced

¹/₄ cup fresh basil leaves, shredded

6 tablespoons freshly grated Parmesan cheese

6 tablespoons extra virgin olive oil

1. Coat 2 disposable aluminum pans with nonstick cooking spray. Set the hollowed-out tomatoes in the pans. If necessary, cut off part of the bottom of the tomatoes so they sit evenly. In a medium-size bowl, combine the zucchini, shallot, basil, and Parmesan. Fill the tomatoes evenly with the mixture. Drizzle each tomato with 1 tablespoon olive oil.

2. Prepare a hot fire in a grill.

3. Place the tomatoes on the grill, cover, and cook until they are bronzed and softened, 8 to 10 minutes. Serve hot, at room temperature, or cold. (If you're going to grill fruit for dessert, place the cover back on the grill so it stays hot.)

Grilled Fish Steaks

Although fish steaks are uniform in thickness and thicker than fish fillets, you grill them the same way, over a hot fire for about 10 minutes per inch of thickness. A halibut steak, for example, is usually about ³/₄ inch thick. That means you would grill the steak for about 7 minutes total, turning once halfway through.

We suggest that you start with halibut or salmon steaks, because they're mild-flavored yet fairly firm in texture, so they stay together well on the grill. When you get the hang of those, try tuna steaks, which you grill to medium or medium-rare, or swordfish steaks, using an oiled perforated grill rack and two big fish spatulas to turn the steaks only once.

In general, fish should not be marinated for more than 30 minutes. Otherwise, the delicate flesh could be "cooked," which is not desirable. **SERVES 4**

> **4 fish steaks**
>
> **Olive oil**
>
> **Fine kosher or sea salt and freshly ground black pepper to taste**

1. Prepare a hot fire in a grill. Oil the grill grate or a perforated grill rack.

2. Brush or spray the steaks on both sides with olive oil. Place the fish on the grill rack and grill for 10 minutes per inch of thickness, turning once halfway through. A fish steak is done when it begins to flake when tested with a fork in the center.

3. Remove from the grill, season with salt and pepper, and serve hot.

 **Crowning Glories**

Serve these steaks with:
Vietnamese Drizzle *(page 87)*
Roasted Red Pepper Sauce *(page 94)*
Hearts of Palm Salad *(page 283)*

Down Under Grilled Fish Steaks with Lime-Ginger Marinade: The tropical climate in the northern part of Australia promotes the growth of citrus and ginger, both distinctive elements in this marinade. We like to use 1-inch-thick swordfish, halibut, or salmon steaks here. In a small bowl, whisk together ¹/₄ cup fresh lime juice (4 to 5 limes), 2 tablespoons vegetable oil, 1 teaspoon Dijon mustard, 1 teaspoon grated fresh ginger (if using a microplane, you don't need to peel), and $1/4$ teaspoon each cayenne pepper and freshly ground black pepper. Arrange 4 fish steaks in a deep baking dish and pour the marinade over. Marinate for up to 30 minutes, turning 2 or 3 times. Remove from the marinade and grill as directed above. Serve hot. **SERVES 4**

Lime-Grilled Swordfish with Charred Tomato-Chipotle Salsa: Our mouths water whenever we think about this big-flavor dish, adapted from one by our barbecue buddy Paul Kirk. We could eat the salsa by the spoonful, but usually we save it to serve with luscious lime-grilled swordfish. In a small bowl, combine 3 tablespoons fresh lime juice, 3 tablespoons olive oil, and 2 minced garlic cloves. Rub the mixture over four 8-ounce swordfish steaks cut 1 inch thick. Place in a baking dish and refrigerate for 30 minutes, then grill as directed above. Serve with Charred Tomato-Chipotle Salsa (page 162). **SERVES 4**

Seared Rare Tuna Steaks with Toasted Sesame Oil: In a small bowl, combine $2/3$ cup soy sauce, $1/4$ cup rice vinegar, 2 tablespoons toasted sesame oil, and 1 tablespoon grated fresh ginger (if using a microplane, you don't need to peel). In a shallow bowl, place four 6-ounce tuna steaks cut at least 1 inch thick. Add $3/4$ cup of the marinade and let sit for 15 minutes, turning the steaks a couple of times. Reserve the rest of the marinade for drizzling over the cooked steaks. Grill as directed above, searing the tuna on both sides, for 5 to 6 minutes total. The tuna should still be rare in the center but browned and charred on the edges. Serve with a drizzle of the reserved marinade. **SERVES 4**

Smoked Fish Fillets

Imagine being able to reach into your freezer and take out a moist, delicious smoked fish fillet whenever you want. In the BBQ Queens' humble opinion, that's a real frozen asset. You are then just minutes away from a fabulous appetizer such as Smoked Fish Pâté with Dill and Lemon (page 276), a brunch dish such as Smoked Trout Benedict with Confetti Hash (right), or that French bistro favorite, smoked haddock with mashed potatoes.

You can smoke any fish fillet, but our favorites are Pacific cod or whitefish, catfish, salmon, trout, and walleye (pike) because of their general availability, great flavor, and pleasing texture. When you're going to the trouble to smoke anything, we always recommend that you smoke intentionally for leftovers that you can wrap and freeze. Don't let an opportunity to give yourself the gift of time— for making future dishes—go up in smoke!

In its simplest and purest form, a fish fillet in the smoker needs little more than oil, salt, and pepper. The oil adds moisture to the fish so it won't dry out. Smoking at 225 to 250°F will take 45 to 60 minutes for fish steaks or fillets. The more fish placed on a smoker, the longer it will take to smoke. Smoked fish will keep, tightly covered, in the refrigerator for up to 2 weeks and in the freezer for up to 3 months. **SERVES 4**

SUGGESTED WOOD: Alder, maple, pecan, or a combination

Two 8-ounce fish fillets

2 tablespoons olive oil

Fine kosher or sea salt and freshly ground black pepper to taste

1. Brush or spray the fillets with the olive oil and season with salt and pepper.

2. Prepare an indirect fire in a smoker.

3. Place the fish in the smoker, close the lid, and smoke at 225 to 250°F until the fish is opaque and the flesh is just beginning to flake when you test it with a fork, 45 to 60 minutes. Serve hot or at room temperature.

Crowning Glories

Smoked fish fillets are delicious served with:
Hearts of Palm Salad (page 283)
Charred Tomato-Chipotle Salsa (page 162)
Hot Shallot Vinaigrette (page 85)

Smoked Fish with Sauce Verte: Easy-to-make *sauce verte*, pale green with fresh herbs, is great with either smoked or grilled fish fillets or steaks. In a blender or food processor, combine 1 cup mayonnaise (lowfat is okay), 1/2 cup roughly chopped fresh Italian parsley, 1/4 cup chopped fresh dill, 1/4 cup chopped fresh tarragon, 1 tablespoon chopped fresh chives, 1 tablespoon tarragon vinegar, and 2 tablespoons drained capers. Process until smooth. Cover and refrigerate for at least 1 hour or up to 3 days to let the flavors blend. Smoke 4 fish fillets as described above. Serve with a dollop of sauce. **SERVES 4**

Smoked Trout Benedict with Confetti Hash: This is one of our favorite ways to enjoy smoked trout—especially if we've smoked it ahead of time and have it on hand in the freezer. For a great presentation, cook the hash in a large skillet, then divide it into 4 mini cast-iron skillets and top with the remaining ingredients. Nestle each small skillet on a

▪▪✕✕✕✕▪

For a simply grilled chicken breast or fish fillet, you want a side dish that is also quick to cook. These delicious vegetable dishes fill the bill.

Haricots Verts with Lemon, Garlic, and Parsley

This dish is adapted from a recipe by Nancy Verde Barr in *Make It Italian* (Alfred A. Knopf, 2002). Normally, we don't go for frozen green beans, but frozen *haricots verts*, those tiny French green beans, have good flavor and a uniform size, and are already trimmed. So why not? This recipe can be doubled or tripled. It just might replace the green bean casserole on your holiday table. The gremolata is also good on grilled chicken breasts, grilled fish fillets or steaks, or any grilled vegetable. **SERVES 4**

One 12-ounce package frozen *haricots verts*

GREMOLATA

3 large cloves garlic, minced

3 tablespoons olive oil

2 tablespoons minced fresh Italian parsley

2 teaspoons grated lemon zest

Fine kosher or sea salt and freshly ground black pepper to taste

1. Bring a pot of salted water to a boil. Add the beans and cook until tender-crisp, 5 to 6 minutes.

2. While the beans are cooking, make the gremolata by combining the garlic, olive oil, parsley, and lemon zest in a small bowl.

3. When the beans are done, drain immediately, plunge into a bowl of ice water, and let cool for 2 minutes. Drain and transfer to a serving bowl. Pour the gremolata over the beans and toss to blend. Season with salt and pepper and serve immediately.

Baby Carrots Braised in Late-Harvest Riesling

Put this dish on to braise before you go out to the grill, and it will be done when your chicken or fish is. After a dinner party, Judith found that she had some wine left over (as is usually the case with dessert wines), so she dreamed up this dish. **SERVES 4**

> 2 tablespoons unsalted butter
> 2 cups baby carrots
> 1/2 teaspoon ground white pepper
> 1/4 teaspoon freshly grated nutmeg
> 1/4 cup late-harvest Riesling or other dessert wine, sherry, or Marsala
> 1/4 cup chicken broth
> Sea salt to taste

In a medium-size saucepan over medium-high heat, melt the butter and stir in the carrots. Sprinkle on the white pepper and nutmeg and stir to coat the carrots. Cook for 2 minutes, stirring. Pour in the wine and broth and bring to a boil. Reduce the heat to low, cover, and simmer until done, about 10 minutes. Season with salt and serve immediately.

Sautéed Baby Spinach with Olive Oil and Garlic

So simple, yet so good! **SERVES 4**

> 2 tablespoons olive oil
> 1/4 teaspoon red pepper flakes
> 2 cloves garlic, cut into slivers
> 1 pound baby spinach leaves
> Kosher or sea salt and freshly ground black pepper to taste

Heat the olive oil in a large skillet over medium-high heat. When the oil is hot, add the red pepper flakes and garlic. Stir, then add the spinach and toss until the leaves have wilted and are glistening, 2 to 3 minutes. Season with salt and pepper and serve immediately.

folded napkin placed on a dinner plate. Have ready 4 small smoked trout fillets (see above). In a skillet, melt 3 tablespoons unsalted butter over medium-high heat. Add 1/2 cup chopped green onions and 1 minced garlic clove and cook, stirring, for 2 minutes. Stir in one 19-ounce package defrosted frozen southern-style hash-brown potatoes (about 3 1/2 cups) and cook, stirring occasionally, until the potatoes have browned. Stir in 1/2 cup chopped roasted red and/or yellow peppers (from a jar) and season with kosher or sea salt and freshly ground black pepper to taste. Set in a preheated 250°F oven to keep warm. To poach the eggs (one at a time), coat a medium-size skillet with nonstick cooking spray and fill halfway with hot water. Bring to a simmer over medium-high heat, then reduce the heat to medium-low. Break 1 large egg into a 1-cup measure. Place the cup, sideways, as close to the simmering water as possible and slide the egg into the water. Repeat with 3 more eggs. Simmer until the whites have set, 3 to 5 minutes. Remove with a slotted spoon and drain on paper towels. To assemble the dish, place one-quarter of the hash on a plate, top with a smoked trout fillet and a poached egg, and spoon a little Food Processor or Blender Hollandaise (page 97) over all. Garnish with fresh herb sprigs. **SERVES 4**

Smoked Fish Pâté with Dill and Lemon: In our book *Fish & Shellfish, Grilled & Smoked* (The Harvard Common Press, 2002), we make this pâté with smoked trout. It's so good that we've branched out to use smoked salmon, catfish, and cod—just as yummy. Remove any remaining skin or bones from 1 cup flaked smoked fish fillet (about 4 ounces) and place in a food processor. Add 1/2 cup (1 stick) softened unsalted butter, 1 tablespoon chopped fresh dill, and 1 teaspoon grated lemon zest and process until smooth. Serve the pâté in a crock, garnished with more chopped fresh dill and surrounded with sesame crackers or slices of French or pumpernickel bread. **MAKES ABOUT 2/3 CUP**

Planked Fish or Shellfish

Planked fish or shellfish is one of the easiest, most foolproof ways you can grill seafood. It won't fall through the grill grate, you don't have to turn it, and if you undercook it, you can always zap it in the microwave for a few seconds.

The **BBQ Queens** plank using a dual-heat fire, meaning that one side of the grill is hot and the other side medium. You put a presoaked plank with the food arranged on it over medium heat, close the grill lid, and cook. (For more information on planking, see Planking 101 on page 42.) Just make sure you have a spray bottle of water handy in case you have a flare-up.

Purchase skinless fish for planking. You want the flesh to touch the wood plank for maximum wood flavor. When you're planking, as in grilling, the thickness of the fish (measured at the thickest part) usually determines the timing. Meaty fish such as tuna and shark, as well as shellfish, will take less time than other fish. For example, a $^1/_2$-inch-thick fish fillet or steak will take 10 to 12 minutes to cook all the way through on a plank. A $^3/_4$-inch-thick fillet or steak will take 12 to 15 minutes. Large shrimp, however, will take only 6 to 8 minutes to cook. We like our halibut and salmon steaks planked until cooked through, but if you like yours served more underdone, adjust the timing. To test whether your fish is done, carefully use the tines of a fork to see whether the fish is beginning to flake in the center but still looks moist. Shellfish should be opaque all the way through. **SERVES 4**

> **One 15 x 6$^1/_2$ x $^3/_8$-inch plank, soaked in water for at least 1 hour before grilling**
> **1 salmon fillet, about $^3/_4$ inch thick, skin removed**
> **Mustard-Mayo-Dill Slather (page 66)**

1. Prepare a dual-heat fire, with a hot fire on one side and a medium fire on the other.

2. Compare the length of the plank with the length of the salmon fillet and trim the salmon to fit the plank, if necessary. Place the salmon on a baking sheet and spread the flesh side with the mustard slather. Bring outside.

3. Place the plank on the grill grate over the hot fire until it begins to char and pop. Turn the plank over and move to the medium-heat side. Carefully place the salmon slather side up on the charred side of the plank. Cover the grill and cook until the fish begins to flake when tested with a fork in the thickest part, 12 to 15 minutes.

 Crowning Glories

Adorn and serve this with:

Chopped fresh herbs

Finely chopped green onions, bell peppers, and tomatoes

Grilled Asparagus (page 117)

Oak-Planked Peppercorn Tuna Steaks with Orange Mayonnaise:

Served on a bed of couscous, this dish is lusciously flavorful, retaining the wonderful texture and taste of fresh tuna. We like our tuna served medium, so if you like yours more rare or more well done, adjust the time on the grill. The mayonnaise is also delicious on other types of planked or grilled fish as well as in chicken salad. Combine $^1/_2$ cup lowfat mayonnaise, $^1/_4$ cup fresh orange juice (1 to 2 oranges), and 1 teaspoon grated orange zest in a bowl. Cover and refrigerate until ready to serve. Place four 4- to 6-ounce tuna steaks cut about $^3/_4$ inch thick on a baking sheet. Lightly spray or brush with olive oil and season with coarse kosher or sea salt to taste. Firmly press 2 tablespoons crushed multicolored peppercorn blend (pink, green, black, and white peppercorns) into the steaks and bring outside. Prepare an oak plank as directed above. Place the steaks on the prepared plank, cover the grill, and cook for about 10 minutes for medium. To serve, place a dollop of the orange mayonnaise on each steak. **SERVES 4**

Cedar-Planked Shrimp Chimichurri:

This is a delicious way to serve shrimp (or scallops) on a plank. Make 1 recipe Chimichurri Sauce (page 346). Place 1 pound peeled and deveined large shrimp in a sealable plastic bag and drizzle with half the sauce. Seal the bag and marinate in the refrigerator for 30 minutes. Bring the shrimp outside. Prepare a cedar plank as directed above. Place the shrimp in a single layer on the prepared plank. Cover the grill and cook until the shrimp are opaque all the way through, 6 to 8 minutes. To serve, drizzle with some of the reserved sauce and pass the rest at the table. **SERVES 4**

▰▰▰▰▰

Salads provide another counterpoint of flavor for a meal from the grill or smoker. Sometimes gently flavored and almost insubstantial, sometimes savory and filling, salads round out a meal with their crunchy fresh texture and great color. For the best flavor, use ingredients in season.

Mediterranean Salad with Lemon-Sumac Vinaigrette

This light, refreshing salad is perfect for the hottest days of summer. Sumac is a dark red powder made from dried sumac berries. In the Midwest, cones of staghorn sumac ripen in late summer and fall and were used by fur traders to make a sour, citrusy drink. Middle Eastern sumac is used as a spice and in blends such as za'atar (combined with sesame, salt, and dried thyme). Sumac is available online from better spice emporiums, such as Penzeys Spices (see Resource Guide, page 446). We love this salad with rotisserie, grilled, or smoked chicken, or with burgers or grilled flatbread. **SERVES 4**

SALAD

2 cups torn romaine lettuce leaves

1/2 cucumber, peeled, seeded, and chopped

1 large ripe beefsteak tomato, chopped

4 green onions

Leaves from 1 bunch fresh mint, coarsely chopped

Leaves from 1 bunch fresh Italian parsley, coarsely chopped

LEMON-SUMAC VINAIGRETTE

1 clove garlic, minced

1/2 teaspoon fine sea salt

Juice of 1/2 lemon

1/4 cup olive oil

1/2 teaspoon ground sumac

1. To make the salad, place all the ingredients in a large salad bowl.

2. To make the vinaigrette, whisk together the garlic, salt, and lemon juice in a small bowl. Drizzle in the olive oil, whisking to blend, then sprinkle in the sumac and whisk again. Pour over the salad, toss, and serve immediately.

Moroccan Orange, Fennel, and Olive Salad

Sweet fennel, tangy oranges, and pungent black olives combine for an impressive salad that will wow guests in any season. We love this paired with grilled, rotisserie, or smoked lamb, chicken, or shellfish. **SERVES 4**

SALAD

2 small fennel bulbs, tops trimmed and bulbs thinly sliced crosswise

2 oranges, peeled and sectioned

24 oil- or brine-cured Niçoise or Kalamata olives, pitted

¹/₂ cup thin, bitter salad greens, such as mizuna or frisée

1 tablespoon snipped fresh chives

ORANGE-FENNEL VINAIGRETTE

¹/₄ cup extra virgin olive oil

Juice of 1 orange

1 tablespoon minced shallot

¹/₂ teaspoon fennel seeds, toasted in a dry skillet over medium heat until fragrant, then ground

1. To make the salad, combine all the ingredients in a large salad bowl.

2. To make the vinaigrette, whisk together all the ingredients in a small bowl. Pour over the salad, toss to blend, and serve immediately.

Kath's Cucumbers

Karen's mother-in-law, Katherine Abernathy, taught her to make these favorite cucumbers for Karen's husband, Dick. Karen likes to jazz them up a bit with minced garlic and dill, but Dick prefers them plain. He doesn't mind if a red onion is used once in a while, though. Karen likes the red onion because it turns the mixture a pretty pale pink. Substitute a can of drained sliced beets for the cucumber, and you have pickled beets. A big plus to these pickled salads is that they keep refrigerated for several days. **SERVES 12**

1 medium-size cucumber, peeled or unpeeled

1 medium-size onion

$1/2$ cup distilled white vinegar

$1^{1}/2$ cups water

6 tablespoons sugar

2 tablespoons salt

1 or 2 cloves garlic (optional), minced

1 teaspoon chopped fresh dill (optional)

Slice the cucumber $1/8$ inch thick. Peel and slice the onion $1/8$ inch thick. In a large glass jar with a tight-fitting lid, alternate slices of cucumber and onion until they reach the top of the jar. Pour in the vinegar, close the lid, and shake to coat. Add the remaining ingredients, close, and gently shake to dissolve the salt and sugar. Taste and adjust the seasoning so that the brine is sweet and sour. This is best made a day ahead and refrigerated to let the flavors develop. It will keep in the refrigerator for up to 2 weeks.

Elaborate Yet Easy Cucumbers in Poppy Seed Dressing

Take the easy way out and buy bottled poppy seed dressing, if you like. We especially enjoy brands made with Vidalia onion. **SERVES 4**

1 cucumber, thinly sliced

¼ cup dried apricots, chopped

¼ cup walnut or pistachio halves, toasted in a 350°F oven until lightly browned, about 15 minutes

2 tablespoons snipped fresh chives

½ cup bottled Vidalia onion–poppy seed dressing

In a large bowl, combine all the ingredients. Serve immediately, or cover and keep refrigerated for up to 1 week.

Cauliflower, Roasted Red Pepper, and Cured Olive Salad

Make this salad early in the day to let the flavors blend. It is colorful and portable, perfect for a bring-a-dish dinner. **SERVES 6 TO 8**

1 large head cauliflower, cut into florets

⅓ cup olive oil

2 cloves garlic, minced

2 teaspoons balsamic vinegar

8 anchovy fillets, chopped

1½ cups pitted oil- or brine-cured olives, drained

1½ cups roasted red peppers (from a jar), drained

¼ cup pine nuts, toasted in a dry skillet over medium heat until golden

2 to 3 teaspoons chopped fresh herbs, such as oregano, thyme, and/or chives

Sea salt and freshly ground black pepper to taste

1. Prepare a large pot of boiling water. Add the cauliflower and blanch for 3 minutes. Drain in a colander.

2.   In a large bowl, whisk together the olive oil, garlic, vinegar, and anchovies. Add the remaining ingredients, including the cauliflower, and toss to blend. Let sit at room temperature for several hours before serving, or refrigerate for up to 1 week.

Hearts of Palm Salad

This is another excellent warm-weather salad that is quick to assemble and can stand at room temperature without any ill effects. Present it in a lovely crystal serving bowl.
SERVES 6

One 14-ounce can hearts of palm, drained and cut into 1-inch pieces
2 cups cherry or grape tomatoes, some cut in half
1/3 cup extra virgin olive oil
3 tablespoons white wine vinegar
1 clove garlic, minced
1/2 teaspoon fine sea salt
1 teaspoon chopped fresh herbs, such as basil, thyme, chives, and/or tarragon
3 tablespoons freshly grated Romano cheese
Freshly ground black pepper to taste

1.   In a medium-size serving bowl, combine the hearts of palm and tomatoes.

2.   In a jar with a tight-fitting lid, combine the olive oil, vinegar, garlic, salt, and herbs and shake vigorously to blend. Pour over the hearts of palm and tomatoes and toss. Sprinkle with the cheese and season with pepper. Serve immediately, let sit at room temperature for several hours before serving, or refrigerate overnight.

Italian Bean Salad

Bean salads can be made several days ahead and kept refrigerated until ready to serve. They can withstand the summer heat on a buffet table, too. SERVES 12

- **1 cup chopped red onion**
- **1 cup seeded and chopped red, green, or yellow bell pepper**
- **One 15-ounce can garbanzo beans, drained and rinsed**
- **Two 15-ounce cans cannellini beans, drained and rinsed**
- **¼ cup red wine vinegar**
- **¼ cup extra virgin olive oil**
- **1 teaspoon freshly ground black pepper**
- **½ teaspoon kosher salt**

In a medium-size serving bowl, combine the onion, bell pepper, and both beans. In a jar with a tight-fitting lid, combine the vinegar, olive oil, pepper, and salt and shake vigorously to blend. Pour over the salad and toss to coat evenly. Serve immediately, or refrigerate for up to 1 week.

Smoked Whole Fish

9 f you have a fisherman in your family, you've heard all the stories about the one that got away. But every so often, you think that *none* got away. You have a glut of fresh fish and don't know what to do.

Why not try smoking a whole fish? You'll end up with a moist, succulent, tender fish with the haunting aroma of wood smoke. Our favorite whole fish to smoke are freshwater trout and ocean fish such as mackerel. Obviously, you'll want a fish that will fit in your grill or smoker, usually in the 3- to 4-pound range.

If you're buying a whole fish, the of freshness is in the eyes—of the beholder and the fish. If the fish's eyes look cloudy, as if they have cataracts, the fish is old and will not taste great. The eyes should be clear and brilliant. A whole fish bought at the store will already be cleaned and scaled for you.

Smoking a whole fish takes 1 to 1½ hours. And because the fish is subjected to the heat for a longer time than fillets or steaks, a basting sauce is a good idea to help keep it moist. Apple juice, apple cider, or a mixture of dry white wine, lemon juice, and melted butter makes for an easy sauce. Remember, the more fish you place in the smoker, the longer it will take to smoke. Serve portions right from the whole fish. A whole smoked fish will keep, tightly covered, in the refrigerator for up to 2 weeks or in the freezer for up to 3 months. **SERVES 4 TO 6**

SUGGESTED WOOD: Apple, cherry, hickory, oak, or pecan

One 3- to 4-pound whole fish, cleaned and scaled

6 sprigs fresh herbs, such as tarragon, dill, chives, and/or Italian parsley

6 thin lemon slices

½ cup dry white wine

¼ cup (½ stick) unsalted butter, melted

¼ cup fresh lemon juice (about 2 lemons)

Coarse kosher or sea salt and freshly ground black pepper to taste

1. Prepare an indirect fire in a smoker.

2. In the cavity of the fish, place the herb sprigs and lemon slices. In a disposable aluminum pan, combine the wine, butter, and lemon juice. Place the fish in the pan and spoon some of the basting liquid over it. Sprinkle with salt and pepper. Place the pan in the smoker, close the lid, and smoke at 225 to 250°F until the fish is opaque and the flesh is just beginning to flake when you test it with a fork, 1½ to 2 hours. Serve hot.

Crowning Glories

Serve your fish up with:

Moroccan Orange, Fennel, and Olive Salad *(page 280)*

Smoked Chile Beurre Blanc *(page 99)*

Roasted Red Pepper Aioli *(page 110)*

Happy, Happy, Happy Hour Salmon: Martini lovers will have most of these ingredients on hand. This recipe is adapted from Karen's *Best Little Barbecue Cookbook* (Celestial Arts, 2000). Serve it with a spring herb risotto and Grilled Asparagus (page 117). In a small saucepan, combine ¼ cup gin or vodka, ¼ cup dry vermouth, ¼ cup fresh lemon juice (about 2 lemons), 3 tablespoons melted unsalted butter, 1 tablespoon prepared horse-radish, ½ teaspoon hot pepper sauce, 1 minced garlic clove, and 2 tablespoons juniper berries. Bring to a boil, then remove from the heat and set aside. Rinse one scaled and cleaned 3- to 4-pound whole salmon and pat dry with paper towels. Place on top of a sheet of heavy-duty aluminum foil large enough to hold the fish. Place 1 sliced lemon and 6 sprigs fresh dill in the cavity of the fish. Crimp 3 sides of the foil to hold in the basting sauce (the fourth side will fold over). Pour the sauce over the salmon, fold the foil over the fish, and crimp the edges together. Place on the grill or smoker rack, close, and smoke as directed above for 1 hour. Open the packet, but make sure the edges stay crimped to hold in the baste. Continue to smoke until the fish is opaque and begins to flake when tested with a fork, about 1 hour more. Serve hot. **SERVES 4 TO 6**

Happy, Happy, Happy Hour Salmon Spread: If you have leftover smoked salmon, turn it into this luscious cocktail spread. In a medium-size bowl, combine 1 cup smoked salmon pieces with one 8-ounce package softened cream cheese, 1 minced garlic clove, ½ tea-spoon hot pepper sauce, 1 teaspoon dillweed, and 2 tablespoons fresh lemon juice (or to taste). Season with fine kosher or sea salt and freshly ground black pepper to taste. Serve with cocktail crackers, small slices of pumpernickel bread, or toasted rounds of French bread. **MAKES ABOUT 2 CUPS**

Apple Cider–Smoked Trout with Horseradish Cream: We love this recipe from our fish book so much, we've adapted it here. Taking the skin off the trout first allows the smoke to penetrate the fish more easily. Just about any fish can be smoked this way. Have ready 1 quart apple cider. Bring a large pot of water to a boil. Using tongs, dip four 14- to 16-ounce cleaned whole trout, one at a time, into the boiling water for 20 to 30 seconds. Remove from the pot and peel off the skin. Brush each trout with ½ cup of the cider, sprinkle with BBQ Queens' All-Purpose Rub (page 49), and place cut side down and splayed open in a disposable aluminum pan. Fill the water pan in your smoker with the remaining apple cider. Place the trout in the smoker, cover, and smoke as directed above until the fish begins to flake when tested with a fork, 1½ to 2 hours. While the trout is smoking, make the horseradish cream by blending together ¾ cup sour cream, 3 tablespoons prepared horseradish, and 3 tablespoons chopped fresh Italian parsley in a small bowl. Season with fine kosher or sea salt and freshly ground black pepper to taste. Serve the trout hot or cold, with a dollop of the cream. **SERVES 4**

Grilled Oysters, Clams, or Mussels in the Shell

Oysters of all kinds, littleneck clams, and mussels are absolutely delicious cooked on the grill, and they look very impressive. Scrub them first under cold running water, then all you have to do is grill them on a perforated grill rack over a hot fire.

You really don't have to worry about overcooking shellfish in the shell, because the shells pop open when they're done. What you do have to worry about is making sure you don't cook any mollusk with a cracked shell or one that is already partially open. Also, any mollusk that doesn't open on the grill should be discarded. **SERVES 4**

36 oysters, littleneck clams, or mussels in the shell

Melted unsalted butter

Fine kosher or sea salt and freshly ground pepper to taste

1. Scrub the oysters under cold running water and discard any that do not close to the touch or have broken shells. Place on an oiled perforated grill rack.

2. Prepare a hot fire in a grill.

3. Place the grill rack over direct heat and close the lid. Grill for 6 to 8 minutes, using grill tongs to remove the mollusks as they pop open and taking care not to spill the juices out of the shells. Transfer to a big bowl and keep warm until ready to serve.

4. To eat, pry each oyster off the shell, dip in melted butter, and season with salt and pepper.

Italian-Style Grilled Lobster

Send someone to the fish market and have someone else fire up the grill. When your lobsters (which you will have had the fishmonger cut in half) arrive, you're ready to grill. Brush both halves of each lobster with olive oil and grill, flesh side down, for 3 to 4 minutes, until you see grill marks. Turn with grill tongs to cook on the shell side until the flesh is opaque all the way through. Serve hot, in the shell, with a drizzle of extra virgin olive oil, a squeeze of fresh lemon juice, and a sprinkling of chopped fresh Italian parsley.

Crowning Glories

Serve these babies with:

Cocktail sauce

Amogio (page 72)

Vietnamese Drizzle (page 87)

Grilled Oysters in Pesto: Now that we're not limited to months with an *r* in them to eat oysters (an old adage), you can grill your favorite oysters and top them with pesto made from fresh summer basil. Enjoy these in their shells as an appetizer or removed from their shells and tossed with hot pasta for a fragrantly delicious main course. This recipe makes more pesto than you really need for the oysters, unless you want to toss them with pasta, but we believe you can never have too much pesto on hand! Cover and refrigerate any leftovers. Grill 36 oysters on the half shell as directed above, spooning about 1 teaspoon prepared pesto over each oyster before they go on the grill. Cook for 3 to 5 minutes, until the pesto is bubbling and the edges of the oysters have begun to curl. Serve hot. **SERVES 4**

Grilled Littleneck Clams with Pernod Butter: Figure 6 to 8 of these small clams per person, says Grill Gal Lisa Mayer (see page 292), then always add an extra dozen or two. There are never any leftovers! To make the Pernod butter, melt 1/2 cup (1 stick) unsalted butter in a small saucepan over medium heat. Remove from the heat and stir in 2 tablespoons Pernod or other anise-flavored liqueur and 3 tablespoons chopped fresh tarragon. Set aside. Grill the clams as directed above and serve on a platter with little cups of the Pernod butter on the side for dipping. **SERVES 4**

Black Fettuccine with Grilled Mussels, Garlic, and Parsley: Black fettuccine is colored with squid ink and makes a dramatic presentation with grilled mussels. Even if you use regular fettuccine, however, the delicate flavors of the grilled mussels and dry white wine make this a singular pasta dish to serve guests. We adapted this recipe from our book *Fish & Shellfish, Grilled & Smoked* (The Harvard Common Press, 2002). Grill 3 pounds mussels as directed above over a hot fire in a grill wok or perforated grill rack using mesquite or hickory wood chips soaked in water for at least 30 minutes before grilling. Set aside to let cool slightly. Meanwhile, cook 1 pound black or regular fettuccine according to the package directions until *al dente*. Drain (reserving $1/4$ cup of the cooking water), return to the pot, toss with 2 tablespoons olive oil, and cover to keep warm. Heat 3 tablespoons olive oil in a medium-size saucepan. Add 1 minced garlic clove and cook, stirring, until golden, 2 to 3 minutes. Pour in $1/4$ cup dry white wine and the reserved pasta cooking water and bring to a boil. Reduce the heat to a simmer and stir in 2 tablespoons chopped fresh Italian parsley. When the mussels are cool enough to handle, remove them from their shells using a paring knife. Add the mussels to the olive oil and wine sauce and stir to combine. Season with fine kosher or sea salt and freshly ground black pepper to taste. Transfer the warm pasta to a large serving bowl. Pour the mussels and sauce over the hot pasta, toss to coat, and serve immediately. **SERVES 4**

Grilled Shrimp, Scallops, or Squid

e hate to admit it, but Karen and Judith remember watching *Queen for a Day* on daytime television during the 1950s. The woman with the best hard-luck story became Queen for a Day, complete with crown, cape, scepter, and lots of prizes.

You don't have to have a hard-luck story to be Queen for a Day at your house. You just have to serve one of these delicious grilled shellfish dishes for ample praise. Choose from shrimp of all sizes (from medium-size to those huge Alaskan spot prawns), large sea scallops, and squid (also called calamari). The trick is not to overcook them, or the texture will be rubbery. (If necessary, pop not-quite-done shellfish in the microwave for 30 seconds on high to finish cooking.) Use a hot fire and a perforated grill rack to cook the fish.

Size does matter when it comes to timing. Smaller shrimp and thin-bodied squid will cook in 2 to 3 minutes total, turning once. Large, meaty sea scallops (the smaller bay scallops are too small for the grill, unless you want to toss them in a grill wok) and Alaskan spot prawns will take about 6 minutes. We prefer to grill shellfish more on one side than the other. For example, grill large sea scallops for 4 minutes on one side, then grill on the other side for 1 to 2 minutes. This technique results in a top "crust" and a softer bottom. **SERVES 4**

1 pound any size shrimp, peeled and deveined, large sea scallops, or cleaned squid (about 12 bodies and 12 tentacles)

Olive oil

Fine kosher or sea salt and freshly ground black pepper to taste

1. Brush or spray the shellfish with olive oil and season with salt and pepper.

2. Prepare a hot fire in a grill.

3. Place the shellfish on a perforated grill rack and grill, turning once, until opaque but still translucent in the center. Smaller shrimp and squid will take about 2 minutes, sea scallops and large prawns about 6 minutes. Serve hot.

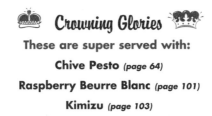

Crowning Glories

These are super served with:

Chive Pesto (page 64)

Raspberry Beurre Blanc (page 101)

Kimizu (page 103)

Grilled Shrimp or Scallops in Thai Green Curry Sauce: Pink shrimp or ivory scallops nestled in a pale green and aromatic sauce is a dish worthy of the finest cubic zirconia tiara. Before grilling, whisk together 3 tablespoons green curry paste and one 11-ounce can unsweetened coconut milk (open the can first and stir the milk with a fork to blend) in a medium-size saucepan. Bring to a boil and cook for 1 minute. Stir in $1/2$ cup finely chopped green onions, 3 kaffir lime leaves (very fragrant green leaves available at Asian markets and better grocery stores; you can freeze them and use frozen) or $1/2$ teaspoon grated lime zest, 1 tablespoon Asian fish sauce, and 1 tablespoon packed light brown sugar. Bring to a boil again and cook for 2 minutes. Keep warm while you grill the shellfish (see above). To serve, ladle the sauce onto individual plates, place the grilled shellfish on top, and garnish with chopped fresh basil and cilantro. **SERVES 4**

Grilled Shrimp with Nuevo Latino Cocktail Sauce: Turn on the CD player and let the Latin music carry you south of the border. Go for hot and spicy! Include some sipping treats, such as Mojitos, Sangria! (page 250), margaritas, or Mexican beer; serve the shrimp in margarita glasses; and everything will be party perfect. In a large bowl, combine $1/2$ cup prepared chili sauce, $1/2$ cup chunky salsa, $1/4$ cup fresh lime juice (4 to 5 limes), $1/4$ cup chopped fresh cilantro, $1/2$ teaspoon hot pepper sauce, and 1 minced garlic clove and mix well. Add about 1 pound grilled shrimp (see above) roughly chopped into bite-size pieces.

(Reserve 6 whole shrimp before chopping.) Place ¼ cup shredded lettuce in the bottom of each of 6 margarita glasses. Divide the shrimp mixture evenly among the glasses. Garnish each glass with a lime wedge, cilantro sprig, and 1 whole shrimp. Serve warm or chilled. **SERVES 6**

Grilled Scallops with Fennel, Red Pepper, and Lemon-Tarragon Vinaigrette: With this

dish's eye-popping presentation and flavor, you won't believe how easy it is to make. We got the original idea from California chef John Ash and took it from there. Trim, quarter, and core 1 large fennel bulb, then slice ¼ inch thick. Prepare a large red bell pepper for grilling, slicing it into strips (see Grilled Peppers, page 142). Brush or spray 12 large sea scallops with olive oil. Grill the fennel and red pepper on a perforated grill rack over a hot fire, turning once, until marked on both sides and tender, about 10 minutes. Transfer to a platter. Grill the scallops as directed above. To serve, divide the fennel slices and pepper strips among 4 plates, place 3 scallops on each plate, and drizzle with Lemon-Tarragon Vinaigrette (page 75). Garnish with fresh tarragon sprigs and serve immediately. **SERVES 4**

Grilled Stuffed Calamari with Thousand-Herb Sauce: If you've had calamari only deep-

fried as an appetizer, you're long overdue for a switch. Make sure your fire is really, really hot before you throw these babies on the grill. Place 1 pound cleaned calamari (about 12 bodies and 12 tentacles) in a medium-size bowl. Add ¼ cup olive oil, ¼ teaspoon red pepper flakes, 1 minced garlic clove, and fine kosher or sea salt and freshly ground black pepper to taste and toss to coat. Cover and marinate in the refrigerator for 30 minutes. In a small bowl, combine ½ cup fresh bread crumbs, 2 tablespoons extra virgin olive oil, the grated zest of 1 lemon, 1 tablespoon coarsely chopped fresh Italian parsley, and ¼ teaspoon red pepper flakes until well blended. Remove the calamari from the marinade. Stuff each calamari with 2 teaspoons of the bread crumb mixture. Season the bodies and tentacles with salt and pepper and grill on a perforated grill rack over a really hot fire for 1 to 2 minutes per side. Serve with Thousand-Herb Sauce (page 192). **SERVES 6**

Grill Gals

She Spends Summers Off at the Jersey Shore Menu

Grilled Prosciutto and Basil–Wrapped Shrimp with Garlic Dipping Sauce
Grilled Bruschetta with Jersey Tomatoes
Grilled Lobster
Blueberry-Peach Tart with Macaroon Crust

Karen's barbecue buddy Lisa Readie Mayer grew up on the New Jersey shore and loves nothing more than spending summer evenings at the beach barbecuing with her family. Lisa is a freelance writer who writes about grills and other outdoor living products. Sometimes her vocation also becomes her avocation, as in this seashore feast.

This end-of-summer dinner party is an annual event at the Mayer house, with husband David and daughters Emily and Hannah pitching in to help. The exact menu varies from year to year, but it always includes foods the area is known for—seafood, Jersey tomatoes, sweet corn, peaches, and blueberries—and much of it is prepared on the grill. Lisa tries to buy whatever she can at her local farmers' market and the seafood market right near the fishing-boat docks.

"We start out with drinks and hors d'oeuvres on our deck overlooking the water," Lisa says. "Dinner is served informally, picnic table style, and we set out colorful sand pails to hold the lobster shells. Dessert is served during a break in the dancing that usually kicks up after dinner."

Grilled Prosciutto and Basil–Wrapped Shrimp with Garlic Dipping Sauce

These skewers are yummy and easy to make, even though they look very sophisticated. **SERVES 8**

24 fresh basil leaves

12 thin slices prosciutto, each cut in half lengthwise

24 extra-large shrimp, peeled and deveined, or large sea scallops

24 bamboo skewers, soaked in water for at least 30 minutes before grilling

GARLIC DIPPING SAUCE

¹/₃ cup red wine vinegar

2 tablespoons Dijon mustard

1 large clove garlic, chopped

1 cup olive oil

1. Place one basil leaf at the short end of a slice of prosciutto and a shrimp on top of the basil. Roll the shrimp in the prosciutto, then thread lengthwise onto a skewer. Repeat with the remaining basil, prosciutto, and shrimp. Place the skewers on a baking sheet and refrigerate until ready to cook.

2. To make the sauce, combine the vinegar, mustard, and garlic in a food processor or blender. With the machine running, add the olive oil in a slow, steady stream. Process until combined. Ten to 15 minutes before you are ready to grill, spoon about one-third of the sauce over the shrimp skewers to marinate. Transfer the rest of the dipping sauce to a small bowl.

3. Prepare a medium-hot fire in a grill. Grill the shrimp, turning often, until opaque, about 6 minutes.

4. Arrange the cooked skewers on a platter and serve with the dipping sauce on the side.

Grilled Bruschetta with Jersey Tomatoes

**To make grilled bruschetta toasts, slice a baguette or other peasant-style bread into
¹/₂-inch-thick slices. Toast the bread on the grill until lightly browned on each side.
Remove from the grill and lightly rub one side of each toast with a peeled garlic clove.
SERVES 8**

> **8 ripe Roma tomatoes, cut in half, seeded, and cut into small dice**
> **¹/₂ cup extra virgin olive oil**
> **¹/₂ teaspoon coarse salt, or to taste**
> **¹/₂ teaspoon freshly ground black pepper, or to taste**
> **12 fresh basil leaves (more or less to taste), torn or snipped into small pieces**
> **1 clove garlic, pressed**
> **Bruschetta toasts (see headnote)**

l.   Combine all the ingredients except the toasts in a medium-size bowl. Let stand at
room temperature for about 30 minutes to meld the flavors. Adjust the seasonings, if
necessary.

2.   To serve, place a spoonful of the tomato mixture on each toast, or serve the topping
and toasts separately and let guests help themselves.

Grilled Lobster

If you've never had lobster on the grill, now is your chance. SERVES 8

> **Eight 1¹/₄- to 1¹/₂-pound lobsters**
> **Melted unsalted butter and cocktail sauce for serving**

l.   Have the fishmonger cut the lobsters in half lengthwise and remove the vein and
sack from the head.

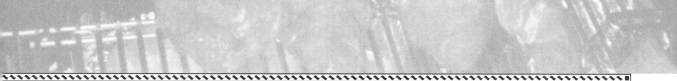

2.   Build a hot fire in a grill.

3.   Oil a perforated grill rack. Place the lobsters cut side down on the grill rack and cook for 6 to 8 minutes. Turn the lobsters over and cook until the flesh is firm and white, another 6 to 8 minutes. Serve with melted butter and cocktail sauce.

Blueberry-Peach Tart with Macaroon Crust

From the crust to the topping, every layer of this dessert is lip-smackin' good. The bonus is that it's also an easy one to put together. If you make it a day ahead, you'll have time to touch up your lipstick and give that 'do another spray before dinner.
MAKES ONE 11-INCH TART; SERVES 10

CRUST

11 soft coconut macaroon cookies (Lisa uses Archway)

1 cup ground pecans

3 tablespoons unsalted butter, melted

FILLING

$^1/_2$ cup heavy cream

One 8-ounce package cream cheese, softened

$^1/_3$ cup sugar

2 teaspoons orange juice

1 teaspoon vanilla extract

$^1/_2$ teaspoon almond extract

TOPPING

2 medium-size ripe peaches, peeled, pitted, and thinly sliced

2 tablespoons fresh lemon juice

1 pint fresh blueberries, picked over for stems

1/2 cup apricot preserves

1. Preheat the oven to 350°F.

2. To make the crust, crumble the macaroons (you should have at least 2 cups). Combine the macaroons, pecans, and melted butter in a large bowl. Press the mixture into an 11-inch tart pan with a removable bottom, pressing it into the bottom and up the sides of the pan. Bake until golden, 15 to 18 minutes. Set on a wire rack to cool.

3. To make the filling, in a chilled medium-size bowl with an electric mixer, beat the heavy cream on medium speed until soft peaks form. Set aside. In a large bowl, beat the cream cheese and sugar together on medium speed until fluffy. Add the orange juice and extracts and beat until smooth. Gently fold in the whipped cream. Spread the mixture evenly into the cooled crust, cover with plastic wrap, and refrigerate for 2 to 4 hours.

4. To make the topping, toss the peach slices with the lemon juice to prevent discoloration. Arrange the peaches and blueberries over the filling. In a small saucepan, heat the apricot preserves until just melted. Brush or spoon the glaze over the fruit. Carefully remove the sides of the pan and transfer the tart to a serving platter. Cut into slices and serve.

Stir-Grilled Shellfish

Shellfish is one of the easiest choices to stir-grill because it cooks fast and doesn't fall apart. If you want to marinate shellfish ahead of time, allow 30 minutes at most. Shrimp is probably the easiest and most widely available shellfish to begin with. We prefer to use a 15-inch grill wok for 2 pounds of shrimp so the shrimp are not crowded and will cook evenly and quickly. If you have a 12-inch grill wok, you may want to grill the shrimp in two batches. This recipe works well for scallops and squid, too, but the time may need to be adjusted slightly. SERVES 4

> 2 pounds large shrimp, peeled and deveined
> 2 to 3 tablespoons olive oil
> 2 to 3 tablespoons lemon pepper seasoning
> ¹/₂ teaspoon kosher salt

1. Place the shrimp in a large bowl. Drizzle with the olive oil, sprinkle with the lemon pepper and salt, and toss to coat.

2. Prepare a hot fire in a grill.

3. Coat a 15-inch grill wok with nonstick cooking spray. Over the sink, add the shrimp and let any excess oil drain off. Place the wok directly over the fire and stir-grill, tossing the shrimp with wooden paddles or grill spatulas until opaque and just firm to the touch, 12 to 15 minutes. Close the lid for 2 to 3 minutes to heat the shrimp all the way through, especially if the outdoor temperature is a bit cool. Serve warm, or let cool, refrigerate, and serve chilled.

Crowning Glories

Stir-grilled shellfish is delicious served over aromatic
scented rice or a thin pasta such as linguine. It is complemented
by any of the following rubs, marinades, or sauces:

Zesty Sugar and Spice Rub (page 52)
Fennel and Orange Marinade (page 72)
Smoked Garlic and Cilantro Cream Sauce (page 93)

"Wonton"-Wrapped Stir-Grilled Shellfish: Use grilled shrimp or scallops and serve as an appetizer or light supper. You'll need 1 pound stir-grilled peeled and deveined large shrimp or bay scallops, twelve 8¼-inch rice paper wrappers, 1 cup rinsed fresh bean sprouts, and 12 fresh basil leaves. Prepare each wrap by placing each rice paper wrapper in a bowl of hot water for 8 to 10 seconds, until completely wet. Lay the wrapper on a damp towel. Place 3 shrimp down the center of the wrapper. Top with sprouts and a basil leaf. Roll the wrapper tightly around the shrimp, folding the ends in. Repeat with the remaining wrappers and shrimp. Serve with Lemon-Tarragon Vinaigrette (page 75). **SERVES 4**

Grilled Squid Linguine with Amogio: Cook 1 pound linguine according to the package directions until *al dente*. Divide the pasta among 4 or 6 plates. Top each with a grilled squid (see headnote) and drizzle with 3 to 4 tablespoons Amogio (page 72). **SERVES 4 TO 6**

Stir-Grilled Scallop Po'boy Sandwiches: In a large bowl, combine 1 pound sea scallops, 2 cups cored and shredded Napa cabbage, and ¾ cup Tandoori Marinade (page 74). Let sit at room temperature for 30 minutes. Using a slotted spoon, remove the scallops and cabbage from the marinade and stir-grill as directed above. Divide the scallops and cabbage among 4 hoagie-style or ciabatta rolls. Serve extra marinade on the side. **SERVES 4**

Here's the Beef

Where's the beef? Right here in this chapter. Americans love beef on the grill, from the popular and economical hamburger to the most expensive steak. People who economize on everything else still like to dine at fancy steakhouses and pay exorbitant prices (compared to other meats) for a prime cut. Beef is primal for Americans. It's all about how our country won the West. So before you decide to throw a steak on the grill or a brisket in the smoker, you need to know how to shop for beef. Let's begin with understanding how beef is graded. The FDA puts beef into three categories—prime, choice, and select (which you rarely see).

The average grocery store usually carries a selection of choice-grade steaks and filets that are $^3/_4$ to 1 inch thick. Butcher shops, upscale grocers, and some specialty gourmet shops offer top choice and even prime (which used to be almost impossible to find) cuts. A butcher will also cut thicker steaks for you.

Steaks for grilling will be prime or choice grade. Let your eyes be your guide and select steaks with a nice, even marbling of fat throughout. The marbling should be thin white veins of fat, which make for tender, juicy, and flavorful eating.

For smoking tougher cuts of meat such as brisket and roasts, choice is often just fine because of the slow cooking time and low temperature, which are the double-barreled secrets to making these cuts of meat desirable and delicious.

It can be confusing shopping for steak, so here's a short rundown of the most popular steaks for the grill. (The same steak may have a different name in different parts of the country. We may use several names for the same steak, so bear with us.) The best and more expensive steaks include Delmonico, boneless rib-eye, Spencer, beauty, filet mignon, tenderloin, *filet de boeuf*, tournedo, Châteaubriand, T-bone, porterhouse, strip, rib, top loin, and shell. Less expensive steaks tend to be thinner and tougher cuts from the shoulder, flank, and round or butt of the cow. These steaks often have a very distinctive grain running through them. They are very flavorful grilled hot and fast to medium-rare, then thinly cut against the grain for best eating. They include shoulder, chuck, London broil, flat iron, blade, sirloin tip, steak tip, cube, minute, skirt, fajita, Philadelphia, flank, charcoal, jiffy, and hangar.

In this chapter, we also tell you how to rotisserie cook and plank beef, and there are certain cuts that take to these treatments better than others. Beef tenderloin works well for grilling, smoking, planking, skewering, and rotisserie cooking—just about anything! For the rotisserie, you want a large boneless roast, whether it's a boneless prime rib, tri-tip, whole beef tenderloin, or sirloin roast.

And, of course, we advise you how to smoke beef. The true American slow-smoked barbecue choice is brisket, but other roasts and tender cuts smoke well, too. Consider sirloin, tri-tip, blade, chuck, rump, rib, boneless rib-eye, tenderloin, standing rib, and beef ribs.

Grilled Burgers 303

Dolled-Up Caesar Burgers 304

Greek-Style Lamb
Burgers with
Cilantro-Mint Chutney 304

Fourth of July Pilgrim
Burgers with Dried
Cranberry Relish 305

Asian Tuna Burgers
with Wasabi Mayo 305

**Grilled Flank,
Skirt, Hangar, or
Other Thin Steak** 307

Bistro-Style Steak with
Red Wine–Shallot Sauce 308

Citrus-Grilled Beef Fajitas 308

Grilled Steak Marinated in
Beer, Herbs, and Morels 309

Grilled Steak Salad with
Caper Vinaigrette 309

NEW WAVE STEAK

*Branding Iron Beef
with Ancho Mayonnaise* 311

*Batayaki Beef with
Spicy Lemon-Soy Sauce* 312

*Beef Filet Salad with
Orange-Cumin Vinaigrette* 313

GRILL GALS: SHE GRILLS
EVERYTHING MENU

*Balsamic-Marinated
Vegetables on the Grill* 314

*Charcoal-Grilled
Rib-Eye Steak* 315

Grilled Boneless Steak 316

Steakhouse-Style
Filet Mignon 317

Grilled Peppercorn
Filet Mignon with
Cognac Sauce 317

Philadelphia Garlic
Rib-Eye Steak 318

Grilled Strip Steak with
Chile–Ginger–Green
Onion Sauce 318

Seduction Strip Steak with
Roquefort-Bacon Butter 318

FAVORITE STEAKHOUSE
SIDE DISHES

Classic Creamed Spinach 319

Fried Onion Slivers 320

Olive Oil Smashed Potatoes 320

*Decadent Garlic
Mashed Potatoes* 321

*Stewed and Scalloped
Tomatoes* 322

Grilled Bone-In Steak 323

Korean-Style
Bone-In Steak 323

Grilled T-Bone Steak with
Smoked Tomato and
Grilled Red Onion Relish 324

Sicilian Bistecca 324

Grilled Thick-Cut Steak 325

Black and Bleu Beef 326

Prairie-Style
Hay-Smoked Steak 326

BISTRO SIDE DISHES

*Haricots Verts Salad with
Mustard-Shallot Vinaigrette* 327

Homemade Frites 328

Celery Root Rémoulade 328

Bistro Grated Carrot Salad 329

Grilled Beef Skewers 330

Grilled Beef Skewers with
Spicy Tomato-Chile Sauce 331

Tamarind and Yogurt
Beef Kabobs with
Warm Pita Breads 331

Beef Skewers with
Quick Peanut Sauce 331

GRILL GALS: SHE GRILLS FOR A
TASTE OF HOME MENU

Kabuli Kabobs 333

*Salata (Afghani Fresh
Chopped Vegetable Salad)* 335

Grilled Beef Tenderloin 336

Grilled Tenderloin with
Sour Cream, Bacon,
and Mushroom Sauce 337

Chez Panisse–Style
Grilled Beef Tenderloin 337

Smoked Beef Tenderloin 338

Peppery Smoked
Beef Tenderloin 339

Smoked Porcini
Beef Tenderloin 339

Smoked Beef BLT 339

GRILL GALS: THIS 'QUE QUEEN IS A
KANSAS CITY GRILL QUEEN MENU

*Grilled Herbed and Spiced
Beef Tenderloin Salad* 341

*Grilled Herbed and Spiced
Beef Tenderloin* 342

*Grilled Turkey Roulade
with Lemon-Basil Sauce* 343

Kathy's Chicken Wings 344

Smoky Meatballs 345

Planked Beef Tenderloin 346

Argentinean Hickory-Planked
Beef Tenderloin with
Chimichurri Sauce 346

Gorgonzola Filet Mignon
on a Plank 347

Slathered Beef Filet
on a Plank 347

Rotisserie Beef Roast 347

Uptown Rotisserie
Beef Roast with
Peppercorn Beurre Blanc 348

Downtown Rotisserie Beef
Roast with BBQ Queens'
Barbecued Beans   348

Lemon Pepper Beef Roast
with Butter Baste   348

Rotisserie Boneless
Prime Rib Roast with
Blackened Seasoning   349

Smoked Beef Rib Roast   349

Smoked Rib Roast with
Yorkshire Pudding   350

Rosemary Pesto
Smoked Rib Roast   350

Smoked Rib Roast
Sandwiches   350

**BBQ BABES: SHE'S A TIARA-TOTIN'
TEXAS QUEEN OF THE 'QUE MENU**

*Slow-Smoked
Texas-Style Brisket*   353

*Mozzarella and Tomato
Salad with Two Dressings*   354

Smoked Brisket   356

Kansas City–Style
Barbecued Brisket   357

Two-Step Shortcut
Barbecued Brisket   358

Barbecued Brisket Dip   358

Burnt Ends   358

Burnt Ends Sandwich   358

**AND NOW FOR SOMETHING
COMPLETELY DIFFERENT**
*Barbecued Corned Beef with
Mustard-Beer Slather and
Smoked Potato Salad*   359

Rustic Reuben   360

Grilled Burgers

To grill an outstanding burger, you *could* follow the meticulous directions in *Cook's Illustrated* magazine, down to patting the burgers so there is an infinitesimal depression in the middle and a corresponding thickness of a few millimeters around the perimeter. As BBQ Queens, we try to limit the use of calipers in cooking. Our mantra is "Keep it simple first, then jazz it up later."

Whether your burger is made from ground beef, turkey, chicken, pork, lamb, fish, or vegetables, make sure it is moist. With beef, you don't want to use lean ground round, or you will get a shoe-leather burger. We like ground chuck with about an 80-to-20 ratio of lean to fat; even 75 to 25 is fine. For turkey, chicken, or tuna, you will be adding ingredients to the ground meat, as you would for a meat loaf. Those extra ingredients will help keep the meat moist.

Don't work the ground meat too much. Gently pat the mixture into a burger, then leave it alone. If you work a burger for more than a minute, that's too long. Just gather the meat together and press it firmly into a burger shape. Ideally, that's about 5 inches in diameter and 1 1/2 to 2 inches high. You need a burger diameter that will fit on your bread or bun, and you want a burger thick enough to stay juicy. As some people have been known to say, this isn't rocket science.

As usual, we prefer a hot fire. Let the burgers cook without turning for 3 to 4 minutes, then turn and cook on the other side. This gives a nice char to the exterior. If you want a more well-done burger, after it has grilled on both sides, move it to a cooler part of the grill (on a raised shelf or on the perimeter) to cook longer. We like to cook extra (rare) burgers for leftovers, then reheat them for lunch the next day.

If you like, brush the cut surfaces of accompanying hamburger buns with melted butter or olive oil and place them cut sides down on the grill grate for about 1 minute, until you have grill marks. Then serve them with the burgers. **SERVES 4**

> **1 pound ground chuck or other ground meat**
> **Fine kosher or sea salt and freshly ground black pepper to taste**
> **Hamburger buns and condiments of your choice**

1. Prepare a hot fire in a grill, with mesquite for a kiss of smoke (see page 13), if you like.

2. Form the ground meat into four 5-inch-diameter burgers, 1 1/2 to 2 inches thick. Grill the burgers for 3 to 4 minutes per side, turning once, for medium-rare. Serve with grilled or plain buns and condiments.

Instead of ketchup and the usual fixin's, try topping your burger with:

Aioli (pages 104–105 and 110)

Simply Delicious Bordelaise Sauce (page 91)

Mustard-Mayo Slather (page 66)

Dolled-Up Caesar Burgers:
These are very similar to what they serve up at the Split T in Oklahoma City. In this part of the country, people prefer their hamburgers "dolled up." We can relate. The Caesar-style dressing has raw egg yolk, so use egg substitute if that is a concern. In a bowl, combine 1 minced garlic clove, 2 to 3 shredded romaine lettuce leaves, 1/2 cup mayonnaise, 1/4 cup freshly grated Parmesan cheese, 1 large egg yolk, 2 tablespoons olive oil, 1/2 teaspoon freshly ground black pepper, and 1 mashed anchovy fillet. Spread on top of each grilled hamburger and serve. **SERVES 4**

Greek-Style Lamb Burgers with Cilantro-Mint Chutney:
You can make burgers from just about any ground meat or fish, but these lamb burgers are really something special. We adapted this recipe from one by Grill Guy Robert Chirico of Greenfield, Massachusetts. The burgers taste very fresh, and the mixture of sirloin and lamb makes for a more economical and milder-tasting blend. Serve them on grilled pita breads, with lettuce leaves and slices of fresh tomato and red onion. The chutney is also delicious with grilled fish or chicken, lamb chops, or kabobs. A little blob of Tzatziki (page 112) on each burger would not go amiss. To make the chutney, combine 1/2 cup plain yogurt, 2 tablespoons finely chopped green onions, 1/4 cup seeded and chopped jalapeños, 1 1/2 tablespoons grated fresh ginger (if using a microplane, you don't need to peel), 3/4 cup chopped fresh cilantro, 1/3 cup fresh mint leaves, 2 minced large garlic cloves, 1/2 teaspoon fine kosher or sea salt, and 1/4 teaspoon sugar in a blender or food processor and blend thoroughly. Cover and refrigerate for at least several hours or up to 24 hours. To make the burgers, combine 1 pound ground sirloin; 1 pound lean ground lamb; 1/2 cup crumbled feta cheese (about 2 ounces); 1/3 cup pitted, drained, and minced oil-cured Kalamata or Niçoise olives; and 1 teaspoon fine kosher or sea salt in a large bowl and mix lightly but thoroughly. Form into 6 patties (each large enough to fit inside a pita bread), handling the meat mixture as little as possible. Brush the patties with 1/4 cup olive oil, then sprinkle with a mixture of 1 teaspoon each ground cumin and ground coriander. Grill as directed above over a medium-hot fire, about 4 minutes per side for medium-rare. During the last few minutes of cooking, place 6 pita breads on the outer edge of the grill and turn to

toast lightly on both sides. Place a patty inside a pita bread pocket, spoon some chutney on top, and serve. **SERVES 6**

Fourth of July Pilgrim Burgers with Dried Cranberry Relish:
You've heard of fusion food, a tasty combination of two different culinary traditions. Well, this is fusion holiday food. Take turkey, cranberries, and Pilgrims from Thanksgiving and dude them up for Fourth of July. Why not? Grill these turkey burgers over medium-high heat so they stay moist. In a large bowl, combine 1^1/$_2$ pounds ground turkey, ^{1}/$_2$ cup seasoned dry bread crumbs, ^{1}/$_2$ cup finely diced onion, 2 minced garlic cloves, 1 teaspoon fine kosher or sea salt, and ^{1}/$_2$ teaspoon ground white pepper. Gently form into four 1-inch-thick burgers. Prepare a medium-hot fire and cook the burgers for 7 to 8 minutes on each side. Serve with mayonnaise, Dried Cranberry Relish (page 175), and lettuce leaves on toasted buns. **SERVES 4**

Asian Tuna Burgers with Wasabi Mayo:
Fellow Harvard Common Press coauthors Jane Murphy and Liz Yeh Singh are the Burger Queens. In *The Great Big Burger Book* (2003), they offer a huge range of burgers, from ground meats to steak sandwiches, with some delicious vegetarian options as well. We love this recipe, which can be made using salmon, shrimp, catfish, tilapia, poultry, beef, pork—you get the picture. We also like to use a fish or meat fillet marinated in mayonnaise. To make the wasabi mayo, combine ^{1}/$_4$ cup plus 2 tablespoons mayonnaise, 3 tablespoons minced green onions, 2 teaspoons grated fresh ginger (if using a microplane, you don't need to peel), 2 teaspoons soy sauce, and 1 teaspoon wasabi paste or powder (available at Asian markets) in a food processor until smooth. Taste and adjust the seasonings. (This will keep, tightly covered, in the refrigerator for up to 1 week.) Cut one ^{3}/$_4$-pound tuna steak into ^{1}/$_4$-inch dice and mince another ^{3}/$_4$-pound tuna steak. Combine the tuna, 2 minced garlic cloves, 2 teaspoons grated fresh ginger, 1 tablespoon toasted sesame oil, 3 tablespoons soy sauce, ^{1}/$_4$ cup chopped green onions, ^{1}/$_2$ teaspoon salt, and ^{1}/$_4$ teaspoon freshly ground black pepper in a large bowl. Form into six 1-inch-thick patties. Grill the burgers over a medium-hot fire until browned on both sides and to the desired degree of doneness (the middle can still be reddish pink), 5 to 7 minutes total. Serve on toasted sesame seed buns and top with the mayo. **SERVES 6**

The BBQ Queens' Burger Condiment Bar

Along with assorted breads and rolls, provide a royal feast of favorites for your next grilled burger bash.

Assorted cheese slices, crumbles, or smoked cheese (see pages 36 and 169–175)

Assorted greens

Crisp-cooked bacon

Sliced tomatoes

Caramelized onions

Bell pepper rings

Grilled onions, mushrooms, peppers, and/or tomatoes (see the vegetables chapter)

Assorted mustards, mayonnaise, and ketchup

Mustard-Mayo Slather (page 66)

Rustic Aioli (page 104)

Ancho Mayonnaise (page 311)

Roquefort-Bacon Butter (page 318)

Thai Chile-Peanut Dressing (page 80)

The Doctor Is In Apricot-Bourbon Barbecue Sauce and variations (page 90)

Grilled Tomatillo Salsa (page 163) or prepared salsa

Chili sauce

Guacamole

Horseradish

Fresh herbs

Grilled Flank, Skirt, Hangar, or Other Thin Steak

The whole steak scene had gotten a bit ho-hum. Very predictable. You knew what cuts were available: rib-eye, strip, sirloin, flank. You knew what to do with them. And then, all of a sudden, things changed. There were new cuts and names, such as beef bavette and skirt, hangar, flat iron, patio, and charcoal steak. Wassup? (as a hip-hop queen might ask).

The change is partly a result of consumer interest in ethnic foods, hence the loose-grained skirt steak (the diaphragm muscle on a steer and the first choice for making great fajitas) and the beef bavette (cut from the flank for the French bistro steak and *frites* combo). Both can be hard to find at the grocery store but are readily available at butcher shops and from online vendors such as Niman Ranch.

In addition, the National Cattlemen's Beef Association, based in Colorado, has championed new "moderately priced" options such as the flat iron steak, cut from the beef chuck, and the western griller, cut from the bottom round. Cube steak, a.k.a. minute steak, has been around for a while. It is cut from the round and cubed twice to tenderize this tasty but tough piece of meat and make it great for grilling (a minute per side, not surprisingly). The hangar steak comes from the flank and is actually a thick muscle. It is much tougher than flank steak but is a bistro favorite and is also referred to as onglet.

All of these steaks have a chewy texture but great beef flavor. You need to tenderize them either by marinating them for at least an hour (preferably 8 hours) or pounding them with a meat tenderizer or mallet. Then you grill them over a hot fire to medium-rare. The final crucial step is slicing them properly to serve. Before you marinate a steak, locate the direction of the grain in the meat, which is easy to do. The grain consists of the lines of muscle fiber, which usually go in one direction. File that information away, grill your steak, and cut the meat against the grain, on the diagonal, holding your knife at a 45-degree angle (so it's slanted, not straight up and down). Perfecto!

For the marinade, we suggest Garlic-Citrus Marinade (page 70), Provençal Red Wine Marinade (page 70), or Homemade Teriyaki Marinade (page 69). **SERVES 4**

> **Marinade of your choice (see headnote)**
>
> **1¹/₂ pounds beef bavette or flank, skirt, hangar, flat iron, or western griller steak**

1. Place the marinade and steak in a sealable plastic bag and refrigerate for at least 1 hour or up to 8 hours.

2. Prepare a hot fire in a grill.

3. Remove the meat from the marinade and pat dry. Grill for 2 to 3 minutes per side for medium-rare. Let the meat rest for 5 minutes, then cut against the grain, on the diagonal and at a 45-degree angle, into slices about ¼ inch thick. Serve warm.

BBQ Tip: Judith's dad, whose family ran a butcher shop in Ohio for several generations, would run a flat steak like flank through the cuber once to tenderize it a little more. Ask the butcher to do that, then go home and marinate the steak before grilling for scrumptious results.

 **Crowning Glories**
Put this over the top with:
Simply Delicious Bordelaise Sauce (page 91)
Potato Gratin with White Cheddar Cheese (page 412)
Haricots Verts with Lemon, Garlic, and Parsley (page 274)

Bistro-Style Steak with Red Wine–Shallot Sauce: In a mortar with a pestle, or with a meat mallet or the edge of a skillet, crush 2 tablespoons black peppercorns. Press the peppercorns and 2 tablespoons coarse kosher or sea salt into the surface of 1½ pounds of the flat steak of your choice. Let rest for 30 minutes. To make the sauce, melt 3 tablespoons unsalted butter in a medium-size skillet over medium heat. Add 1 cup minced shallot (about 8 medium-size shallots) and cook, stirring, until transparent, about 5 minutes. Stir in ¾ cup dry red wine and ¾ cup beef broth and simmer until very thick, about 30 minutes. Season with kosher or sea salt and freshly ground black pepper to taste. Keep warm. When ready to grill, spray the coated steaks lightly with olive oil and grill over a hot fire, 2 to 3 minutes per side for rare. Let rest for 5 minutes, then slice against the grain and serve with the warm sauce, Homemade Frites (page 328), Dijon mustard, and fresh watercress. **SERVES 4**

Citrus-Grilled Beef Fajitas: These are the definitive fajitas. Substitute the same weight in boneless, skinless chicken breasts, if you like. Make 1 recipe of Garlic-Citrus Marinade (page 70). Place 1½ pounds of the flat steak of your choice in a sealable plastic bag and pour the marinade over. Seal the bag and marinate in the refrigerator for at least 2 hours or overnight. Prepare 1 recipe Stir-Grilled Vegetables (page 166) and keep warm. Grill the steak for 2 to 3 minutes on each side for medium-rare, or until the beef is to your desired doneness. Let rest for several minutes before slicing against the grain. To serve, place garnishes such as guacamole, chopped tomato, shredded lettuce, salsa, and shredded cheese in attractive bowls on the table. Arrange the meat, stir-grilled vegetables, and warm flour tortillas on a large platter and let your family or guests have at it. **SERVES 6**

Grilled Steak Marinated in Beer, Herbs, and Morels: This is a hearty yet lean dish of prairie favorites—wheat beer, steak, and morels—adapted from a recipe by midwesterner-at-heart Larry Forgione, who made his mark at An American Place in New York City. In a large bowl, combine 1 cup amber or wheat beer, 1¹/₂ cups chicken broth, 1 cup tomato juice, ¹/₄ cup dried morels or ¹/₂ cup fresh morels, 2 tablespoons chopped fresh oregano, 2 tablespoons chopped fresh thyme, 1 tablespoon Worcestershire sauce, ¹/₂ teaspoon hot pepper sauce, and 2 bay leaves. Pour half of the marinade into a baking dish and reserve the other half. Place 1¹/₂ pounds flat or thin steak of your choice in the dish, turning to coat. Marinate for 1 hour at room temperature, turning the steak every 15 minutes. Meanwhile, melt 2 tablespoons unsalted butter in a medium-size skillet over medium-high heat. Add 2 tablespoons chopped green onions and cook, stirring, until tender, about 4 minutes. Add the reserved marinade and heat through. Season with fine kosher or sea salt and freshly ground black pepper to taste. Keep warm. Remove the steak from the marinade and pat dry. Sprinkle with salt and pepper and grill as directed above. Let rest for 5 minutes, then slice against the grain, nap with the sauce, and serve. **SERVES 4**

Grilled Steak Salad with Caper Vinaigrette: This is cooking for the sexes. Women want a light dish, men want meat. They get both in this refreshing yet man-pleasing salad any time of the year. For easy entertaining, layer the salad ingredients (minus the flank steak and vinaigrette) in a bowl, cover, and refrigerate for several hours or overnight. In a small bowl, combine 2 tablespoons drained capers, 3 tablespoons fresh lemon juice, ¹/₂ cup red wine vinegar, 1 cup extra virgin olive oil, and fine kosher or sea salt and freshly ground black pepper to taste. Place 1¹/₂ pounds flank steak in a sealable plastic bag and pour half of the vinaigrette over the meat. Seal the bag and marinate in the refrigerator for at least 1 hour or overnight. In a large salad bowl, assemble ¹/₂ sliced large red onion, 8 ounces sliced fresh mushrooms, 1 cup grape tomatoes, 12 ounces trimmed fresh green beans cooked in boiling water until just crisp (about 3 minutes), 1 cup drained marinated artichoke hearts cut into bite-size pieces, and 1 bunch coarsely chopped watercress or fresh Italian parsley. Grill the steak as directed above, then let the meat rest for 5 minutes. Slice against the grain, then place on top of the salad. Pour the reserved vinaigrette over the salad and toss to blend. Serve immediately. **SERVES 6**

New Wave Steak

America's fascination and fixation with steak dates back only a hundred years or so. It became popular when the West opened up in the 1870s and cowboys drove herds of wild Texas longhorns, descended from cattle abandoned by the Spanish, up to the railroad cars in Abilene, Kansas.

In these years right after the Civil War, the "carpetbagger steak" came into being—a thick steak with a pocket cut in the side that was stuffed with fresh oysters, then cooked on a griddle for city folk. Cowboys herding the rowdy, rangy longhorns north from the southernmost tip of Texas enjoyed steak and beans most nights for supper. However, they enjoyed their tough and lean longhorn steak charred and well done, cooked to death in a cast-iron skillet over an open fire. (Perhaps "enjoyed" is not quite the right term.)

America's cattle industry—and a more tender steak's popularity—began to grow as European cattle breeds such as the Hereford and Aberdeen Angus were introduced to this country and cross-bred with the longhorn. By the late 1800s, a good steak sizzled on a hot griddle was what workingmen wanted when they ate out in cow towns such as Kansas City and Omaha.

In the 1950s, steak entered another evolutionary cycle. Charcoal briquettes, developed as an offshoot business to make use of wooden crates left over from automobile manufacturing at the Ford plant in Detroit, tempted a whole new generation of men to get outside and grill that steak. Charcoal grilling added a spectacular flavor dimension that we still crave.

Flash forward to the 1960s and 1970s, when college-age baby boomers discovered world travel. Cheap airfares, a "do your own thing" ideal, and a good dose of wanderlust sent a whole generation abroad. It's no accident that Julia Child was so successful in introducing French cooking to an American audience at this time. We were open to new ideas and eager to learn. Châteaubriand, *steak au poivre*, and steak Diane became familiar haute cuisine dishes.

Steak is still what we crave today, whether we're queens or kings. According to steak expert William Rice, retired *Chicago Tribune* columnist and author of *Steak Lover's*

Cookbook (Workman, 1997), "The steak dinner is the feast of choice for special occasions and a symbol of American well-being and prosperity."

In the recipes that follow, a new wave of creativity takes steak into the new millennium.

Branding Iron Beef with Ancho Mayonnaise

This recipe is adapted from one created by chef Dan Palmer and featured in Judith's *Prairie Home Cooking* (The Harvard Common Press, 1999). Toasting the ancho chile brings out the flavor, which is milder in heat than a jalapeño or serrano. **SERVES 4 AS AN APPETIZER**

> 1 pound sirloin tip
> Extra virgin olive oil
> Fine kosher or sea salt and freshly ground black pepper to taste
> 1 small dried ancho chile, cut in half, stemmed, and seeded
> 1 cup good-quality mayonnaise
> 2 tablespoons capers, drained, for garnish

1. If your outdoor grill has enough BTUs to blacken redfish, build a very hot fire in the grill. If not, heat a cast-iron skillet on the hottest burner on your stove. (Open the windows and turn on the exhaust fan if cooking indoors, because this will create lots of smoke.) Paint all sides of the sirloin tip with olive oil and season with salt and pepper. When the grill or skillet is extremely hot, blacken the beef for about 1 minute on each side, then remove from the heat.

2. While the beef is cooling, heat a small skillet over high heat. Add the ancho chile and toast until fragrant, 1 to 2 seconds on each side. Transfer to a small bowl and add just enough hot water to cover. Let steep for about 10 minutes. Remove the chile and pat dry. Place in a food processor with the mayonnaise and process until smooth and slightly pink. Cover and refrigerate.

3.   When the beef is completely cool, wrap in plastic and put in the freezer to firm (but not freeze), 20 to 30 minutes. If you have one, use a mandoline to cut the beef paper-thin and arrange the slices around the perimeter of 4 chilled serving plates. If you wish, pour the ancho mayonnaise into a squeeze bottle and squirt a design over the beef; you can also drizzle the mayonnaise over. Garnish each plate with capers and serve immediately.

Batayaki Beef with Spicy Lemon-Soy Sauce

Batayaki is a Japanese cooking style in which thin slices of meat and small cut vegetables are cooked right at the table and served with a dipping sauce and steamed rice. Do this inside using a grill pan or electric grill or outside using a grill wok or perforated grill rack. **SERVES 4**

SPICY LEMON-SOY SAUCE

Juice of 1 lemon

¹/₄ cup soy sauce

1 teaspoon Korean chile bean sauce (*kochujang*) or other hot pepper paste

1 teaspoon toasted sesame oil

¹/₂ teaspoon dashi (instant Oriental soup stock; available at Japanese markets)

1 cup thinly shredded daikon (Oriental radish)

1 bunch green onions, cut into 2-inch pieces

1¹/₂ pounds sirloin tip, very thinly sliced

12 fresh shiitake mushrooms, stems removed and caps sliced

1 large yellow onion, sliced and separated into rings

8 ounces fresh bean sprouts, rinsed

5 tablespoons vegetable oil

1.   To make the sauce, combine all the ingredients in a small bowl. Ladle into 4 individual bowls and top each with ¹/₄ cup daikon and 1 tablespoon green onions.

2.   Brush the beef slices, mushrooms, onion, and bean sprouts with the vegetable oil. Using a hot electric skillet at the table or a grill pan on the stovetop over high heat, or using a grill wok or perforated grill rack on a hot grill outside, cook the beef, mushrooms,

and onion on both sides until done to your satisfaction. Sizzle the bean sprouts a little bit. Arrange the cooked foods on a platter and serve, having guests dip them into the sauce as desired.

Beef Filet Salad with Orange-Cumin Vinaigrette

This dish, adapted from a recipe in William Rice's *Steak Lover's Cookbook* (Workman, 1997), is one that Monique King, chef at Chicago's Soul Kitchen, serves at room temperature. **SERVES 4**

> **Two 8-ounce filet mignon steaks, about 1 inch thick, at room temperature**
>
> **1 tablespoon olive oil**
>
> **8 cups mesclun or mixed baby greens**
>
> **ORANGE-CUMIN VINAIGRETTE**
>
> **3 tablespoons extra virgin olive oil**
>
> **1 tablespoon fresh orange juice**
>
> **1 tablespoon sherry vinegar**
>
> **1 1/2 teaspoons minced green onions**
>
> **1 teaspoon grated orange zest**
>
> **1/4 teaspoon ground cumin**
>
> **Kosher or sea salt and ground white pepper to taste**

1. Prepare a hot fire in a grill.

2. Pat the steaks dry and lightly coat with the olive oil. Grill for 2 to 3 minutes per side for medium-rare. Set aside and let cool.

3. Put the greens in a large bowl.

4. To make the vinaigrette, combine all the ingredients in a small bowl. Pour all but 1 tablespoon over the greens, tossing to coat evenly. Divide the greens among 4 plates. Cut the steaks into 1/4-inch-thick slices and arrange the slices on top of the greens. Drizzle the remaining dressing on top and serve.

Grill Gals

She Grills Everything Menu

Balsamic-Marinated Vegetables on the Grill
Charcoal-Grilled Rib-Eye Steak

Celina Tio is the executive chef at the renowned American Restaurant in Kansas City. Her previous position was with Disney in Orlando, Florida. She has more energy than two chefs put together and enjoys rock climbing in her spare(!) time. When she has friends over for dinner or caters a meal during the summer, she favors a dish she calls "Everything Grilled"—basically, a charcoal-grilled rib-eye steak accompanied by grilled vegetables that have been marinated in balsamic vinegar. It all cooks at the same time, and cleanup is easy. We find that cooking the vegetables—especially the onion slices, which can fall apart—on a perforated grill rack is the way to go.

Balsamic-Marinated Vegetables on the Grill

Who doesn't like balsamic vinegar? Nobody we know. This marinade darkens and deepens the flavors of the grilled vegetables. If you like, use a perforated grill rack so you don't lose any vegetables to the flames. SERVES 6

> ¹/₂ cup olive oil
>
> ¹/₄ cup balsamic vinegar
>
> 1 eggplant, ends trimmed and sliced ¹/₄ inch thick
>
> 2 zucchini, ends trimmed and sliced on the diagonal ¹/₄ inch thick

1 yellow summer squash, ends trimmed and sliced on the diagonal 1/4 inch thick

3 Yukon Gold potatoes, sliced 1/4 inch thick

2 red onions, sliced 1/4 inch thick

4 portobello mushrooms, stems and gills removed

1. Combine the olive oil and vinegar in a large sealable plastic bag. Add the vegetables, seal, and marinate for at least 1 hour.

2. When ready to cook, prepare a hot fire in a grill.

3. Remove the vegetables from the marinade and place in a large bowl. Grill the onions, potatoes, and mushrooms directly on the grill grate until soft, about 7 minutes per side. Transfer to a large platter and keep warm.

4. Place an oiled grill wok or perforated grill rack over the grill grate. Grill the eggplant, zucchini, and yellow squash until soft, about 4 minutes per side. Depending on the size of your grill rack, you may need to grill these in 2 batches.

5. Just before the last batch of vegetables goes on the grill, you may begin grilling the steaks. Arrange the cooked vegetables on the platter and serve with the steaks.

Charcoal-Grilled Rib-Eye Steak

SERVES 6

Six 8-ounce rib-eye steaks, 3/4 inch thick

Kosher or sea salt and freshly ground black pepper to taste

1. Prepare a hot fire in a grill.

2. Season the steaks with salt and pepper. Grill for 7 minutes per side for medium. Place on a platter and serve hot.

Grilled Boneless Steak

Boneless steaks come in all shapes, sizes, and degrees of tenderness, from the chewy charcoal steak cut from the beef chuck to the more tender and flavorful sirloin or strip steak to the fabulously tender filet mignon.

The BBQ Queens' favorites are the filet mignon and rib-eye, great steaks for the grill because of their tenderness and good marbling of fat throughout. Cut from the long piece of rib section meat known as standing rib roast or prime rib, boneless rib-eye steaks are usually about 3/4 inch thick. Filet mignon can be cut into steaks up to 3 inches thick, but Grill Gals like us prefer 1-inch cuts.

We love really tender boneless steaks grilled over mesquite charcoal or on a gas grill. The key is a hot-as-you-can-get-it fire. We both like our tender steaks steakhouse style—with a spice rub or flavoring paste applied to the meat, which is then cooked over a hot fire to get a charred crust, while the center remains rare to medium.

Strip steak, also known as Kansas City or New York strip, is a he-man kind of steak—thick, meaty, full of beef flavor, and somewhat chewy. Karen's husband, Dick, loves this cut, so they grill it a lot at their house. Cut from the hindquarter or the middle section of the steer's back, the strip steak starts out as a T-bone steak, part tenderloin and part top loin. The butcher cuts out the tenderloin from one side of the T-bone, then removes the T-bone area entirely and—voilà!—a boneless, elongated strip steak, usually cut about 1 inch thick.

Because strip, sirloin, or chuck steaks are a little chewier than rib-eye or filet mignon, we use a slightly lower fire—medium-hot rather than hot. Full-flavored strip steaks and their like need a sauce or accompaniment with big flavor as well. You can marinate a strip steak, but we prefer an accompanying sauce, condiment, or relish for a better flavor contrast. We love this best served with Smoked Tomato and Grilled Red Onion Relish (page 324), Chile–Ginger–Green Onion Sauce (page 318), or Roquefort-Bacon Butter (page 318). You can grill this steak indoors using a grill pan, if you wish. We're gonna give you a lot of recipes for this type of steak, because there are so many ways to enjoy it.

SERVES 4

Four 8-ounce filet mignon, rib-eye, boneless sirloin, or strip steaks, 1 inch thick
Olive oil
Coarse kosher or sea salt and freshly ground black pepper or lemon pepper seasoning to taste

1. Brush the steaks lightly with olive oil and season with salt and pepper. Set aside.

2. Prepare a hot fire in a grill.

3. Close the lid and grill for 3 minutes per side for medium-rare.

Crowning Glories

Keep it simple and serve with a baked potato and a green salad, or
have a rhinestone-tiara kind of night and top your steaks with:

Simply Delicious Bordelaise Sauce (page 91)

Smoked Tomato and Grilled Red Onion Relish (page 324)

Rustic Béarnaise Sauce (page 98)

Roasted Cherry Tomatoes with Frizzled Herbs (page 208)

Steakhouse-Style Filet Mignon: The secret to great steakhouse steak flavor is to sear the meat over high heat in a seasoned cast-iron skillet or a heavy anodized grill pan—indoors or out—similar to blackening fish. If your outdoor grill doesn't have the upper-level BTUs to do this, use your stovetop indoors. (Open the windows and turn your kitchen fan on high—this is smoky business.) Searing will produce that blackened, charred exterior and rarish, pink, juicy interior you're looking for—what's termed "black and blue" by New York steakhouses. For a really divine version, spread Porcini Paste (page 65) on the filets and omit dipping them in butter or oil. Prepare a hot fire in a grill or turn your stovetop burner to high, and heat a cast-iron skillet or grill pan over the coals or burner until the bottom begins to turn gray, about 20 minutes. Have ready four 6-ounce filet mignon steaks cut about 2 inches thick. Pour 2 tablespoons clarified butter or olive oil on a plate and dip each steak in it. Sear the steaks for 2 to 3 minutes per side for medium-rare, a little longer for medium. Season with salt and pepper. Accompany with Classic Creamed Spinach (page 319) and Fried Onion Slivers (page 320). **SERVES 6**

Grilled Peppercorn Filet Mignon with Cognac Sauce: This dish deserves a *real* rhinestone tiara! You'll need a seasoned cast-iron skillet you can use on the grill. Prepare a hot fire and place the skillet over direct heat for 20 to 30 minutes before grilling. Meanwhile, press $1/4$ cup cracked black peppercorns and kosher salt to taste into the surface of four 6- to 8-ounce filet mignon steaks cut $1^1/_2$ to 2 inches thick. Spray the filets with olive oil and place in the hot skillet. Close the grill and cook until a thick crust forms on the bottom, 7 to 8 minutes. Turn and dot each with $1^1/_2$ teaspoons unsalted butter. Close the grill and cook for another 7 to 8 minutes for medium-rare. Transfer the steaks to a plate near the grill to keep warm. Add $1/4$ cup heavy cream, $1/4$ cup cognac, and $1/2$ cup demi-glace (made from concentrate that you can get at gourmet shops and better grocery stores) or good-quality chicken broth to the skillet. Whisk together, then cook until slightly thickened, 3 to 4 minutes. Nap each filet with sauce and serve. **SERVES 4**

Philadelphia Garlic Rib-Eye Steak: In a shallow pie pan, make a paste of $1/4$ cup minced garlic (about 8 cloves), $1/4$ cup olive oil, $1/4$ cup sweet Hungarian paprika, 1 teaspoon seasoned salt, and 1 teaspoon freshly ground black pepper. Dredge four 8-ounce, 1-inch-thick rib-eye (or other boneless) steaks in this mixture and let marinate at room temperature for 30 minutes. Grill the steaks over a hot fire for 3 minutes per side for medium-rare. Serve with Grilled Asparagus (page 117) and a potato casserole (see pages 412–413). **SERVES 4**

Grilled Strip Steak with Chile–Ginger–Green Onion Sauce: In a small skillet, heat 1 tablespoon vegetable oil over medium-high heat. Add 1 teaspoon minced garlic, 1 teaspoon grated fresh ginger (if using a microplane, you don't need to peel), and $1/4$ teaspoon red pepper flakes. Cook, stirring, until the garlic and ginger have softened, about 4 minutes. Stir in $1/2$ cup mirin (a sweet Japanese wine) or sweet sake, $1/4$ cup soy sauce, and 1 tablespoon sugar and bring to a boil. In a small jar with a tight-fitting lid, place 2 tablespoons cornstarch and 1 tablespoon cold water. Cover and shake to blend. Whisk the mixture into the sauce until thickened, about 5 minutes. Keep warm while you grill four 8-ounce, 1-inch-thick strip steaks as directly above. Just before serving, stir $1/4$ cup sliced green onions into the sauce. Slice the steak and serve with the sauce spooned over. This sauce is also good with grilled fish, chicken, pork, or vegetables. **SERVES 4**

Seduction Strip Steak with Roquefort-Bacon Butter: Food writer M. F. K. Fisher had menus to both seduce—and un-seduce—would-be lovers. Use this dish for taste-bud seduction, at the very least (unless your intended doesn't like blue cheese, of course). To make the butter, place 2 sticks unsalted butter minus 1 tablespoon in a medium-size bowl. Melt the remaining 1 tablespoon butter in a small skillet over medium heat. Add 6 diced shallots and cook, stirring, until browned, about 6 minutes. Transfer to the bowl along with 3 slices crumbled crisp-cooked bacon, $1/2$ cup crumbled Roquefort or other blue cheese, 1 tablespoon snipped fresh chives, and 1 tablespoon Worcestershire sauce. Using a fork or potato masher, mash the butter and place in the middle of a sheet of waxed paper or plastic wrap. Partially cover and roll into a long cylinder. Cover and refrigerate until firm, about 2 hours. (This may be stored in a sealed plastic bag in the freezer for up to 6 months.) Grill four 8-ounce, 1-inch-thick strip steaks as directed above. Serve topped with large pats of the butter, which will pleasingly melt over the hot steaks. Also try the butter on grilled or smoked chicken or pork or on a baked potato. **SERVES 4**

Since the time the first American steakhouses graced the big cities, side dishes like these have offered counterpoint flavors to the great taste of steak.

Classic Creamed Spinach

Creamed spinach has been a classic American steakhouse favorite for generations, and for good reason. Fresh baby spinach makes the most tender side dish, almost melting in your mouth. Mellow with cream and gently spiced with freshly grated nutmeg, this is good enough to enjoy on its own, but it's also delicious with steak, roast chicken, or fish or shellfish. SERVES 4

> 1½ pounds fresh spinach, washed well and trimmed of heavy stems
>
> 1 tablespoon unsalted butter
>
> 1 tablespoon all-purpose flour
>
> ¾ cup half-and-half
>
> Kosher or sea salt, ground white pepper, and freshly grated nutmeg to taste

1. Place the spinach, with the rinse water still clinging to it, in a large pot. Turn the heat to high and cover. When steam begins to escape from under the lid, about 3 minutes, remove the pot from the heat, leave the cover on, and let the spinach steam while you make the sauce.

2. In a small saucepan, melt the butter over medium heat. Stir in the flour and cook until the flour smell disappears, about 2 minutes. Whisk in the half-and-half and stir to remove any lumps. Let the sauce come to a boil to thicken. Stir into the spinach and season with salt, white pepper, and nutmeg. Serve immediately.

Fried Onion Slivers

Judith loves to serve these with filet mignon or rib-eye steak, along with creamed spinach. The Bravo restaurant chain serves these slivers atop a grilled chicken and feta cheese salad with citrus dressing. (Yum!) You'll think of even more ways to enjoy them. We use a mandoline to cut the onion paper-thin and a candy thermometer to check the temperature of the oil. (You also may use an electric skillet or deep-fat fryer.) These "slivers" are actually the thinnest of thin onion rings. SERVES 4

> 1 large yellow onion, sliced paper-thin
> 1/2 cup all-purpose flour
> 3 cups peanut oil
> Fine sea salt to taste

1. Toss the onion slices with the flour in a medium-size bowl until well coated.

2. Heat the peanut oil in a deep saucepan or electric skillet to 350°F. Fry the onions in batches, without crowding them, until golden brown, 7 to 8 minutes. Remove from the oil using a slotted spoon and drain on paper towels. Immediately season with salt. Keep warm in a low oven until all the slices have been fried. Serve immediately.

Olive Oil Smashed Potatoes

So easy, and so good! Use the best olive oil you can find, because this flavors the potatoes. SERVES 4

> 4 large baking potatoes, peeled and roughly chopped
> 1/4 cup extra virgin olive oil, or to you taste
> 1 teaspoon fine sea salt
> 1 teaspoon freshly ground black pepper or ground white pepper

1. Place the potatoes in a medium-size saucepan with enough water to cover. Bring to a boil and continue to boil until the potatoes are tender, 12 to 15 minutes.

2. Drain off the water and use a potato masher or fork to smash the potatoes with the olive oil in the pan. Season with salt and pepper and serve hot.

Decadent Garlic Mashed Potatoes

Julia Child was always ahead of her time. This recipe first appeared on her *French Chef* television program in the 1970s. Today, it's a perfect accompaniment to grilled steak. **SERVES 6 TO 8**

GARLIC SAUCE

2 heads garlic (about 30 cloves)
¹/₄ cup (¹/₂ stick) unsalted butter
2 tablespoons all-purpose flour
1 cup milk, heated

MASHED POTATOES

2¹/₂ pounds baking potatoes, peeled and roughly chopped
¹/₄ cup (¹/₂ stick) unsalted butter
3 to 4 tablespoons heavy cream to taste
Fine kosher or sea salt and freshly ground black pepper to taste

1. To make the sauce, separate the garlic cloves from the heads and drop them into boiling water. Boil for 2 minutes, drain, and peel. (This blanches and mellows the garlic so it's not overpowering.) In a small, heavy saucepan, melt the butter over medium-low heat. Add the peeled garlic cloves and flour and cook for 2 minutes. Whisk in the hot milk and continue to whisk until thick and creamy, about 5 minutes. Keep warm.

2. Meanwhile, make the mashed potatoes. Place the potatoes in a large saucepan with salted water to cover. Bring to a boil and continue to boil until tender, 15 to 20 minutes. Drain off the water and use a potato masher or fork to mash the potatoes in the pan, adding the butter, cream and salt and pepper. Mash in the garlic sauce and serve hot.

Stewed and Scalloped Tomatoes

There are stewed tomatoes and there are stewed tomatoes. Some come straight from the can and are just heated up. Others, like this recipe, are graced with a few simple but delicious additions—such as crème fraîche—that make all the difference. **SERVES 6 TO 8**

> ¹/₂ cup sour cream (lowfat is okay)
>
> ¹/₂ cup heavy cream
>
> **Two 15-ounce cans stewed tomatoes, with their juice**
>
> **2 cups fresh bakery or artisanal bread cut into 1-inch cubes**
>
> ¹/₄ cup (¹/₂ stick) unsalted butter, melted

1. Preheat the oven to 350°F. Butter a 13 x 9-inch baking dish.

2. In a large bowl, whisk together the sour cream and heavy cream to make crème fraîche. Fold in the tomatoes and spoon half the mixture into the prepared pan. Dot the top with half the bread cubes and drizzle with half the butter. Spoon the remaining tomato mixture on top of the bread cubes, then dot the surface with the remaining bread cubes and drizzle with the remaining butter. Bake until bubbling and browned, 25 to 30 minutes. Serve hot.

Grilled Bone-In Steak

Sometimes you just gotta have a primeval hunk of grilled meat with a bone to gnaw. Happily, you have lots of choices for this type of steak. A premium rib steak is a rib-eye with the bone left in, tender and juicy from the marbling of fat throughout. The T-bone, cut from the short loin, has a tender filet mignon side and a chewier New York or strip steak side, with a T-shaped bone separating them. The bigger porterhouse is a T-bone steak on steroids, with a more generous portion on the filet side. A chewier, beefier strip steak can also have the bone left in. In that case, it could be called a Kansas City, New York strip, Delmonico, shell, or club steak—depending on where you live and shop. Most bone-in steaks are cut about 1 inch thick.

We like a hot fire and a simple preparation for this kind of steak. Just a little brush of olive oil and maybe a spicy rub (or simply salt and pepper), and you're good to go. **SERVES 4**

> **4 bone-in steaks of your choice, about 1 inch thick**
>
> **Olive oil**
>
> **Cajun Steak Rub (page 58) or fine kosher or sea salt and freshly ground black pepper to taste**

1. Brush or spray the steaks with olive oil.

2. Prepare a hot fire in a grill.

3. Grill the steaks on each side for 3 to 4 minutes for medium-rare. An instant-read meat thermometer inserted in the center near the bone should register 140°F.

Crowning Glories

Enjoy your steak in glorious nakedness (its, not yours, though that's an idea) or gild it with your choice of:

Simply Delicious Bordelaise Sauce *(page 91)*

Mustard-Cornichon Beurre Blanc *(page 100)*

Rustic Béarnaise Sauce *(page 98)*

Korean-Style Bone-In Steak: A Korean-style marinade flavors this steak before it sizzles on the grill. In a large sealable plastic bag, combine ⅓ cup soy sauce; 2 tablespoons rice wine, rice vinegar, or dry sherry; 1 teaspoon toasted sesame oil; 3 tablespoons vegetable oil;

1 finely chopped small red chile (with or without seeds); 4 minced garlic cloves; ¹/₄ cup sugar; and 4 thinly sliced green onions. Add 4 bone-in steaks cut about 1 inch thick, seal, and marinate in the refrigerator for at least 2 hours or up to 8 hours, turning the meat at least once. When ready to grill, remove from the marinade, pat dry, and grill as directed above. **SERVES 4**

Grilled T-Bone Steak with Smoked Tomato and Grilled Red Onion Relish: In a small skillet, heat 2 tablespoons olive oil over medium heat. Add 2 minced garlic cloves and cook, stirring, until golden, about 4 minutes. Combine with 2 tablespoons drained capers in a medium-size bowl. Set aside. Slice 2 medium-size red onions, arrange the slices on a microwavable tray, and precook in the microwave on high for 1¹/₂ to 2 minutes. Brush the onion slices with 1 tablespoon olive oil, place in a grill basket, and grill for 10 to 12 minutes, turning once. Peel 2 smoked tomatoes (see page 37) and chop the tomato pulp coarsely. Chop the grilled onions. Toss the tomatoes and onions with the garlic oil and capers. Season with kosher or sea salt and freshly ground black pepper to taste. Grill 4 T-bone steaks cut about 1 inch thick as directed above. Spoon the relish over the steaks and serve. This relish also is good with grilled fish, chicken, or pork. **SERVES 4**

Sicilian Bistecca: Culinary wizard Gino Corte's family came to Kansas City from a Sicilian farming community—Poggioreale, about 40 minutes inland from the port city of Palermo. They brought with them the tradition of their own amogio marinade plus seasoned bread crumbs to add flavor notes to everything from artichokes to chicken. In America, where beef was plentiful and relatively cheap, they added that treatment to steak, and it's delicious. First, make the Corte family's version of amogio by whisking together ¹/₃ cup olive oil, ¹/₄ cup fresh lemon juice (about 2 lemons), 4 minced garlic cloves, several fresh oregano sprigs or 1 teaspoon dried oregano, 10 cracked black peppercorns, and 3 large bay leaves in a medium-size bowl. Place 2 large bone-in steaks cut 1 inch thick in a glass dish or sealable plastic bag. Pour in the marinade, cover or seal, and refrigerate for at least 2 hours, turning the meat several times. Meanwhile, cut several slices from a good loaf of bread and toast on a baking sheet in a preheated 350°F oven for about 15 minutes. Let cool, then process into crumbs in a food processor or blender. In a medium-size bowl, mix together ³/₄ cup of the bread crumbs, ¹/₂ teaspoon dried oregano, and fine kosher or sea salt and freshly ground black pepper to taste. Remove the steaks from the marinade, without patting them dry. Transfer the bread crumbs to a large plate and dredge the steaks in the crumbs to coat evenly. The steaks should have a thick crust of crumbs. Grill as directed above, first coating the grill grate well with oil. Serve with lemon wedges. **SERVES 4 TO 6**

Grilled Thick-Cut Steak

Keep it simple, stupid, could be the slogan for this type of steak. Grill one huge slab of beef, then slice it and serve. It's easier to cook a thick-cut steak just right, because there's a greater margin of error than with a thinner steak. Grill a thick steak for a minute or two longer, and it's no big deal.

Steaks that are cut thickly usually come from the sirloin or hip section. These include the triangular-shaped tri-tip from the bottom sirloin and the really thick porterhouse from the rib section. Sometimes you'll see them packaged as "double sirloin," but mostly you have to ask the butcher to cut this type of steak for you.

A huge slab of meat like this can go with any kind of flavoring, from Asian or Italian to French bistro or American prairie.

Because this type of steak is more tender than a skirt or flank steak, just cut it across the grain into slices of whatever thickness you want. **SERVES 8 TO 12**

> **1 large or 4 smaller steaks of your choice, 2 to 3 inches thick**
> **Olive oil**
> **Fine kosher or sea salt and freshly ground black pepper to taste**

1. Brush or spray the steaks with olive oil.

2. Prepare a hot fire in a grill.

3. Grill the steaks for 12 to 15 minutes per side for medium-rare. An instant-read meat thermometer inserted in the center should register 140°F.

4. Season with salt and pepper and let rest for 10 to 15 minutes before slicing against the grain and serving.

 *Crowning Glories*

Serve this with:
Rustic Grill-Roasted Potato Salad *(page 148)*
Grilled Goat Cheese Tomatoes *(page 160)*
Matchstick-cut cucumber, daikon radish, and green onions
with Vietnamese Drizzle *(page 87)*
Grilled Mushrooms *(page 132)* **with**
Wheat Beer Vinaigrette *(page 77; see headnote for sauce variation)*

Black and Bleu Beef: The term "black and blue (or bleu)" refers to a steak that's charred on the outside and rare on the inside—our personal favorite way of grilling a thick steak. You'll need a hotter than hot fire or a really hot, seasoned large cast-iron griddle or skillet. Brush melted unsalted butter or olive oil on the surface of four 2-inch-thick filet mignon steaks and season with coarse kosher or sea salt and freshly ground black pepper to taste. Wait until you can hold your hand over the fire (or griddle or skillet) for only 3 to 4 seconds, then put the steaks on. Let sizzle for 6 to 7 minutes, turn over, and let sizzle for 6 to 7 minutes more, until an instant-read meat thermometer inserted in the center registers 130°F. Serve with Rustic Béarnaise Sauce (page 98) for an out-of-body experience. **SERVES 4**

Prairie-Style Hay-Smoked Steak: "The following recipe will yield, I promise you, one of the best steaks you have ever eaten," says Kansas City barbecuer Ardie Davis, a.k.a. Remus Powers, Ph.B. (see page 44). Ardie's recipe appeared in Judith's *Prairie Home Cooking* (The Harvard Common Press, 1999), and we repeat it here—we know a good thing when we taste it. From Kansas City, we drive north or south beyond suburbia to farm country, where we buy cider and doughnuts, and a small bale of hay. (You can also buy hay at feed stores.) You actually grill this steak, but the hay smokes as it smolders, giving the steak a little kiss of smoke. You have to use a charcoal grill for this recipe, as the hay has to burn away, and that could clog the jets of a gas grill. You need 1 huge tri-tip or porterhouse steak or 4 Kansas City strip steaks cut 2 to 3 inches thick. Place a large handful (about 3 cups for all of you type A's) of hay (or wheat straw) on a platter and set the steaks on the hay. Sprinkle lightly with 1 tablespoon coarse kosher or sea salt and let sit at room temperature for about 2 hours. You want the moisture from the steaks to permeate the hay. Prepare a hot fire in a charcoal grill and use oak chips for a kiss of smoke (see page 13). Remove the steaks from the hay (pick off any stray pieces from the meat), reserving the moistened hay, and grill for about 3 minutes on each side. Using grill mitts, carefully remove the grate with the steaks still on it and set aside. Drop the hay over the hot coals and return the grate to the grill. Cover and grill-smoke the steaks for 15 to 20 minutes, turning them so both sides absorb the smoky flavor. When medium-rare to medium, about 140°F on an instant-read meat thermometer, transfer to a platter, drizzle with 1 tablespoon extra virgin olive oil, and season with kosher or sea salt and freshly ground black pepper to taste. Pass lemon wedges at the table. **SERVES 4**

┃▪▟▟▟▟▟┃

"Bistro style" has become a buzzword for somewhat sophisticated yet casual food. Envision zinc-topped bars, black-and-white tile flooring, colorful dishes served on plain white china, and a Gallic flair to it all. We love bistro side dishes with all kinds of plainly grilled or smoked foods. Our hands-down favorite is Haricot Verts Salad with Mustard-Shallot Vinaigrette, which we enjoyed at a bistro in the eighth arrondissement of Paris. A few days later, we shopped the local markets and made it from taste memory when we stayed at Anne Willan's Château du Fey in Burgundy with our culinary book club. Don't fret, though; all of these dishes are *magnifique*!

Haricots Verts Salad with Mustard-Shallot Vinaigrette

Haricots verts are those tiny, thin French green beans that start to come on the market in late spring. Judith grows them in her garden. These beans should be cooked until just slightly crunchy, then dressed warm with the vinaigrette. Use a lighter olive oil, not extra virgin, as you don't want the olive oil flavor to dominate here. If you want the beans to stay a vivid green, plunge them into ice water after cooking, let cool, and then drain before proceeding with the recipe. SERVES 4

> 1 pound *haricots verts* or young, thin green beans, tops trimmed
>
> MUSTARD-SHALLOT VINAIGRETTE
> 1 large shallot, diced
> 1 tablespoon Dijon mustard
> 1/4 cup white wine vinegar
> 1/2 cup olive oil
> Fine kosher or sea salt and freshly ground black pepper to taste

1. Put the beans in a large pot with enough water to cover. Bring to a boil and cook until crisp-tender, 1 to 2 minutes. Drain in a colander and rinse under cold running water for 30 seconds to refresh the color but still keep them slightly warm. Let drain for 1 minute, then transfer to a serving bowl.

2.   To make the vinaigrette, whisk the shallot, mustard, and vinegar together in a small bowl. Slowly drizzle in the olive oil, whisking to blend. Season with salt and pepper. Pour over the beans, toss to coat, and serve immediately.

Homemade Frites

Basically, these are homemade French fries, but they sound better as *frites*, don't they? The secrets to great *frites* include cutting them thin and keeping the oil at or around 350°F. A deep fryer is great, but you can also use an electric skillet or a deep skillet and a candy thermometer. **SERVES 4 TO 6**

> **4 large Idaho potatoes, peeled**
> **Vegetable oil for frying**
> **Coarse kosher or sea salt to taste**

1.   Cut the potatoes lengthwise into ¼-inch-thick slices, then cut each slice into ¼-inch-wide strips. Place the strips in a bowl of ice water for 15 minutes.

2.   Drain the water from the potatoes and pat very dry with paper towels.

3.   Add 2 inches of vegetable oil to a deep fryer or skillet. If using a skillet, place over medium-high heat. When the oil reaches 350°F, place half the potatoes in the hot oil and cook, turning if necessary, until the potatoes turn golden brown, 5 to 7 minutes. Transfer to paper towels and season with salt. Keep warm in a low oven while you prepare the second batch. Serve immediately.

Celery Root Rémoulade

Bulbous, knobby celery root—which tastes like a cross between celery and potato—is a traditional European vegetable usually available in American markets during the cooler months. You can quarter and peel it, then grate it in a food processor for serving raw in a salad like this one. Or peel it, cut it into cubes, and sauté it in olive oil for a wonderful change from fried potatoes. Either way, work fast, as celery root tends to darken (like raw potato). True Parisian rémoulade is mustard-based, not like our New Orleans rémoulade, which is more like tartar sauce. This recipe is adapted from one by the well-known cookbook author and Francophile Patricia Wells, the BBQ Queens' American friend in Paris. SERVES 4 TO 6

 ½ cup sour cream
 ½ cup heavy cream
 2 tablespoons fresh lemon juice
 2 tablespoons Dijon mustard (we prefer the Maille brand for this)
 One 1-pound celery root
 Coarse kosher or sea salt and freshly ground black pepper to taste

1.   In a large bowl, whisk together the sour cream and heavy cream until smooth. Whisk in the lemon juice and mustard. Set aside.

2.   Peel and quarter the celery root, then grate in a food processor or by hand on the large holes of a box grater. As you grate each quarter, transfer it to the dressing in the bowl and stir to coat. This keeps the celery root from darkening. Season with salt and pepper. Serve at room temperature or chilled.

Bistro Grated Carrot Salad

This is simplicity itself. SERVES 4 TO 6

 4 cups finely shredded carrot (about 6 medium-size carrots)
 1 tablespoon fresh lemon juice
 1 tablespoon olive oil
 2 tablespoons tarragon or raspberry vinegar
 Finely chopped fresh Italian parsley for garnish

Place the grated carrot in a large bowl. In a small bowl, stir together the lemon juice, olive oil, and vinegar. Drizzle the dressing over the carrot and toss to blend. Serve at once, garnished with parsley.

Grilled Beef Skewers

The BBQ Queens decree that skewered beef is only as good as the beef you buy. With that said, our choices for skewering include beef from good-quality cuts such as rib-eye steak, sirloin, and tenderloin. You can also vary the type of skewer you use (see pages 29–32 for your options and how to grill skewers), from the standard bamboo skewer, which needs to be soaked in water for at least 30 minutes before grilling, to fresh rosemary branches. If you can, buy flat bamboo skewers, or purchase two-prong metal skewers so the meat won't spin on the stick. You can also thread the meat onto two skewers, which accomplishes the same thing as the double-prong metal skewers. (See how clever we are!)

While the beef skewers are grilling, grill Cheesy Grilled Pepper Boats (page 143) or Char-Grilled Baby Summer Squash (page 155) as an accompaniment. Drizzle a dipping sauce over the finished skewers, if you like. We are particularly fond of amogio, which we also use to marinate the beef before grilling. **SERVES 6**

> 1¹/₂ pounds boneless sirloin, cut into 24 cubes
>
> 1 recipe Amogio (page 72) or 1³/₄ cups bottled Italian-style vinaigrette
>
> 6 wooden skewers, soaked in water for at least 30 minutes before grilling

1. Place the beef in a baking dish or sealable plastic bag and pour half the amogio over. Cover or seal and refrigerate for at least 30 minutes or up to 2 hours.

2. Prepare a hot fire in a grill.

3. Thread the beef cubes onto the skewers, 4 to a skewer. Grill, turning once with grill tongs, for 3 to 4 minutes per side for medium. Drizzle a little of the remaining amogio on each skewer and serve.

Crowning Glories

Try making beef skewers sprinkled with a spicy rub (before grilling)
or served with a side sauce, such as:

Tricolored Peppercorn Rub (page 62)

Asian Barbecue Sauce (page 90)

Peanut Butter Dipping Sauce (page 118)

Grilled Beef Skewers with Spicy Tomato-Chile Sauce: This delicious Thai-style sauce is a great dipping sauce for beef, pork, fish, or poultry. In a medium-size skillet over medium heat, heat 1 tablespoon red pepper flakes for about 1 minute. Add 1 cup chopped white onion, 4 chopped garlic cloves, and 4 chopped Roma tomatoes and cook, stirring, for 5 to 7 minutes. In a large bowl, combine ¼ cup Asian fish sauce, the juice and grated zest of 2 limes, and ¼ cup firmly packed dark brown sugar. Add the tomato mixture and combine using a hand-held blender (or process in an electric blender). Don't overblend; you want the sauce to be a little chunky. Grill the beef skewers as described above and serve with the sauce. **SERVES 6**

Tamarind and Yogurt Beef Kabobs with Warm Pita Breads: Begin with a small bowl filled with ½ cup hot water. Add 1 to 2 ounces tamarind pulp (available at Asian markets), soaking it for about 30 minutes. In a large bowl, combine 1½ cups plain yogurt, 3 tablespoons unsweetened coconut milk, 2 tablespoons ground coriander, 1 tablespoon ground cumin, and 1 teaspoon chili powder. Drain the tamarind pulp and add the liquid to the yogurt mixture. Transfer half of the sauce to a small serving bowl and reserve. Cut 1½ pounds boneless sirloin into 24 cubes and marinate in the remaining sauce for about 1 hour. Drain, then thread the beef onto skewers and grill as directed above. While grilling, warm 6 pita breads on the grill. Serve the beef with the pitas and reserved yogurt sauce for dipping. **SERVES 6**

Beef Skewers with Quick Peanut Sauce: In a small bowl, combine ¼ cup crunchy peanut butter, ¼ cup unsweetened coconut milk, 1 tablespoon ground cumin, 1 teaspoon red pepper flakes, ½ teaspoon ground cinnamon, and kosher salt to taste. (If you like a thicker sauce, use either more peanut butter or less coconut milk.) Grill the skewers as directed above and serve with the sauce. **SERVES 6**

Grill Gals

She Grills for a Taste of Home Menu

Kabuli Kabobs

Salata (Afghani Fresh Chopped Vegetable Salad)

Entrepreneur and go-getter Latifa Raoufi grew up in Kabul, Afghanistan, during the 1950s and 1960s. Her father was a diplomat working for King Shah Zahir and the Afghani royal family. Latifa's family, who spoke Farsi, lived in the old section of upper-class Kabul when her father wasn't on diplomatic assignment in New York, Cairo, or Bombay. Photos taken during the 1960s show a thriving city, with the clear blue Kabul River, landscaped parks, beautiful old flat-roofed buildings of sun-bleached mud brick, a crowded central bazaar with many vendors, the rounded domes of mosques, and the Hindu Kush mountains in the background. Just beyond Kabul were lush irrigated fields where all kinds of vegetables and fruits were grown.

"In the 1950s, Kabul looked like the city of Lyon in France," remembers Latifa, who was a little girl then. "It was beautiful. We had so much luxury. We bought all of our food fresh."

In the kitchen compound, the Raoufi family had four raised brick hearths, each made from two mud-brick squat pillars with an iron grill rack placed atop them. Wood and charcoal fires burned under the grill racks. Pots and pans were coated on the outside with mud for easier cleanup after cooking over the open fire. "When the pots were cleaned, the maids would take them outside again and coat them with fresh mud," Latifa recalls. "Then they would turn the pots upside down to dry in the sun."

When the Soviets invaded Afghanistan in 1979, Latifa fled the country in a daring escape, hidden in the back of a truck with only a little money and her passport. She came to the United States and has made a success of her life here. But when she gets homesick from time to time, she goes to the kitchen to re-create taste memories from another time, another place.

Kabuli Kabobs

A traditional evening meal in pre-1979 Kabul might have five different courses. The first course might include grilled flatbreads with different fillings (such as Bolani, page 182) and kabobs served on platters and eaten out of hand. As a sweet ending to a meal, the Raoufi family often ate dried fruits and nuts, accompanied by green tea flavored with ground cardamom. Make the kabobs the day before you plan to serve them, because they need to be refrigerated overnight. The onion also may be prepared the day before. **SERVES 10**

BEEF TENDERLOIN KABOBS

3 pounds beef tenderloin, cut into 2 x 1-inch pieces

Juice of 2 lemons

1 head garlic, cloves minced

¼ teaspoon cayenne pepper, or more to taste

½ teaspoon kosher or sea salt

MINCED BEEF KABOBS

1 pound ground sirloin

2 tablespoons ground coriander

1 bunch fresh cilantro, minced

4 cloves garlic, minced

Juice of 1 lemon

1 large egg

1 large onion, peeled

Juice of 1 lemon

¼ teaspoon kosher or sea salt

20 wooden skewers, soaked in water for at least 30 minutes before grilling

10 flatbreads or pita breads

2 large ripe tomatoes

Edible flowers and fresh cilantro or mint sprigs for garnish

1. To make the beef tenderloin kabobs, rinse the meat, pat dry, and place in a large dish or sealable plastic bag. In a small bowl, combine the lemon juice, garlic, cayenne, and salt. Pour over the meat, cover or seal, and marinate in the refrigerator overnight, turning several times.

2. To make the minced beef kabobs, combine all the ingredients in a medium-size bowl, using your hands or a rubber spatula to blend. Cover and refrigerate overnight.

3. Cut the onion into quarters, then cut each quarter into paper-thin half-moons. Place the onion slices in a colander and rinse well with water. Transfer to a medium-size bowl and sprinkle with the lemon juice and salt. Set aside to marinate for at least 1 hour or overnight.

4. Prepare a medium-hot fire in a grill.

5. Thread the marinated beef tenderloin kabobs onto 10 of the skewers and set aside. Form the cold minced beef mixture into ten 6-inch logs. Thread each log lengthwise onto a skewer (handle the logs gently so they don't fall apart). Grill all the kabobs until still a bit pink in the middle, turning once, 5 to 10 minutes total.

6. To serve, arrange the flatbreads on a platter. Cut the tomatoes into quarters. Place the kabobs on top of the breads. Garnish with the marinated onion slices, tomato quarters, flowers, and herb sprigs. Serve hot or at room temperature.

To eat the kabobs in the traditional way, place a flatbread on your plate and slide the kabobs off 2 skewers (one of each type) into the center of the bread. Add some tomatoes and onions (or Salata; right) and wrap the flatbread around the filling.

Salata (Afghani Fresh Chopped Vegetable Salad)

Kabuli cooks have special ways to tame the fire and tears provoked by fresh onions, as you will see in this recipe. Use *salata* as you would *pico de gallo*, a relish made with hot and sweet peppers, other vegetables, and seasonings. SERVES 6

2 large onions, peeled

1/4 teaspoon fine kosher or sea salt

Juice of 2 lemons

2 large ripe tomatoes

1 medium-size cucumber, peeled

Juice of 1 lime

1.   Cut the onions into quarters, then cut each quarter into paper-thin half-moons. Place the onion slices in a colander and rinse well with water. Transfer to a medium-size bowl and sprinkle with the salt and lemon juice. Set aside for at least 1 hour to marinate.

2.   Cut the tomatoes into quarters, then cut each quarter into paper-thin half-moons and place in a large bowl. Cut the cucumber in half lengthwise, then cut into paper-thin slices. Add to the bowl. Stir in the marinated onion, then the lime juice. Toss to blend and taste for seasoning. Add more salt or lime juice, if necessary. Serve at room temperature.

Grilled Beef Tenderloin

This dish has become special occasion or holiday fare in Judith's family. Although pricey, beef tenderloin repays your outlay with a great entrée—and great leftovers—requiring minimal effort. The BBQ Queens like to grill beef tenderloin with a little char on the exterior, leaving the interior rosy and juicy.

We prefer a plain grilled tenderloin accompanied by a jazzy sauce or two, but you can soak, sprinkle, slather, or sauce this cut to your heart's content. It will always be delicious. Have your butcher prepare the tenderloin first by removing the silverskin and tying it up into a nice, evenly shaped roast.

Grilling a great beef tenderloin starts with a really hot fire—preferably one made with mesquite charcoal—but you can still have a mighty fine tenderloin on a gas grill. You'll want the heat very hot to get that char.

It's also important to turn the tenderloin every 4 to 5 minutes so it cooks evenly all over. During the last 10 minutes of cooking, insert an instant-read meat thermometer in the middle of the meat and watch it as you would a new hairdresser—like a hawk. You can always zap an underdone tenderloin in the microwave, but a well-done tenderloin can't be fixed. (You don't want to see the BBQ Queens cry, now, do you?)

For a royal feast, serve your tenderloin with Grilled Asparagus (page 117) and/or Grilled Mushrooms (page 132). **SERVES 10 TO 12**

> **One 6- to 8-pound beef tenderloin, trimmed of any fat and silverskin**
> **Melted unsalted butter**
> **Fine kosher or sea salt and freshly ground black pepper to taste**

1. Brush the tenderloin with melted butter, then season with salt and pepper.

2. Prepare a hot fire in a grill, using mesquite chips for a kiss of smoke (see page 13), if you like.

3. Place the tenderloin on the grill, close the lid, and grill, turning a quarter turn every 5 minutes for the first 10 minutes. Turn, brush again with melted butter, and insert a heatproof meat thermometer in the middle of the tenderloin. Continue to grill with the lid closed until the thermometer registers 130°F (for rare) or the meat is firm yet a little springy to the touch, 10 to 12 minutes.

4. Remove from the grill and let rest for 5 minutes. Remove the twine, slice, and serve to frenzied accolades.

BBQ Tip: Judith learned a few beef tenderloin tips from her father. One is to watch for when whole beef tenderloin goes on sale. Then buy it, bring it home, and sharpen that knife. You can get extra savings on beef tenderloin if you trim it yourself, which is easy to do. The whole tenderloin will have a thick end and taper down to a thin end. Trim off any fat and silverskin. Cut the size tenderloin you want to grill whole, then cut the rest of the tenderloin into 1-inch-thick steaks. Cut the tapered end into chunks for kabobs. Wrap well and freeze until you're ready to grill, up to 3 months.

 Crowning Glories

Why hold back? Gild that beef lily with one of the following:

Poblano Cream Sauce *(page 93)*

Smoked Chile Beurre Blanc *(page 99)*

Peppercorn Beurre Blanc *(page 102)*

Grilled Tenderloin with Sour Cream, Bacon, and Mushroom Sauce: When Judith's family grills a tenderloin, this is the sauce they serve with it, adapted from a recipe in the Junior League of Pasadena's *California Heritage Cookbook* (Doubleday, 1976). In a large skillet, cook 12 ounces sliced bacon until crisp, then transfer to paper towels to drain. Pour off all but 2 tablespoons of the fat and cook 4 ounces sliced fresh mushrooms until softened, 3 to 5 minutes. Transfer to a medium-size bowl and let cool. When cooled, add 1¹/₂ cups sour cream, 2 teaspoons prepared horseradish, 1 tablespoon grated onion (we use a microplane grater), and 2 tablespoons finely chopped fresh Italian parsley and mix. Crumble the bacon into the sauce and mix again. Grill the tenderloin as described above and serve with the sauce on the side. **SERVES 8**

Chez Panisse–Style Grilled Beef Tenderloin: It was a perfect spring night in Berkeley, California—a light breeze, the air a little cool and clear. The BBQ Queens were dining at Chez Panisse—or should we say paying long overdue homage to culinary queen and Grill Gal Alice Waters, who confesses that her "picky eater" childhood birthday menu was always green beans and rare charcoal-grilled steak. We had a fabulous meal, a fabulous experience. When you enjoy beef tenderloin prepared this way, adapted from Waters's *Chez Panisse Menu Cookbook* (Random House, 1982), you'll share in the fabulous-ness. Place one 6- to 8-pound trimmed beef tenderloin in a deep casserole dish. Scatter 2 sliced medium-size onions, 2 crumbled bay leaves, and 10 to 12 black peppercorns around the beef. Pour one 750 ml bottle dry red wine over the beef, then add 10 to 12 sprigs fresh Italian parsley and ¹/₂ cup olive oil. Cover and refrigerate, turning several times, for up to 12 hours. When ready to grill, remove the meat from the marinade and pat dry. Brush with olive oil and season with kosher or sea salt and freshly ground black pepper to taste. Grill as directed above, then slice and serve. **SERVES 8**

Smoked Beef Tenderloin

When you really want to wow your guests, serve them a beef tenderloin that's slightly charred on the outside, smoky and tender inside.

The only trick to this is our two-step process of putting grill marks on the meat first, then smoking it, because this speeds up the process a bit and makes for a better presentation. But you don't want to build a fire in a grill *and* a smoker. That's just not queenly; it's fussy.

Here's how we do it. If we're using a charcoal or gas grill as a smoker, we simply sear the tenderloin over direct heat, then move it over to the indirect side to smoke. If we're using a three-part bullet-shaped water smoker, we place the smoker's grill rack over the bottom third (which contains the heating element or coals) and sear the meat on the grill rack. Then we remove the grill rack, place the middle section of the smoker back over the heating element or coals, place the grill rack back on top of the middle section, cover, and smoke the tenderloin as usual. If we're using a traditional smoker, we use a grill pan indoors to get the grill marks, then put the meat in the smoker.

Because the beef tenderloin is so thick and meaty, we prefer a smoke that will match its heft—mesquite or hickory. **SERVES 8**

SUGGESTED WOOD: Mesquite or hickory

¹/₄ cup olive oil

2 cloves garlic, minced

1 tablespoon finely chopped fresh rosemary

¹/₂ teaspoon fine kosher or sea salt

Freshly ground black pepper to taste

One 4-pound beef tenderloin, at room temperature, trimmed of any fat and silverskin

1.   In a small bowl, combine the olive oil, garlic, rosemary, salt, and pepper. Slather the beef with the mixture and set aside.

2.   Prepare an indirect fire in a smoker.

3.   On the direct side of the smoker or in a grill pan over high heat indoors, sear the meat on all sides until you can see grill marks. Remove from the heat.

4.   Place the beef in a disposable aluminum pan in the smoker. Insert a heatproof meat thermometer in the center of the meat. Cover and smoke at 225 to 250°F until the internal temperature is 135 to 140°F for rare, about 3 hours. Remove from the smoker, remove the thermometer from the meat, and wrap tightly in plastic. Allow to rest for 15 to 20 minutes, then unwrap, slice, and serve.

 *Crowning Glories*

This is heavenly served with:
Simply Delicious Bordelaise Sauce *(page 91)*
White Truffle Aioli *(page 105)*
Smoked Chile Beurre Blanc *(page 99)*

Peppery Smoked Beef Tenderloin: Make 1 recipe Tricolored Peppercorn Rub (page 62), add ¹/₄ cup olive oil, and slather over a 4-pound trimmed beef tenderloin. Smoke as directed above. Slice and serve with Peppercorn Beurre Blanc (page 102) for a beaucoup fabulous finish. **SERVES 8**

Smoked Porcini Beef Tenderloin: Use Porcini Paste (page 65) to slather a 4-pound trimmed beef tenderloin. Smoke as directed above. During the last hour of smoking, add portobello mushrooms to smoke as directed on page 134. To serve, slice the tenderloin and drizzle the meat and portobellos with Simply Delicious Bordelaise Sauce (page 91). **SERVES 8**

Smoked Beef BLT: Begin with an artisanal loaf of bread, such as Asiago-herb or rosemary-garlic. Slather 1 slice of bread with mustard and another with aioli (see pages 104–105 and 110). Layer thin slices of the smoked beef (as much as you like) on the bread. Top with 3 slices crisp-cooked bacon, a crisp fresh lettuce leaf, and a couple thin slices of homegrown tomatoes. **SERVES 1**

Grill Gals

This 'Que Queen Is a Kansas City Grill Queen Menu

Grilled Herbed and Spiced Beef Tenderloin Salad
Grilled Herbed and Spiced Beef Tenderloin
Grilled Turkey Roulade with Lemon-Basil Sauce
Kathy's Chicken Wings
Smoky Meatballs

'Que Queen team member Kathy Smith is also a member of our Kansas City Cookbook Club. We all cook, eat, and share recipes at least once a month. When the cookbook club meets at Kathy's house, she almost always prepares something from the grill. She and her husband, Don, have traveled to South America and are particularly fond of Brazilian cuisine. This comes through in the recipes Kathy favors, which often have the earthy taste of ground cumin and coriander, plus fresh cilantro.

Kathy, along with 'Que Queen Dee Barwick, cooks up huge quantities of from-scratch soups and casseroles for the homeless. Volunteers deliver the food weekly to homeless people around the city.

An avid cookbook and food magazine devotee, Kathy scours the pages of books and magazines to add new recipes to her repertoire. Her salad is great alone or with other freshly grilled or leftover grilled meats, such as poultry, shellfish, or pork. The turkey roulade recipe can be made ahead and refrigerated, then sliced and served cold. It would also be divine in place of the beef on the salad.

Grilled Herbed and Spiced Beef Tenderloin Salad

Kathy found this recipe in an old *Food & Wine* magazine. While testing it, we decided that it would also be delicious with pork tenderloin, poultry, or even shrimp. Kathy heartily agreed. Here is our revised version. **SERVES 6**

DRESSING

1/2 cup mayonnaise

1/2 cup freshly grated Romano cheese

3 tablespoons Dijon mustard

3 tablespoons fresh lime juice

2 anchovy fillets, mashed

2 cloves garlic, minced

1 tablespoon Worcestershire sauce

Tabasco sauce to taste

Kosher salt and freshly ground black pepper to taste

SALAD

2 large heads romaine lettuce

4 large ripe beefsteak tomatoes, cut into wedges

2 large ripe avocados, peeled, pitted, and diced

6 slices bacon, cooked crisp and crumbled

1 small red onion, chopped

1/2 cup salted sunflower seeds, CornNuts, or other salty nuts

2 pounds Grilled Herbed and Spiced Beef Tenderloin (recipe follows), thinly sliced

1. To make the dressing, combine all the ingredients in a medium-size bowl. Stir to blend and check the seasoning. Cover and refrigerate until ready to use. (The dressing may be made a day ahead.)

2. To make the salad, rinse and dry the lettuce and tear into bite-size pieces. Toss with half the dressing. Mound on a large platter and surround with the tomato wedges and diced avocado. Sprinkle the bacon, onion, and sunflower seeds over the salad. Arrange the sliced meat on top and serve, passing the remaining dressing at the table.

Grilled Herbed and Spiced Beef Tenderloin

Take advantage of this delicious marinade and use it for fish, shellfish, pork, and poultry, too. Add a satay or Peanut Butter Dipping Sauce (page 118), and you'll be in flavor heaven. **SERVES 6**

> ¼ cup chopped fresh Italian parsley
> ¼ cup chopped fresh cilantro
> 2 tablespoons extra virgin olive oil
> 1 tablespoon ground coriander
> 1 tablespoon ground cumin
> 2 cloves garlic, minced
> 1 tablespoon coarse kosher salt
> 2 tablespoons freshly ground black pepper
> 2 pounds beef tenderloin, trimmed of any fat and silverskin
> Handful of wood chips, soaked in water for at least 30 minutes before grilling

1. In a large, shallow glass dish, combine all the ingredients except the beef and wood chips. Stir to blend, then add the meat and turn to coat thoroughly. Cover and refrigerate for 1 to 2 hours.

2. Prepare a hot indirect fire in a grill.

3. Remove the meat from the marinade and pat dry. Grill over the hot fire, searing it by turning it a quarter turn at a time until well browned all over, about 12 minutes total.

4. Place the meat on the indirect side of the grill and tent with heavy-duty aluminum foil or cover with a disposable aluminum pan. Add the wood chips to the fire. Close the lid and roast-smoke until an instant-read meat thermometer inserted in the thickest part of the beef registers 125 to 130°F for medium-rare, 25 to 30 minutes. Transfer to a platter and let rest for 10 to 15 minutes before slicing.

Grilled Turkey Roulade with Lemon-Basil Sauce

This is another adaptable recipe, which Kathy first discovered in an issue of Gourmet magazine. Try substituting chicken paillards or beef tenderloin for the turkey and, of course, adjusting the cooking time for the meat you choose. SERVES 6

> **One 2-pound turkey tenderloin**
> **Kosher salt and freshly ground black pepper to taste**
> **One 12-ounce jar fire-roasted red peppers, drained and cut into strips**
> **4 ounces Brie, cut into strips**
> **1 cup sour cream**
> **Juice and grated zest of 1 lemon**
> **¹/₂ cup chopped fresh basil**

1. Place the turkey on a cutting board and cut in half crosswise. Pound each half as you would to create a paillard (see page 191). Season with salt and pepper, then divide the red pepper slices evenly between them, leaving a ¹/₄-inch border around the edges. Place the Brie on top of the peppers. Gently roll up each turkey fillet so the filling stays in place and does not squeeze out. Tie the roulades with kitchen twin in 3 or 4 places. Season again with salt and pepper. Cover and refrigerate for 1 to 4 hours.

2. In a small bowl, combine the sour cream, lemon juice and zest, and basil. Cover and refrigerate until ready to serve.

3. Prepare a medium-hot indirect fire in a grill.

4. Grill the roulades directly over the fire, searing them on all sides, about 15 minutes total. Move to the indirect side of the grill and close the lid. Cook for about 10 minutes, then open the grill, turn the roulades, close the lid, and cook for another 5 to 10 minutes, until an instant-read meat thermometer inserted in the center of each registers 170°F.

5. Transfer to a cutting board and let stand for 10 to 15 minutes. Remove the twine carefully and cut into ¹/₂-inch-thick slices. Serve warm with the sauce.

Kathy's Chicken Wings

Kathy is an adventurous cook. She likes to follow a recipe exactly first, then experiment the second time around. You won't need to do that with this classic chicken wing recipe. It's a winner just as it is. Try serving it with our Creamy Blue Cheese Dressing (page 111). SERVES 10 TO 12

> **3 pounds chicken wings**
> **1 teaspoon kosher or sea salt**
> **1 teaspoon sweet Hungarian paprika**
> **1 teaspoon onion powder**
> **1 teaspoon lemon pepper seasoning**
> **¹/₂ teaspoon red pepper flakes**
> **¹/₂ teaspoon garlic powder**

1. Rinse the wings and pat dry. In a large sealable plastic bag, combine the remaining ingredients. Add the chicken, seal the bag, and shake to coat evenly. Place the wings on a baking sheet and let stand at room temperature for 30 to 60 minutes.

2. Prepare a hot fire in a grill.

3. Grill the wings in a single layer, turning and rotating, for 20 to 30 minutes. They are done when the joints move easily and can be torn apart. Serve hot.

Smoky Meatballs

Ever try meatballs on the grill or in the smoker? If not, here's your chance. We start with Kathy's very good recipe, which makes big meatballs that won't fall through the grill grate. These can also be baked at 350°F for 30 to 40 minutes or sautéed over high heat for 20 to 25 minutes. Serve them with marinara sauce, horseradish cocktail sauce, or Spicy Tomato-Chile Sauce (page 331). **MAKES 12 MEATBALLS**

> 1 pound ground beef
>
> 3 large eggs
>
> ¹/₂ cup fresh Italian bread crumbs
>
> ¹/₂ cup freshly grated Romano cheese, or more to taste
>
> 3 cloves garlic, minced
>
> 2 tablespoons chopped fresh Italian parsley
>
> 2 tablespoons chopped fresh basil
>
> ³/₄ teaspoon kosher salt
>
> ¹/₂ teaspoon freshly ground black pepper

1. In a large bowl, combine all the ingredients. Shape into 12 large meatballs. Place in a covered container and refrigerate for at least 8 hours to allow the flavors to meld and the meatballs to firm up.

2. To grill the meatballs, prepare a hot fire. Grill for about 15 minutes, turning several times so they are charred all over. To smoke the meatballs, prepare an indirect fire at 250°F. Place the meatballs directly on the grill grate or in a disposable aluminum pan on the indirect side of the smoker. Smoke for 1 hour. Serve hot.

Planked Beef Tenderloin

We love to plank, and anything that is tender planks well. Our sublime beef tenderloin is perfection. Favored woods for planking beef are oak, maple, pecan, and hickory. Fruitwood planks are nice, too, but you may have to cut your own. For detailed instructions on planking, see page 42.

Serve planked tenderloin with A Platter of Fresh Tomatoes (page 206), Fiesta Bread (page 178), and an earthy Cabernet or a fruity Merlot. It doesn't get much easier—or better—than this. **SERVES 4**

Four 4-ounce beef tenderloin steaks, ³/₄ inch thick

Fine kosher or sea salt and freshly ground black pepper to taste

One 15 x 6¹/₂ x 3/8-inch oak or maple plank, soaked in water for at least 1 hour before grilling

1. Prepare a dual-heat fire, with a hot fire on one side and a medium fire on the other.

2. Place the tenderloin steaks on a baking sheet, season with salt and pepper, and bring outside. Place the plank over direct heat for 4 to 5 minutes, until it begins to smoke and pop. Turn the plank over and move to the medium-heat side. Carefully place the steaks on the charred side of the plank. Cover and cook until an instant-read meat thermometer inserted in the center registers 125 to 130°F for medium-rare, about 12 minutes. Serve hot.

Crowning Glories

You can dress these steaks up with a fancy rub, drizzle with a vinaigrette, or serve with a scrumptious side sauce:

BBQ Queens' Photo Op Barbecue Rub *(page 58)*

Hot Shallot Vinaigrette *(page 85)*

Smoked Chile Beurre Blanc *(page 99)*

Bourbon-Mustard Cream Sauce *(page 377)*

Argentinean Hickory-Planked Beef Tenderloin with Chimichurri Sauce: Argentinean restaurants often serve *churrasco* beef that is planked upright around a blazing fire. This recipe gives you much the same flavor, but in an easier preparation. The sauce—made with four different fresh herbs, along with garlic and sherry vinegar—is a robust accompaniment to the gentle smokiness of the beef. To make the sauce, in a food processor combine ¹/₂ cup fresh Italian parsley leaves, ¹/₄ cup fresh cilantro leaves, ¹/₄ cup fresh mint leaves, 2 tablespoons fresh oregano leaves, $^1/_4$ cup chopped yellow onion, 3 peeled garlic cloves, $^1/_2$ teaspoon cayenne pepper, $^1/_2$ teaspoon fine kosher or sea salt, $^1/_2$ teaspoon freshly ground black pepper, $^1/_3$ cup olive oil, $^1/_3$ cup sherry vinegar, and $^1/_4$ cup water. Process until smooth. (The sauce is best served the same day but will keep, covered, in the refrigerator for up to 5 days.) Prepare the planked beef as directed above using a hickory plank. Serve with the sauce. **SERVES 4**

Gorgonzola Filet Mignon on a Plank: Plank the tenderloin steaks as directed above, first placing 1 tablespoon crumbled Gorgonzola on top of each filet. Serve with additional crumbled Gorgonzola on the side and big fat grilled asparagus spears (see page 117). **SERVES 4**

Slathered Beef Filet on a Plank: Plank the steaks as directed above, first slathering each one with 1 to 2 tablespoons Porcini Paste (page 65). **SERVES 4**

Rotisserie Beef Roast

Once you've rotisserie cooked your first rib-eye or sirloin tip roast, there's no going back to plain old roasting. The flavor of smoke and char is a sensational component to the tender meatiness of the beef. To us, roasted-in-the-oven prime rib is now a little lackluster. We prefer rib-eye roasts for tenderness, but sirloin tip or tri-tip roasts are also mighty tasty, if just a little chewier.

Because rotisserie cooking is a bit of a production, why not make it part of the theatrics of entertaining a crowd? Judith recently made this dish for her son Nick's college graduation party, and nary a speck was left over. **SERVES 12**

> **One 6-pound boneless rib-eye or sirloin tip roast, rolled and tied**
> **2 cloves garlic, cut into slivers**
> **2 tablespoons olive oil**
> **1 tablespoon fresh lemon juice**
> **Kosher or sea salt and freshly ground black pepper to taste**

1.   Make 1-inch-deep slits in the roast in several places, then press the garlic slivers into the slits. Combine the olive oil and lemon juice in a cup and rub the roast all over with it. Season with salt and pepper.

2. Set up a grill for rotisserie cooking (see page 33). Prepare a medium fire (around 350°F). Push the rotisserie rod through the center of the roast so it is balanced, then place on the spit. Cover and roast until an instant-read meat thermometer inserted in the center registers 120°F for rare or 140°F for medium-rare, about 2 hours.

3. Place the roast on a serving platter and tent with aluminum foil to keep warm. Let rest for 20 minutes before slicing and serving.

 **Crowning Glories**

Rotisserie beef roast is delicious served with a fancy-schmancy beurre blanc or plain old barbecue sauce; heirloom vegetables, baked beans, or potato salad; or:

Grilled Onions with Thyme and Garlic Cream (page 138)

Potato Gratin with White Cheddar Cheese (page 412)

Grilled Asparagus (page 117)

Uptown Rotisserie Beef Roast with Peppercorn Beurre Blanc: We don't mind the hot flashes we get from *this* combination! It's wonderful. Simply substitute Tricolored Peppercorn Rub (page 62) for the salt and pepper when you're preparing the roast for the spit. Rotisserie cook the roast as directed above. Serve with a double (or triple) recipe of Peppercorn Beurre Blanc (page 102). (Make the beurre blanc one batch at a time, but keep all the batches warm together in one pan.) **SERVES 12**

Downtown Rotisserie Beef Roast with BBQ Queens' Barbecued Beans: This is closer to the down-home barbecuer's idea of barbecue. Substitute BBQ Queens' All-Purpose Rub (page 49) for the salt and pepper when you're preparing the roast for the spit. Rotisserie cook the roast as directed above, but instead of an 11 x 9-inch disposable pan with liquid under the roast, top it with a second pan of BBQ Queens' Barbecued Beans (page 107). Cook the beans with the roast, stirring them every 30 minutes. (The beans will catch all the delicious drippings.) Serve the beef and beans with Smoky Barbecue Sauce (page 90). **SERVES 12**

Lemon Pepper Beef Roast with Butter Baste: This treatment makes sirloin tip taste as luscious as rib-eye roast. Substitute lemon pepper seasoning for the black pepper when you're preparing the roast for the spit. Rotisserie cook the roast as directed above, basting with a brushful of softened unsalted butter (about 1 stick total) every 15 minutes. **SERVES 12**

Rotisserie Boneless Prime Rib Roast with Blackened Seasoning: This is perfect for a New Year's Day feast or a Super Bowl gathering. Substitute your favorite blackened seasoning or Cajun Steak Rub (page 58) for the pepper when you're preparing the roast for the spit. Rotisserie cook the roast as directed above. Let rest for 15 minutes before slicing. **SERVES 12**

Smoked Beef Rib Roast

A standing rib roast often is the main culinary attraction for a special occasion or holiday dinner. Generally, it is cooked in the oven, but the BBQ Queens are here to tell you that there's a more savory and memorable way to serve this expensive holiday classic. Smoke that sucker!

A smoked rib roast has all that good char on the exterior, and the somewhat bland meat of your mother's standard roasted rib roast is revved up with a smoky flavor. Even traditionalists who don't like anyone messing with their holiday favorites love beef roast this way. By using the smoker, you also free up the oven for other dishes. You can have someone keep an eye on it outside (and get him out from underfoot in the kitchen). Hie thee hence to the smoker for this dish. The BBQ Queens have spoken.

Because the beef roast is so thick and meaty, we prefer to match it with a thick and meaty smoke—mesquite or hickory. Just don't use too much. With smoke, as with makeup, more is not necessarily better.

Go uptown with the roast and serve a wine-enriched sauce or Yorkshire Pudding (page 350), or go downtown with traditional barbecue fixin's—your pick. **SERVES 8**

SUGGESTED WOOD: Mesquite or hickory

One 4- to 6-pound standing rib roast, at room temperature
1/4 cup olive oil
1 tablespoon granulated garlic
1/2 cup cracked black peppercorns

1. Prepare a fire in a smoker.

2. Trim some of the white fat from the roast. Discard it or save it for Yorkshire Pudding (below). Rub the roast with the olive oil and press the granulated garlic and cracked pepper into the meat. Insert a heatproof meat thermometer in the center of the roast. Place fat side up on a rack in the smoker. Cover and smoke at 225 to 250°F, until the meat thermometer registers 140°F for rare, 3 to 3¹/₂ hours.

3. Remove the roast from the smoker, remove the thermometer, and wrap the roast tightly in plastic wrap. Allow to rest for 15 to 20 minutes, then unwrap, slice, and serve.

Crowning Glories

Smoked beef rib roast is wonderful with:

Mediterranean-Style Stir-Grilled Mushrooms and Olives *(page 168)*

BBQ Queens' Smoked Potato Casserole *(page 153)*

Cheesy Italian Pesto Bread *(page 177)*

Smoked Rib Roast with Yorkshire Pudding: If you're going to the trouble of making a smoked rib roast, why not go all out and make decadent Yorkshire pudding? If you've never had really good Yorkshire pudding—a cross between a soufflé and a risen savory pancake—now's your chance. When you're trimming the white fat from the rib roast, reserve 1 cup. Smoke the roast as described above. About 45 minutes before you're ready to eat, preheat the oven to 450°F. In a heavy, square glass baking dish, combine the fat, ¹/₄ teaspoon freshly ground black pepper, and ¹/₂ teaspoon granulated garlic. Cover loosely with aluminum foil and place in the oven for 7 to 10 minutes, until the fat has melted and slightly browned. Meanwhile, in a small bowl, whisk 2 large eggs. Add 1 cup all-purpose flour, 1 cup whole milk, ¹/₄ teaspoon fine kosher or sea salt, and 2 tablespoons vegetable oil and whisk to a smooth batter. Remove the baking dish from the oven and carefully pour the batter over the hot fat. Return the baking dish to the oven and bake for 10 minutes, then reduce the oven temperature to 350°F and bake until puffed and golden, another 10 to 15 minutes. Cut immediately into squares and serve hot with slices of rib roast. **SERVES 8**

Rosemary Pesto Smoked Rib Roast: A big, beefy roast can stand up to the assertive flavor of Rosemary Pesto (page 62), so slather it on the meat, then smoke as described above. **SERVES 8**

Smoked Rib Roast Sandwiches: If you have any leftover smoked rib roast (which is doubtful), make these memorable sandwiches. Start with crusty ciabatta or other artisanal bread, cut into 12 to 16 slices. In a small bowl, combine $^1/_2$ cup mayonnaise, 1 teaspoon prepared horseradish, and 1 teaspoon Cajun or blackened seasoning of your choice. Slather half the bread slices with the mayonnaise mixture. Layer on slices of smoked rib roast and arugula or other assertive greens and top with the remaining bread slices. Then dig in! **SERVES 6 TO 8**

Fourth of July All-American Barbecue

The BBQ Queens have an extra-special reason for celebrating the Fourth of July. On that day, America made a bold step in declaring its independence from England, King George III, and his queen! That paved the way for democracy—and opened the door to real rhinestone royalty like us. Two centuries later, you can become whatever kind of queen you want to be—BBQ, Sweet Potato, or even Silver Queen Corn Queen. Like the athletic shoe ads say, just do it!

The same goes for putting on a big barbecue bash (and we mean barbecue as in slow smoking, not grilling). Nothing else will do but red, white, and blue for Uncle Sam's birthday. Decorate with miniature flags stuffed in bouquets of red and blue carnations and lots of baby's breath. Fire up that smoker and put in the brisket, beans, and potatoes. Post your favorite male courtier outside (with a supply of beer) and have him keep an eye on things. Meanwhile, because you know everyone's coming, you can bake a cake (see pages 394–397). Howd'yado, howd'yado, howd'yado!

Fourth of July All-American Barbecue Menu

Smoked Brisket (page 356)

BBQ Queens' Barbecued Beans (page 107)

BBQ Queens' Smoked Potato Casserole (page 153)

Smoky Barbecue Sauce (page 90)

S'mores (page 262)

Toasted Coconut Ice Cream with Hot Fudge Ganache and Toasted Pecans (page 440)

BBQ Babes

She's a Tiara-Totin' Texas Queen of the 'Que Menu

Slow-Smoked Texas-Style Brisket
Mozzarella and Tomato Salad with Two Dressings

Dotty Griffith (above, left) was born and raised on Texas barbecue—beef brisket barbecue to be exact. Texas is cattle country, and beef is king of this state. So when we asked Dotty if she would be one of our BBQ Babes and share her delicious brisket recipe with us, her reply was that she'd be honored. We say to Dotty, "Back at ya!"

Dotty is the dining editor and restaurant critic for the *Dallas Morning News*. Formerly, Dotty was the paper's food editor, and that's when Karen first met her and became her publisher for a collection of restaurant recipes titled *Dallas Cuisine* (Two Lane Press, 1993). This now out-of-print cookbook includes a wonderful mozzarella and tomato salad recipe from Paula Lambert (above, right), owner of the renowned Mozzarella Company in Dallas (and a good friend of Dotty's). We include it here and suggest serving it with BBQ Babe Paris Permenter's Texas-Style Pinto Beans (page 106).

Slow-Smoked Texas-Style Brisket

Dotty says, "Brisket is a big, flat, stringy piece of meat, but when slow-smoked, it becomes fork tender and delicious." Her method for cooking brisket is to allow about one hour of cooking per pound of meat, plus a little more in case the fire gets too low or the meat's just tough and stubborn. "And remember," Dotty says, "brisket, like any other meat on the barbecue, takes longer to cook when the weather is cold."

Another Texas buddy of Dotty's is Dean Fearing, lauded chef of the Mansion on Turtle Creek in Dallas. His tip for perfect brisket is an internal temperature of 185 to 200°F. If the meat registers 210°F, it will be too dry. SERVES 10 TO 12

SUGGESTED WOOD: Oak or mesquite

One 8- to 10-pound beef brisket, left untrimmed (it should have a thick layer of fat on one side)

1/2 cup Texas Two-Steppin' Mesquite Rub (page 59), or kosher or sea salt and freshly ground black pepper to taste

8 to 10 wood chunks, soaked in water for at least 1 hour before grilling, or 2 to 3 cups wood chips, soaked in water for at least 30 minutes before grilling

Warm barbecue sauce of your choice for serving (optional)

Dill pickle slices, sliced onion, and/or pickled jalapeños for serving

1. Generously coat all sides of the brisket, particularly the fat layer, with the rub. Cover and let the meat come to room temperature, about 1 hour.

2. If using a charcoal smoker, prepare an indirect fire. Add the wood chunks when the temperature inside the smoker is about 300°F. When the fire has burned down to glowing embers or the coals are covered with gray ash (225 to 250°F), place a pan of water over the fire. Place the brisket on the grate beside the water pan but not directly over the heat.

If using a gas grill, turn on one burner and close the lid. Heat the grill to 225 to 250°F. Put the wood chips in a smoker box or in an aluminum foil packet poked with holes and place directly over the flames. Place a pan of water over the flames, too. Place the brisket on the grate beside the water pan but not directly over the heat.

3.   Close the lid and smoke the brisket, turning every hour or so. Tend the charcoal fire by adding wood (or wood embers from a separate fire) or coals to keep it from going out and to keep the temperature inside the smoker at 225 to 250°F. Keep a steady 225 to 250°F internal temperature inside the gas grill by adjusting the temperature knob. The brisket is done when it is charred and tender and an instant-read meat thermometer inserted in the center registers 180 to 190°F, 8 to 10 hours.

4.   Remove the brisket from the smoker or grill and allow to rest for about 20 minutes. Trim off the fat layer and cut the brisket into thin slices across the grain. Serve with warm barbecue sauce, if desired. (Or stack several slices in a sandwich bun spread lightly with barbecue sauce.) Serve with pickles, onions, and jalapeños on the side.

Mozzarella and Tomato Salad with Two Dressings

Paula Lambert is a cheesemaker who founded the Mozzarella Company in Dallas in 1982. We especially love her handcrafted fresh mozzarella. This recipe is adapted from Dotty's book _Dallas Cuisine_. SERVES 4

> **1 pound fresh mozzarella**
> **2 large ripe beefsteak tomatoes**
> **8 lettuce leaves**
> **Dressing of your choice (recipes follow)**
> **Fresh basil or cilantro leaves for garnish**

Slice the mozzarella and tomatoes uniformly about ¼ inch thick. Alternate the slices over the lettuce on a platter or on individual salad plates. Drizzle with dressing, garnish with basil leaves, and serve.

Basil Vinaigrette

You can also use this as a drizzle over grilled or smoked meats, fish, or vegetables.
MAKES ABOUT $^1/_2$ CUP

> **$^1/_4$ cup olive oil**
> **2 tablespoons balsamic vinegar**
> **6 to 8 fresh basil leaves**
> **Kosher salt and freshly ground black pepper to taste**

Combine all the ingredients in a food processor and whirl until well blended. Taste for salt and pepper.

Southwestern Dressing

This yummy dressing also goes well with poultry and fish and can be used as a marinade or basting sauce, too. **MAKES ABOUT $^1/_2$ CUP**

> **$^1/_4$ cup olive oil**
> **2 tablespoons red wine vinegar**
> **1 clove garlic, chopped**
> **1 tablespoon chopped fresh cilantro leaves**
> **2 tablespoons chopped canned green chiles**
> **Fine kosher salt and freshly ground black pepper to taste**

Combine all the ingredients in a small bowl and whisk to blend.

Smoked Brisket

Beef brisket comes from the front end of the steer, basically the breast area. It's a tough, stringy piece of meat, which makes it perfect for long, slow cooking. Many people have slow roasted a brisket in the oven with the traditional onion gravy to follow, but slow smoking a brisket gives it even more flavor.

The BBQ Queens recommend two methods for smoking your brisket: the long way—about 15 hours—in the smoker, or the shortcut method, which we explain below. We love both, but the reality is, you don't always have 15 hours to tend a fire outdoors.

If you *are* going to devote that much time to a recipe, we think you should get some bang for your buck and smoke two briskets at once. Wrap and freeze one, if you like, to serve for another occasion. Plus, two briskets will yield enough burnt ends for a couple of tasty sandwiches (see page 358). If you choose to smoke only one brisket, cut the recipe in half and smoke for 8 hours total.

We slather the brisket first with a mustard mixture, then sprinkle on a zesty, spicy rub. Then it's into the smoker, where we baste it occasionally with apple juice. When it's done, we slice it on the diagonal, across the grain of the meat (as you do for flank steak), for maximum tenderness. Lots of barbecuers cut a notch in the corner of the meat before it goes on the smoker so they know which way the grain runs; after the brisket has smoked and shrunk, it can be hard to tell.

Make sure you save any trimmings from your smoked brisket. If necessary, freeze them to use later in heavenly BBQ Queens' Barbecued Beans (page 107) or Barbecued Brisket Dip (page 358). **SERVES 24**

SUGGESTED WOOD: Apple, hickory, pecan, or a combination; a little mesquite mixed in is quite good, but mesquite alone can be too bitter for long smoking

Two 10- to 12-pound beef briskets
2 recipes Mustard-Mayo Slather (page 66)
2 recipes BBQ Queens' All-Purpose Rub (page 49)
1 quart apple juice

1. Brush the briskets all over with the slather, then sprinkle evenly with the rub. Set aside for 15 minutes, until the surface of the meat is tacky to the touch.

2. Prepare an indirect fire in a smoker.

3. Cover and smoke the briskets at 225 to 250°F. After 2 hours, start basting with apple juice every 30 minutes. The briskets are done when you can insert a grill fork into the meat and twist easily. An instant-read meat thermometer inserted in the thickest part should register 165°F. This will take about 15 hours total.

4. Let the meat rest for 15 minutes, then slice on the diagonal and across the grain, arrange on a platter, and serve.

BBQ Tip: The meat will stay juicier if you slice it ¼ inch thick. If it is not fall-apart tender, however, it is better to slice it paper-thin. Or, if you prefer chopped or pulled brisket, slice it 1 inch thick, then pull the meat apart. If the meat doesn't pull easily, chop it up. Toss it with a small amount of BBQ Queens' Love Potion for the Swine (page 89) for a sublime touch.

 **Crowning Glories**

Smoked brisket is traditionally served piled high on a
nondescript white bread and topped with barbecue sauce, such as
Smoky Barbecue Sauce (page 90); also serve it with:
BBQ Queens' Barbecued Beans *(page 107)*
BBQ Queens' Smoked Potato Casserole *(page 153)*
Layered Vinegar Slaw *(page 80)*

Kansas City–Style Barbecued Brisket: There are two main styles of barbecued brisket—Texas style, which is mildly smoked and very tender, and Kansas City style, which is more heavily smoked and slightly chewy. For KC style, you need to coat the briskets with olive oil, then sprinkle on a rub composed of ½ cup sweet Hungarian paprika, ¼ cup cayenne pepper, ¼ cup granulated garlic, and ¼ cup freshly ground black pepper. Use hickory wood for the smoke flavor. Smoke the briskets at 225 to 250°F for 12 hours and begin basting every 30 minutes with apple juice after 4 hours of cooking. After 12 hours, remove the briskets from the smoker, wrap well in a double thickness of plastic wrap and a sheet of heavy-duty aluminum foil, and return to the smoker. (At 225 to 250°F, the plastic wrap will not melt.) Smoke the briskets for another 2 to 3 hours, until tender. Unwrap, slice, and serve. **SERVES 24**

Two-Step Shortcut Barbecued Brisket: Sometimes you end up with a moister brisket by taking a shortcut. You still get the smoky flavor this way, but you also get a juicier end result. Slather and rub the briskets as described above and smoke for 3 hours, basting twice with apple juice. Then bring them inside, wrap in 2 sheets of aluminum foil, and finish in a preheated 300°F oven for 3 to 3½ hours. The briskets are done when you can pierce the meat with a fork and twist easily. Unwrap, slice, and serve. **SERVES 24**

Barbecued Brisket Dip: Smoke for leftovers, we always say. With all the time you've spent smoking a brisket, it only makes sense to freeze some for dishes like this that you can make later. We adapted our recipe from one by our barbecue buddy Ardie Davis, also known as Remus Powers, Ph.B. To make the dip, in a large bowl combine 1 pound (about 2 cups) chopped barbecued brisket; ½ cup chopped onion; 1 minced garlic clove; 1¼ cups barbecue sauce of your choice; one 4-ounce can drained and chopped jalapeños; one 8-ounce package softened cream cheese; and ⅓ cup freshly grated Pecorino Romano, Asiago, or Parmesan cheese. Spoon into a greased 13 x 11-inch baking dish and bake at 350°F until browned and bubbling, 20 to 30 minutes. Serve hot with French bread or crackers. **SERVES 8**

Burnt Ends: When you're doing several briskets at a time, you can make a tasty dish of burnt ends. Burnt ends come from the thinnest part of the brisket, which is too thin to slice. After the brisket has come out of the smoker, trim off the burnt ends. Chop them into small, bite-size pieces, then brush them with the mustard slather and sprinkle with the rub (see above). Put them in a disposable aluminum pan, tightly wrap with foil, and return to the smoker (or a 300°F oven) for 1 to 2 hours, until you can shred them easily. **MAKES 2 TO 4 CUPS**

Burnt Ends Sandwich: One of our favorite decadent sandwiches—the Poor Russ—is made from burnt ends of both beef brisket and pork butt, courtesy of Jack Fiorella's Jack Stack in Kansas City. To make a burnt ends sandwich, use burnt ends that have been slow cooked twice as described above, then shredded and piled on a slice of bread. Add lots of barbecue sauce and top with another bread slice. That's durn good eatin'. **SERVES 1**

Barbecued Corned Beef with Mustard-Beer Slather and Smoked Potato Salad

Sometimes it's good to leave Venus for Mars and get a guy's take on barbecue. Plus, a girl's got to have some guy friends, right? Former Chicago superstation WGN anchor Dave Eckert has two not-so-secret passions—slow-smoked barbecue and great wine. Now taping another season of *Culinary Travels with Dave Eckert*, shown on public television stations nationwide, Eckert loves to experiment with barbecue and pair different smoked meats with wines.

For a recent gathering at his Liberty, Missouri, home, Eckert dreamed up this new take on corned beef and offered it to the BBQ Queens to try. Our decree: divine! Dave's advice: "Try to find a corned beef brisket that has a decent layer of fat on one side. This will help keep the meat tender during the cooking process." And make sure you cook for leftovers, because this barbecued corned beef makes a killer Rustic Reuben (page 360). **SERVES 8**

SUGGESTED WOOD: Oak

CORNED BEEF WITH MUSTARD SLATHER

One 5-pound corned beef brisket

One 12-ounce bottle Carolina-style mustard-based barbecue sauce

One 12-ounce can or bottle beer

SMOKED POTATO SALAD

2 pounds small new potatoes, pricked all over with a paring knife

2 bunches green onions, sliced

1 cup mayonnaise

Kosher or sea salt and ground white pepper to taste

Hearty, peasant-style rye bread for serving

1.   To prepare the brisket, rinse and pat dry. Prepare a mop by combining about half the bottle of barbecue sauce with half the beer. (Drink the rest!) Stir well. The mop should be runny but still have the full flavor of the sauce. (A thicker mixture with more sauce will have a tendency to burn.)

2.   Prepare an indirect fire in a grill or smoker.

3.   Place the brisket fat side up on the indirect side of the grill and smoke at 250°F. Using a brush or dish mop, slather the meat thoroughly with the mop and close the lid. Mop the meat every 30 to 45 minutes. The brisket should brown slowly but not burn. If the meat is turning black too quickly, turn down the heat or close the vents on the grill to lower the temperature. If the meat is not browning, move the brisket closer to the heat.

4.   After about 2 hours, flip the brisket over and continue mopping.

5.   To make the potato salad, arrange the potatoes on the rack of the grill or smoker. Remove the potatoes from the smoker after 2 hours. They should fall apart when pierced with a fork. (The brisket, depending on its size and the heat of your grill, should be done at about the same time.) Combine the potatoes, green onions, mayonnaise, and salt and pepper in a large bowl. Gently pierce the potatoes so they make a chunky salad.

6.   To serve, cut the brisket on the diagonal, against the grain of the meat, into thin slices. Serve with the warm smoked potato salad and the bread. Pass the rest of the barbecue sauce at the table.

Rustic Reuben: Pile thin slices of barbecued corned beef on a slice of artisanal rye bread. Top with drained deli sauerkraut, a slice of Swiss cheese, a dollop of mustard-based barbecue sauce, and another slice of bread. Coat a skillet with nonstick cooking spray and grill over medium-high heat on both sides until the bread is toasted and the cheese has melted. Serve hot. **SERVES 1**

Bringing Home the Bacon: Pork

Pork is probably the meat that gains the most from both the hot fire of the grill and the low heat of the smoker. From grilled thin-cut pork chops, which take minutes, to smoked pork butt, which takes hours, and all the goodies in between, you've got mighty good eatin'. 👑 When the BBQ Queens go out to strut our saucy stuff, we're constantly amazed at the number of people who still haven't grilled a pork tenderloin. If you're one of them, this chapter is especially for you. You have definitely been missing out. 👑 For hot and fast grilling, we recommend already-tender cuts such as chops, pork tenderloin, and sausages. Try those very thin breakfast-style pork chops grilled the Roman *scottadito* (to scorch the fingers) way as we do in our master recipe for Grilled Lamb Chops (page 420). Yum! Grill Gal Julie Fox's pork tenderloin, marinated in a heady blend of Worcestershire sauce and mustard, tastes fabulous (page 391).

You'll want a big cut of pork for the rotisserie, such as a pork loin (which also tastes great slow smoked). For low and slow smoking, we recommend a tougher cut, such as a pork butt or ribs. And when you anoint either one with BBQ Queens' Love Potion for the Swine (page 89), you'll understand why we gave that name to that barbecue sauce.

Now, get oinking out there.

Grilled Hot Diggity Dogs   365

Grilled Chicken and Apple
Sausage with Honey-
Almond Grilling Glaze   365

Grilled Seafood Sausage with
Cucumber and Tzatziki   366

Wisconsin Dilly Beer Brat
Sandwiches   366

*Rebecca's 'Que Queen
Extraordinaire Spicy
Pork Sausage*   367

Smoked Sausage   368

Smoked Italian Sausage
and Artichoke Soup   369

BBQ Queens' Choucroute
Garnie with Smoked
Bratwurst   369

Red Beans and Rice with
Smoked Sausage   369

**BBQ BABES: SHE'S A POWDERPUFF
AT HEART MENU**

*Bill's Better Than the Average
Barbecue Sauce*   370

Cheesy Wild Rice   371

Pistachio Sausage   372

*Spiral Herbed Smoked
Pork Loin with
Apricot-Dijon Glaze*   373

Fresh Fruit Tart   374

**Grilled Thick-Cut
Pork Chops**   376

Grilled Pork Chops with
Red Wine, Vinegar, and
Herb Marinade   377

Grilled Pork Chops with
Honey-Apple Marinade
and Baste   377

Grilled Pork Chops
with Bourbon-Mustard
Cream Sauce   377

DEVILISHLY GOOD EGGS

Classic Deviled Eggs   379

Caper-Stuffed Eggs   380

*Deviled Eggs with
Grilled Shrimp*   380

Mediterranean Stuffed Eggs   381

**Grilled Thin-Cut Pork
Chops, Pork Steaks,
or Ham Steaks**   382

Vinegar-Mopped Country
Cured Ham Steaks   382

Sweet Chops or Ham
Steaks with Brown
Sugar Basting Sauce   383

Ham, Cheddar, and
Apricot Chutney Pizza   384

Smoked Pork Ribs   384

Asian-Style Ribs   385

Raspberry Barbecued Ribs   385

Country-Style Ribs   386

*Indoor-Outdoor Kiss of
Fire and Smoke Ribs*   387

**Grilled Pork Tenderloin or
Center-Cut Pork Loin Fillet**   388

Sesame and Soy–Marinated
Pork Tenderloin   389

Grilled Pork Tenderloin
with Cilantro-Peanut
Dipping Sauce   389

Grilled Pork Tenderloin with
Chipotle Dipping Sauce   389

Grilled Pork Tenderloin
with Mustard-Herb
Dipping Sauce   389

**GRILL GALS: SHE WANTS Y'ALL
TO COME OVER FOR DINNER MENU**

*Grilled Pork Tenderloin in
Worcestershire Marinade*   391

*Slow-Simmered Baby
Lima Beans*   392

Asiago-Garlic Grits   392

Lemon-Scented Peach Crisp   393

YOU TAKE THE CAKE

*Cranberry-Almond Torte
with Cranberry Drizzle*   394

*Orange Marmalade
Bundt Cake*   396

*Grilled Pound Cake with
Hot Fudge Ganache
and Sweetened Berries*   397

Rotisserie Pork Loin   398

Herb-Marinated Rotisserie
Pork Loin   398

Ancho and Chipotle–Rubbed
Rotisserie Pork Loin   399

Bourbon Pecan-Stuffed
Rotisserie Pork Loin   399

Rotisserie Pork Loin
Sandwiches   399

**BBQ BABES: SHE'S THE FLOWER
OF THE FLAMES MENU**

*Raspberry and Mustard–
Glazed Pork Roast*   400

*Kiss of Smoke Beef
Tenderloin Black Forest*   402

*Cola-Marinated Smoked
Flank Steak*   403

Smoked Pork Loin   404

Slathered and Rubbed
Smoked Pork Loin   405

Tuscan-Style Porchetta   405

BBQ Queens'
Choucroute Garnie   405

NOT ON THE DISCOVERY CHANNEL: SMOKE-ROASTING

Smoke-Roasted Pork Loin with Herbed Pear Stuffing   407

Smoke-Roasted Potatoes with Garlic and Rosemary   408

Smoked Pork Butt   409

Spicy Orange Barbecued Pork Butt   410

Butts in a Bag   410

Piggy Sandwich   411

Double-Smoked Ham   411

POTATO CASSEROLES WITH A ROYAL TOUCH

Potato Gratin with White Cheddar Cheese   412

Oven-Roasted Saffron Potatoes   413

Double-Smoked Ham with Pineapple-Ginger Salsa   414

Karen's Double-Smoked Ham Salad Sandwiches   414

RISE AND SHINE: BREAKFAST IN THE GREAT OUTDOORS

Campfire Skillet Scones   415

Breakfast S'mores   416

Grilled Hot Diggity Dogs

On the Midwest, where we both live, we're in sausage heaven. Ethnic groups of all kinds settled in our region, bringing their best sausage varieties with them. In Kansas City alone, we can find all kinds of Slavic, German, Polish, Italian, Cajun, Chinese, Swedish, and French sausages—even English bangers.

We're also blessed to have great markets (such as Whole Foods Market) that offer boutique sausages made from salmon, chicken, turkey, buffalo, and the more common pork and beef. So if you haven't done so already, it's time to graduate from the hot dog to something **MORE** (as the queen of inspirational day-to-day living, Sarah Ban Breathnach, would say).

Grilling great unsmoked link sausage means a medium to medium-hot fire and turning them frequently with grill tongs. Sausage already has fat in the mixture, which will sizzle out during cooking, so you don't need olive oil. It's already seasoned, too, so you don't need salt and pepper. If you like, you can glaze the sausage as you grill it with barbecue sauce. To see whether sausage is done, slice it in the thickest part; if the juices run clear and the interior looks cooked through, it is. To be extra safe, you could use an instant-read meat thermometer inserted in the center; when it registers 170°F, your sausage is fully cooked.

Smoked sausage is not usually grilled, but you can brush it with olive oil and get some grill marks on it, if you like. You can also grill breakfast sausage patties, using a perforated grill rack and keeping a spray bottle with water handy for flare-ups. **SERVES 8**

2 pounds link sausage, such as Italian, Polish, andouille, chicken, or bratwurst

1. Prepare a medium fire in a grill.

2. Grill the sausage, turning every 4 to 5 minutes, until cooked through, 10 to 15 minutes total, depending on the diameter of the sausage. Serve hot.

Crowning Glories

Have a griller's feast and serve your sausage with mountains of:
Grilled Potatoes *(page 147)*
Grilled Peppers *(page 143)*
Grilled Onions *(page 137)*

Grilled Chicken and Apple Sausage with Honey-Almond Grilling Glaze: The glaze adds
a touch of savory sweetness to the sausage. Grill 2 pounds chicken and apple link sausage

as directed above, brushing with Honey Almond Grilling Glaze (page 88) and turning frequently. **SERVES 8**

Grilled Seafood Sausage with Cucumber and Tzatziki: Slice an English cucumber paper-thin; sprinkle with 1 teaspoon chopped fresh dill, 1/2 teaspoon ground white pepper, and 1/2 teaspoon garlic salt; arrange on a platter. Grill 2 pounds seafood link sausage as directed above, then place over the cucumber. Pass a bowl of Tzatziki (page 112) at the table, along with Wood-Grilled Flatbreads (page 176), if desired. **SERVES 8**

Wisconsin Dilly Beer Brat Sandwiches: In Wisconsin, grilling a brat is an art form, much like smoking a slab of ribs is in Kansas City. When the weather permits at the "frozen tundra of Lambeau Field," and sometimes when it doesn't, Green Bay Packers fans fire up their grills in the parking lot and wolf down a few of these delicious sandwiches to keep warm. Putting the brats in cold water before grilling ensures juicy sausage, and the beer pot serves two purposes: to add a last touch of flavor to the grilled brats and to keep them warm before serving. Thinly slice 1 large white onion, then separate into rings. In a large bowl, combine 1/2 cup sugar, 2 teaspoons kosher or sea salt, 1 teaspoon dillweed, 1/4 cup water, and 1/2 cup distilled white vinegar. Add the onion rings, submerging them in the marinade. Cover and refrigerate, stirring occasionally, for at least 1 hour. An hour before grilling, put 12 bratwurst sausage in a pan of cold water. Make a beer pot by pouring three 12-ounce bottles microbrew beer into a clean 3-pound coffee can or other similar container that can sit on the side of the grill. Grill the sausage and, as they're cooked, place them in the beer pot. Cut 1 dozen hard rolls or kaiser rolls almost in half horizontally and toast them cut sides down on the grill. To serve, split each brat lengthwise and place in a toasted roll. Place some dilly onion rings on top of the brat and add your favorite condiments. **SERVES A HUNGRY DOZEN**

Rebecca's 'Que Queen Extraordinaire Spicy Pork Sausage

Beckie Baker has been on two barbecue teams that compete in contests around the country. One is the glittery 'Que Queens, to which Karen and Judith belong. The other was Powderpuff Barbecue, a team that included her husband, John, and friends Bill and Janeyce Michel-Cupito. Beckie says, with her characteristic quirky humor, that "even though my main responsibility was mascot, I was also responsible for the sausage category. It was not a mandatory category, so there was not a lot I could screw up. This is the final recipe, after several trials and changes." SERVES 10 TO 12

> One 5-pound boneless Boston butt or pork shoulder, trimmed of some fat
>
> 2 tablespoons fine kosher or sea salt
>
> 2 tablespoons freshly ground black pepper
>
> 3 tablespoons crumbled dried sage
>
> 1 teaspoon ground coriander
>
> ¹/₂ to 1¹/₂ teaspoons cayenne pepper, to your taste
>
> 1 tablespoon crumbled dried thyme
>
> 1¹/₄ teaspoons sugar
>
> ¹/₄ cup chopped garlic
>
> 1 cup apple juice

1. Cut the pork into chunks. Attach a ¹/₈-inch plate to a meat grinder and finely grind the pork in batches, twice.

2. In a large bowl, combine all the remaining ingredients. Add the ground pork and mix thoroughly. Form the mixture into patties or logs before grilling. Or use the meat grinder's stuffing attachment to stuff the mixture into lengths of 31- to 34-millimeter rinsed pork casings, available at wholesale meat companies. Tie off the sausage at 6- to 8-inch intervals with kitchen twine. The sausage will keep in the refrigerator for up to 1 week and in the freezer for 4 to 6 months.

BBQ Tip: When grilling link sausage, sprinkle 1 envelope unflavored gelatin over 4 cups warm water in a medium-size bowl. Let the gelatin soften, then dissolve, until the liquid is a light, clear beige. Add 1 tablespoon light corn syrup. Soak the sausage links in the mixture for 10 minutes before grilling, then baste with the mixture while grilling. The mixture will caramelize, giving the sausage a nice color and slight sweetness.

Smoked Sausage

ecause sausage is often a category at barbecue competitions, many teams have developed their own sausage recipes (see Beckie Baker's and Janeyce Michel-Cupito's recipes on pages 367 and 372). The teams lovingly tend their homemade sausage as the links bronze to a fine turn on the smoker, along with the ribs, pork butt, brisket, and other goodies they are also smoking for the contest.

The BBQ Queens love a good, smoked hot sausage, but we probably wouldn't fire up the smoker in the backyard for sausage alone. Like smoked vegetables, we are more likely to smoke sausage alongside something else: a whole chicken, ribs, a brisket, or whatever else we're cooking.

Also, you don't have to make your own to enjoy sausage. In Kansas City, we're lucky to have three wonderful Italian sausage companies that make sweet and mild or hot and spicy varieties that are wonderful smoked. Smoke whatever sausage you like best. Even already-smoked sausage is delicious with another kiss of smoke, much like Double-Smoked Ham (page 411).

Smoked sausage can be kept in the refrigerator for up to 2 weeks or in the freezer for up to 3 months. It's one of our favorite convenience foods, ready to thaw and eat as is or as part of a soup, stew, or casserole.

Smoked over fruitwood, this dish has big flavor with very few calories. **SERVES 4**

SUGGESTED WOOD: Apple, hickory, or pecan

**1 to 2 pounds link sausage, such as Italian, Polish, or bratwurst, 1¹/₂ to
2 inches in diameter**

1. Prepare a fire in a smoker.

2. Place the sausage in a disposable aluminum pan, cover, and smoke at 225 to 250°F until cooked through and bronzed, 2 to 2¹/₂ hours. Serve hot.

 Crowning Glories

Smoked sausage is stellar topped with:
Stir-Grilled Vegetables (page 166)
Raspberry-Jalapeño Barbecue Sauce (page 90)
Grated or sliced cheese, such as provolone, cheddar, or mozzarella

Smoked Italian Sausage and Artichoke Soup: The smokiness of the sausage ratchets up the flavor of this soup, adapted from a recipe in Judith's *Prairie Home Cooking* (The Harvard Common Press, 1999). If you use canned fire-roasted tomatoes (such as the Muir Glen brand), so much the better. In a large soup pot, sauté 1 diced red onion and 2 minced garlic cloves in 2 tablespoons olive oil over medium-high heat until softened, about 5 minutes. Cut 1 pound smoked Italian link sausage (see above), one 14-ounce can drained or one 9-ounce package defrosted frozen artichoke hearts, and one 28-ounce can undrained whole Roma tomatoes into bite-size pieces and add to the pot. Pour in 3 cups chicken broth, then add 1 teaspoon each dried oregano, dried basil, and fennel seeds. Bring to a boil, reduce the heat to medium-low, and simmer, uncovered, for 30 minutes. If desired, add 1/4 pound penne and cook until *al dente*, about 15 minutes more. Taste for seasoning and serve. **SERVES 6**

BBQ Queens' Choucroute Garnie with Smoked Bratwurst: Substitute 1 pound smoked bratwurst (see above) for the Polish sausage in BBQ Queens' Choucroute Garnie (page 405) for a rib-sticking entrée when you entertain in cold weather. **SERVES 10 TO 12**

Red Beans and Rice with Smoked Sausage: This dish is pure comfort food, whether you're Cajun or not. Traditionally, already-smoked andouille is used, but the recipe tastes great with any smoked hot and spicy pork sausage. In a large slow cooker or large pot, combine 2 pounds dried red kidney beans, 2 pounds smoked link sausage (see above), 1/2 pound diced smoked pork jowl (available at the butcher counter), 1/2 cup chopped yellow onion, 1/2 cup seeded and chopped green bell pepper, 1 tablespoon vegetable oil, 2 tablespoons sugar, and kosher or sea salt to taste. Mix together and add enough water to cover by 1 inch. Cook on low for 10 hours, stirring occasionally all the way to the bottom of the pan, until the beans are tender and the mixture has thickened. Serve over rice. **SERVES 10 TO 12**

BBQ Babes

She's a Powderpuff at Heart Menu

Bill's Better Than the Average Barbecue Sauce
Cheesy Wild Rice
Pistachio Sausage
Spiral Herbed Smoked Pork Loin with Apricot-Dijon Glaze
Fresh Fruit Tart

Janeyce Michel-Cupito (above, left) never does anything halfway. For years, she put her all into a very successful retail career. During that time, she and her husband, Bill, along with their friends John and Beckie Baker (see Beckie's sausage recipe on page 368), formed the Powderpuff Barbeque team, which competed on the barbecue contest circuit—very successfully, of course. Along the way, they garnered lots of ribbons and several state championships.

The team created many of their own recipes to wow the judges. Because they're not competing anymore and have gone on to new pursuits, Janeyce can share some of their best barbecue secrets here.

Bill's Better Than the Average Barbecue Sauce

This recipe originated when Janeyce's barbecue team needed a new sauce and the team members decided to have a contest among themselves. Janeyce's husband, Bill, wanted to do a really basic, nothing-to-object-to sweet red sauce, so he found some basic recipes, plugged them into the computer, averaged the ingredients, and made this sauce. He won, and they've been enjoying his sauce ever since. **MAKES ABOUT 6 CUPS**

Three 6-ounce cans tomato paste
3 cups cider vinegar
$^1/_2$ cup Worcestershire sauce

1 1/2 cups firmly packed light or dark brown sugar

1/3 cup light corn syrup

1/2 cup honey

1/3 cup molasses

1 medium-size onion, finely minced

2 tablespoons sweet Hungarian paprika

1 tablespoon freshly ground black pepper

2 tablespoons celery salt

2 tablespoons granulated garlic

1 tablespoon liquid smoke flavoring

Combine all the ingredients in a 3-quart saucepan. Bring to a boil, reduce the heat to low, and simmer for about 2 hours, until the flavors blend. Use immediately, or pour into a covered container and keep refrigerated for several months.

Cheesy Wild Rice

This is a wonderful accompaniment to slow-smoked ribs, turkey, pork loin, beef brisket, or chicken. SERVES 6 TO 8

One 6-ounce package long-grain and wild rice mix

4 ounces fresh mushrooms, sliced or chopped

2 1/2 cups water

One 10-ounce package frozen chopped spinach, defrosted

3/4 cup chopped onion

1 tablespoon unsalted butter

2 teaspoons Dijon mustard

1/4 teaspoon freshly grated nutmeg

One 8-ounce package cream cheese, cubed

1. Preheat the oven to 375°F. In a 13 x 9-inch baking dish, combine the rice mix and mushrooms.

2. In a medium-size saucepan, combine the water, spinach, onion, butter, and mustard. Bring to a boil, remove from the heat, and stir in the nutmeg and cream cheese until melted and smooth. Pour over the rice mixture.

3. Bake, covered with aluminum foil, until browned and bubbling, about 40 minutes. Remove from the oven and let stand for 10 minutes before serving.

Pistachio Sausage

This is one of Janeyce's to-die-for sausage recipes. It tastes great either grilled or slow smoked. SERVES 10 TO 12

> **3 pounds coarsely ground pork butt**
>
> **¹/₂ cup unsalted shelled pistachios**
>
> **1 tablespoon minced fresh Italian parsley**
>
> **1 tablespoon fine kosher or sea salt**
>
> **1 teaspoon freshly ground black pepper, plus more for coating**
>
> **¹/₂ teaspoon red pepper flakes**
>
> **1 clove garlic, minced**

1. In a large bowl, combine all the ingredients. Divide the mixture into 4 parts. Roll each portion into a long roll about 1¹/₂ inches in diameter. Wrap in plastic and refrigerate overnight to blend the flavors.

2. Prepare a medium-hot fire in a grill. Unwrap each roll and coat with pepper.

3. Grill until all sides are nicely browned and an instant-read meat thermometer inserted in the center of a roll registers 160°F, about 12 minutes. To serve, slice each roll into portions.

Spiral Herbed Smoked Pork Loin with Apricot-Dijon Glaze

This dish looks as great as it tastes. It's a wonderful entrée to serve a crowd. The herb filling creates a spiral design when you slice the pork loin. SERVES 10 TO 12

SUGGESTED WOOD: A combination of apple, oak, and hickory

$^1/_4$ cup ($^1/_2$ stick) unsalted butter

$^1/_2$ cup finely minced onion

2 tablespoons finely minced fresh Italian parsley

2 tablespoons finely minced fresh sage

2 tablespoons finely minced fresh rosemary

Fine kosher or sea salt and freshly ground black pepper to taste

One 4-pound boneless pork loin roast, cut and pounded with a tenderizer to form a $^1/_2$-inch-thick rectangle

1 recipe Apricot-Dijon Glaze (recipe follows)

1.   Melt the butter in a small skillet over medium heat. Add the onion and cook, stirring, until soft, about 5 minutes. Add the herbs and season with salt and pepper. Stir, remove from heat, and let cool for 10 minutes. Spread over the pork loin rectangle. Roll up the pork loin, starting from a long end and tying with kitchen twine at 3-inch intervals. Place in a disposable aluminum pan.

2.   Prepare a fire in a smoker.

3.   Cover and smoke over indirect heat at 225 to 250°F until an instant-read meat thermometer inserted in the thickest part of the roast registers 160°F and the meat is quite tender, 4 to 5 hours. During the last hour of cooking, brush the meat every 15 minutes with the glaze. Let rest for 15 minutes before slicing and serving.

Apricot-Dijon Glaze

The sweetness of the apricot preserves and the savory Dijon mustard and balsamic vinegar create a sweet yet savory glaze for all kinds of smoked pork, turkey, or chicken dishes. **MAKES ABOUT 1 CUP**

> 1/4 cup apricot preserves
>
> 1/4 cup Dijon mustard
>
> 1/4 cup cider vinegar
>
> 1 tablespoon balsamic vinegar
>
> 1 large clove garlic, minced
>
> 1/4 teaspoon cayenne pepper

Combine all the ingredients in a small bowl. This glaze will keep, covered, in the refrigerator for up to 2 weeks.

Fresh Fruit Tart

This is a lovely light dessert for after the heavy barbecue meal. **MAKES ONE 10-INCH TART; SERVES 8**

> **CRUST**
>
> 1/2 cup sliced almonds
>
> 1/2 cup shelled hazelnuts
>
> 1/4 cup Splenda granular sweetener
>
> 1/4 cup whey protein powder (available in the health food section of better grocery stores)
>
> 1/2 teaspoon ground cinnamon
>
> 6 tablespoons (3/4 stick) unsalted butter, cut into 6 pieces

FILLING

One 8-ounce package cream cheese, softened

$^1/_4$ cup Splenda granular sweetener

$^1/_2$ teaspoon almond extract

TOPPING

Fruit of your choice, such as fresh strawberries, kiwis, raspberries, and/or oranges, or canned apricots

2 tablespoons fresh lemon juice

$^1/_2$ teaspoon almond extract

$^1/_3$ cup sugar-free apricot preserves

1.   Preheat the oven to 400°F.

2.   To make the crust, coat a 10-inch tart pan with nonstick cooking spray. In a food processor, process the almonds and hazelnuts until finely ground. Add the Splenda, whey protein powder, cinnamon, and butter and process until the mixture starts to come together into a mass. With your fingers, press the mixture evenly into the prepared pan. Bake for 5 minutes, then remove from the oven and let cool. Place in the refrigerator until cold to the touch.

3.   To make the filling, combine the cream cheese, Splenda, and almond extract in the food processor. Process until smooth, then spread in the cold crust.

4.   To make the topping, prepare the fruit: slice the strawberries, peel and thinly slice the kiwis, use the raspberries whole, peel and section the oranges, or slice the apricots. Arrange over the filling in slightly overlapping circles. In a small bowl, mix the lemon juice, almond extract, and apricot preserves together until smooth, then brush over the fruit. This tart is best served the same day it is made. Serve at room temperature or chilled.

Grilled Thick-Cut Pork Chops

Thick-cut pork chops—usually center cut from the loin and at least 1 inch thick, bone-in or boneless—can be delicious. In our part of the country, the Midwest, these chops are called Iowa chops. Traditionally, thick pork chops were served "carpetbagger style"—stuffed with a bread crumb and celery dressing—quickly browned on both sides and then braised in chicken broth until tender. We love these chops on the grill, too, but there is a trick to getting them just right: temperature. You need medium heat to produce flavorful and just done, yet still juicy, chops. A bath in a marinade beforehand helps, too.

Over medium heat, cooking will take about 10 minutes per side for a 1-inch-thick chop, longer for thicker chops. For a little razzle-dazzle, try seasoning them with Porcini Paste (page 65) or Spicy Orange Rub (page 51) or marinating them in Garlic-Citrus Marinade (page 70) or Rosemary-Mustard Marinade (page 71) before grilling.

All of these recipes also work well with veal chops. Once the province of upscale Italian restaurants, veal chops are now becoming more popular on the grill. **SERVES 4**

Four center-cut pork chops, 1 inch thick (about 11 ounces each)
Olive oil
Fine kosher or sea salt and freshly ground black pepper to taste

1. Prepare a medium fire in a grill.

2. Brush or spray the chops on both sides with olive oil. Grill directly over the fire for about 10 minutes per side, or until an instant-read meat thermometer inserted in the thickest part of the chop registers 155°F. Season with salt and pepper and serve hot.

 *Crowning Glories*

A simply grilled thick-cut pork chop is delicious served with:

Smoked Chile Beurre Blanc *(page 99)*
Winter Blood Orange, Fennel, and Black Olive Relish *(page 424)*
Potato Gratin with White Cheddar Cheese *(page 412)*

Grilled Pork Chops with Red Wine, Vinegar, and Herb Marinade: This marinade, in the European hunter's tradition of preparing wild boar, tastes great with pork chops. In a baking dish or sealable plastic bag, combine 1 cup dry red wine, $1^{1}/_{2}$ tablespoons red wine vinegar, 1 teaspoon juniper berries, 2 bay leaves, 2 tablespoons chopped fresh rosemary, and 3 chopped garlic cloves. Add four 1-inch-thick center-cut pork chops, turning to coat. Cover or seal and marinate in the refrigerator for at least 4 hours or up to 8 hours, turning several times. When ready to cook, remove the chops from the marinade and transfer the marinade to a saucepan. Bring to a boil and cook for 2 minutes, swirling in 2 tablespoons unsalted butter. Grill the chops as directed above and serve the sauce over them. **SERVES 4**

Grilled Pork Chops with Honey-Apple Marinade and Baste: The sweetness of the honey and apple cider accentuates the sweetness of the pork. In a baking dish or sealable plastic bag, combine $1^{1}/_{2}$ cups apple cider, $^{1}/_{4}$ cup fresh lemon juice (about 2 lemons), $^{1}/_{4}$ cup soy sauce, 2 tablespoons clover or other medium-colored honey, 1 minced garlic clove, and kosher or sea salt and freshly ground black pepper to taste. Add four 1-inch-thick center-cut pork chops, turning to coat. Cover or seal and marinate in the refrigerator for at least 4 hours or up to 24 hours, turning several times. When ready to cook, remove the chops from the marinade and transfer the marinade to a saucepan. Bring to a boil and cook for 2 minutes, then swirl in 2 tablespoons unsalted butter. Grill the chops as directed above, basting with the cooked marinade every 3 minutes. Serve hot. **SERVES 10**

Grilled Pork Chops with Bourbon-Mustard Cream Sauce: This sauce is a true "crowning glory" to a luscious, moist chop hot off the grill. In a small saucepan, bring $^{1}/_{2}$ cup bourbon to a boil and continue to boil until reduced by half, about 5 minutes. Set aside. In a medium-size skillet, melt 2 tablespoons unsalted butter over medium-high heat. Add 2 tablespoons finely chopped onion and 1 cup thinly sliced fresh mushrooms. Cook, stirring, until the onion is transparent and the mushrooms are lightly browned, about 5 minutes. Stir in $^{1}/_{8}$ teaspoon dried thyme, 1 tablespoon Dijon mustard, $^{1}/_{2}$ cup heavy cream, and the reduced bourbon and cook for 1 minute to blend the flavors. Keep warm. Grill the pork chops as directed above. Top the chops with the sauce, sprinkle with chopped fresh Italian parsley, and serve. **SERVES 4**

Devilishly Good Eggs

Karen's family holds bragging rights to making unusually good deviled eggs. The trick, says Karen, is to hard-boil the eggs and peel them while they are still warm. Then combine the yolk mixture ingredients while still warm, too. It goes without saying, they are best when served the day they are made.

A true deviled egg always has a little something hot in it, such as hot sauce, red pepper flakes, or a spicy pepper blend, as well as something a little sour, such as vinegar, to take away the "eggy" taste. If you skip the hot stuff, you have just a stuffed egg. But oh what stuffings you can create! Try adding any leftover grilled or smoked fare to the stuffing mixture, such as chopped grilled shrimp, chicken, or pork. Even chopped grilled bell peppers and onions are "eggsellent" choices.

Quick-as-a-wink flavored deviled eggs are only a tube of sun-dried tomato paste, anchovy paste, or tapenade (black olive paste) away. Just add 1 to 2 tablespoons of your favorite paste to the Classic Deviled Eggs recipe below.

As BBQ Queens, we recommend that you invest in containers or plates with indentations made specifically for deviled eggs.

How to Hard-Boil an Egg:
Place the eggs in a single layer in a saucepan. Fill with cold water to cover. Place over medium heat until the water just begins to boil. Lower the heat slightly and cook for 5 minutes. Remove the pan from the heat and let sit for 8 minutes. Drain the hot water from the pan and replace with cold tap water. Let sit for a couple of minutes more. Then peel the eggs, while still warm. They will be perfect.

Classic Deviled Eggs

Delicious served as an appetizer or side dish with your barbecue. MAKES 12

6 hard-boiled large eggs, still warm

3 tablespoons mayonnaise

1 tablespoon Dijon mustard

1 tablespoon fresh lemon juice

1 teaspoon Worcestershire sauce, preferably white

¹/₈ teaspoon hot pepper sauce

Fine kosher or sea salt and freshly ground black pepper to taste

Finely chopped fresh chives for garnish (optional)

1. Peel the eggs, then cut in half lengthwise. Remove the yolks from the whites and place the yolks in a small bowl. Place the whites cut side up on a plate and set aside.

2. Mash the yolks with a fork. Add the mayonnaise, mustard, lemon juice, Worcestershire, and hot sauce and mash until the mixture just begins to be smooth. Season with salt and pepper.

3. Stuff the whites with the yolk mixture, mounding the tops. If desired, sprinkle with chives. Cover loosely and refrigerate for at least 1 hour or up to 8 hours. The eggs will keep, covered, in the refrigerator for 2 to 3 days but are best eaten the day they are made.

Caper-Stuffed Eggs

These are a little tangier and more piquant than regular deviled eggs. MAKES 24

> **12 hard-boiled large eggs, still warm**
> **¹/₂ cup extra virgin olive oil**
> **2 tablespoons fresh lemon juice**
> **¹/₄ cup chopped fresh Italian parsley**
> **3 tablespoons plus 1 teaspoon capers, drained**
> **Fine kosher or sea salt and freshly ground black pepper to taste**

1. Peel the eggs, then cut in half lengthwise. Remove the yolks from the whites and place the yolks in a small bowl. Place the whites cut side up on a plate and set aside.

2. Mash the yolks with a fork. Add ¹/₄ cup of the olive oil, the lemon juice, the parsley, 3 tablespoons of the capers, and the salt and pepper. Mash until the mixture just begins to be smooth. Gradually blend in the remaining ¹/₄ cup olive oil until smooth and fluffy. Taste for salt and pepper.

3. Stuff the whites with the yolk mixture, mounding the tops. Sprinkle the eggs with the remaining 1 teaspoon capers. Cover loosely and refrigerate for at least 1 hour or up to 8 hours. The eggs will keep, covered, in the refrigerator for 2 to 3 days but are best eaten the day they are made.

Deviled Eggs with Grilled Shrimp

This is a great way to use leftover grilled shrimp. You may substitute salad shrimp, crabmeat, or smoked trout. MAKES 12

> **6 hard-boiled large eggs, still warm**
> **3 tablespoons mayonnaise**
> **1 tablespoon Dijon mustard**
> **1 tablespoon fresh lemon juice**
> **¹/₈ teaspoon hot pepper sauce**
> **¹/₄ cup plus 1 tablespoon chopped grilled shrimp (see page 289)**
> **Fine kosher or sea salt and freshly ground black pepper to taste**

1.   Peel the eggs, then cut in half lengthwise. Remove the yolks from the whites and place the yolks in a small bowl. Place the whites cut side up on a plate and set aside.

2.   Mash the yolks with a fork. Add the mayonnaise, mustard, lemon juice, and hot sauce and mash until the mixture just begins to be smooth. Add ¹/₄ cup of the shrimp. Season with salt and pepper.

3.   Stuff the whites with the yolk mixture, mounding the tops. Top each egg with a bit of the remaining 1 tablespoon chopped shrimp. Cover loosely and refrigerate for at least 1 hour or up to 8 hours. The eggs will keep, covered, in the refrigerator for 2 to 3 days but are best eaten the day they are made.

Mediterranean Stuffed Eggs

Cured olives and roasted red peppers are to die for in these incredible party-perfect eggs. MAKES 24

> **12 hard-boiled large eggs, still warm**
> **¹/₂ cup extra virgin olive oil**
> **2 tablespoons fresh lemon juice**
> **¹/₄ cup plus 1 tablespoon pitted, drained, and chopped oil- or brine-cured olives**
> **¹/₄ cup chopped roasted red peppers (homemade, see page 145, or from a jar)**
> **Fine kosher or sea salt and freshly ground black pepper to taste**

1.   Peel the eggs, then cut in half lengthwise. Remove the yolks from the whites and place the yolks in a small bowl. Place the whites cut side up on a plate and set aside.

2.   Mash the yolks with a fork. Add ¹/₄ cup of the olive oil, the lemon juice, ¹/₄ cup of the olives, the red peppers, and salt and pepper. Mash until the mixture just begins to be smooth. Gradually blend in the remaining ¹/₄ cup olive oil until smooth and fluffy. Taste for salt and pepper.

3.   Stuff the whites with the yolk mixture, mounding the tops. Sprinkle the eggs with the remaining 1 tablespoon olives. Cover loosely and refrigerate for at least 1 hour or up to 8 hours. The eggs will keep, covered, in the refrigerator for 2 to 3 days but are best eaten the day they are made.

Grilled Thin-Cut Pork Chops, Pork Steaks, or Ham Steaks

We wish we were as lean and mean as these quick-to-prepare thin-cut pork chops, pork steaks, and ham steaks. They are perfect for weeknight suppers or feeding a crowd because they cook up so fast and easy.

Tender pork chops cut from the loin can be bone-in or butterflied (with the bone out and opened like a book for even faster cooking). Pork steaks are a tougher cut of meat, usually cut from the pork shoulder, and do well with a bit of a marinade. Ham steaks can be sliced about 1/2 inch thick from a boneless precooked ham. Ham will cook the quickest because it has already been precooked and needs only to heat through and develop those pretty grill marks.

Grill fresh fruit at the same time. Fresh pineapple slices and peach and plum halves are wonderful accompaniments to pork and cook quickly. **SERVES 4**

> **Four bone-in pork chops or steaks, boneless butterflied pork chops, or ham steaks, 1/2 inch thick**
>
> **2 tablespoons mustard of your choice**

1. Prepare a hot fire in a grill.

2. Slather the meat on both sides with the mustard. (It can be applied several hours in advance and allowed to marinate in the refrigerator.) Place the meat directly over the fire. Grill until the meat is juicy and slightly pink in the center, 3 to 4 minutes per side.

Crowning Glories

Serve your chops or steaks with:
Fennel and Orange Drizzling Sauce *(page 73)*
Red Cabbage and Apple Slaw *(page 83)*

Vinegar-Mopped Country Cured Ham Steaks: You have probably heard of Smithfield ham, a country cured ham that is saltier and drier than most hams. Have a Smithfield ham or a similar brand sliced about 1/2 inch thick for this recipe. Grill it with a mustard slather as directed above for 4 to 5 minutes per side, but in addition, mop it with a baste of 1/4 cup strong black coffee and 1/4 cup cider vinegar. This lip-smackin' treat is dynamite for breakfast, served with eggs and stone-ground grits seasoned with butter, fine kosher or sea salt, and ground white pepper to taste. **SERVES 4**

Sweet Chops or Ham Steaks with Brown Sugar Basting Sauce:

Throw some fresh pineapple slices or peach halves on the grill along with the chops or steaks and use this sweet basting sauce on both. To make the sauce, melt ¼ cup (½ stick) unsalted butter in a small saucepan. Remove from the heat and whisk in ½ cup firmly packed light or dark brown sugar; 2 tablespoons each fresh lemon juice, grated orange zest, and dry mustard, and ½ teaspoon red pepper flakes. Grill the chops or steaks over a medium-hot fire, basting with the sauce. **SERVES 4**

The 'Que Queens Versus the Male Chauvinist Pigs in the Battle of the Sexes Barbecue Contest

Mid-morning: "Luckily, the charity teams only competed in three categories: pork, brisket, and ribs. The pork shoulder and beef brisket had been on the fire since midnight. At mid-morning, they were ready to go in the warming box after several dips in the sauce. The Queens didn't marinate with sauce until the end, but they did put a marinade on the pork shoulder and a dry rub on the ribs and brisket before they started the cooking process."

Noon: "It was time to get on the tiaras and the royal sashes. The queens had separated their ribs, pulled their pork and sliced their brisket. . . They had put out their wares, one meat category at a time. . . Participants paid their two bucks and picked up a ballot and a sample from each tray. . . And . . . Once again, the women beat the men in the barbeque Battle of the Sexes."

Check out this and other adventures of Heaven Lee in *Revenge of the Barbeque Queens* (St. Martin's Press, 1997), one of a series of culinary mystery novels written by our fellow 'Que Queen Lou Jane Temple.

Ham, Cheddar, and Apricot Chutney Pizza: This pizza is a snazzy way to use leftover ham or turkey. You can buy a jar of chutney, but this homemade version is really a snap. Combine 1¹/₂ cups apricot preserves, ¹/₂ teaspoon grated fresh ginger (if using a microplane, you don't need to peel), ¹/₂ cup golden raisins, 1 minced garlic clove, 2 tablespoons fresh lemon juice, 1 teaspoon ground cinnamon, and ¹/₂ teaspoon ground white pepper in a medium-size bowl. (This will keep, covered, in the refrigerator for several weeks.) To make the pizza, begin with a flatbread such as a pita bread or Boboli as your base. Spread 2 to 3 tablespoons Dijon mustard over the bread. Thinly slice 4 to 5 ounces grilled ham and scatter over the pizza. Sprinkle 1 cup finely shredded cheddar cheese over the meat. Finish by spooning small dollops of the chutney over everything. Bake for about 10 minutes in a preheated 350°F oven. **SERVES 6 TO 8**

Smoked Pork Ribs

When competition barbecuers start talking about ribs, they divide into four camps: those who favor St. Louis–cut ribs, Kansas City–cut ribs, spareribs, and baby back ribs. St. Louis–cut and Kansas City–cut ribs and spareribs are all bigger and tougher than baby backs, coming from the side of the hog. Because we're kinder, gentler, and daintier than those beefy barbecue guys, we prefer the smaller and more tender baby backs, which come from the area on either side of the backbone. If presented with a platter of heavenly smoked spareribs, however, takers we will be.

Our all-female barbecue team, the 'Que Queens, has won the Battle of the Sexes Barbecue Contest in Kansas City several times with the following recipe. Don't cringe at the thought of squeeze-bottle margarine and honey. This glazing technique really does make the ribs melt-in-your-mouth good!

As a side note, when we were preparing these ribs for a St. Louis television program, we met a young television anchorwoman. She remarked on our tiaras and said she had one of her own. Like a complete dork, Judith asked what kind of queen she was. This former Miss America, Debbye Turner, graciously answered. Then she taught us the four queen waves, which we pass on to you on page 224.

One bit of essential technique is to pull off the membrane from the underside of the ribs in one motion. We usually use needle-nose pliers (or heavy-duty tweezers) for this, grabbing a corner of the membrane, then pulling and tugging until we get it all off. The ribs have to be cold when you do this, or you can't grab the membrane easily. Do it the night before, then sprinkle with the rub, cover, and refrigerate for the best flavor. **SERVES 8**

SUGGESTED WOOD: A combination of hickory and cherry

3 whole slabs (1 to 1¹/₂ pounds each) baby back ribs

Memphis Blue-Ribbon Rib Rub (page 49) or Prizewinning Rib Rub (page 50)

1 cup clover or other medium-colored honey

One 12-ounce squeeze bottle Parkay margarine

One 14-ounce ounce bottle smoky, spicy barbecue sauce of your choice

1. The day before cooking, remove the membrane from the back of the ribs. Sprinkle with the rub on both sides. Cover and refrigerate overnight.

2. Prepare an indirect fire in a smoker.

3. Cover and smoke the ribs at 225 to 250°F. After 2 hours, the rib meat should have pulled back from the tips of the bones. Turn the ribs over and drizzle with half of the honey and half of the margarine. Brush to distribute the honey and margarine evenly over the surface of the meat. Cover and cook for 30 minutes.

4. Turn the ribs again, drizzle with the remaining honey and margarine, and brush the meat again. Cover and cook for 30 minutes.

5. As a glaze, brush the ribs on both sides with some of the barbecue sauce, then smoke for a final 15 minutes. To serve, leave as whole slabs or cut into individual ribs. Serve the remaining sauce on the side.

Crowning Glories

Barbecued ribs are traditionally served with:

BBQ Queens' Barbecued Beans (page 107)

BBQ Queens' Smoked Potato Casserole (page 153)

BBQ Queens' Love Potion for the Swine (page 89)

Asian-Style Ribs: Instead of a typical barbecue rub, make a triple batch of Zesty Sugar and Spice Rub (page 52) or Five-Spice Asian Paste (page 64) and sprinkle or slather on the ribs. Smoke and baste with the honey and margarine as directed above, then finish with Asian Barbecue Sauce (page 90) during the last 30 minutes of smoking. Brush the ribs with some of the sauce to glaze them, then serve the rest at the table. **SERVES 8**

Raspberry Barbecued Ribs: Flower of the Flames barbecue guru Karen Putman (see page 400) inspired this recipe. After you've removed the membrane from the ribs, brush them with one 12-ounce bottle raspberry vinaigrette. Cover and refrigerate overnight. The next day, remove the ribs from the marinade, pat dry, and sprinkle with Memphis

Blue-Ribbon Rib Rub (page 49) or Prizewinning Rib Rub (page 50). Smoke and baste with the honey and margarine as directed above, then finish with Raspberry-Jalapeño Barbecue Sauce (page 90) during the last 30 minutes of smoking. Brush the ribs with some of the sauce to glaze, then serve the rest at the table. **SERVES 8**

Country-Style Ribs: Country-style ribs aren't ribs at all, but fingers of boneless meat cut from the pork shoulder—the same cut of meat known as pork butt. Country-style ribs also benefit from slow smoking, and they're usually tender in about 2 hours. To make these, slather 4 pounds country-style ribs with Mustard-Mayo Slather (page 66) and sprinkle with either Memphis Blue-Ribbon Rib Rub (page 49) or Prizewinning Rib Rub (page 50). Cover and smoke at 225 to 250°F for about 2 hours, turning halfway through (these don't get the honey-Parkay treatment). The ribs are done when they feel tender when pierced with a knife. Serve with your favorite barbecue sauce on the side. **SERVES 8**

Indoor-Outdoor Kiss of Fire and Smoke Ribs

Our editor, Pam Hoenig, coaxed us into trying oven-roasted ribs finished on the outdoor grill for a kiss of fire. She acknowledged that for passionate barbecuers this method may seem sacrilegious. Although they don't have the depth of flavor that slow-smoked ribs do, they're still mighty tasty.

The trick to this recipe is preparing two or more slabs at a time, so they can be layered on top of each other and rotated during the oven-roasting process, which keeps the meat moist. Then take them out to the grill to finish. If you don't want to venture outdoors at all (not a queenly thing to do, mind you), the ribs can be sauced and finished in the oven as well. Brush them with barbecue sauce, lay them out flat (not layered), and roast for a final 15 minutes. We like a spicy sauce to finish, but any kind of glaze would do.

Leftover slabs can be double-wrapped in aluminum foil, then plastic wrap, and frozen for up to 3 months. Defrost, unwrap, place on a baking sheet, and warm in a 350°F oven until heated through. SERVES 8

> 4 whole slabs (1 to 1¹/₂ pounds each) baby back ribs
> ¹/₂ cup Ole Hickory Rub (page 60)
> 1 cup hickory chips, soaked in water for at least 30 minutes before grilling
> 2 cups BBQ Queens' Love Potion for the Swine (page 89)

1. Preheat the oven to 350°F. Line a baking sheet with aluminum foil.

2. Remove the membrane from the back of the ribs with a paring knife, heavy-duty tweezers, or needle-nose pliers. Sprinkle 2 tablespoons of the rub on the top of each slab of ribs. Stack the ribs in two piles on the prepared baking sheet. Bake for about 2¹/₂ hours, rotating the ribs every 30 to 45 minutes.

3. Remove the ribs from the oven. (At this point, the ribs could be cooled, wrapped in foil, and refrigerated for up to 2 days before finishing on the grill.)

4. Prepare a hot fire in a grill, adding the hickory chips.

5. Brush both sides of the ribs with sauce and place on the grill. Turn and baste the ribs with additional sauce. Grill for about 15 minutes, until the sauce has caramelized.

Grilled Pork Tenderloin or Center-Cut Pork Loin Fillet

It amazes us how many people have never grilled pork tenderloin or the new, more economical center-cut pork loin fillet. If you're one of those people, this recipe is for you. We give it our royal seal of approval. In a single word and with a wave of our tongs, pork tenderloin is superb!

Pork tenderloin or center-cut pork loin fillet is a great party food. Several tenderloins can go on the grill at once. The meat holds well and can be served hot, at room temperature, or chilled. We once char-grilled 30 tenderloins for a barbecue party of 100 dietitians. It was our first foray into catering, so it was quite by accident that they turned out beautifully. Here's how we did it: We charred about 10 tenderloins at a time over a very hot fire of mesquite hardwood lump charcoal. This took only 7 to 8 minutes per batch, and the pork was crispy on the outside and very rare on the inside. We transferred the charred pork to a cooler and transported it to the dinner destination. Then we cut it into 2-inch-thick slices, placed the slices in a hotel chafing dish, and set the dish out on the buffet. An hour later, the buffet opened. Our pork was a perfect medium and the hit of the party.

Be sure to purchase pork tenderloin or center-cut pork loin fillet, not pork loin roast. Pork tenderloin often comes two tenderloins to a package; a single center-cut pork loin fillet is usually available in about a 1 1/2-pound package. Tenderloins vary in weight from 8 to 16 ounces. Plan on a serving size of 8 ounces—the same for the larger and slightly chewier pork loin fillet. If not all of the meat is eaten, you'll have leftovers for eating cold with peanut dipping sauce, and there's nothing wrong with that.

SERVES 8

> 4 pork tenderloins or 2 center-cut pork loin fillets (3 1/2 to 4 pounds total)
> 2 tablespoons olive oil
> Fine kosher or sea salt and freshly ground black pepper to taste

1. Prepare a hot fire in a grill.

2. Lightly coat the tenderloins with the olive oil and season with salt and pepper. Place directly over the fire. Grill the tenderloins for 2 to 3 minutes per side (the center-cut pork loin fillets for 5 to 7 minutes per side), turning a quarter turn at a time, until an instant-read meat thermometer inserted in the thickest part registers 145°F and the meat is juicy and slightly pink in the center.

3. Let rest for about 5 minutes, then cut on the diagonal into 1- to 2-inch-thick slices. Transfer to a platter and serve.

Crowning Glories

This meat is delicious served with:

Hearts of Palm Salad *(page 283)*
Grilled Asparagus *(page 117)*
Grilled romaine *(page 127)*

Sesame and Soy–Marinated Pork Tenderloin: Try this pungent Asian-style marinade with just about any meat, fish, or vegetable. In a large bowl, combine ½ cup soy sauce, 2 tablespoons toasted sesame oil, 2 minced garlic cloves, and 5 thin slices peeled fresh ginger. Place the tenderloins (or loin fillets) in the bowl, cover, and marinate in the refrigerator for 1 to 2 hours. Grill as directed above and serve. **SERVES 8**

Grilled Pork Tenderloin with Cilantro-Peanut Dipping Sauce: In a small bowl, combine ¾ cup crunchy peanut butter, ¼ cup soy sauce, ¼ cup rice vinegar, ¼ cup fresh lime juice (4 to 5 limes), 2 tablespoons jalapeño honey, 1 tablespoon toasted sesame oil, and 1 to 2 tablespoons chopped fresh cilantro. To make a thinner sauce, add a little more lime juice. Grill the tenderloins (or loin fillets) as directed above. Serve hot or chilled with this sauce on the side. **SERVES 8 AS A MAIN COURSE OR 16 TO 20 AS AN APPETIZER**

Grilled Pork Tenderloin with Chipotle Dipping Sauce: This simple sauce can be mildly spicy or red-hot depending on the amount of chipotle chiles used. Try it with beef and shellfish, too. In a food processor, combine 2 cups prepared chili sauce, 1 canned chipotle chile in adobo sauce plus 1 teaspoon sauce, 1 tablespoon honey, 1 tablespoon fresh lemon juice, and ½ teaspoon kosher salt. Pulse 2 or 3 times to chop the chipotle and blend. Grill the tenderloins (or loin fillets) as described above and serve with the sauce. **SERVES 8**

Grilled Pork Tenderloin with Mustard-Herb Dipping Sauce: The BBQ Queens come from sturdy European stock. Judith has quite a bit of German blood; Karen is half Slavic and is married to Dick, whose family is of German descent. Why are we telling you this? Because we love mustard and mustard sauces. Another member of barbecue royalty, "the Baron of Barbecue," otherwise known as Paul Kirk, is a master at making sauces and rubs. Here we have adapted one of the recipes from his most recent book, *Paul Kirk's Championship Barbecue* (The Harvard Common Press, 2004). In a medium-size bowl, combine 2 cups sour cream, ¼ cup German-style whole-grain mustard, ¼ cup Dijon mustard, 1 tablespoon snipped fresh chives, 1 tablespoon chopped fresh tarragon, 1 tablespoon brandy, ½ teaspoon kosher salt, and ¼ teaspoon freshly ground black pepper. Grill the tenderloins (or loin fillets) as directed above. Serve with the sauce on the side. **SERVES 8**

Grill Gals

She Wants Y'all to Come Over for Dinner Menu

Grilled Pork Tenderloin in Worcestershire Marinade
Slow-Simmered Baby Lima Beans
Asiago-Garlic Grits
Lemon-Scented Peach Crisp

Judith's sister, Julie Fox, never used to say "y'all," but she does now that she lives in Atlanta. Although she's still not into sweetened ice tea, Julie loves to frequent the farmers' market near her home to buy great regional produce. In July, she brings home boxes of juice-running-down-your-arm Georgia peaches and tender fresh baby lima beans for a grill menu that Scarlett O'Hara would have loved. Unlike some who might think that women "don't know nuthin' 'bout grillin'," Julie is the grillmaster in her household.

She marinates the pork tenderloins the night before, slowly simmers the lima beans after she comes home from the market on Saturday morning, and then bakes the peach crisp and stirs up the grits right before she sizzles the pork on her gas grill. The bonus with this menu is that *everything* tastes as good or even better the next day.

Grilled Pork Tenderloin in Worcestershire Marinade

The hearty, savory marinade is also yummy with chicken and steaks. SERVES 8

WORCESTERSHIRE MARINADE

$^1/_2$ cup olive oil

$^1/_4$ cup soy sauce

$^1/_2$ cup Worcestershire sauce

2 tablespoons Dijon mustard

$^3/_4$ teaspoon kosher or sea salt

1 tablespoon freshly ground black pepper

$^1/_2$ cup red or white wine vinegar

2 tablespoons chopped fresh Italian parsley

2 cloves garlic, minced

$^1/_2$ cup fresh lemon juice (3 to 4 lemons)

Four 8-ounce pork tenderloins, trimmed of any fat and silverskin
Olive oil

1. To make the marinade, combine all the ingredients in a large baking dish. Reserve 1 cup of the marinade and refrigerate. Place the pork tenderloins in the remaining marinade, turn to coat, cover with plastic wrap, and refrigerate for 4 hours or overnight.

2. Prepare a hot fire in a grill.

3. Remove the pork from the marinade, discarding the marinade. Pat dry with paper towels and spray with olive oil. Grill until an instant-read meat thermometer inserted in the thickest part registers 145°F for medium, about 5 minutes per side.

4. Let rest for 10 minutes before slicing. Meanwhile, bring the reserved marinade to a boil over high heat, drizzle over the tenderloin slices on a platter, and serve.

Slow-Simmered Baby Lima Beans

If you have bad memories of big old lima beans, stop right there. These young whipper-snappers are tender, toothsome, and flavorful. **SERVES 8**

> **4 cups fresh or three 10-ounce packages defrosted frozen baby lima beans**
> **4 cups water**
> **1¹/₂ tablespoons chicken flavor base (available in the soup section of most grocery stores)**
> **4 slices bacon, cooked crisp and crumbled**

Place all the ingredients in a large saucepan and bring to a boil. Reduce the heat to low, cover, and simmer until the beans are tender, 3 to 4 hours. Check periodically, adding more water, if necessary. Serve hot.

Asiago-Garlic Grits

There are cheese grits and then there are *these* cheese grits! If you can't find stone-ground grits, use the old-fashioned kind, not instant. It's okay to use quick-cooking grits, but they will take less time to cook and be less textured than stone-ground grits. **SERVES 8**

> **2 cups water**
> **1 cup chicken broth**
> **1 tablespoon chopped garlic**
> **1 cup white or yellow stone-ground grits**
> **1 cup heavy cream**
> **1 cup freshly grated Asiago cheese**
> **Fine kosher or sea salt and ground white pepper to taste**

Combine the water, broth, and garlic in a large saucepan. Bring to a boil and slowly whisk in the grits. Cook over low heat, stirring frequently, until the grits thicken to a porridge consistency, about 15 minutes. Remove from the heat and stir in the cream and cheese. Season with salt and white pepper and serve.

Lemon-Scented Peach Crisp

We love the tart taste of lemon with everything—especially peaches. SERVES 8

> **6 cups peeled, pitted, and sliced fresh peaches**
> **2 cups sugar**
> **1 tablespoon quick-cooking tapioca**
> **Juice and grated zest of 1 lemon**
> **1 cup all-purpose flour**
> **1/2 cup (1 stick) unsalted butter, softened**

1. Preheat the oven to 375°F. Butter a 13 x 9-inch baking dish.

2. In a large bowl, combine the peaches, 1 cup of the sugar, the tapioca, and lemon juice. Spoon into the prepared baking dish. In a medium-size bowl, combine the remaining 1 cup sugar, the flour, and lemon zest. Using your fingers, rub the butter into the flour mixture to form large crumbs. Sprinkle these evenly over the fruit. Bake until lightly browned and bubbly, about 35 minutes. Serve warm.

Unfussy, big-flavor, homemade cakes are perfect to serve a crowd at your backyard feast—or for totin' over to someone else's. We've rounded up three of our favorite cakes that pay big dividends for minimal time and effort. We think it's a good idea to give your guests some time to digest all that savory food from the grill or smoker before offering them a sweet treat, perhaps with a coffee bar.

Cranberry-Almond Torte with Cranberry Drizzle

Our friend (and fellow culinary instructor and cookbook author) Ann Lund brought this torte to a meeting, where it was promptly devoured. Everyone asked for the recipe— the highest praise. Ann says she keeps bags of cranberries in the freezer year-round just to use for this easy-to-assemble cake. And the drizzle is divine. MAKES ONE 9-INCH TORTE; SERVES 8

CRANBERRY-ALMOND TORTE

1 cup sugar

One 8-ounce can almond paste

1/4 cup (1/2 stick) unsalted butter, softened

3 large eggs

1 tablespoon vanilla extract

1/4 cup all-purpose flour

2 cups frozen cranberries (don't defrost them)

CRANBERRY DRIZZLE

One 11-ounce can frozen cranberry juice concentrate, defrosted

1/4 cup sugar

1 tablespoon cornstarch

1 tablespoon cold water

3 tablespoons amaretto or other almond-flavored liqueur

1. Preheat the oven to 350°F. Grease and flour a 9-inch springform pan.

2. To make the torte, in a food processor, process the sugar, almond paste, butter, eggs, and vanilla together until smooth. Transfer the batter to a bowl. Stir in the flour, then the still-frozen cranberries. Spoon into the prepared pan and bake until a cake tester inserted in the center comes out clean, 35 to 40 minutes.

3. Let cool on a wire rack for 15 minutes, then run a knife around the pan to loosen the torte. Remove the pan and let the torte cool completely.

4. To make the drizzle, combine the cranberry juice concentrate and sugar in a medium-size saucepan and bring to a boil. Stir together the cornstarch and cold water, then stir the mixture into the juice and let boil for 1 minute. Remove from the heat and stir in the amaretto.

5. To serve, slice the torte and pour a little drizzle over each slice. Store any leftover torte, covered, at room temperature for 4 to 5 days. Store the drizzle in the refrigerator for up to 1 week.

Orange Marmalade Bundt Cake

This Bundt cake is a simpler version of the famous cake from author Jan Karon's Mitford series of novels about the fictional North Carolina town. The secret? (Don't faint!) A doctored-up cake mix. This is delish. SERVES 8 TO 12

CAKE

One yellow cake mix with pudding

4 large eggs

$1/2$ cup vegetable oil, such as canola, corn, or light olive oil

1 cup orange juice

1 tablespoon grated orange zest

ORANGE SYRUP AND MARMALADE TOPPING

$1/2$ cup orange juice

$1/4$ cup sugar

One 12-ounce jar orange marmalade, melted and cooled

$1/3$ cup lowfat sour cream

3 cups whipped cream (about $1^1/2$ cups heavy cream, whipped to firm peaks) or lowfat whipped topping

Threads of orange zest from 1 orange for garnish

1. Preheat the oven to 325°F. Generously grease a 12-cup tube or Bundt pan.

2. To make the cake, in a large bowl mix together the cake mix, eggs, oil, orange juice, and zest with an electric mixer until smooth. Pour into the prepared pan and bake until a cake tester inserted near the center comes out clean, 55 to 60 minutes. Set on a wire rack.

3. To make the topping, combine the orange juice and sugar in a small bowl, stirring until dissolved. Poke lots of holes in the top of the hot cake with a toothpick. Slowly pour the juice over the cake, making sure that it is absorbed. Let the cake cool completely, then loosen the sides with a knife and remove from the pan. Set on the rack again.

4. Spread the melted orange marmalade over the cake. Combine the sour cream and whipped cream and spread over the marmalade. Sprinkle the top with the orange zest. Refrigerate for at least 2 hours before serving. Store in the refrigerator, covered, for up to 3 days.

Grilled Pound Cake with Hot Fudge Ganache and Sweetened Berries

Pound cake is a delicious basic that can be served with fresh seasonal fruit or frozen fruit. Pair the cake and fruit with a favorite dessert sauce, such as lemon, vanilla, or chocolate, or a liqueur, and garnish with fresh lemon balm or spearmint leaves or citrus zest. Or make the whole thing into a sundae with ice cream or sorbet.

You can find prepared pound cake in the freezer or bakery section of most grocery stores or make your own from a mix or from scratch. SERVES 8

> **4 cups fresh seasonal berries, such as strawberries, blueberries, or raspberries**
> **$^1/_2$ cup sugar, or to taste**
> **1 pound cake**
> **Hot Fudge Ganache (page 440)**

1. About 30 minutes before serving, place the berries in a bowl and sprinkle with the sugar. This will bring out the juice in the berries.

2. Cut the pound cake into slices and toast on a clean grill over medium-high heat until grill marks appear, about 2 minutes per side. (Or toast in a toaster.) Serve the toasted pound cake with a spoonful of sweetened berries and a drizzle of ganache.

Rotisserie Pork Loin

Rotisserie pork loin is a great crowd-pleaser. It stays moist and juicy, it slices beautifully, and it tastes fabulous. And unlike the queens of yore, you don't need any minions (scullery maids, knife boys, wenches in general) to help you. The rotisserie does all the work, and you take all the credit. In about 3 hours, you have a spectacular entrée that is wonderful served with a complementary sauce, or with a green salad and a potato casserole (see pages 412–413).

Check the maximum weight that your rotisserie motor can handle, then buy your pork loin. Cook two at a time and plan for delicious leftovers. **SERVES 6 TO 8**

> **One 5- to 6- pound boneless pork loin roast**
>
> **1 recipe Mustard-Mayo-Orange Slather (page 66)**
>
> **1 recipe Spicy Orange Rub (page 51)**

1. Brush the pork loin all over with the slather and sprinkle evenly with the rub. Let sit at room temperature for 15 minutes, until the slather feels tacky to the touch.

2. Set up your grill for rotisserie cooking (see page 33). Prepare a medium fire (around 350°F). Push the rotisserie rod through the center of the roast so that the meat is balanced, then place on the spit. Cover and cook until an instant-read meat thermometer inserted in the center registers 145°F for medium, 3 to 4 hours total. (If you like your pork more well done, aim for 155 to 165°F.) Let rest for 10 minutes before slicing and serving.

Crowning Glories

Rotisserie pork loin is dynamite served with a sauce, such as:

Fennel and Orange Drizzling Sauce *(page 73)*

The Doctor Is In Apricot-Bourbon Barbecue Sauce *(page 90; you can glaze the pork with*
this or serve it on the side)

Raspberry-Jalapeño Barbecue Sauce *(page 90; you can glaze the pork*
with this or serve it on the side)

Herb-Marinated Rotisserie Pork Loin: This is another way to go with pork loin, marinating

it instead of using a slather and rub. We love this dish served with a complementary but different herb sauce, such as Thousand-Herb Sauce (page 192) or Chimichurri Sauce (page

346). To make the marinade, combine 2 fresh bay leaves or 1 teaspoon powdered bay leaf, 1 teaspoon dried thyme, 6 minced garlic cloves, the juice of 2 lemons, and $1/4$ cup olive oil in a small bowl. Brush the mixture all over the loin. Cover with plastic wrap and refrigerate for at least 1 hour or overnight. Season with kosher or sea salt and freshly ground black pepper to taste, then cook on the rotisserie as directed above. **SERVES 6 TO 8**

Ancho and Chipotle-Rubbed Rotisserie Pork Loin: You can find ground chipotle and ancho chile in the grocery store under the McCormick label or buy them from your favorite spice emporium. In a small bowl, mix together 1 tablespoon ground chipotle chile, 1 tablespoon ground ancho chile, $1/4$ cup grated onion, 1 tablespoon minced garlic, 2 tablespoons olive oil, 1 tablespoon ground cumin, 2 teaspoons coarse kosher or sea salt, and 1 teaspoon freshly ground black pepper. Wearing rubber gloves or using a rubber spatula, rub the paste all over the pork loin. Cover with plastic wrap and marinate in the refrigerator for at least 6 hours or overnight. Unwrap and cook on the rotisserie as directed above. **SERVES 6 TO 8**

Bourbon Pecan-Stuffed Rotisserie Pork Loin: The bourbon in the stuffing and marinade brings out the natural sweetness in the pork. We love this! (Because we're so sweet ourselves.) Have the butcher butterfly a 5- to 6-pound pork loin for you. To make the stuffing, finely snip (using kitchen shears) $1/2$ cup dried apricots, $1/2$ cup sweetened dried cranberries, and $1/2$ cup sweetened dried pineapple into a medium-size bowl. Pour over 1 cup bourbon and let soak and soften for 1 hour, then stir in $1/2$ cup finely chopped pecans. Drain the liquid from the stuffing, reserving it. Spread the stuffing over the surface of the pork loin, leaving a 1-inch border. Roll up and tie at 4-inch intervals with kitchen twine. Place the rolled pork loin in a large sealable plastic bag, pour in the reserved stuffing liquid, and turn to coat. Seal the bag and marinate in the refrigerator for at least 1 hour or overnight, turning occasionally. Season with kosher or sea salt and freshly ground black pepper to taste, then cook on the rotisserie as directed above. This is great served with The Doctor Is In Apricot-Bourbon Barbecue Sauce (page 90). **SERVES 6 TO 8**

Rotisserie Pork Loin Sandwiches: Depending on which rotisserie pork loin you make, you can enjoy the leftovers in one of the following sandwiches: sliced Rotisserie Pork Loin with sliced ripe tomatoes, pitted, drained, and sliced oil- or brine-cured Kalamata olives, arugula, and aioli (see pages 104–105 and 110) on country bread; shredded Ancho and Chipotle–Rubbed Rotisserie Pork Loin with assorted greens or *pico de gallo* and Chipotle Vinaigrette (page 86), rolled up in a flour tortilla; sliced Bourbon Pecan-Stuffed Rotisserie Pork Loin with shredded iceberg lettuce and The Doctor Is In Apricot-Bourbon Barbecue Sauce (page 90) on ciabatta. **SERVES AS MANY AS YOU HAVE LEFTOVERS FOR**

BBQ Babes

She's the Flower of the Flames Menu

Raspberry and Mustard–Glazed Pork Roast
Kiss of Smoke Beef Tenderloin Black Forest
Cola-Marinated Smoked Flank Steak

When she began barbecuing on the competition circuit in the mid-1980s, Karen Putman was one of the few women in the game. And she was a big winner. Her fellow competitors dubbed her "the Flower of the Flames." Her barbecue was and still is a force to be reckoned with, and we're proud to say she's one of the original 'Que Queens. She has won hundreds of barbecue and chef competition awards, national and international. Here are some of her greatest hits.

Raspberry and Mustard–Glazed Pork Roast

One of Karen's signature flavors is raspberry, combined here with orange juice and zest, spicy barbecue sauce, and whole-grain mustard to make a superb glaze that you can almost drink as an elixir—the true sign of a queenly sauce. **SERVES 8**

RASPBERRY AND MUSTARD GLAZE

1 1/2 cups spicy barbecue sauce of your choice

One 12-ounce bag individually frozen raspberries, defrosted

2 tablespoons grated orange zest

1/4 cup fresh orange juice (1 to 2 oranges)

1/4 cup whole-grain mustard

1 teaspoon finely grated fresh ginger (if using a microplane, you don't need to peel)

¹/₂ teaspoon fine kosher or sea salt

¹/₄ teaspoon cayenne pepper

One 3¹/₂- to 4-pound boneless pork loin roast, tied

4 or 5 apple wood chunks (optional), soaked in water for at least 1 hour before grilling

1. To make the glaze, combine all the ingredients in a medium-size bowl. Divide in half, using one half for basting and reserving the other half for serving.

2. Prepare an indirect fire with a temperature of 250°F.

3. Place a wire rack 4 to 6 inches over a drip pan, then place the roast on the rack. Cover the grill, opening the vents slightly. Cook the roast for 45 minutes and turn. To maintain a constant temperature, add more charcoal and the apple wood chunks, if desired. Cover and continue to cook, basting the roast with the glaze every 10 minutes for the next 45 minutes of cooking. The roast is done when there is still a slight tinge of pink in the center and an instant-read meat thermometer inserted in the center registers 160 to 165°F.

4. Remove from the grill, wrap in plastic, and let stand for 15 minutes before slicing. Serve with the reserved glaze.

Kiss of Smoke Beef Tenderloin Black Forest

Chef Putman creates recipes all the time, and she often enters them in culinary contests, which she usually wins. In this one, she first sears the tenderloins over a hot fire, then transfers them to the indirect side of a grill to finish cooking and get that kiss of smoke. Her concoction for beef tenderloin is an elegant way to serve a crowd. Be sure to serve Decadent Garlic Mashed Potatoes (page 321) with this. Nothing else will do. **SERVES 16**

SUGGESTED WOOD: Cherry

One 16-ounce can pitted dark sweet cherries, drained
4 large cloves garlic, minced
$\frac{1}{2}$ cup dry red wine, such as a Burgundy or Cabernet Sauvignon
$\frac{1}{3}$ cup extra virgin olive oil
Two 5-pound beef tenderloins, trimmed of any fat and silverskin
Fine kosher or sea salt and freshly ground black pepper to taste

1. In a medium-size bowl, combine the cherries, garlic, wine, and olive oil. Cover and refrigerate overnight so the flavors will meld.

2. Prepare a hot indirect fire in a grill.

3. Split the tenderloins lengthwise, but not all the way through. Fill each with the cherry mixture and tie closed at 2-inch intervals with kitchen twine.

4. Grill the meat directly over the hot fire for 10 minutes per side, turning a quarter turn at a time. Move the tenderloins to the indirect side of the grill, cover, and grill until an instant-read meat thermometer inserted in the thickest part registers 120°F for medium-rare and 135°F for medium, 10 to 15 minutes. Slice and serve.

Cola-Marinated Smoked Flank Steak

Coca-Cola makes for a very southern marinade that is sometimes used to glaze smoked ham and other cuts of pork. Chef Putman shows her creativity by applying this to a beef flank steak, a cut that is usually grilled. **SERVES 6 TO 8**

SUGGESTED WOOD: Fruitwood, hickory, mesquite, oak, or maple

One 4- to 5-pound flank steak

COLA MARINADE

2 cups cola (Karen uses Coca-Cola)
1 cup vegetable oil
1 cup distilled white vinegar
3 cloves garlic, minced
Fine kosher or sea salt and freshly ground black pepper to taste

1. Place the meat in a shallow dish or sealable plastic bag.

2. To make the marinade, combine all the ingredients in a large bowl. Pour two-thirds of it over the meat. Reserve the rest for basting. (Keep refrigerated until ready to use.) Cover or seal and marinate in the refrigerator for at least 8 hours or overnight.

3. Prepare a 200°F fire in a smoker or grill.

4. Remove the meat from the marinade, discarding the marinade. Place in the smoker, cover, and smoke for 6 to 7 hours, basting with the reserved marinade every 30 minutes after the first hour of cooking. The meat is done when it is tender and an instant-read meat thermometer inserted in the thickest part registers about 180°F. Slice on the diagonal and serve.

Smoked Pork Loin

nstead of a safe for our crown jewels, we regard the freezer as the true repository of our culinary gems. We like to buy pork loin on sale, then stow it in the freezer to become a frozen asset. There are so many delicious ways to cook a pork loin on the grill or in the smoker. You can brush on a mustard slather, then sprinkle with a rub, or go for a more basic treatment, as we suggest here.

When a family in Judith's neighborhood was undergoing a medical crisis, Judith smoked a large pork loin and made it the centerpiece of a dinner she brought over to them. The report back was that nary a speck was left over the next day. People in distress have to eat, and what better time to have the food be really, really good? **SERVES 8 TO 10**

SUGGESTED WOOD: Apple, cherry, hickory, oak, or a combination

One 5- to 6-pound boneless pork loin roast

¹/₄ cup olive oil

3 tablespoons freshly ground black pepper

1 tablespoon garlic salt

2 cups apple juice

1. Brush the pork with the olive oil, then sprinkle with the pepper and garlic salt. Set aside for 15 minutes.

2. Prepare an indirect fire in a smoker.

3. Cover and smoke the pork loin at 225 to 250°F for about 30 minutes per pound. After half an hour, start basting with the apple juice every 30 minutes. The pork loin is done when an instant-read meat thermometer inserted in the center registers 145°F, 3 to 3¹/₂ hours. Let rest for 15 minutes, then slice and serve.

 Crowning Glories

Smoked pork loin is delicious served with:

Honeyed Barbecue Sauce *(page 90; glaze the pork with this or serve it on the side)*

Smoked (or Grilled) Onion Marmalade *(page 141)*

Pineapple-Ginger Salsa *(page 414)*

Slathered and Rubbed Smoked Pork Loin: You can smoke pork loin using the same preparation as for Rotisserie Pork Loin (page 398). Try slathering a 5- to 6-pound boneless pork roast with Mustard-Mayo-Orange Slather (page 66), then sprinkling on Spicy Orange Rub (page 51). Let sit for at least 15 minutes, until the surface feels tacky to the touch. Place the roast in a disposable aluminum pan and smoke as directed above. A great finishing touch would be Fennel and Orange Drizzling Sauce (page 73). **SERVES 8 TO 10**

Tuscan-Style Porchetta: When Judith and her family went to Tuscany, this rolled and tied roast with a savory filling was part of the Fourth of July feast they enjoyed outdoors. In Tuscany, you can buy roasted porchetta—with its thick collar of fat—at market stalls or butcher shops. We lightened it up a little and smoked instead of roasted it, so you won't miss that collar of fat, we promise! Have your butcher butterfly a 5- to 6-pound boneless pork roast. Combine 2 cups peeled garlic cloves and $1/2$ cup olive oil in a baking dish and bake at 350°F until softened, 30 to 40 minutes. Let cool. In a food processor, puree 1 bunch fresh Italian parsley with the roasted garlic, any olive oil remaining in the pan, and the juice of 1 lemon. Spread three-quarters of the paste over the surface of the pork loin, then sprinkle with $1^1/2$ teaspoons freshly ground black pepper, 1 teaspoon fine kosher or sea salt, and $1^1/2$ teaspoons fennel seeds. Roll up from a long side and tie with kitchen twine at intervals. Slather the remaining paste over the rolled loin, place in a disposable aluminum pan, and smoke as directed above. **SERVES 8 TO 10**

BBQ Queens' Choucroute Garnie: Some of Karen's family is from Yugoslavia and Judith's from Germany, so this dish is soul food to us. Use smoked pork loin as the centerpiece of a hearty sauerkraut supper with all the trimmings. It's a great recipe to serve a crowd on a cold night. Preheat the oven to 350°F. In a large roasting pan, place a 5- to 6-pound pork loin smoked as described above, 2 pounds drained deli or freshly made sauerkraut (not canned), 2 tablespoons juniper berries, 2 tablespoons caraway seeds, 1 cup dry white wine, 1 cup chicken broth, 4 large or 8 small bratwurst sausage, and 1 pound smoked or Polish link sausage. Cover and braise for 1 hour. Check periodically, adding more wine and broth, if necessary. Serve hot, with whole-grain mustard and freshly grated horse-radish to pass at the table. **SERVES 10 TO 12**

Not on the Discovery Channel: Smoke-Roasting

Sometimes necessity really is the mother of invention.

When the BBQ Queens traveled far to do a cooking class at a school that shall remain nameless, we realized that only one inept person—who took 15 minutes to chop an onion—was going to help us prepare the four-course dinner. The school also had no smoker (which they assured us they had). Luckily, we had brought a small one with us. But that meant we couldn't slow smoke a pork roast and a potato dish *and* get everything else ready.

First, shock set in, then momentary panic. Finally, we talked ourselves down from the ledge and knew we had to pull this off some way. That's when we invented our version of smoke-roasting—although we found out later that lots of barbecuers, such as Paul Kirk, had come to the technique under similar circumstances.

Smoke-roasting is a combination of low and slow smoking (at 225 to 250°F) and hot and fast roasting (at 450°F). You use both your smoker and your oven. You can either smoke first and roast later, or the opposite. Your food will be a little crispier if you smoke first and roast later (which we prefer), a little softer if you roast and then smoke. What you get is roasted food with a touch of caramelization and a smoky aroma and flavor. Heavenly!

Smoke-roasting works with any dish that you would just roast, namely pork or beef roasts, whole chickens or turkeys, or vegetable dishes.

Smoke-Roasted Pork Loin with Herbed Pear Stuffing

We adapted one of our own recipes from *Easy Grilling & Simple Smoking* (Pig Out Publications, 1997) for this dish. Have your butcher butterfly the roast. Smoking it takes about 2 hours; smoke-roasting saves you a sometimes crucial half-hour. But the big benefit is the flavor and texture. **SERVES 6 TO 8**

SUGGESTED WOOD: Apple or cherry

HERBED PEAR STUFFING

2 tablespoons unsalted butter

4 ripe but firm pears, peeled, cored, and chopped

1 medium-size yellow onion, diced

4 stalks celery, diced

3 sprigs fresh tarragon, chopped

1 tablespoon chopped fresh oregano

1 tablespoon chopped fresh rosemary

$1/2$ teaspoon freshly grated nutmeg

$1/2$ teaspoon ground allspice

4 slices homemade or good-quality store-bought bread, crumbled

One 3- to 4-pound boneless pork loin roast, butterflied

$1/2$ teaspoon fine kosher or sea salt, or more to taste

Ground white pepper to taste

2 tablespoons freshly ground black pepper

2 teaspoons garlic salt

3 cups apple juice

1 or 2 yellow onions, cut in half

1. Prepare an indirect fire in a smoker.

2. To make the stuffing, melt the butter in a large skillet over medium heat. Add the pears, onion, celery, herbs, and spices and cook, stirring often, until the onion is

translucent, 6 to 8 minutes. Stir in enough of the bread crumbs to bind the mixture together, then remove from the heat.

3.   Lay the butterflied pork loin on a work surface and season with the salt and white pepper. Spread the stuffing over the meat. Roll up the loin, starting with a long side. Tie the roll together at intervals with kitchen twine. Sprinkle with the black pepper and garlic salt. Place the tied and rolled pork loin in a disposable aluminum pan with 2 cups of the apple juice and the onion halves.

4.   Smoke at 225 to 250°F, with the lid closed, for 1 hour. Meanwhile, preheat the oven to 400°F.

5.   Transfer the roast to the oven and baste with the remaining 1 cup apple juice. Cook until an instant-read meat thermometer inserted in the center registers 155°F, about 30 minutes. Remove from the oven. Let sit for 10 minutes before slicing and serving.

Smoke-Roasted Potatoes with Garlic and Rosemary

This is a splendid way to update regular roasted potatoes with a kiss of smoke. SERVES 6

> **3 large baking potatoes, peeled and quartered**
> **3 large sweet potatoes, peeled and quartered**
> **10 large cloves garlic, peeled**
> **1/2 cup olive oil**
> **2 tablespoons fresh rosemary leaves**
> **Fine kosher or sea salt and freshly ground black pepper to taste**

1.   Prepare an indirect fire in a smoker.

2.   In a large disposable aluminum pan, combine the potatoes and garlic. Drizzle with the olive oil and toss to blend. Sprinkle with the rosemary, season with salt and pepper, and toss again. Smoke at 225 to 250°F, with the lid closed, for 1 hour. Meanwhile, preheat the oven to 400°F.

3.   Toss the potatoes again, then transfer to the oven and finish cooking until the potatoes are fork tender, about 30 minutes. Serve hot.

Smoked Pork Butt

Pork butt is a large, usually boneless (the shoulder blade is removed), somewhat cylindrical piece of meat from the upper shoulder of a hog. Pork butt is also sold as Boston butt. A pork butt weighs anywhere from 3½ to 9 pounds, and it's muscular, riddled with fat, and chewy, chewy, chewy. That is, until you slow smoke it. Then it's fabulous—smoky, moist, meltingly tender, and full of flavor. The same goes for the pork shoulder blade roast (bone-in). It takes longer to smoke but is very tasty and often cheap to buy.

You can either slice or pull apart a slow-smoked pork butt to serve as is, with a sauce, or piled on bread, Carolina-style, with a vinegary coleslaw on top—the Piggy Sandwich (page 411). It's where the bun meets the butt, and it's delicious.

The BBQ Queens recommend smoking two smaller pork butts, because that will save you some time. Two 3½-pound pork butts will still take about 8 hours to slow smoke, but a 7-pound pork butt could take 10 to 12 hours. We love to use apple, hickory, oak, pecan, or a combination of these woods and slow smoke at a constant temperature of 225 to 250°F.

We slather our pork butts with a mustard mixture, sprinkle on a zesty rub, and then smoke for a good 8 hours, maybe longer, depending on the weather. We baste occasionally with apple juice. When it's done, people just salivate as we pull it apart. The charred exterior, tender pink interior, and delicious aroma are irresistible. Pork butt is a great smoked meat to serve a crowd.

Hoisin sauce is wonderful slathered all over pork butt. In the spring and summer, when fresh herbs are plentiful, be sure to chop some and add to whatever slather you plan to use.

Make sure you save any trimmings from your smoked pork butt. If necessary, freeze them to use later in heavenly BBQ Queens' Barbecued Beans (page 107). **SERVES 12**

SUGGESTED WOOD: Apple, pecan, oak, or hickory, or a combination

Two 3½-pound boneless pork butts
Mustard-Mayo Slather (page 66)
BBQ Queens' All-Purpose Rub (page 49)
2 cups apple juice

1. Brush the pork butts with the slather, then sprinkle with the rub. Set aside for 15 minutes, until the surface of the meat is tacky to the touch.

2. Prepare an indirect fire in a smoker.

3.   Cover and smoke the pork butts at 225 to 250°F. After 4 hours, start basting with apple juice every 30 minutes. The butts are done when you can insert a grill fork into the meat and twist, about 4 hours more. An instant-read meat thermometer inserted in the center should register 165°F. Pull the meat apart while it is still hot, arrange on a platter, and serve.

Crowning Glories

**Barbecued pork butt is traditionally served piled on a bun and
topped with a vinegary coleslaw, or serve with:**
BBQ Queens' Barbecued Beans (page 107)
BBQ Queens' Smoked Potato Casserole (page 153)
Smoky Barbecue Sauce (page 90)

Spicy Orange Barbecued Pork Butt: Traditional barbecued pork butt, a staple category at barbecue competitions, is nothing short of wonderful. But if you prepare it a lot, sometimes you get a hankerin' for pork butt a different way. This is it. Use Mustard-Mayo-Orange Slather (page 66) and sprinkle the pork butts with Spicy Orange Rub (page 51). Slow smoke as directed above, then accompany with Fennel and Orange Drizzling Sauce (page 73). **SERVES 12**

Butts in a Bag: We couldn't resist this. The name alone made us chuckle. We got this unusual but folksy recipe from Ardie Davis, known on the barbecue circuit as Remus Powers, Ph.B. Like beer can chicken, this recipe has developed a following, and for good reason—it works! The only extras you need, in addition to our basic slow-smoked pork butts, are 4 medium-size brown paper grocery bags, about the size for a small order of groceries. Slather and rub the 2 pork butts as directed above with the slather and rub of your choice, then smoke them for 4 hours. Slide each pork butt into a grocery bag, then double-bag it by sliding the open end of the bag into a second grocery bag. The idea is to totally enclose the pork butt. Place the bagged butts in the smoker and continue to smoke, without basting, for another 4 hours, until the meat is tender. (Don't worry, the bags won't burn at 250°F. Don't try this, though, if you use a kamado-style smoker, which smokes foods at a higher heat.) Remove the bags, pull apart the meat, and serve this moister, even more delicious pork butt. **SERVES 12**

Piggy Sandwich: In the Carolinas, barbecued pork sandwiches are an art form and one of the best ways to enjoy slow-smoked pork butt. Finely chop some of the hot pork butt, mix it with a little barbecue sauce, if you like, and pile some of the meat on the bottom of a toasted bun. Top with a vinegar-based coleslaw, such as Layered Vinegar Slaw (page 80), crown with the top of the bun, and you're in hog heaven! **SERVES 1**

Double-Smoked Ham

Yes, we know that precooked ham is smoked once already. And we know you shouldn't experiment with new dishes on dinner guests—or cooking school students. But we found out how wonderful a double-smoked ham tastes while experimenting, er, we mean teaching a class, in Indiana.

You can double-smoke two different kinds of ham. The easiest one to use is a good-quality, presliced bone-in ham. Because it is presliced, the smoke penetrates farther into the meat in a shorter amount of time—about an hour is just fine—even tented with aluminum foil in a stovetop smoker (see page 34). You don't want to smoke a sliced ham for very long, or it will dry out.

But if you want a mahogany-colored ham with lots of smoke and have some time on your hands, don't buy the spiral cut. Instead, purchase either a country cured whole ham, such as a Smithfield, or a precooked whole ham, such as a Hormel Cure 81. You need the covering on the outside of the ham so that the inner meat doesn't dry out. You'll be able to smoke this whole ham for anywhere from 2 to 10 hours, depending on your desire for smokiness.

You don't even need a glaze on a double-smoked ham, but this one is fairly simple. **SERVES 8 TO 10**

SUGGESTED WOOD: Apple, hickory, pecan, or oak, or a combination

MUSTARD-APRICOT GLAZE

2 cups apricot preserves

2¹/₂ teaspoons dry mustard

1¹/₂ tablespoons cider vinegar

One 5- to 7-pound bone-in precooked or smoked ham (shank or butt)

20 whole cloves

I.   To make the glaze, combine all the ingredients in a small bowl.

Potato Casseroles with a Royal Touch

Having a number of rich and hearty potato casseroles in your culinary arsenal is as important as knowing the four queen waves (see page 224). Whether you're grilling or smoking (or broiling, frying, poaching, or baking) the main part of your dinner, a potato casserole always comes in handy. You can feed vegetarians, children, the elderly, terminally hungry adolescent boys, picky eaters, those who need fattening up, and those who don't. Here are two of the BBQ Queens' favorites.

Potato Gratin with White Cheddar Cheese

This comes from our culinary instructor and friend Ann Lund, author of her self-published *Dining in Style*. We first tried this at a Somerset Vineyard dinner in Kansas (yes, you read that right). The Burgundy-style wines were wonderful, and one of the stars of the gourmet potluck gathering was this gratin. In company, we were both circumspect and only ate a small square each. At home, we would have cut ourselves a generous slab! We use a mandoline to cut the potatoes. This gratin takes about 2 hours to bake, but it's well worth the time and energy. Don't plan on any leftovers. **SERVES 12 TO 16**

3 cups heavy cream

¾ cup finely chopped shallot

2 teaspoons chopped fresh rosemary

2 teaspoons kosher or sea salt

¾ teaspoon freshly ground black pepper

4 pounds russet potatoes, peeled and sliced ¼ inch thick

2 cups finely shredded sharp white cheddar cheese

1.   Preheat the oven to 375°F. Butter a 13 x 9-inch baking dish.

2.   Pour the cream into a microwave-safe bowl and heat on high for 2 minutes. Or pour into a medium-size saucepan and warm over medium heat. Remove from the heat and stir in the shallot, rosemary, salt, and pepper. Cover and let infuse for 30 minutes.

3.   Layer half the potato slices in the prepared baking dish, overlapping them to fit. Sprinkle with three-quarters of the cheese. Arrange the remaining potatoes on top of the cheese and pour the cream mixture over. Sprinkle with the remaining cheese.

4.   Cover with aluminum foil and bake for 1 hour. Remove the foil and bake until the top is golden and bubbling, about 45 minutes. Let cool for 10 minutes before cutting into squares.

Oven-Roasted Saffron Potatoes

We prefer new or red potatoes for the color of their skins paired with the wonderful tinge of yellow from the saffron. Serve these amazingly aromatic potatoes with grilled pork, lamb, or fish. SERVES 8

> **1 large pinch of saffron threads (about ¹/₂ teaspoon)**
> **2 cups chicken broth**
> **16 small new or red potatoes, cut in half**
> **1 tablespoon unsalted butter, melted**
> **Fine kosher or sea salt and cracked black peppercorns to taste**

1.   Preheat the oven to 400°F. Oil a large baking dish.

2.   Carefully toast the saffron in a small saucepan over high heat for 1 minute. Immediately add the broth, stir to blend, and bring to a simmer.

3.   In a large bowl, toss the potatoes with the melted butter and season with salt and cracked pepper. Arrange in the prepared dish and pour the saffron broth over all. Roast, turning the potatoes once, until they are tender and the broth has reduced to a rich glaze, 20 to 30 minutes. Serve immediately.

2.   Coat the ham with the glaze, reserving any leftover glaze. Stud the ham with the cloves and let stand for 1 hour to marinate.

3.   Meanwhile, prepare an indirect fire in a smoker.

4.   Put the ham in a disposable aluminum pan and place in the smoker. Cover and smoke at 225 to 250°F. Baste with additional glaze and pan juices after the first hour of smoking. Continue to smoke until the ham is bronzed and reaches the desired smokiness. A spiral-cut ham will take at least 1 hour or up to 2 hours without drying out. A whole ham will take 2 to 8 hours. Remove from the smoker and serve.

👑 Crowning Glories 👑
Double-smoked ham is out of this world served with:
Layered Vinegar Slaw *(page 80)*
Potato Gratin with White Cheddar Cheese *(page 412)*
Texas-Style Pinto Beans *(page 106)*

Double-Smoked Ham with Pineapple-Ginger Salsa:
The smoky ham is so good you'll dice it for soup, put it in pasta, and make decadent hoagie sandwiches with it. Or you can serve it sliced with a delicious condiment on the side, such as this salsa. Combine the following ingredients in a food processor: 2 cups peeled, cored, and chopped fresh pineapple; 3 tablespoons peeled and chopped fresh ginger; 1/4 cup firmly packed light brown sugar; and 1/4 cup fresh lime juice (4 to 5 limes). (This salsa will keep in the refrigerator for up to 1 week.) Smoke the ham as directed above and serve with the salsa.
SERVES 8 TO 10

Karen's Double-Smoked Ham Salad Sandwiches:
Karen has been making ham salad sandwiches for years, and her coworkers Mary Ann Duckers and Dee Barwick proclaim them the best. When Judith heard this, she quizzed Karen on what she did to make them so special. Because Karen doesn't use a recipe, it took several questions to figure out the secret: she added the hard-boiled eggs while still warm. To make the ham salad, hard-boil 4 or 5 large eggs (see page 378). While the eggs are cooling a bit, process several chunks of double-smoked ham in a food processor. You need about 2 cups ground ham. Add 1/4 cup mayonnaise, 2 tablespoons Dijon mustard, and 2 tablespoons fresh lemon juice and pulse. Peel the eggs while still warm and put them in the food processor whole. Pulse to combine. Spread the slightly warm ham salad on 4 slices of fresh sourdough bread, top with 4 more bread slices, and enjoy. **SERVES 4**

Rise and Shine: Breakfast in the Great Outdoors

You should have a breakfast picnic at least once in your life, preferably on a cool and sunny May morning before the bugs have come to life again. A breakfast outdoors is perfect for a family gathering. The kids can run around, and the adults can get breakfast on the grill and the table.

Bring everything (freshly brewed coffee in a large thermos, for example) to a park, or relax in your own backyard, with the coffeemaker perking in the kitchen. Scramble the eggs or sauté the hash in a large greased skillet over a medium-hot fire in the grill, Girl Scout style.

Double-Smoked Ham *(page 411)*
Scrambled eggs
Smoked Trout Benedict with Confetti Hash *(page 273)*
Campfire Skillet Scones (recipe follows) with butter, jams, and jellies
Breakfast S'mores (recipe follows)

Campfire Skillet Scones

Portable and pleasing, these scones are adapted from a recipe in Judith's *Prairie Home Breads* (The Harvard Common Press, 2001). Her first experience with campfire cooking was during Girl Scout weekends at Camp Butterworth in Loveland, Ohio. If you're camping, simply place the dry ingredients in a sealable plastic bag, then mix up the batter right before you bake the scones. The key is a large, seasoned cast-iron skillet.

MAKES 8 SCONES

2 cups all-purpose flour

2 tablespoons sugar

2¹/₂ teaspoons baking powder

1 teaspoon fine kosher or sea salt

2 teaspoons cream of tartar

3 tablespoons instant nonfat dry milk

6 tablespoons (³/₄ stick) unsalted butter, cut into small pieces

¹/₄ cup water

1 large egg, lightly beaten

1. Prepare a medium-hot campfire or grill fire. Grease a well-seasoned 12-inch cast-iron skillet. In a medium-size bowl, combine the dry ingredients. With your fingertips, work in the butter until the mixture resembles coarse crumbs. Stir in the water and egg until a dough forms.

2. Turn the dough out onto a floured work surface. Flour your hands and pat or press the dough into an 8-inch round about ¹/₂ inch thick. Cut the round into 8 wedges and arrange the wedges about ¹/₂ inch apart in the skillet.

3. Place the pan over the campfire or grill fire and cook until the scones have risen and are browned on top, 10 to 15 minutes. Serve warm.

Breakfast S'mores

Send the kids to look for suitable twigs. Then thread a piece of fruit or two (try fresh banana or pineapple chunks, whole firm strawberries, or large peach or nectarine slices), along with a marshmallow, onto each twig and roast over the grill or campfire until the marshmallow gets squishy. Eat right away.

A Little Lamb

Some people still need their arms twisted to try lamb. If you're one of those (and even if you're not), read on. Gone are the days when older mutton was dressed as younger lamb, with a stronger flavor than we really liked. Sometimes the only lamb available was imported, frozen, from New Zealand. Today you can often get delicious, tender lamb that is raised locally. It's lighter in color, finer in flavor, and not at all strong. When paired with garlic, herbs, dry wines, and other seasonings, lamb is one of the BBQ Queens' favorite meats to grill or smoke. We love grilled butterflied leg of lamb and those thin little lamb chops cooked over a hot, hot, hot fire.

There are two tricks to achieving great-tasting lamb. One is to trim off as much of the hard white fat as you can, because this can contribute a stronger flavor than you might like. The second is to grill or rotisserie cook lamb to a medium doneness at most. Well-done lamb on the grill or rotisserie can be dry and strong-flavored. (By contrast, slow-smoked lamb is delicious well done. The smoke counteracts the stronger well-done flavor, and the longer, slower cooking time results in a very tender and juicy meat.)

One reason to eat more lamb—from chops to burgers to skewers to racks to leg cuts—is that there is so much you can do with it on the grill, smoker, or rotisserie. For the grill, we recommend smaller, more tender cuts, such as chops, lamb loin, rack of lamb, or steaks (or cubes of meat destined for skewers) cut from the leg. For the outdoor smoker, we recommend larger cuts of meat that benefit from long, slow cooking, such as boneless butterflied or bone-in leg of lamb, rack of lamb, or lamb shoulder. And for the rotisserie, a boneless butterflied leg of lamb is just perfect.

We hope that we've piqued your interest in baaaaarbecued lamb, and we encourage you to experiment with several of our recipes in this chapter.

Grilled Lamb Chops 420

Lamb Chops with
Chiles and Mint 421

Lamb Chops with
Rosemary, Garlic,
and Lemon Baste 421

Spring Grill Platter
with Aioli 421

Grilled Rack of Lamb 422

Rosemary Pesto
Rack of Lamb 423

Grilled Marinated Rack of
Lamb with Apricot and
Cognac-Cabernet Sauce 423

Baaaaarbecued
Rack of Lamb 423

FOUR SEASONS OF RELISH

Winter Blood Orange, Fennel,
and Black Olive Relish 424

Springtime Strawberry,
Toasted Almond, and
Spinach Relish 425

Summer Tomato, Pine Nut,
and Caper Relish 425

Autumn Roasted Red Pepper
and Cannellini Bean Relish 426

Grilled Lamb Skewers 427

Mediterranean-Rubbed
Lamb Kabobs with
Lemon Butter Drizzle 428

Sambar-Spiced South
Indian Lamb Kabobs
with Tomato, Garlic,
and Chile Chutney 428

Tapas-Style Lamb
Brochettes 428

Grilled Leg of Lamb 429

Simple Stuffed
Leg of Lamb 430

Rustic Spinach Pesto–Stuffed
Leg of Lamb 430

Grilled Lamb, Pear,
and Pistou Salad 430

Rotisserie Leg of Lamb 431

Rotisserie Leg of Lamb
with Smoked Ratatouille 432

Pasta Salad with Rotisserie
Lamb and Eggplant 432

Rotisserie Lamb
Sandwiches with
Matchstick Vegetables
and Tzatziki 433

BBQ BABES: SHE CONDUCTS A ROTISSERIE SMEAR CAMPAIGN MENU

Garlic-Marinated Rolled
Leg of Lamb 434

Smear of Your Choice:
Sweet Moroccan Spice Paste,
Santa Fe Herb Paste, or
Mediterranean Herb Paste 435

Sweet-Hot Mustard-Glazed
Salmon 437

Smoked Leg of Lamb 438

Smoked Butterflied
Leg of Lamb Pinot Noir 438

Tandoori-Marinated
Smoked Butterflied
Leg of Lamb 439

BBQ Queens' Smoked
Stuffed Leg of Lamb 439

EASY AS 1-2-3 ICE CREAMS AND SORBETS

Toasted Coconut Ice Cream
with Hot Fudge Ganache
and Toasted Pecans 440

Fresh Peach Crumble
Ice Cream 441

Pineapple Sorbet in Grilled
Pineapple Rings 442

Grilled Lamb Chops

Succulently thin baby lamb chops, grilled in the Roman *scottadito* (to scorch the fingers) way, are best when they're treated in the simplest manner. Bone-in chops cut from either the shoulder or the loin work well in this dish. Flatten the meat first (as you would for boneless, skinless chicken breasts; see page 191) with the side of a saucer or the flat side of a chef's knife. Don't try to flatten the bones; just leave them be. Then give the chops a touch of olive oil, a sprinkling of fresh rosemary, and the high heat of the grill. You want the chops seared and somewhat charred on the outside yet moist and tender inside. In this case, flare-ups from the olive oil are your friend!

These chops get done so quickly that you'll want to have everything else prepared and ready to go. Serve them, rustic style, on a platter garnished with lemon wedges. **SERVES 4**

12 thin lamb chops, cut from the shoulder or loin, pounded to a ¹/₂-inch thickness

¹/₄ cup olive oil

2 teaspoons fresh rosemary leaves

Coarse kosher or sea salt and coarsely ground black pepper to taste

Lemon wedges for garnish

1. Place the lamb chops in a single layer in a baking dish or on a baking sheet. Drizzle with the olive oil and turn to coat each chop. Sprinkle the rosemary over the chops, then marinate for 15 to 30 minutes at room temperature.

2. Prepare a hot fire in a grill.

3. When the coals are at their hottest, season the chops with salt and pepper. Remove from the marinade and place on the grill rack. As the olive oil drips onto the coals, you will have flare-ups, but that's good. The flames will rise up for several seconds, then die down, giving your chops a bit of char. (Keep a spray bottle of water nearby just in case things get out of hand.) Cook the chops for 1 to 2 minutes per side, until definite grill marks appear, for medium-rare. Serve on a platter with lemon wedges.

🜲 Crowning Glories 🜲

Bring these babies forth topped with your choice of:

Smoked Chile Beurre Blanc *(page 99)*

Raspberry Beurre Blanc *(page 101)*

Chimichurri Sauce *(page 346)*

Lamb Chops with Chiles and Mint: A fresh-tasting chile and mint paste flavors the lamb before grilling. In a bowl, using a fork, make a paste of 2 minced garlic cloves, the juice of 1/2 lemon, 2 seeded and minced small hot chiles, 1/2 cup chopped fresh mint, 1/2 cup olive oil, and kosher or sea salt and freshly ground black pepper to taste. Spread the paste over 12 thin lamb chops pounded to a 1/2-inch thickness. Marinate at room temperature for 15 to 30 minutes, then grill as directed above. **SERVES 4**

Lamb Chops with Rosemary, Garlic, and Lemon Baste: Spread Rosemary, Garlic, and Lemon Baste (page 68) over 12 thin lamb chops pounded to a 1/2-inch thickness. Marinate at room temperature for 15 to 30 minutes, then grill as directed above. **SERVES 4**

Spring Grill Platter with Aioli: We like aioli, that wonderful garlicky mayonnaise, on just about everything. And we like to experiment with riffs on the traditional wintertime Provençal aioli platter of cooked salt cod and roasted vegetables. The virtues of an updated aioli platter are that it looks appealingly rustic, tastes great, and is perfect for casual entertaining. Make 1 recipe Rustic Aioli (page 104) ahead of time and keep covered in the refrigerator. Drizzle fingerling or new potatoes with olive oil and sprinkle with kosher or sea salt and freshly ground black pepper to taste. Roast in a 400°F oven until tender, 35 to 40 minutes, then keep warm. Grill 12 thin lamb chops pounded to a 1/2-inch thickness as directed above. Prepare 1 recipe Grilled Asparagus (page 117) at the same time. Heap the lamb chops in the middle of a platter, then surround them with the asparagus, roasted potatoes, and pitted and drained oil- or brine-cured Niçoise or Kalamata olives. Serve the aioli on the side. **SERVES 4**

Grilled Rack of Lamb

Of you love rack of lamb roasted, you'll really love it grilled. The key is a medium-hot fire, turning the lamb every 15 minutes, and cooking it medium-rare. Serve it with Mustard-Cornichon Beurre Blanc (page 100), and you'll be in heaven.

For the mildest flavor, buy the best and youngest lamb you can find. Today's lamb is grain-fed, which gives it great flavor and texture. Naturally tender, lamb should have a deep pinkish red to a dull brick red color, and the fat should be hard, white, and waxy.

Have the butcher remove the chine bone and attached feather bones from the racks and trim the fat and tissue from the rib bones, a process known as "frenching the bones." To french the bones yourself, take a sharp boning or paring knife and trim the meat back from the bones about 1 inch down the rib.

When you are served rack of lamb in a restaurant, the bones usually have frilly paper "hats" on the ends. You can buy these "chop frills" in gourmet shops, but the lamb is just as good without them.

SERVES 4 TO 6

> **4 racks of lamb (about 1¹/₂ pounds each), trimmed of fat and frenched**
> **Olive oil**
> **Coarse kosher or sea salt and ground white pepper to taste**

1. Prepare a medium-hot fire in a grill.

2. Rub the lamb with olive oil, then season with salt and white pepper.

3. Grill the lamb, with the lid down and turning every 15 minutes, until an instant-read meat thermometer inserted in the thickest part registers 135 to 140°F for medium-rare, about 45 minutes. Transfer to a cutting board and let rest for 10 minutes before cutting into chops and serving.

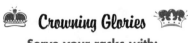

Crowning Glories

Serve your racks with:

Basil Oil Mashed Potatoes *(page 258)*
Peppercorn Beurre Blanc *(page 102)*
Pistachio-Pomegranate Sauce *(page 96)*

Rosemary Pesto Rack of Lamb: When it's going to be roasted, rack of lamb usually gets some kind of mustard or herb paste slathered on it. That's not practical when you grill it, as the paste falls off when you turn the lamb. But Rosemary Pesto (page 62) works well. Slather it all over each rack of lamb and marinate, covered, in the refrigerator for at least 4 hours or up to 12 hours. Then grill as directed above and serve with Roasted Red Pepper Sauce (page 94). **SERVES 4 TO 6**

Grilled Marinated Rack of Lamb with Apricot and Cognac-Cabernet Sauce: Luscious! Use the demi-glace concentrate you can buy at gourmet shops or better grocery stores and reconstitute it, or substitute good-quality chicken broth. In a medium-size bowl, whisk together 2 cups olive oil, 1/2 cup chopped garlic (that's not a typo!), 10 sprigs fresh thyme, 6 sprigs fresh rosemary, and 1 tablespoon cracked black peppercorns. Place the lamb in a baking pan large enough to hold it and drizzle the marinade over. Cover and re-frigerate, turning several times, for at least 4 hours or up to 12 hours. When ready to grill, remove the lamb from the marinade and pat dry. While the lamb is grilling as directed above, make the sauce by combining 1 cup Cabernet Sauvignon, 6 sprigs fresh thyme, 3 sprigs fresh rosemary, 3 finely chopped shallots, and 5 minced garlic cloves in a medium-size saucepan over high heat. Bring to a boil and let continue to boil until reduced to 1/3 cup, about 10 minutes. (Go out and turn the lamb, then come back in.) Remove the herb sprigs and whisk in 1 1/2 cups reconstituted demi-glace and 1/3 cup apricot preserves until smooth. Keep at a simmer. Right before serving, whisk in 1 tablespoon cognac and 2 tablespoons unsalted butter until the butter melts. Serve the racks of lamb napped with the sauce. Pass the rest of the sauce at the table. **SERVES 4 TO 6**

Baaaaarbecued Rack of Lamb: Rack of lamb is most often roasted or grilled, but you can also slow smoke it. Set up an indirect fire in your grill (see pages 10–12), using the wood of your choice (we like apple, pecan, or hickory with lamb). Paint the lamb with a mustard slather (see page 66) and sprinkle with garlic salt and lemon pepper seasoning. Place the lamb on your grill or smoker. Cook, with the lid down, at 250 to 300°F until an instant-read meat thermometer inserted in the thickest part registers 135 to 140°F for medium-rare, 2 to 3 hours. Let rest for 15 minutes before serving. **SERVES 4 TO 6**

Relish is a wonderful accompaniment to simply grilled fish, chicken, pork, beef, or lamb and can be tailored to what's available seasonally. A relish is composed of fruit and/or vegetables, oil, and seasonings, and is uncooked. Here are four recipes to whet your appetite and grace your plate.

Winter Blood Orange, Fennel, and Black Olive Relish

Blood oranges, which are smaller, more reddish orange, and slightly more puckery than other varieties, come on the market in January and February. Grab some up to make this relish. Before sectioning the oranges, grate the rind into a freezer bag to save for other dishes. **SERVES 4**

> 4 blood oranges, peeled and sectioned
>
> 1 fennel bulb, trimmed, quartered, cored, and thinly sliced
>
> 1 medium-size red onion, thinly sliced and separated into rings
>
> ¹/₂ cup pitted oil- or brine-cured black olives, such as Gaeta or Kalamata, drained
>
> ¹/₂ cup extra virgin olive oil
>
> Fine kosher or sea salt and freshly ground black pepper to taste

In a medium-size bowl, combine the orange sections, fennel, onion, and olives. Drizzle with olive oil, season with salt and pepper, and stir to blend. This is best served the same day at room temperature.

Springtime Strawberry, Toasted Almond, and Spinach Relish

Use tender baby spinach and juicy sweet strawberries. SERVES 4

> 1 cup fresh strawberries, hulled and cut in half
>
> 1/4 cup sliced almonds, toasted in a dry skillet over medium heat until medium brown
>
> 1 cup baby spinach leaves
>
> 1/4 cup balsamic vinegar
>
> 1/4 cup extra virgin olive oil
>
> Kosher salt and freshly ground black pepper to taste

In a medium-size bowl, combine the strawberries, almonds, and spinach. Drizzle with the vinegar and olive oil, season with salt and pepper, and stir to blend. This is best served the same day at room temperature.

Summer Tomato, Pine Nut, and Caper Relish

Use the juiciest, freshest cherry tomatoes for this aromatic and delicious relish. SERVES 4

> 16 small cherry tomatoes, cut in half
>
> 1/4 cup pine nuts, toasted in a dry skillet over medium heat until medium brown
>
> 1/4 cup golden raisins
>
> 2 tablespoons capers, drained
>
> 1/2 cup pitted oil- or brine-cured black olives, such as Gaeta or Kalamata, drained
>
> 1/2 cup extra virgin olive oil
>
> Kosher salt and freshly ground black pepper to taste

In a medium-size bowl, combine the tomatoes, pine nuts, raisins, capers, and olives. Drizzle with the olive oil, season with salt and pepper, and stir to blend. This is best served the same day at room temperature.

Autumn Roasted Red Pepper and Cannellini Bean Relish

You can throw this one together in minutes. SERVES 4

One 15-ounce can cannellini beans, drained and rinsed

¹/₂ cup chopped roasted red peppers (homemade, see page 145, or from a jar)

¹/₂ cup finely chopped fresh basil

1 clove garlic, minced

¹/₄ cup extra virgin olive oil

Kosher salt and freshly ground black pepper to taste

In a medium-size bowl, combine the beans, red peppers, basil, and garlic. Drizzle with the olive oil, season with salt and pepper, and stir to blend. This is best served the same day at room temperature.

Grilled Lamb Skewers

Grilling lamb on a skewer seems like a simple thing to do. Flavor some chunks of lamb with something, thread them onto a stick, and then grill and eat. People do this all over the world. And therein lies the difficulty—choosing a few from the many, many recipes for this dish.

Karen acquired a taste for tapas from her travels in Spain and Portugal. Judith loves south Indian food from her London days. And we both love Mediterranean food. So deciding on which flavors we wanted to showcase here was relatively easy. Just know that you can take these skewers in any direction you like, from Greek (marinated in a vinaigrette with oregano and mint) to French (slathered with Rosemary Pesto, page 62) to Persian (soaked in Tandoori Marinade, page 74, then served with plain yogurt and a sprinkling of sour-tasting sumac on pita bread) to California cool (marinated in Rosemary-Mustard Marinade, page 71, then served with fresh avocado slices and cherry tomatoes).

You can also vary the type of skewer you use (see page 29 for your options and how to grill skewers), from the standard bamboo skewer, which needs to be soaked in water for at least 30 minutes before grilling, to fresh rosemary branches or spikes of sugarcane. In the case of metal skewers, the BBQ Queens like to use two-prong skewers so the meat doesn't spin on the stick.

We prefer to use boneless leg of lamb for skewers, but lamb loin (expensive but tender) and lamb shoulder (cheap but chewy) work as well. Trim off any fat and gristle and try to keep the cubes as uniform as possible, because they will cook more evenly if they're the same size.

While the lamb skewers are grilling, you could also grill onions (page 137), squash (page 154), and/or tomatoes (page 159) at the same time. **SERVES 6**

2 pounds lean, boneless leg of lamb, trimmed of fat and cut into 1 1/2-inch cubes

1 cup vinaigrette of your choice, homemade or bottled

1/4 cup extra virgin olive oil

1. Place the lamb in a sealable plastic bag and pour the vinaigrette over. Seal and refrigerate for 1 to 2 hours (preferable) or up to 12 hours.

2. Prepare a hot fire in a grill.

3. Remove the lamb from the marinade and thread onto 6 skewers, leaving a little room between the pieces. Pour the olive oil into a small bowl. Carry the oil with a basting brush and the skewers out to the grill. Grill the skewers, turning and basting with oil, for about 8 minutes, until the meat is browned but still pink in the center. Serve hot.

Crowning Glories

Serve these with your choice of:

Bolani (*page 182*)

Fennel and Orange Drizzling Sauce (*page 73*)

Kimizu (*page 103*)

Mediterranean-Rubbed Lamb Kabobs with Lemon Butter Drizzle: Tender pieces of lamb cut from the leg work well for this recipe. The kabobs can be served with rice or couscous and grilled onion slices (see page 138). Place the lamb cubes in a bowl and sprinkle with about 1 teaspoon Lavender Salt (page 55) and freshly ground black pepper to taste. Cover and refrigerate for 1 to 2 hours. Meanwhile, make the Lemon Butter Drizzle (page 87). Grill the kabobs as directed above, basting with the drizzle. **SERVES 6**

Sambar-Spiced South Indian Lamb Kabobs with Tomato, Garlic, and Chile Chutney: Serve this dish with a pitcher of fresh lemonade to which you've added 1 teaspoon or more bottled rose water for a refreshing hot-weather meal. To make the marinade, in a small bowl combine 4 teaspoons ground coriander, 1 teaspoon ground cumin, $^1/_4$ teaspoon cayenne pepper, $^1/_4$ teaspoon freshly ground black pepper, and $^1/_4$ teaspoon turmeric. Add $^1/_3$ cup vegetable oil, 2 minced garlic cloves, 2 teaspoons finely grated fresh ginger (if using a microplane, you don't need to peel), $^1/_4$ teaspoon ground fennel seeds (use a mortar and pestle), 1 teaspoon kosher or sea salt, and $^1/_4$ cup finely chopped fresh tomato. Place 2 pounds lamb cubes (see above) in a sealable plastic bag. Pour the spice mixture over the lamb, seal the bag, and marinate in the refrigerator for 1 to 2 hours (preferable) or up to 12 hours. Meanwhile, make the chutney. Combine 2 cups chopped fresh tomatoes, 2 minced garlic cloves, 2 teaspoons seeded and minced green chile (such as serrano, Thai, or jalapeño), and $^1/_4$ cup finely chopped fresh cilantro. Add fresh lemon juice and kosher or sea salt to taste. (This can be made up to 1 day in advance and refrigerated.) Skewer, grill, and baste the lamb with olive oil as directed above. Serve with the chutney. **SERVES 6**

Tapas-Style Lamb Brochettes: Enjoy these skewers with a pitcher of Sangria! (page 250) or small glasses of chilled fino sherry. Place 2 pounds lamb cubes in a sealable plastic bag and add half 1 recipe Chimichurri Sauce (page 346) mixed with 1 teaspoon sweet Hungarian paprika. Seal the bag and marinate in the refrigerator for 1 to 2 hours (preferable) or up to 12 hours. Skewer, grill, and baste with olive oil as directed above. Serve the brochettes drizzled with the remaining sauce. **SERVES 6**

Grilled Leg of Lamb

Pamper yourself royally by having your butcher butterfly a leg of lamb. Otherwise, it will take you at least 15 minutes to do the trimming, and unless you are really adept at this, the lamb will look as if you massacred the poor thing. So call in the order, then waltz into the butcher shop and go home with a pretty cut of meat.

For this simple recipe, we are grilling the lamb flat. We're not pounding it out to an even thickness, but you can, if you wish, especially if you plan to stuff and roll it. This is something you can also ask the butcher to do.

Another delicious and timesaving tip is to buy a prepared pesto or tapenade (black olive paste) to spread on the lamb, then roll and tie it. Now we're talking tasty, easy, and pretty when sliced.

Lamb is best cooked medium-rare, 125 to 130°F at the thickest part of the meat. Well done is not a pleasant option, because the meat will be tough and dry. If there are thinner portions of the leg, they will automatically cook more, so you can please all of your guests with medium-rare and medium lamb from the same prepared leg. **SERVES 8**

> **One 6- to 7-pound leg of lamb, boned, trimmed of fat, and butterflied**
> **¹/₂ cup Dijon mustard**
> **Kosher salt and freshly ground black pepper to taste**

1. Place the butterflied lamb in a shallow dish, slather the mustard on both sides, and season with salt and pepper. Cover and refrigerate for at least 4 hours or up to 12 hours.

2. Prepare a medium-hot fire in a grill.

3. Grill the lamb over medium-high heat until nicely browned and an instant-read meat thermometer inserted in the thickest part registers 125 to 130°F for medium-rare to medium, about 15 minutes per side. Let rest for 10 to 15 minutes, then slice, arrange on a platter, and serve.

Crowning Glories

Anoint your leg before grilling with your choice of:
Rosemary Salt *(page 56)*
Southwest Heat *(page 215)*
Texas Two-Steppin' Mesquite Rub *(page 59)*

Simple Stuffed Leg of Lamb: Preparing this recipe may be as easy as opening your pantry or refrigerator door. Do you see any store-bought condiments that can be spread on your leg of lamb? Maybe a jar of marmalade with a sprinkling of garlic, or some mint jelly mixed with chopped fresh mint from your garden? Do you have any garlic, sun-dried tomato, or anchovy paste that comes in a tube? What about a jar of chutney or a porcini mushroom sauce? Of course, you can also thumb through the rubs and marinades chapter for appealing recipes. To begin, lay out a butterflied and flattened 6- to 7-pound leg of lamb and slather it on one side with about 1 cup prepared pesto, tapenade (black olive paste), or other condiment of your choice. Roll up lengthwise, jellyroll style, and tie with kitchen twine at 1-inch intervals. Grill over a medium-hot fire for about 10 minutes per side, turning it a quarter turn each time, until an instant-read meat thermometer inserted in the center registers 125 to 130°F for medium-rare to medium. Let rest for 10 to 15 minutes before slicing and serving. **SERVES 8**

Rustic Spinach Pesto–Stuffed Leg of Lamb: This takes just a bit more effort. To make the spinach mixture, heat 3 tablespoons olive oil in a medium-size skillet over high heat. Add 1 pound roughly chopped fresh spinach leaves and 2 minced large garlic cloves and cook, stirring, for about 2 minutes. Transfer the cooked spinach to a medium-size bowl. Add $^1/_2$ cup fresh bread crumbs, $^1/_4$ cup golden raisins, $^1/_4$ cup pine nuts, $^1/_4$ cup chopped fresh Italian parsley, one 3-ounce package softened cream cheese, $^1/_2$ teaspoon fine kosher or sea salt, and $^1/_2$ teaspoon freshly ground black pepper and mix well. Lay out a butterflied and flattened 6- to 7-pound leg of lamb and spread with the spinach mixture. Roll up lengthwise, jellyroll style, and tie with kitchen twine at 1-inch intervals. Grill over a medium-hot fire for about 10 minutes per side, turning it a quarter turn each time, until an instant-read meat thermometer inserted in the center registers 125 to 130°F for medium-rare to medium. Let rest for 10 to 15 minutes before slicing and serving. **SERVES 8**

Grilled Lamb, Pear, and Pistou Salad: This is a great way to use grilled lamb leftovers. Chop sliced grilled lamb into bite-size pieces so that you have about 1 cup. Arrange salad greens on 4 plates and top with the grilled lamb. Peel and core 1 ripe but firm pear, cut into thin slices, and place over the lamb. In a small bowl, whisk together 2 tablespoons freshly grated Parmesan cheese, 16 coarsely chopped fresh basil leaves, $^1/_4$ cup olive oil, and $2^1/_2$ tablespoons balsamic vinegar. Season with kosher or sea salt and freshly ground black pepper to taste. Drizzle the dressing over the salads and serve. For a great garnish, draw a vegetable peeler over a large, flat piece of Parmesan cheese, letting the thin shavings fall directly onto the salads. **SERVES 4**

Rotisserie Leg of Lamb

Even people who say they don't like lamb, like lamb cooked this way. The first key is to buy fresh lamb, not frozen, for a better flavor. Locally raised is better yet. The second key it to trim the lamb of most of the fat, which can carry a stronger flavor. The third key is to get the exterior of the lamb caramelized and charred on the outside and cooked to medium doneness—at the most!—on the inside. A steady 350°F on the grill and a meat thermometer are your trusty culinary friends.

There's so much you can do, serving-wise, with a leg of lamb. Serve it high style, sliced and napped with a wonderful sauce, such as piquant Mustard-Cornichon Beurre Blanc (page 100). Serve it more casually, Mediterranean style, with warm pita bread, hummus, and a fresh salad. Add any leftovers to a big-flavor pasta salad. **SERVES 6 TO 12**

> **One 4- to 9-pound leg of lamb, boned (have your butcher do this for you) and trimmed of fat**
>
> **1 recipe Provençal Red Wine Marinade (page 70)**

1. Place the lamb in a baking dish and pour the marinade over. Cover with plastic wrap and marinate in the refrigerator for at least 4 hours or overnight, turning it several times.

2. Remove the lamb from the marinade, shaking off any excess. Transfer the remaining marinade to a medium-size saucepan, bring to a boil, and continue to boil for 5 minutes, then set aside.

3. Set up your grill for rotisserie cooking (see page 33). Prepare a medium fire (around 350°F). Place a rotisserie clamp on the end of the lamb. Push the rotisserie rod through the center of the lamb so the meat is balanced, secure the other clamp, and place on the spit. Insert a heatproof meat thermometer in the thickest part of the meat, away from the bone. Make sure it is positioned so that you can read it and it will turn freely as the meat turns. Place the spit on the rotisserie. Cover and cook the lamb, basting every 30 minutes with the reserved marinade, until the thermometer registers 135 to 140°F for medium-rare, 2 to 2¹/₂ hours. Let rest for 15 minutes before slicing and serving.

Crowning Glories

**Rotisserie leg of lamb is delicious served with a
fresh tomato salad and warm flatbread or with:**

Smoked Garlic and Cilantro Cream Sauce *(page 93)*

Tomato-Fennel Sauce *(page 95)*

Tzatziki *(page 112)*

Rotisserie Leg of Lamb with Smoked Ratatouille:

Why not do two things at once when you're cooking the lamb? Smoked ratatouille is a new twist on the Provençal classic: the marinade and juices that drip from the lamb will flavor the vegetables. Peel 1 medium-size eggplant and cut into large chunks. Place in a double thickness of disposable aluminum pans (one placed inside the other) along with 1 pint cherry or grape tomatoes, 2 medium-size zucchini cut into large chunks, 1 yellow onion cut into large chunks, 1 teaspoon dried herbes de Provence, 1/2 cup olive oil and 6 peeled garlic cloves. Toss well to blend. Place the pans under the lamb on the spit and add 1 cup water. Cover and cook as directed above. Slice the lamb and serve with the ratatouille. **SERVES 6 TO 12**

Pasta Salad with Rotisserie Lamb and Eggplant:

If you know that your leg of lamb isn't likely to be consumed in one meal, plan ahead to make this yummy salad with the leftovers. The salad can be served warm, at room temperature, or chilled, but we like it best at room temperature. Before you rotisserie the lamb, place 2 cups diced but not peeled eggplant in a double thickness of disposable aluminum pans (one placed inside the other) and drizzle with 2 tablespoons olive oil. Place the pans under the lamb and cook until the eggplant is tender, about 1 hour. Let cool, cover, and refrigerate. The next day, arrange one 12-ounce bag baby spinach leaves on 4 to 6 plates. Cook 1/2 pound small dried pasta (penne, farfalle, wheels, or rings) according to the package directions until *al dente*. Drain well and toss with 1 tablespoon olive oil. Transfer the pasta to a large bowl. With a wooden spoon, mix in the reserved eggplant, 2 cups finely chopped rotisserie lamb; 2 teaspoons drained capers; and 8 pitted, drained, and sliced oil- or brine-cured Kalamata olives. To a triple recipe of Lemon-Garlic Mayonnaise (page 103), add 1 teaspoon fresh thyme leaves and 1 teaspoon grated lemon zest. Stir to combine. Spoon the mayonnaise over the pasta mixture and toss well to blend. Serve over the baby spinach leaves. **SERVES 4 TO 6**

Rotisserie Lamb Sandwiches with Matchstick Vegetables and Tzatziki: Instead of the Provençal Red Wine Marinade, use a double recipe of Tandoori Marinade (page 74) to marinate the lamb. Prepare 1 recipe Tzatziki (page 112). Rotisserie cook the lamb as directed above. Meanwhile, use the julienne blade on a mandoline or food processor (or a chef's knife) to cut 2 small zucchini, 1 peeled and seeded cucumber, 1 peeled carrot, and 1 small red onion into matchsticks. Place in a medium-size bowl, add 1 cup of the tzatziki, and toss. Slice the lamb, slip slices into warm pita breads, and add a spoonful of the vegetables to each. Pass the rest of the tzatziki at the table. **SERVES 6 TO 8**

BBQ Babes

She Conducts a Rotisserie Smear Campaign Menu

Garlic-Marinated Rolled Leg of Lamb
Smear of Your Choice: Sweet Moroccan Spice Paste, Santa Fe Herb Paste, or Mediterranean Herb Paste
Sweet-Hot Mustard-Glazed Salmon

We may be queens in our working lives, but we're basically nice girls at heart. If we were going to start a smear campaign, we'd prefer the kind that our culinary instructor and cookbook author friend Diane Phillips conducts. She concocts all kinds of delicious savory pastes and glazes to smear on food as it cooks on the rotisserie in her southern California backyard. She likes cooking that way so much, she created an entire cookbook of recipes—*The Ultimate Rotisserie Cookbook* (The Harvard Common Press, 2002)—from which we adapted these dishes.

Maybe you wouldn't do all of these dishes on the same day, or maybe you would. The lamb takes longer and by the time it's resting, ready to be carved, you've got the salmon twirling around in the rotisserie basket. Or you could do the salmon first and serve it warm or chilled as an appetizer, then serve the lamb as the main course.

Garlic-Marinated Rolled Leg of Lamb

The garlic marinade works well with any of the three pastes, so decide on your flavor and enjoy the results. **SERVES 6**

GARLIC MARINADE

$^1/_2$ **cup olive oil**
$^1/_4$ **cup red wine vinegar**
4 cloves garlic, minced

1 1/2 teaspoons fine kosher or sea salt

1/2 teaspoon freshly ground black pepper

One 3- to 4-pound boneless rolled leg of lamb, tied

Flavoring paste of your choice (recipes follow)

1. To make the marinade, combine all the ingredients in a 1-gallon sealable plastic bag.

2. Add the lamb to the bag, seal, and marinate in the refrigerator for at least 6 hours or overnight.

3. Remove the lamb from the marinade and pat dry. Smear your choice of paste over the lamb and cook on the rotisserie as directed on page 431 until an instant-read meat thermometer inserted in the thickest part registers 155°F for medium, 2 to 2 1/2 hours.

4. Remove the lamb from the spit, cover loosely with aluminum foil, and let rest for 10 to 15 minutes. Remove the twine and carve the lamb. Serve hot.

Sweet Moroccan Spice Paste

We love coriander and cumin together, the yin and yang of flavors, as in this heady paste, which is delicious on chicken, pork, or lamb. MAKES ABOUT 1/2 CUP

3 cloves garlic, minced

2 tablespoons olive oil

2 tablespoons firmly packed light brown sugar

1/2 teaspoon sweet Hungarian paprika

1/4 teaspoon ground coriander

1/4 teaspoon ground cumin

Combine all the ingredients in a small bowl. This paste will keep, covered, in the refrigerator for up to 2 days.

Santa Fe Herb Paste

Various levels of heat and a sweet spiciness make this herb and spice paste a winner on beef, lamb, or pork. **MAKES ABOUT 1 CUP**

> $^1/_2$ cup finely chopped fresh cilantro
>
> $^1/_4$ cup olive oil
>
> 2 tablespoons firmly packed light brown sugar
>
> 2 tablespoons fresh lime juice
>
> 2 teaspoons ground cumin
>
> 5 cloves garlic, minced
>
> 1 dried ancho chile, crushed

Combine all the ingredients in a small bowl. This paste will keep, covered, in the refrigerator for up to 3 days.

Mediterranean Herb Paste

Assertively flavored, this paste is great on anything destined for the grill. **MAKES ABOUT $^1/_2$ CUP**

> Grated zest of 2 lemons
>
> 6 cloves garlic, minced
>
> 2 tablespoons chopped fresh rosemary
>
> 1 tablespoon Dijon mustard
>
> $1^1/_2$ teaspoons fine kosher or sea salt
>
> 1 teaspoon freshly ground black pepper
>
> Pinch of red pepper flakes

Combine all the ingredients in a small bowl. This paste will keep, covered, in the refrigerator for up to 4 days.

Sweet-Hot Mustard-Glazed Salmon

There are so many delicious ways to do salmon on the grill. This recipe is yet another. Serve over mixed field greens as a main dish salad, or with Tzatziki (page 112) or Charred Tomato-Chipotle Salsa (page 162) as an appetizer. **SERVES 6**

> **1 cup Dijon mustard**
> **1/2 cup clover or other medium-colored honey**
> **1 tablespoon fresh lemon juice**
> **2 pounds salmon fillets**

1. Coat a rotisserie basket with nonstick cooking spray.

2. In a small saucepan over medium heat, combine the mustard, honey, and lemon juice. Bring to a simmer.

3. Reserve half of the glaze for serving. Liberally brush the other half over the salmon, then cook on the rotisserie as directed in the box on page 40 until just cooked through, 15 to 20 minutes. The center will still be a bit undercooked, but it will continue to cook once removed from the heat.

4. Remove the salmon from the basket and brush with the reserved glaze. Serve immediately, or refrigerate and serve cold.

Smoked Leg of Lamb

When the bone is removed and the meat butterflied, a leg of lamb is even easier to smoke. Pamper yourself royally by having your butcher butterfly a leg of lamb, or do it yourself, if you like. You can flavor lamb in so many ways and accompany it with so many different side dishes that we wonder why more people don't smoke it. We've decided that we're now on a mission—a butterflied leg of lamb mission. This is a great dish to serve at a gathering, and with the recent upsurge of interest in Middle Eastern food, you can enjoy smoked leg of lamb as part of a traditional American barbecue or a Mediterranean feast. **SERVES 6 TO 8**

SUGGESTED WOOD: **Apple, cherry, hickory, oak, or pecan**

One 6- to 8-pound leg of lamb, boned, trimmed of fat, and butterflied
¼ cup olive oil
2 tablespoons minced garlic
3 tablespoons lemon pepper seasoning

1. Prepare an indirect fire in a smoker.

2. Rub the butterflied leg of lamb all over with the olive oil, garlic, and lemon pepper. Place the lamb in the smoker, cover, and smoke at 225 to 250°F until an instant-read meat thermometer inserted in the thickest part registers 140 to 145°F for medium-rare, 3 to 4 hours. Let rest for 15 minutes before slicing and serving.

Crowning Glories

Smoked leg of lamb is delicious served with:
Oven-Roasted Saffron Potatoes *(page 413)*
Chimichurri Sauce *(page 346)*
Classic Creamed Spinach *(page 319)*

Smoked Butterflied Leg of Lamb Pinot Noir: Now you don't have to wonder which wine to serve with lamb. It says it all in the title. We love this accompanied by a vinaigrette-dressed spinach, pasta, or rice salad tossed with crumbled goat cheese, toasted pine nuts, and dried currants. For the Pinot Noir marinade, whisk together 2 cups olive oil, 1 cup Pinot Noir or other dry red wine, 1 sliced red onion, 1 tablespoon chopped garlic, 3 bay leaves, 1 tablespoon dried herbes de Provence, and 1 teaspoon lemon pepper seasoning. Place the lamb in a shallow pan or sealable plastic bag and add the marinade. Cover or seal and let marinate in the refrigerator for at least 1 hour or up to 12 hours. Drain and pat dry, then smoke as directed above. **SERVES 6 TO 8**

Tandoori-Marinated Smoked Butterflied Leg of Lamb: For a Mediterranean spin on this
recipe, place the lamb in a shallow pan or sealable plastic bag and add 1 recipe Tandoori Marinade (page 74). Cover or seal and marinate in the refrigerator overnight. Drain and pat dry, then smoke as directed above. Serve with grilled pita bread and Tzatziki (page 112). **SERVES 6 TO 8**

BBQ Queens' Smoked Stuffed Leg of Lamb: We've adapted this recipe from one in *Easy
Grilling & Simple Smoking with the BBQ Queens* (Pig Out Publications, 1999). We like to use a combination of hickory and apple wood for this dish. The hickory provides a heavier smoke, while the apple supplies sweetness. Make the stuffing by trimming 1 pound fresh spinach of any heavy stems. Take 10 to 12 large leaves and stack them on top of one another. Roll into a cigar shape and cut crosswise into $1/8$-inch shreds. Repeat with the remaining spinach. In a medium-size skillet, heat 3 tablespoons olive oil over high heat. Stir in the spinach and 2 minced large garlic cloves. Cook, tossing and stirring often, for about 2 minutes, until the moisture has evaporated from the spinach. Transfer to a medium-size bowl and add $1/2$ cup fresh bread crumbs, $1/4$ cup golden raisins, $1/4$ cup pine nuts, $1/4$ cup chopped fresh basil, one 3-ounce package softened cream cheese, $1/2$ teaspoon fine kosher or sea salt, and $1/4$ teaspoon freshly ground black pepper. Mix well. Lay out the butterflied and trimmed leg of lamb and spread with the spinach mixture. Roll up lengthwise, jelly-roll style, and tie at 1-inch intervals with kitchen twine. Smoke as directed above until an instant-read meat thermometer inserted in the thickest part registers at least 160°F for medium, 5 to 6 hours. Let rest for 15 minutes before slicing and serving. **SERVES 6 TO 8**

Nothing cools the palate after a spicy barbecue meal like ice cream or sorbet. As "the BBQ Queen of Easy," Karen has found some delicious shortcuts to homemade ice cream. We know you'll like the fact that you don't have to make the custard the day before, then chill it overnight. These recipes are for when you have a spur-of-the-moment yen for good ice cream.

If you want to add crunch to any of these ice creams, get creative with store-bought granola cereal, your favorite cookies (store-bought or homemade, crumbled), or toasted nuts (pecans, almonds, walnuts, or others).

Made from canned fruit in heavy syrup, the sorbets included here don't get any easier.

Toasted Coconut Ice Cream with Hot Fudge Ganache and Toasted Pecans

Judith and her father introduced Karen to Aglamesi's coconut ice cream in Cincinnati. Their favorite way to devour this delicious treat is topped with hot fudge ganache and toasted pecans. Divine! MAKES ABOUT 1 QUART

 1 cup pecan halves

 TOASTED COCONUT ICE CREAM

 1 cup sweetened flaked coconut
 3 cups heavy cream
 1 tablespoon coconut extract

 HOT FUDGE GANACHE

 1 cup heavy cream
 1 1/2 cups semisweet chocolate chips

1.   Preheat the oven to 350°F. Spread the pecans on a baking sheet and bake until the nuts begin to brown and smell toasted, about 10 minutes. Set aside to cool. (The nuts will keep in the freezer for several months.)

2.   To make the ice cream, spread the flaked coconut on a baking sheet and bake until it begins to brown, 8 to 10 minutes. Remove from the oven and set aside to cool.

3.   Pour the heavy cream and coconut extract into an ice cream maker and begin to freeze according to the manufacturer's directions. After 5 minutes, add the cooled coconut and finish freezing the ice cream.

4.   To make the ganache, place the heavy cream in a large glass bowl and microwave on high until it just begins to boil, 2 to 3 minutes. Or bring the cream to a boil in a small, heavy saucepan on the stovetop. Remove from the microwave or heat, add the chocolate chips, and let sit for 5 minutes (do not stir). Gently stir the mixture to create a shiny, dark chocolate sauce. (This will keep in the refrigerator for up to 1 month.)

5.   Serve the ice cream topped with ganache and a handful of toasted pecans.

Fresh Peach Crumble Ice Cream

When the dog days of summer hit, your hair goes limp, and not even a tiara can perk up your "do," buy some juicy ripe peaches at the farmers' market and get out your bowl and spoon for a real summer treat. MAKES ABOUT 1 QUART

> **2 large ripe peaches**
> **3 cups heavy cream**
> **1 teaspoon almond extract**
> **1 cup crumbled shortbread cookies**

1.   Peel the peaches over a bowl to catch any of the juices. Slice the peaches or cut into chunks, discarding the pits. Set aside.

2. Pour the heavy cream and almond extract into an ice cream maker and begin to freeze according to the manufacturer's directions. After 5 minutes, add the peaches and crumbled cookies. Finish freezing the ice cream, then serve.

Pineapple Sorbet in Grilled Pineapple Rings

Grill Gal Melanie Barnard first shared this sorbet recipe with us while she was representing the Canned Food Alliance. We thought the pineapple sorbet was so delicious and easy to make that we've made variations using canned plums, mandarin oranges, grapefruit sections, and cherries. Freeze the unopened can of crushed pineapple for at least 2 days before making this recipe. We love to use it to doll up grilled fresh pineapple rings. SERVES 6

PINEAPPLE SORBET

One 20-ounce can crushed pineapple in heavy syrup, frozen in the unopened can

3 tablespoons dark rum or 2 teaspoons rum flavoring

3 tablespoons well-stirred canned cream of coconut

GRILLED PINEAPPLE RINGS

1 large fresh pineapple, peeled and cored

1. To make the sorbet, submerge the unopened can of frozen pineapple in hot water for 1 minute. Open the can and pour the pineapple and syrup into a food processor. Process until smooth. Add the rum and cream of coconut and process to mix. Serve immediately, or freeze for up to 8 hours before serving.

2. To make the pineapple rings, right before serving, cut the pineapple into 1-inch-thick-rings and place on a medium-hot grill. Grill until the pineapple has browned and softened, about 2 minutes per side. To serve, place a scoop of pineapple sorbet in each grilled pineapple ring.

Mandarin Orange Sorbet: Freeze 2 unopened 10-ounce cans mandarin oranges overnight or for at least 8 hours to make sure they're frozen solid. Proceed as directed above, substituting 3 tablespoons orange-flavored liqueur or orange extract for the rum and cream of coconut. For extra zing, add 1 tablespoon grated orange zest. MAKES ABOUT 2½ CUPS

Resource Guide

BARBECUE AND GRILL MANUFACTURERS

Many manufacturers produce outdoor barbecues and grills. Only a few are listed here. We suggest that you visit a local dealer that offers a variety of grills, as well as service. Happy grilling and smoking!

Alfresco Gourmet Grills
7039 East Slauson Boulevard
Commerce, GA 90040
(888) 383-8800
www.alfrescogrills.com
Manufacturer of gas grills and smokers. Outdoor kitchen concepts with bartending centers and refrigeration units.

Barbeques Galore
U.S. Headquarters
10 Orchard Road, Suite 200
Lake Forest, CA 92630
(800) 752-3085
www.bbqgalore.com
Australian gas grill manufacturer with a U.S. retail division of more than 60 stores nationwide. Also carries barbecue utensils, accessories, books, woods, charcoal, and more.

BBQ Pits by Klose
2216 West 34th Street
Houston, TX 77018
(800) 487-7487
www.bbqpits.com
David Klose carries ready-made smokers in just about every size—from 24-inch models to huge commercial rigs. Also custom-makes smokers.

Big Green Egg
3414 Clairmont Road
Atlanta, GA 30319
(404) 321-4658
www.biggreenegg.com
Large producer of an egg-shaped, ceramic kamado combination smoker/grill that cooks at a higher temperature than traditional cookers.

Brinkmann Corporation
4215 McEwen Road
Dallas, TX 75244
(800) 527-0717
www.thebrinkmanncorp.com
Manufacturer of bullet-shaped charcoal and electric water smokers and grills.

Cajun Grill/Percy Guidry Manufacturing
204 Wilson Street
Lafayette, LA 70501
(800) 822-4766
www.cajungrill.com
Manufacturers of the Cajun Grill and the Cajun Smoker, plus a variety of barbecue accessories, rubs, and sauces.

Char-Broil/W.C. Bradley
P.O. Box 1240
Columbus, GA 31902
(800) 352-4111
www.charbroil.com
Manufacturer of gas and electric grills and barbecue accessories. Also the maker of the New Braunfels heavy-gauge steel smokers and grills.

CM International
P.O. Box 60220
Colorado Springs, CO 80960
(888) 563-0227
www.cameronssmoker.com
Manufacturer of the Camerons Stovetop Smokers. Also a supplier of wood grilling and baking planks and fine wood chips, including corncob pellets and pecan shells.

Cookshack
2304 North Ash Street
Ponca City, OK 74601
(800) 423-0698
www.cookshackamerica.com
Manufacturer of residential and commercial barbecues, grills, cookstoves, ranges, and ovens.

DCS (Dynamic Cooking Systems)
5800 Skylab Road
Huntington Beach, CA 92647
(800) 433-8466
www.dcsappliances.com
Manufacturer of upscale stainless steel gas grills.

Empire Comfort Systems
918 Freeburg Avenue
Belleville, IL 62220
(800) 443-8648
www.broilmaster.com
Manufacturer of the Broilmaster gas grills, smokers, and portable cookers.

Fiesta Gas Grills
One Fiesta Drive
Dickson, TN 37055
(800) 396-3838
www.fiestagasgrills.com
Manufacturer of mid-priced gas grills and barbecues.

Grills to Go
5659 West San Madele Way
Fresno, CA 93722
(877) 869-2253
www.grillstogo.com
Manufacturer of towable commercial charcoal, wood, and gas barbecue grills.

Hasty-Bake
7656 East 46th Street
Tulsa, OK 74145
(800) 426-6836
www.hastybake.com
Manufacturer of the Hasty-Bake oven, a charcoal grill/smoker that has a pulley system to raise and lower the grill grates over the fire. Side door for refueling is nifty, too.

Kingfisher Kookers
1107 South Main
Kingfisher, OK 73750
(866) 542-5665
www.kingfisherkookers.com
Manufacturer of Kingfisher Kookers, grills and smokers in all shapes and sizes.

KitchenAid
P.O. Box 218
St. Joseph, MI 49084
(800) 422-1230
www.kitchenaid.com
Major appliance manufacturer of, among other products, outdoor cooking systems, refrigeration products, and refreshment systems.

Magma Products
3940 Pixie Avenue
Lakewood, CA 90712
(800) 866-2462
www.magmaproducts.com
Manufacturers of Del Mar and Magma brands. These gas and charcoal cookers are compact units professionally designed for boats and small patios.

Napoleon Gourmet Grills
214 Bayview Drive
Barrie, Ontario
Canada L4N 4Y8
(888) 726-2220
www.napoleongrills.com
Manufacturer of stainless steel gas and charcoal grills.

Robert H. Peterson Company
14742 East Proctor Avenue
City of Industry, CA 91746
(800) 332-0240
www.rhpeterson.com
Manufacturer of the widely distributed and popular Fire Magic grills. Models include smokers and charcoal, gas, electric, and infrared grills.

Traeger Industries
P.O. Box 829
1385 East College Street
Mount Angel, OR 97362
(800) 872-3437
www.traegerindustries.com
Manufacturer of the original electric-powered wood pellet grill/smoker. Compressed wood pellets are funneled into the firebox and provide both fuel and flavor.

Viking Range Corporation
111 Front Street
Greenwood, MS 38930
(888) 845-4641
www.vikingrange.com
Manufacturer of stainless steel gas grill outdoor kitchens and professional-quality appliances for the home.

Weber-Stephen Products Co.
200 East Daniels Road
Palatine, IL 60067-6266
(800) 446-1071
www.weber.com
Manufacturer of the original Weber grill since 1951. Grills, smokers, and all their accessories, as well as the Weber Smokey Mountain Cooker, a charcoal chimney starter, and more.

Wolf Appliance Company
P.O. Box 44848
Madison, WI 53744
(800) 332-9513
www.wolfappliance.com
Manufacturer of stainless steel outdoor gas grills, as well as professional indoor kitchens for the home.

BARBECUE BOOKS, SPICES, CATALOGS, NEWSLETTERS, AND CLASSES

Passionate barbecuers are always in search of information about outdoor cooking. Give some of these companies a try.

BBQ Queens
www.bbqqueens.com
Official online site of the BBQ Queens, Karen Adler and Judith Fertig. Features tips and recipes for outdoor cooking, where the BBQ Queens are teaching culinary classes, and information about their books.

Grill Lover's Catalog
P.O. Box 1300
Columbus, GA 31902
(800) 241-8981
www.grilllovers.com
Catalog offering charcoal and gas grills, cookbooks, sauces and seasonings, and accessories for the grill.

Kansas City *Bullsheet*
Kansas City Barbeque Society
11514 Hickman Mills Drive
Kansas City, MO 64134
(800) 963-5227
www.rbjb.com/rbjb/kcbs.htm
Monthly newspaper published by the Kansas City Barbeque Society featuring everything barbecue.

Lawry's Foods
222 East Huntington Drive
Monrovia, CA 91016
(626) 930-8870
www.lawrys.com
Manufacturer of good-quality marinades and spice blends available at grocery stores nationwide.

McCormick & Company
226 Schilling Circle
Hunt Valley, MD 21031
(800) 632-5847
www.mccormick.com
Manufacturer of good-quality spices and flavorings available at grocery stores nationwide.

National Barbecue News
P.O. Box 981
Douglas, GA 31534-0981
(800) 385-0002
www.barbecuenews.com
Monthly newspaper featuring barbecue events and columns. Also the official newspaper of the National Barbecue Association.

Old World Spices & Seasonings Company
4601 Emanuel Cleaver II Boulevard
Kansas City, MO 64130
(800) 241-0070
www.oldworldspices.com
Manufacturer of spices, sauces, and seasonings, including custom products.

Paul Kirk Pitmaster Classes
(800) 963-5227
(816) 765-5891
E-mail: bbqbaron@hotmail.com
Paul Kirk, the Baron of Barbecue, presents one-day classes in which students spend 12 grueling hours cooking and presenting the four competition barbecue meats—brisket, pork butt, pork ribs, and chicken. Classes are usually organized by state or local barbecue association. Barbecue videos and sauces are also available.

Penzeys Spices
19300 West Janacek Court
Brookfield, WI 53045
(800) 741-7787
www.penzeys.com
Online source and catalog sales for spices, herbs, and seasonings. Fresh products are available in larger quantities, too.

Pig Out Publications
207 East Gregory
Kansas City, MO 64114
(800) 877-3119
www.pigoutpublications.com
BBQ Queen Karen Adler owns this company, which offers more than 200 barbecue cookbooks.

The Spice House
1031 North Old World Third Street
Milwaukee, WI 53203
(414) 272-0977
www.thespicehouse.com
Large selection of spices and seasonings.

Vanns Spices
6105 Oakleaf Avenue
Baltimore, MD 21215
(800) 583-1693
www.vannsspices.com
High-quality spices and seasonings with no chemicals or additives. Private labeling and custom blending offered.

Zach's Spice Company
1001 Georgia Avenue
Deer Park, TX 77536
(800) 460-0521
www.zachsspice.com
Specializes in ingredients for barbecuing and grilling in general, as well as those for making sausage, dry rubs, and barbecue sauces.

WOOD PRODUCTS

Look for wood products at stores nearby because they are moderately expensive to ship. However, some specialty woods and wood products are available only in certain regions of the country. If you can't find something locally, try these sources.

Acadian Woods
117 Twenty-fifth Avenue
Madawaska, ME 04756
(321) 698-5826
www.acadian-woods.com
Manufacturer of white cedar grilling and baking planks from the northern Maine woods.

American Wood Products
9540 Riggs Street
Overland Park, KS 66212
(800) 223-9046

Bags of mesquite lump charcoal, as well as a variety of woods—mesquite, pecan, hickory, grape, oak, apple, cherry, sassafras, peach, and alder—in logs, slabs, chunks, and chips.

Barbecuewood.com
P.O. Box 8163
Yakima, WA 98098
(509) 961-3420
www.barbecuewood.com

A variety of wood grilling and baking planks in alder, cherry, cedar, maple, white oak, and hickory. Also wood chunks and chips in hard-to-find varieties such as apricot, as well as all the usual woods used for smoking.

BBQr's Delight
P.O. Box 8727
6109 Celia Road
Pine Bluff, AR 71611
(877) 275-9591
www.bbqrsdelight.com

Compressed wood pellets for fuel and smoke in hickory, mesquite, pecan, apple, cherry, oak, black walnut, mulberry, orange, Jack Daniel's, sugar maple, and more.

Blue Moon Woods
P.O. Box 207
2350 Sopchoppy Highway
Sopchoppy, FL 32358-0207
(888) 959-9291
www.bluemoonwoods.com

A unique line of presoaked wood products that come in convenient pull-ring cans placed directly on the grill. You grill, the wood smokes, and there is no mess. Presoaked woods come in hickory, pecan, mesquite, oak, wild cherry, and more.

Chigger Creek Products
4200 Highway D
Syracuse, MO 65354
(660) 298-3188
www.bbqads.com/chigger/chigger.htm

Hardwood lump charcoal, as well as a variety of woods—hickory, apple, cherry, pecan, grape, sugar maple, alder, oak, mesquite, peach, sassafras, persimmon, pear, apple-hickory, and cherry-oak blends—in chips, chunks, and logs.

CM International
See page 444.

Wood grilling and baking planks.

Fairlane Bar-BQ Wood
12520 Third Street
Grandview, MO 64030
(816) 761-1350

Specializes in mesquite, pecan, hickory, oak, apple, cherry, and sassafras chunks.

Peoples Woods
75 Mill Street
Cumberland, RI 02864
(800) 729-5800
www.peopleswoods.com

Natural lump charcoal and smoking woods.

Sautee Cedar Company
328 Commerce Boulevard, Unit 8
Bogart, GA 30622
(866) 728-8332
www.sauteecedar.com

Aromatic western red cedar grilling planks. Custom packaging available.

WW Wood
P.O. Box 398
Pleasanton, TX 78064
(830) 569-2501
www.woodinc.com

Smoking and grilling woods.

Measurement Equivalents

Please note that all conversions are approximate.

Liquid Conversions

U.S.	Metric
1 tsp	5 ml
1 tbs	15 ml
2 tbs	30 ml
3 tbs	45 ml
1/4 cup	60 ml
1/3 cup	75 ml
1/3 cup + 1 tbs	90 ml
1/3 cup + 2 tbs	100 ml
1/2 cup	120 ml
2/3 cup	150 ml
3/4 cup	180 ml
3/4 cup + 2 tbs	200 ml
1 cup	240 ml
1 cup + 2 tbs	275 ml
1 1/4 cups	300 ml
1 1/3 cups	325 ml
1 1/2 cups	350 ml
1 2/3 cups	375 ml
1 3/4 cups	400 ml
1 3/4 cups + 2 tbs	450 ml
2 cups (1 pint)	475 ml
2 1/2 cups	600 ml
3 cups	720 ml
4 cups (1 quart)	945 ml (1,000 ml is 1 liter)

Weight Conversions

U.S./U.K.	Metric
1/2 oz	14 g
1 oz	28 g
1 1/2 oz	43 g
2 oz	57 g
2 1/2 oz	71 g
3 oz	85 g
3 1/2 oz	100 g
4 oz	113 g
5 oz	142 g
6 oz	170 g
7 oz	200 g
8 oz	227 g
9 oz	255 g
10 oz	284 g
11 oz	312 g
12 oz	340 g
13 oz	368 g
14 oz	400 g
15 oz	425 g
1 lb	454 g

Oven Temperature Conversions

°F	Gas Mark	°C
250	1/2	120
275	1	140
300	2	150
325	3	165
350	4	180
375	5	190
400	6	200
425	7	220
450	8	230
475	9	240
500	10	260
550	Broil	290

Index

A

Aioli
  Easy, The Doctor Is In, 110
  platter, ideas for, 135
  Rustic, 104
  and Smoked Potato Gratin,
    152–53
  variations on, 110
  White Truffle, 105
Almond
  Cookie Brittle, 264–65
  -Cranberry Torte with Cranberry
    Drizzle, 394–95
  -Honey Grilling Glaze, 88
  Joy Brittle, 265
  Toasted, Strawberry, and Spinach
    Relish, Springtime, 425
Apple and Red Cabbage Slaw, 83
Apple-Rosemary Salsa, 234
Apples, Grilled Stuffed, 244
Apricot and Cognac-Cabernet Sauce,
  423
Apricot and Cognac-Glazed Duck,
  241
Apricot-Bourbon Barbecue Sauce,
  The Doctor Is In, 90
Apricot Chutney, 384
Apricot-Dijon Glaze, 374
Apricot-Mustard Glaze, 411
Artichoke(s)
  –Pecorino Romano Glaze, Planked
    Chicken Breasts with, 194
  Pizza, Grilled, on Parmesan-Herb
    Crust, 185–86
  and Smoked Italian Sausage Soup,
    369
Asparagus
  and Beef Saddlebags, Smoky,
    171–72
  Grilled, 117
  Asian-Style, with Peanut Butter
    Dipping Sauce, 118
  Frittata, 118
  with Shaved Parmigiano-
    Reggiano, 118
  Spring Grill Platter with Aioli,
    421
  Vegetable Platter with Fresh
    Basil Vinaigrette, 129–30
  Stir-Grilled, with Chicken and
    Shaved Parmigiano-Reggiano,
    199

B

Bacon
  -Roquefort Butter, 318
  Smoked Beef BLT, 339
  Sour Cream, and Mushroom
    Sauce, 337
Baker, Beckie, 367
Barbecue Sauce
  Apricot-Bourbon, The Doctor Is
    In, 90
  BBQ Queens' Love Potion for the
    Swine, 89
  Bill's Better Than the Average,
    370–71
  glazing foods with, 15, 26
  variations, 90
Barwick, Dee, 340
Basil
  Fresh, Vinaigrette, 85
  Lemon Sauce, 343
  Mayonnaise, 213
  Oil Mashed Potatoes, 258
  Vinaigrette, 355
Bastes
  applying to grilled foods, 14–15
  applying to smoked foods, 26
  Brown Sugar Basting Sauce, 383
  Honey-Apple, 377
  Lemon Butter Drizzle, 87
  liquid mixtures for, 15, 26
  Orange-Ginger, 261
  Orange-Honey, 246
  Rosemary, Garlic, and Lemon, 68
Battle of the Sexes Barbecue Contest,
  197
Bean(s)
  Baked, Easy Southern-Style, 109
  Baked, Jazzy Java, 108
  Barbecued, BBQ Queens', 107
  Cannellini, and Roasted Red
    Pepper Relish, Autumn, 426
  Haricots Verts Salad with Mustard-
    Shallot Vinaigrette, 327–28
  Haricots Verts with Lemon, Garlic,
    and Parsley, 274
  Lima, Baby, Slow-Simmered, 392
  Pinto, Texas-Style, 106–7
  Red, and Rice with Smoked
    Sausage, 369
  Salad, Italian, 284
Béarnaise Sauce, Rustic, 98
Beef
  buying, 299–300
  Grilled
    and Asparagus Saddlebags,
      Smoky, 171–72
    Batayaki, with Spicy Lemon-Soy
      Sauce, 312–13
    best cuts for, 300
    Black and Bleu, 326
    Branding Iron, with Ancho
      Mayonnaise, 311–12
    Burgers, 303
    Burgers, Dolled-Up Caesar, 304
    Fajitas, Citrus-Grilled, 308–9
    Filet Mignon, Peppercorn, with
      Cognac Sauce, 317–18

Beef, Grilled (*cont.*)
Filet Mignon, Steakhouse-Style, 317
Filet Salad with Orange-Cumin Vinaigrette, 313
grilling times, 16
Kabobs, Kabuli, 333–34
Kabobs, Tamarind and Yogurt, with Warm Pita Breads, 331
Sicilian Bistecca, 324
Skewers, 330
Skewers with Quick Peanut Sauce, 331
Skewers with Spicy Tomato-Chile Sauce, 331
Smoky Meatballs, 345
Steak, Bistro-Style, with Red Wine–Shallot Sauce, 308
Steak, Bone-In, 323
Steak, Bone-In, Korean-Style, 323–24
Steak, Boneless, 316–17
Steak, Flank, Skirt, Hangar, or Other Thin, 307–8
Steak, Prairie-Style Hay-Smoked, 326
Steak, Rib-Eye, Charcoal-Grilled, 315
Steak, Rib-Eye, Philadelphia Garlic, 318
Steak, Strip, Seduction, with Roquefort-Bacon Butter, 318
Steak, Strip, with Chile–Ginger–Green Onion Sauce, 318
Steak, T-Bone, with Smoked Tomato and Grilled Red Onion Relish, 324
Steak, Thick-Cut, 325
Steak Marinated in Beer, Herbs, and Morels, 309
Steak Salad with Caper Vinaigrette, 309
Tenderloin, 336–37
Tenderloin, Chez Panisse–Style, 337–38
Tenderloin, Herbed and Spiced, 342–43
Tenderloin, Herbed and Spiced, Salad, 341–42
Tenderloin with Sour Cream, Bacon, and Mushroom Sauce, 337
testing for doneness, 16, 17
marinating times, 67
Planked
Gorgonzola Filet Mignon, 347
Hickory-, Tenderloin, Argentinean, with Chimichurri Sauce, 346–47
Slathered, 347
Tenderloin, 346
Rotisserie Roast, 347–48
Boneless Prime Rib, with Blackened Seasoning, 349
Downtown, with BBQ Queens' Barbecued Beans, 348
Lemon Pepper, with Butter Baste, 348
Uptown, with Peppercorn Beurre Blanc, 348
Smoked
best cuts for, 300
BLT, 339
Brisket, 356–57
Brisket, Barbecued, Dip, 358
Brisket, Kansas City–Style Barbecued, 357
Brisket, Texas-Style Slow-Smoked, 353–54
Brisket, Two-Step Shortcut Barbecued, 358
Burnt Ends, 358
Burnt Ends Sandwich, 358
Corned, Barbecued, with Mustard-Beer Slather, 359–60
Flank Steak, Cola-Marinated, 403
Rib Roast, 349–50
Rib Roast, Rosemary Pesto, 350
Rib Roast Sandwiches, 350–51
Rib Roast with Yorkshire Pudding, 350
Rustic Reuben, 360
Smoky Meatballs, 345
Tenderloin, 338–39
Tenderloin, Kiss of Smoke, Black Forest, 402
Tenderloin, Peppery, 339
Tenderloin, Porcini, 339
testing for doneness, 28
timetable for, 27
Smoked Greek Stuffed Tomatoes, 164
steaks, popularity of, 310–11
steaks, types of, 300
Stovetop Smoked Tenderloin, 39
Super Sicilian Sandwich, 184
Beurre Blanc
Mustard-Cornichon, 100
Peppercorn, 102
Raspberry, 101
Smoked Chile, 99
Blueberry-Peach Tart with Macaroon Crust, 295–96
Bordelaise Sauce, Simply Delicious, 91
Boss Hawg barbecue team, 197
Bourbon-Mustard Cream Sauce, 377
Bourbon Pecan-Stuffed Rotisserie Pork Loin, 399
Bread(s). *See also* Pizza
Bolani (Afghani Flatbreads with Fresh Herb Filling), 182
Bruschetta with Jersey Tomatoes, 294
Campfire Skillet Scones, 415–16
Cheesy Italian Pesto, 177
Fiesta, 178
grilled, testing for doneness, 16
Rustic, with Smoked Tomato and Basil Butter, 177–78
Sticks, Grilled Leaf-Wrapped, 181–82
Wood-Grilled Flatbreads, 176
Broccoli Slaw, Crunchy, with Thai Chile-Peanut Dressing, 80
Burgers
Caesar, Dolled-Up, 304
condiments for, 306
Fourth of July Pilgrim, with Dried Cranberry Relish, 305
Grilled, 303
grilled, testing for doneness, 17
grilling times, 16
Lamb, Greek-Style, with Cilantro-Mint Chutney, 304–5
preparing, tips for, 303
Tuna, Asian, with Wasabi Mayo, 305
"Burgers," Grilled Portobello Mushroom, 133
"Burgers," Grilled Tomato, with Herbed Cream Cheese, 160

Butter. *See also* Beurre Blanc
  Lemon Drizzle, 87
  Pernod, 288
  Roquefort-Bacon, 318
  Smoked Tomato and Basil, 177–78

C

Cabbage. *See also* Sauerkraut
  Blue Cheese Coleslaw, 79
  Frozen Asset Slaw, 82
  Grilled Greens, 126–27
  Layered Vinegar Slaw, 80–81
  Red, and Apple Slaw, 83
  Red, and Radicchio, Grilled, with
    Herbed Caesar Dressing, 127
Caesar Burgers, Dolled-Up, 304
Caesar Dressing, Herbed, 127
Caesar Salad, Curlicue Chicken,
  196–97
Caesar Salad, Grilled Romaine, 127
Caesar Vinaigrette, Citrus, 84
Cake
  Cranberry-Almond Torte with
    Cranberry Drizzle, 394–95
  Grilled Pound, with Hot Fudge
    Ganache and Sweetened
    Berries, 397
  Orange Marmalade Bundt, 396–97
Calamari. *See* Squid
Caper, Tomato, and Pine Nut Relish,
  Summer, 425
Caper-Stuffed Eggs, 380
Caper Vinaigrette, 309
Carrot(s)
  Baby, Braised in Late-Harvest
    Riesling, 275
  Grated, Salad, Bistro, 329
  Vegetable Ribbon Skewers, 156
Cauliflower, Roasted Red Pepper, and
  Cured Olive Salad, 282–83
Celery Root Rémoulade, 328–29
charcoal, hardwood, 8
charcoal briquettes, 8
charcoal chimney, 8–9
charcoal grills
  adding smoke flavors, 11, 21, 24
  adjusting temperature in, 25
  lighting fire in, 8–9
  preparing direct fire in, 10–11
  preparing indirect fire in, 11, 19
  rotisserie unit on, 33
  selection criteria, 4

  signs of hot fire in, 13
  smoking foods in, 11, 19, 25
Cheese
  Asiago-Garlic Grits, 392–93
  Blue, Coleslaw, 79
  Blue, Dressing, Creamy, 111
  Brie and Basil–Stuffed Turkey
    Breast, 227
  Cheesy Grilled Pepper Boats, 143
  Cheesy Italian Pesto Bread, 177
  Cream, Herbed, Grilled Tomato
    "Burgers" with, 160
  Fennel and Feta Salad, 128
  Fiesta Bread, 178
  Goat, and Grilled Vegetable
    Terrine, 130–31
  Goat, and Tapenade, Smoked
    Vegetable Confit on Country
    Bread with, 158
  Goat, Cream Sauce, Smoked
    Turkey, and Sun-Dried
    Tomatoes, Penne with, 227
  Goat, Grilled Eggplant, and
    Peppers with Balsamic-
    Thyme Vinaigrette, 124
  Goat, Grilled Portobellos with
    Garlic, Pine Nuts, Basil, and,
    133
  Goat, Grilled Tomatoes, 160
  Goat, Herbed, or Boursin, Grilled
    Drumsticks or Thighs Stuffed
    with, 211–12
  Gorgonzola Filet Mignon on a
    Plank, 347
  Grilled, in a Sarong, 128
  Grilled Artichoke Pizza on
    Parmesan-Herb Crust, 185–86
  Grilled Asparagus with Shaved
    Parmigiano-Reggiano, 118
  Grilled Eggplant Roll-Ups with
    Feta-Olive-Lemon Filling, 126
  Grilled Pizza with Caramelized
    Onions and Brie, 180–81
  Ham, Cheddar, and Apricot
    Chutney Pizza, 384
  Mozzarella and Tomato Salad with
    Two Dressings, 354–55
  Pecorino Romano–Artichoke
    Glaze, 194
  Planked
    Hickory-, with Dried Cranberry
    Relish, 175

    Maple-, with Tricolored Peppers,
    175
    Semisoft, 174
  Roquefort-Bacon Butter, 318
  Smoked
    Cheesy Smashed Potatoes, 170
    Dip, Crunchy, 170
    Dip, Homemade Vegetable
    Crisps with, 170–71
    Goat, Salad, 170
    Gouda and Tomato Pasta Salad,
    173
    Mozzarella, Tomato, and Fresh
    Basil Salad, 173
    Sandwich, Grilled, Smoky, 173
    Semisoft, 172–73
    Smoky Beef and Asparagus
    Saddlebags, 171–72
    Soft, 169–70
    Stovetop, Soft, 36
    -Stuffed Bone-In Chicken Breasts,
    Grilled, 200–201
    White Cheddar, Potato Gratin
    with, 412–13
Cherry(ies)
  Dried Sweet, –Port Sauce, 237
  Kiss of Smoke Beef Tenderloin
    Black Forest, 402
Chicken
  Grilled
    and Apple Sausage with Honey-
    Almond Grilling Glaze,
    365–66
    Burgers, 303
    Butterflied, Rosemary-Scented,
    205
    Drumsticks or Thighs Stuffed
    with Herbed Goat Cheese or
    Boursin, 211–12
    grilling times, 16
    half a chicken, method for, 201
    Hot Diggity Dogs, 365
    testing for doneness, 16, 17, 201
    Wings, Kathy's, 344
    Wings Amogio, 211
    Wings and Things, 210–11
    Wings and Things, Sizzling,
    with Sage Butter and Romano
    Cheese, 211
  Grilled Bone-In, Skin-On Breasts,
    199–200
    Cheese-Stuffed, 200–201

Chicken, Grilled Bone-In, Skin-On
    Breasts (cont.)
    and Fresh Greens Salad, 201
    Pesto, Sandwich with Cranberry
      Preserves, 201
  Grilled Boneless, Skinless Breasts,
    191
    Cubano, with Picadillo Olive
      Salsa, 192
    Indoors, 192
    Lemonata, 192
    Sicilian, One-Dish-Meal, 192–93
    with Thousand-Herb Sauce, 192
  Grilled, Skewers, 195
    Caesar Salad, Curlicue, 196–97
    Chopstix, with Gingered
      Teriyaki Glaze, 196
    Satay, 196
  marinating times, 67
  Planked Boneless, Skinless Breasts,
    193–94
    Balsamic-Thyme, with Peppers
      and Onions, 194
    with Pecorino Romano–
      Artichoke Glaze, 194
  Rotisserie, 217–18
    French Tarragon, 218
    Puerto Rican–Style, 218
    Sandwich, Karen's Famous,
      218–19
  Smoked
    Barbecued, on Fire, 213
    Breasts, and Green Chile Soup,
      216
    Breasts, with Southwest Heat,
      215
    Italian Barbecued, 220
    Pulled, Salad with Basil
      Mayonnaise, 213
    Rosemary-Garlic, 220
    Salad, Chopped, 213
    Sesame-Soy Marinated, 221
    testing for doneness, 28
    timetable for, 27
    and Vegetable Lasagna, 221
    Whole, 219–20
    whole, method for, 201
    Wings and Things, 212
  Stir-Grilled
    Asian Lettuce Wraps, 168–69
    with Asparagus and Shaved
      Parmigiano-Reggiano, 199

and Summer Vegetable Pasta
  with Fresh Basil Vinaigrette,
  199
  Tequila-Lime, 199
  and Vegetables, 198
Chile(s)
  Ancho Mayonnaise, 311–12
  Charred Tomato–Chipotle Salsa,
    162–63
  Chipotle Barbecue Sauce, 90
  Chipotle Dipping Sauce, 389
  Chipotle Vinaigrette, 86
  –Ginger–Green Onion Sauce, 318
  Green, and Smoked Chicken Soup,
    216
  Grilled, Rellenos with Baby
    Shrimp, 143–44
  Grilled, Sauce, Pick a Peck of,
    145–46
  Poblano Cream Sauce, 93
  Raspberry-Jalapeño Barbecue
    Sauce, 90
  Smoked, Beurre Blanc, 99
  smoked, preparing, 140
  Smoked Chicken Breasts with
    Southwest Heat, 215
  Smoky Chipotle Corn Pudding,
    122–23
  Southwestern Dressing, 355
  Southwest Heat, 215
  Tomato, and Garlic Chutney, 428
Chimichurri Sauce, 346–47
Chive Pesto, 64
Chocolate
  Almond Joy Brittle, 265
  -Coconut-Macadamia Bars, 262–63
  Hot Fudge Ganache, 440–41
  –Peanut Butter Bars, 263
  S'mores, 262
  White, –Cranberry Brittle, 265
Chutney
  Apricot, 384
  Cilantro-Mint, 304
  Tomato, Garlic, and Chile, 428
Cilantro
  -Mint Chutney, 304
  -Peanut Dipping Sauce, 389
  Santa Fe Herb Paste, 436
  and Smoked Garlic Cream Sauce,
    93–94
Clams, Grilled
  with Lemon Butter Drizzle, 268

Littleneck, with Pernod Butter, 288
  in the Shell, 287
Coconut
  Almond Joy Brittle, 265
  Chocolate-Macadamia Bars, 262–63
  Toasted, Ice Cream, 440–41
Cognac and Apricot Glaze, 241
coleslaw. See Slaws
Colwin, Laurie, 63
Corn
  cobs and husks, grilling with, 23
  Grilled, 119
    Green Chile and Smoked
      Chicken Soup, 216
    Layered Salad, 120
    Relish, Southwestern-Style, 120
    and Smoked Vegetable Pudding,
      120
  Smoked
    Chipotle Pudding, Smoky, 122–23
    Green Chile and Smoked
      Chicken Soup, 216
    Ham, and Hominy Casserole,
      123
    in the Husks, 121–22
    Sliced Tomato, and Slivered Red
      Onion Salad, 122
    and Tomato Salad, Fresh, 203
Cornish Game Hens
  Grilled, à la Chez Panisse, 246
  Grilled Game Birds, 245
  with Orange-Honey Baste, 246
Cranberry(ies)
  -Almond Torte with Cranberry
    Drizzle, 394–95
  Bourbon Pecan-Stuffed Rotisserie
    Pork Loin, 399
  Dried, Relish, Hickory-Planked
    Cheese with, 175
  -Orange Salsa, 227
  –White Chocolate Brittle, 265
Cucumber(s)
  Elaborate Yet Easy, in Poppy Seed
    Dressing, 282
  Grilled Gazpacho, 155
  Kath's, 281
  Tzatziki, 112

D

Davis, Ardie, 44
Desserts
  Almond Cookie Brittle, 264–65

Almond Joy Brittle, 265
Blueberry-Peach Tart with
    Macaroon Crust, 295 96
Chocolate-Coconut-Macadamia
    Bars, 262–63
Chocolate–Peanut Butter Bars, 263
Cranberry-Almond Torte with
    Cranberry Drizzle, 394–95
Fresh Fruit Tart, 374–75
Fresh Peach Crumble Ice Cream,
    441–42
Grilled Pound Cake with Hot
    Fudge Ganache and
    Sweetened Berries, 397
Lemon-Scented Peach Crisp, 393
Mandarin Orange Sorbet, 442
Orange Marmalade Bundt Cake,
    396–97
Pecan Pie Bars, 263–64
Pineapple Sorbet in Grilled
    Pineapple Rings, 442
Rice Krispie Treats, 265
S'mores, 262
Toasted Coconut Ice Cream with
    Hot Fudge Ganache and
    Toasted Pecans, 440–41
White Chocolate–Cranberry
    Brittle, 265
Dips
Barbecued Brisket, 358
Crunchy Smoked Cheese, 170
Smoky Cheese, Homemade
    Vegetable Crisps with, 170–71
dressings. See Salad dressings;
    Vinaigrettes
drinks. See Sangria!
Duck
domestic, about, 236
Grilled
    Breast, Salad, 237
    Paillards, 235
    Paillards with Dried Sweet
        Cherry–Port Sauce, 237
    whole, method for, 236
Smoked
    Apricot and Cognac-Glazed, 241
    on a Beer Can, 239
    Breasts, 239
    with Five-Spice Asian Paste, 239
    Whole, 238
    whole, method for, 236
    and Wild Rice Soup, 239

wild, about, 236
Dukka, 61

E

Eggplant
Grilled, 123–24
    Balsamic-Marinated Vegetables
        on the Grill, 314–15
    –Garlic Sauce, Fettuccine with,
        126
    Peppers, and Goat Cheese with
        Balsamic-Thyme Vinaigrette,
        124
    Roll-Ups with Feta-Olive-Lemon
        Filling, 126
    Salad, Warm Asian, 125
    Spread, Sonoma Farmers'
        Market, 124–25
    Vegetable and Goat Cheese
        Terrine, 130–31
    Vegetable Platter with Fresh
        Basil Vinaigrette, 129–30
Smoked
    Pasta Salad with Rotisserie
        Lamb and, 432
    Rotisserie Leg of Lamb with
        Smoked Ratatouille, 432
    Vegetable Confit, 158
    Vegetable Confit on Country
        Bread with Tapenade and
        Goat Cheese, 158
Eggs
Beelzebub's Bloody Marys, 204
Caper-Stuffed, 380
Deviled, Classic, 379
Deviled, with Grilled Shrimp,
    380–81
Grilled Asparagus Frittata, 118
hard-boiling, 378
Mediterranean Stuffed, 381
Smoked Trout Benedict with
    Confetti Hash, 273–76
electric grills, 5, 9–10, 24, 25
electric smoker ovens, 10, 12–13, 21,
    24
Elk, Drunk, 242–43

F

Fajitas, Citrus-Grilled Beef, 308–9
Fennel
    Blood Orange, and Black Olive
        Relish, Winter, 424

and Feta Salad, 128
Grilled, and Red Potato Salad, 148
Grilled, Red Pepper, and Lemon-
    Tarragon Vinaigrette, Grilled
    Scallops with, 291
Orange, and Olive Salad,
    Moroccan, 280
and Orange Drizzling Sauce, 73
and Orange Marinade, 72–73
Salt, 56
-Tomato Sauce, 95
Fish
Grilled
    Asian Tuna Burgers with Wasabi
        Mayo, 305
    cooking times for, 256
    general rules for, 256
    grilling times, 16
    preparing for grill, 256
    Skewers, 259–60
    testing for doneness, 16, 17
Grilled Fillets, 257
    with Basil Oil Mashed Potatoes
        and Warm Citrus Garnish,
        258
    Caribbean Grouper on Sugar
        Cane Skewers, 260–61
    Herb-, 258
    Japanese-Style, 258–59
    Skewers, 259–60
    Sweet-Hot Mustard-Glazed
        Salmon, 437
    Veracruzano, 258
Grilled Steaks, 271
    Lime-, Swordfish with Charred
        Tomato-Chipotle Salsa, 272
    with Lime-Ginger Marinade,
        Down Under, 271–72
    Seared Rare Tuna Steaks with
        Toasted Sesame Oil, 272
    Skewers, 259–60
    Thai-Style Halibut on
        Lemongrass Skewers, 260
marinating times, 67, 256
Oak-Planked Peppercorn Tuna
    Steaks with Orange
    Mayonnaise, 278
Planked, 277
rotisserie cooking, 40
Smoked
    Apple Cider–, Trout with
        Horseradish Cream, 286–87

Fish, Smoked (*cont.*)
    cooking times for, 256
    general rules for, 256
    Happy, Happy, Happy Hour
        Salmon, 286
    Happy, Happy, Happy Hour
        Salmon Spread, 286
    preparing for smoker, 256
    Whole, 285
    Smoked Fillets, 272–73
        Pâté with Dill and Lemon, 276
        with Sauce Verte, 273
        Smoked Trout Benedict with
          Confetti Hash, 273–76
        Smoked Tomato with Tuna,
          Lemon, and Herbs, 165
    substitution chart, 254–55
Fox, Julie, 390
Frittata, Grilled Asparagus, 118
Fruit. *See also specific fruits*
    Breakfast S'Mores, 416
    Fresh, Tart, 374–75
    Grilled Duck Breast Salad, 237

G

Game Birds. *See also* Duck
    Grilled, 245
        Cornish Game Hens à la Chez
          Panisse, 246
        Cornish Game Hens with
          Orange-Honey Baste, 246
        Quail Salad with Spiced Pears
          and Mushrooms, Warm,
          246–47
    Smoked
        and Pasta, 249
        Pheasant and Quail, Bacon-
          Wrapped, 248
        pheasant breasts, 249
        preparing for cooking, 236
        Salad, 248
        Small, 247–48
Garlic
    -Citrus Marinade, 70
    -Herb Pizza Dough, 180
    Marinade, 434–35
    Mashed Potatoes, Decadent, 321
    Rib-Eye Steak, Philadelphia, 318
    and Rosemary, Smoke-Roasted
        Potatoes with, 408
    -Rosemary Smoked Chicken, 220
    Sauce, 321

Sauce, Dipping, 293
Smoked
    and Cilantro Cream Sauce,
        93–94
    preparing, 140
    and Tomatoes, Fettuccine with,
        165
    Tuscan-Style Porchetta, 405
gas grills
    adding "kiss of smoke," 13–14
    adding smoke flavors, 12, 13–14,
        20, 21, 24
    adjusting temperature in, 25
    lighting, 9
    natural gas for, 3
    preparing direct fire in, 11
    preparing indirect fire in, 12, 20
    propane fuel for, 3
    rotisserie cooking on, 33
    selection criteria, 3–4
    smoking foods in, 12, 20
Gazpacho, Grilled, 155
Gingered Teriyaki Glaze, 196
Ginger-Pineapple Salsa, 414
Glaze
    applying to grilled foods, 15
    applying to smoked foods, 26
    Apricot and Cognac, 241
    Apricot-Dijon, 374
    barbecue sauces used as, 15, 26
    Gingered Teriyaki, 196
    Honey-Almond Grilling, 88
    Mustard-Apricot, 411
    Orange and Tarragon, 261
    Pecorino Romano–Artichoke,
        194
    Raspberry and Mustard, 400–401
    sugar-based, types of, 15, 26
Gravy, Traditional Rotisserie Turkey,
    229
Greasehouse University, 44
Greens. *See also* Cabbage; Fennel;
    Lettuce; Spinach
    Beef Filet Salad with Orange-
        Cumin Vinaigrette, 313
    Fennel and Feta Salad, 128
    Fresh, and Grilled Chicken Salad,
        201
    Grilled, 126–27
    Grilled Cheese in a Sarong, 128
    Grilled Lamb, Pear, and Pistou
        Salad, 430

    Grilled Radicchio and Red
        Cabbage with Herbed Caesar
        Dressing, 127
    Smoked Game Bird Salad, 248
    Smoked Goat Cheese Salad, 170
    Warm Grilled Quail Salad with
        Spiced Pears and Mushrooms,
        246–47
Gremolata, 274
Griffith, Dotty, 352
grilling foods, 8–17
    adding smoke flavors, 11, 12,
        13–14, 20
    bastes for, 14–15
    compared with smoking foods, 2
    doneness, testing for, 16–17
    doneness chart for, 16
    glazes for, 15
    grilling times, 15–17
    grilling timetable, 16
    heat temperatures for, 13
    lid position for, 11, 14
    methods and tips for, 14–15
    rotisserie cooking, 33, 40
    stir-grilling, 32
    utensils for, 6–7, 41
grills. *See also specific grill types*
    baskets for, 6, 40
    cleaning, 14
    lid position for, 11, 14
    preparing food for, 14
    racks for, 6
    types of, 2–3
Grits, Asiago-Garlic, 392–93
Grits, Smoked Tomato, 164
Grouper, Caribbean, on Sugar Cane
    Skewers, 260–61

H

Halibut, Thai-Style, on Lemongrass
    Skewers, 260
Ham
    Double-Smoked, 411–14
        with Pineapple-Ginger Salsa, 414
        Salad Sandwiches, Karen's, 414
        Stovetop, 38
    Grilled
        Cheddar, and Apricot Chutney
          Pizza, 384
        Steaks, 382
        Steaks, Country Cured, Vinegar-
          Mopped, 382–83

Steaks, Sweet, with Brown
Sugar Basting Sauce, 383
Smoked Corn, and Hominy
Casserole, 123
Hearts of Palm Salad, 283
Herb(s). *See also specific herbs*
adding smoky flavor with, 23
Chimichurri Sauce, 346–47
flavoring grilled foods with,
30–31
Fresh, Aioli, 110
Frizzled, Roasted Cherry Tomatoes
with, 208
-Grilled Fish, 258
Herbed Caesar Dressing, 127
-Lemon Marinade, Aromatic,
68–69
-Marinated Rotisserie Pork Loin,
398–99
Mediterranean Salad with Lemon-
Sumac Vinaigrette, 279–80
Sauce Verte, 273
stalks, as brushes, 15
stalks, as skewers, 29, 30–31
Thousand-, Sauce, 192
Hollandaise, Food Processor or
Blender, 97
Hominy, Smoked Corn, and Ham
Casserole, 123
Honey-Almond Grilling Glaze, 88
Honey-Apple Marinade and Baste,
377
Honey-Basted Smoked Onions, 141
Honeyed Barbecue Sauce, 90
Honey-Orange Baste, 246
Horseradish Aioli, 110
Horseradish Cream, 286–87
Horseradish Sauce, Spicy, 223
Hughes, Betty, 171

I

Ice Cream, Fresh Peach Crumble,
441–42
Ice Cream, Toasted Coconut, 440–41

J

Jamison, Cheryl, 214

K

Kallas, Rose, 171
Kamado grills, 5, 10, 12, 21
Kansas City Barbeque Society, 44, 232

Kimizu, 103
Kirk, Paul, 44, 46

L

Lamb
cooking, tips for, 418
Grilled
best cuts for, 418
Brochettes, Tapas-Style, 428
Burgers, 303
Burgers, Greek-Style, with
Cilantro-Mint Chutney, 304–5
Chops, 420
Chops with Chiles and Mint,
421
Chops with Rosemary, Garlic,
and Lemon Baste, 421
grilling times, 16
Kabobs, Mediterranean-Rubbed,
with Lemon Butter Drizzle,
428
Kabobs, Sambar-Spiced South
Indian, with Tomato, Garlic,
and Chile Chutney, 428
Leg of, 429
Leg of, Rustic Spinach
Pesto–Stuffed, 430
Leg of, Simple Stuffed, 430
Pear, and Pistou Salad, 430
Rack of, 422
Rack of, Marinated, with
Apricot and Cognac-Cabernet
Sauce, 423
Rack of, Rosemary Pesto, 423
Skewers, 427
Spring Grill Platter with Aioli,
421
testing for doneness, 16, 17
marinating times, 67
Rotisserie
and Eggplant, Pasta Salad with,
432
Leg of, 431
Leg of, Garlic-Marinated Rolled,
434–35
Leg of, with Smoked
Ratatouille, 432
Sandwiches with Matchstick
Vegetables and Tzatziki, 433
Smoked
best cuts for, 418
Leg of, 438

Leg of, Butterflied, Pinot Noir,
438–39
Leg of, Butterflied, Tandoori-
Marinated, 439
Leg of, Stuffed, BBQ Queens',
439
Rack of, Baaaaarbecued, 423
testing for doneness, 28
timetable for, 27
Smoked Greek Stuffed Tomatoes,
164
Lasagna, Smoked Chicken and
Vegetable, 221
Lavender Salt, 55
Leblang, Bonnie Tandy, 266
Lemongrass Marinade, 74
Lemon(s)
Amogio, 72
Basil Sauce, 343
Butter Drizzle, 87
-Garlic Mayonnaise, 103
Grilled Chicken Lemonata, 192
-Herb Marinade, Aromatic, 68–69
-Soy Sauce, Spicy, 312
-Sumac Vinaigrette, 279–80
-Tarragon Vinaigrette, 75–76
Lettuce
Curlicue Chicken Caesar Salad,
196–97
Grilled Greens, 126–27
Grilled Romaine and Green
Onions with Lemon and
Olives, 127–28
Grilled Romaine Caesar Salad, 127
Mediterranean Salad with Lemon-
Sumac Vinaigrette, 279–80
Wraps, Stir-Grilled Asian, 168–69
Lime(s)
Garlic-Citrus Marinade, 70
-Tequila Marinade, 73
Lobster, Grilled, 294–95
Lobster, Grilled, Italian-Style, 288

M

Macadamia-Chocolate-Coconut Bars,
262–63
Mango-Lemon Sauce, 92
Marinades
Amogio, 72
Cola, 403
compared with vinaigrettes, 67
Fennel and Orange, 72–73

Marinades (*cont.*)
Garlic, 434–35
Garlic-Citrus, 70
Honey-Apple, 377
Lemon Butter Drizzle, 87
Lemongrass, 74
Lemon-Herb, Aromatic, 68–69
Lime-Ginger, 271–72
Red Wine, Provençal, 70
Red Wine, Vinegar, and Herb, 377
Rosemary-Mustard, 71
Sesame and Soy, 389
Sesame-Soy, 221
Tandoori, 74–75
Tequila-Lime, 73
Teriyaki, Homemade, 69
for vegetables, reusing, 119
Worcestershire, 391
working with, 67
Marmalade, Smoked (or Grilled) Onion, 141
Mayer, Lisa Readie, 292
Mayonnaise. *See also* Aioli
Ancho, 311–12
Basil, 213
Lemon-Garlic, 103
Mustard-Mayo-Dill Slather, 66
Mustard-Mayo-Orange Slather, 66
Mustard-Mayo Slather, 66
Mustard-Mayo-Tarragon Slather, 66
Orange, 278
Wasabi, 305
Meatballs, Smoky, 345
Michel-Cupito, Janeyce, 370
Moose, Debbie, 202
Mushroom(s)
Bourbon-Mustard Cream Sauce, 377
Grilled, 132
Balsamic-Marinated Vegetables on the Grill, 314–15
Batayaki Beef with Spicy Lemon-Soy Sauce, 312–13
Portobello, "Burgers," 133
Portobellos with Garlic, Pine Nuts, Basil, and Goat Cheese, 133
Smoked Chicken and Vegetable Lasagna, 221

Grilled Artichoke Pizza on Parmesan-Herb Crust, 185–86
Grilled Steak Salad with Caper Vinaigrette, 309
Porcini Paste, 65
Smoked, 134
Bisque, 136
PLT, 136
Porcini Beef Tenderloin, 339
Smoked Chicken and Vegetable Lasagna, 221
Stuffed, 136
Sour Cream, and Bacon Sauce, 337
Stir-Grilled
and Olives, Mediterranean-Style, 168
Vegetables, Thai-Style, in Lemongrass Marinade, 167
Warm Grilled Quail Salad with Spiced Pears and, 246–47
Mussels, Grilled
with Garlic and Parsley, Black Fettuccine with, 288–89
in the Shell, 287
Mustard
Apricot-Dijon Glaze, 374
-Apricot Glaze, 411
-Bourbon Cream Sauce, 377
-Cornichon Beurre Blanc, 100
-Glazed Salmon, Sweet-Hot, 437
-Herb Dipping Sauce, 389
-Mayo-Dill Slather, 66
-Mayo-Orange Slather, 66
-Mayo Slather, 66
-Mayo-Tarragon Slather, 66
and Raspberry Glaze, 400–401
-Shallot Vinaigrette, 327–28

N

Nut(s). *See also* Almond
Bourbon Pecan-Stuffed Rotisserie Pork Loin, 399
Chocolate-Coconut-Macadamia Bars, 262–63
Dukka, 61
Peanut-Thai Chile Dressing, 80
Pecan Pie Bars, 263–64
Pistachio-Pomegranate Sauce, 96
Pistachio Sausage, 372
Toasted Pecans, 440–41

O

Olive(s)
Black, Blood Orange, and Fennel Relish, Winter, 424
Cured, Cauliflower, and Roasted Red Pepper Salad, 282–83
and Fire-Roasted Tomato Topping, Grilled Pizza with, 180
Orange, and Fennel Salad, Moroccan, 280
Queen-Size Spiced, 145
Salsa, Picadillo, 192
Stir-Grilled, and Mushrooms, Mediterranean-Style, 168
Onion(s)
Caramelized, and Brie, Grilled Pizza with, 180–81
Fried, Slivers, 320
Grilled, 137
Green, 138
Green, and Romaine, with Lemon and Olives, 127–28
Marmalade, 141
Red, and Smoked Tomato Relish, 324
Red, and Sweet Potato Skewers, 151
Red, Slices, 138
Soufflé, 138
with Thyme and Garlic Cream, 138–39
Planked, and Peppers, Balsamic-Thyme Chicken with, 194
Smoked, 139–41
Honey-Basted, 141
Marmalade, 141
Pickled Brewpub, 142
Tart, 141
Orange(s)
Blood, and Raspberry Sauce, 92
Blood, Fennel, and Black Olive Relish, Winter, 424
-Cumin Vinaigrette, 313
Fennel, and Olive Salad, Moroccan, 280
and Fennel Drizzling Sauce, 73
and Fennel Marinade, 72–73
-Fennel Vinaigrette, 280
Garlic-Citrus Marinade, 70
-Ginger Baste, 261
-Ginger Baste, Aussie Shrimp on the Barbie with, 261

-Honey Baste, 246
Mandarin, Sorbet, 442
Marmalade Bundt Cake, 396–97
Mayonnaise, 278
Rub, Spicy, 51
and Tarragon Glaze, 261
Order of the Magic Mop, 44
Oyster(s), Grilled
in Pesto, 288
Prosciutto, and Bay Leaf Skewers, 267
in the Shell, 287

P

Pasta
Black Fettuccine with Grilled
Mussels, Garlic, and Parsley, 288–89
Fettuccine with Grilled
Eggplant–Garlic Sauce, 126
Fettuccine with Smoked Garlic and
Tomatoes, 165
Grilled Squid Linguine with
Amogio, 298
Linguine with Smoked Butternut
Squash, Fresh Sage, and
Morel Cream Sauce, 158
One-Dish-Meal Grilled Chicken
Sicilian, 192–93
Penne with Smoked Turkey,
Goat Cheese Cream Sauce,
and Sun-Dried Tomatoes, 227
Salad, Smoked Gouda and Tomato, 173
Salad with Rotisserie Lamb and
Eggplant, 432
Smoked Chicken and Vegetable
Lasagna, 221
Smoked Game Birds and, 249
Stir-Grilled Chicken and Summer
Vegetable, with Fresh Basil
Vinaigrette, 199
Pastes
about, 46
Chive Pesto, 64
Five-Spice Asian, 64–65
Mediterranean Herb, 436
Porcini, 65
Rosemary Pesto, 62–63
Santa Fe Herb, 436
Sweet Moroccan Spice, 435

Peach-Blueberry Tart with Macaroon
Crust, 295–96
Peach Crisp, Lemon-Scented, 393
Peach Crumble Ice Cream, Fresh, 441–42
Peanut Butter
–Chocolate Bars, 263
Cilantro-Peanut Dipping Sauce, 389
Dipping Sauce, Asian-Style
Asparagus with, 118
Quick Peanut Sauce, 331
Peanut-Thai Chile Dressing, 80
Pear, Grilled Lamb, and Pistou Salad, 430
Pears, Spiced, and Mushrooms,
Warm Grilled Quail Salad
with, 246–47
Pecan Pie Bars, 263–64
Pecans, Toasted, 440–41
Pecan-Stuffed Bourbon Rotisserie
Pork Loin, 399
Peppercorn Beurre Blanc, 102
Peppercorn Rub, Tricolored, 62
Pepper(s). See also Chile(s)
Grilled, 142–43
Boats, Cheesy, 143
Eggplant, and Goat Cheese with
Balsamic-Thyme Vinaigrette, 124
Gazpacho, 155
Red, Fennel, and Lemon-
Tarragon Vinaigrette, Grilled
Scallops with, 291
Sauce, Pick a Peck of, 145–46
Tricolored, Maple-Planked
Cheese with, 175
Vegetable and Goat Cheese
Terrine, 130–31
Vegetable Platter with Fresh
Basil Vinaigrette, 129–30
Grill-Roasted, 145
Mediterranean Stuffed Eggs, 381
Roasted Red, Aioli, 110
Roasted Red, and Cannellini Bean
Relish, Autumn, 426
Roasted Red, Cauliflower, and
Cured Olive Salad, 282–83
Roasted Red, Sauce, 94
smoked, preparing, 140
Smoked Chile Beurre Blanc, 99

Stir-Grilled
Balsamic-Thyme Vegetables, 167
Red Bell, with Garlic and
Thyme, 168
Vegetables, 166
Pesto
Aioli, 110
Bread, Cheesy Italian, 177
Chive, 64
Grilled Oysters in, 288
Rosemary, 62–63
Pheasant and Quail, Bacon-Wrapped
Smoked, 248
Pheasant breasts, smoked, 249
Phillips, Diane, 434
Pineapple
Bourbon Pecan-Stuffed Rotisserie
Pork Loin, 399
-Ginger Salsa, 414
Sorbet in Grilled Pineapple Rings, 442
Pistachio-Pomegranate Sauce, 96
Pistachio Sausage, 372
Pizza
Dough, Food Processor, 179
Dough, Garlic-Herb, 180
Grilled, 179–80
Artichoke, on Parmesan-Herb
Crust, 185–86
with Caramelized Onions and
Brie, 180–81
with Fire-Roasted Tomato and
Olive Topping, 180
Ham, Cheddar, and Apricot
Chutney, 384
party, ideas for, 181
plank cooking, 42–43
Pomegranate-Pistachio Sauce, 96
Porcini Beef Tenderloin, Smoked, 339
Porcini Paste, 65
Pork. See also Bacon; Ham
Grilled
Burgers, 303
Chops, Sweet, with Brown
Sugar Basting Sauce, 383
Chops, Thick-Cut, 376
Chops, Thin-Cut, 382
Chops with Bourbon- Mustard
Cream Sauce, 377
Chops with Honey-Apple
Marinade and Baste, 377

Pork, Grilled (*cont.*)
    Chops with Red Wine, Vinegar,
      and Herb Marinade, 377
    grilling times, 16
    Hot Diggity Dogs, 365
    Loin Fillet, Center-Cut, 388
    Ribs, Indoor-Outdoor Kiss of
      Fire and Smoke, 387
    Sausage, Pistachio, 372
    sausage links, tips for, 367
    Steaks, 382
    Tenderloin, 388
    Tenderloin, Sesame and Soy-
      Marinated, 389
    Tenderloin in Worcestershire
      Marinade, 391
    Tenderloin with Chipotle
      Dipping Sauce, 389
    Tenderloin with Cilantro-Peanut
      Dipping Sauce, 389
    Tenderloin with Mustard-Herb
      Dipping Sauce, 389
    testing for doneness, 16, 17
    Wisconsin Dilly Beer Brat
      Sandwiches, 366
  marinating times, 67
  Rotisserie Loin, 398
    Ancho and Chipotle-Rubbed,
      399
    Bourbon Pecan-Stuffed, 399
    Herb-Marinated, 398–99
    Sandwiches, 399
  Sausage, Spicy, Rebecca's 'Que
    Queen Extraordinaire, 367
  Smoked
    BBQ Queens' Choucroute
      Garnie, 405
    Bratwurst, BBQ Queens'
      Choucroute Garnie with, 369
    Butt, 409–10
    Butt, Spicy Orange Barbecued,
      410
    Butts in a Bag, 410
    Loin, 404
    Loin, Slathered and Rubbed,
      405
    Loin, Spiral Herbed, with
      Apricot-Dijon Glaze, 373
    Piggy Sandwich, 411
    Ribs, 384–85
    Ribs, Asian-Style, 385
    Ribs, Country-Style, 386

Ribs, Rasberry Barbecued,
  385–86
Roast, Raspberry and
  Mustard–Glazed, 400–401
Sausage, 368
Sausage, Italian, and Artichoke
  Soup, 369
Sausage, Red Beans and Rice
  with, 369
Stovetop, Tenderloin, 38–39
testing for doneness, 28
timetable for, 27
Tuscan-Style Porchetta, 405
Smoke-Roasted Loin, with Herbed
  Pear Stuffing, 407–8
Potato(es). *See also* Sweet Potato(es)
  Gratin with White Cheddar
    Cheese, 412–13
  Grilled, 147
    Antipasto Skewers, 151
    Balsamic-Marinated Vegetables
      on the Grill, 314–15
    Red, and Fennel Salad, 148
    Skewered, 149–50
    Whole, 148
  Grill-Roasted, Salad, Rustic, 148
  Homemade Frites, 328
  Homemade Vegetable Crisps with
    Smoky Cheese Dip, 170–71
  Mashed, Basil Oil, and Warm
    Citrus Garnish, Grilled Fish
    with, 258
  Mashed, Decadent Garlic, 321
  Oven-Roasted Saffron, 413
  Salad, Creamy Dijon, for a Crowd,
    151
  Smashed, Olive Oil, 320
  Smashed, Smoked Cheesy, 170
  Smoked, 152
    and Aioli Gratin, 152–53
    Casserole, BBQ Queens', 153
    New or Fingerling, Platter, 153
    Salad, 359–60
    Soup, 153
  Smoked Trout Benedict with
    Confetti Hash, 273–76
  Smoked Turkey Hash, 231
  Smoke-Roasted, with Garlic and
    Rosemary, 408
Powderpuff Barbeque team, 367,
  370
Prather, Rozane Miceli, 183

Pudding
  Chipotle Corn, Smoky, 122–23
  Grilled Corn and Smoked
    Vegetable, 120
  Yorkshire, Smoked Rib Roast with,
    350
Putman, Karen, 400

Q

Quail
  Grilled, Salad with Spiced Pears
    and Mushrooms, Warm,
    246–47
  Grilled Game Birds, 245
  Smoked, and Pheasant, Bacon-
    Wrapped, 248
  Smoked Small Game Birds, 247–48
Queen waves, 224–25

R

Radicchio
  Grilled Greens, 126–27
  and Red Cabbage, Grilled, with
    Herbed Caesar Dressing, 127
Raoufi, Latifa, 332
Raspberry
  Barbecued Ribs, 385–86
  Beurre Blanc, 101
  and Blood Orange Sauce, 92
  -Jalapeño Barbecue Sauce, 90
  and Mustard Glaze, 400–401
Relish
  Blood Orange, Fennel, and Black
    Olive, Winter, 424
  Dried Cranberry, 175
  Grilled Corn, Southwestern-Style,
    120
  Roasted Red Pepper and Cannellini
    Bean, Autumn, 426
  Smoked Tomato and Grilled Red
    Onion, 324
  Strawberry, Toasted Almond, and
    Spinach, Springtime, 425
  Tomato, Pine Nut, and Caper,
    Summer, 425
Rice
  Durn Good, 243
  Wild, and Smoked Duck Soup, 239
  Wild, Cheesy, 371–72
Rosemary
  -Apple Salsa, 234
  Garlic, and Lemon Baste, 68

-Garlic Smoked Chicken, 220
Mediterranean Herb Paste, 436
-Mustard Marinade, 71
Pesto, 62–63
Pesto Rack of Lamb, 423
Pesto Smoked Rib Roast, 350
Salt, 56
-Scented Grilled Butterflied
    Chicken, 205
rotisserie cooking, 33, 40
Rubs
    about, 46
    All-Purpose, BBQ Queens', 49
    Barbecue, BBQ Queens' Photo Op,
        58–59
    Dukka, 61
    Fair for Fowl, 51
    Fennel Salt, 56
    Fireworks, 60
    Lavender Salt, 55
    Lemon Pepper, Spicy Red-Hot, 53
    McCormick seasonings, 59
    Mesquite, Texas Two-Steppin', 59
    Ole Hickory, 60–61
    Orange, Spicy, 51
    pantry ingredients for, 50
    Peppercorn, Tricolored, 62
    Rib, Memphis Blue-Ribbon, 49
    Rib, Prizewinning, 50
    Rosemary Salt, 56
    Smoked Hickory Salt, 57
    Southwest Heat, 215
    Spicy, Savory Seasoned Salt, 56–57
    Steak, Cajun, 58
    Sugar and Spice, Zesty, 52

S

Saffron Potatoes, Oven-Roasted, 413
Saffron Vinaigrette, 76
Salad. See also Slaws
    Bean, Italian, 284
    Beef Filet, with Orange-Cumin
        Vinaigrette, 313
    Cauliflower, Roasted Red Pepper,
        and Cured Olive, 282–83
    Celery Root Rémoulade, 328–29
    Chicken Caesar, Curlicue, 196–97
    Dijon Potato, Creamy, for a
        Crowd, 151
    Eggplant, Warm Asian, 125
    Elaborate Yet Easy Cucumbers in
        Poppy Seed Dressing, 282

Fennel and Feta, 128
Fresh Corn and Tomato, 203
Fresh Greens and Grilled Chicken,
    201
Grated Carrot, Bistro, 329
Grilled Corn Layered, 120
Grilled Duck Breast, 237
Grilled Herbed and Spiced Beef
    Tenderloin, 341–42
Grilled Lamb, Pear, and Pistou, 430
Grilled Quail, with Spiced Pears
    and Mushrooms, Warm,
    246–47
Grilled Radicchio and Red
    Cabbage with Herbed Caesar
    Dressing, 127
Grilled Red Potato and Fennel, 148
Grilled Romaine and Green
    Onions with Lemon and
    Olives, 127–28
Grilled Romaine Caesar, 127
Grilled Steak, with Caper
    Vinaigrette, 309
Grill-Roasted Potato, Rustic, 148
Haricots Verts, with Mustard-
    Shallot Vinaigrette, 327–28
Hearts of Palm, 283
Kath's Cucumbers, 281
Mediterranean, with Lemon-
    Sumac Vinaigrette, 279–80
Mozzarella and Tomato, with Two
    Dressings, 354–55
Orange, Fennel, and Olive,
    Moroccan, 280
Pasta, with Rotisserie Lamb and
    Eggplant, 432
A Platter of Fresh Tomatoes, 206–7
Pulled Smoked Chicken, with Basil
    Mayonnaise, 213
Roma Tomato, Italian, 207
Salata (Afghani Fresh Chopped
    Vegetable), 335
Smoked Chicken, Chopped, 213
Smoked Corn, Sliced Tomato, and
    Slivered Red Onion, 122
Smoked Game Bird, 248
Smoked Goat Cheese, 170
Smoked Gouda and Tomato Pasta,
    173
Smoked Mozzarella, Tomato, and
    Fresh Basil, 173
Smoked Potato, 359–60

Smoked Tomato with Tuna,
    Lemon, and Herbs, 165
Salad dressings. See also Vinaigrettes
    Creamy Blue Cheese, 111
    Herbed Caesar, 127
    Southwestern, 355
    Thai Chile-Peanut, 80
Salmon
    Planked, 277
    Smoked, Happy, Happy, Happy
        Hour, 286
    Smoked, Happy, Happy, Happy
        Hour, Spread, 286
    Sweet-Hot Mustard-Glazed, 437
Salsa
    Charred Tomato–Chipotle, 162–63
    Cranberry-Orange, 227
    Grilled Tomatillo, 163
    Picadillo Olive, 192
    Pineapple-Ginger, 414
    Rosemary-Apple, 234
Salt
    Fennel, 56
    Lavender, 55
    Rosemary, 56
    Smoked Hickory, 57
    Spicy, Savory Seasoned, 56–57
    types of, 54–55
Sandwiches
    Burnt Ends, 358
    Double-Smoked Ham Salad,
        Karen's, 414
    Grilled Cheese, Smoky, 173
    Pesto Chicken, with Cranberry
        Preserves, 201
    Piggy, 411
    Rotisserie Chicken, Karen's
        Famous, 218–19
    Rotisserie Lamb, with Matchstick
        Vegetables and Tzatziki, 433
    Rotisserie Pork Loin, 399
    Rotisserie Turkey, Day-After, 229
    Rustic Reuben, 360
    Smoked Beef BLT, 339
    Smoked PLT, 136
    Smoked Rib Roast, 350–51
    Smoked Turkey and Monterey Jack
        Club, 231
    Smoked Vegetable Confit on
        Country Bread with
        Tapenade and Goat Cheese,
        158

Sandwiches (cont.)
  Stir-Grilled Scallop Po'boy, 298
  Super Sicilian, 184
  Wisconsin Dilly Beer Brat, 366
Sangria!, 250
Sauce. See also Aioli; Barbecue Sauce;
    Salsa
  Ancho Mayonnaise, 311–12
  Apricot and Cognac-Cabernet, 423
  BBQ Queens' Love Potion for the
    Swine, 89
  Béarnaise, Rustic, 98
  Bordelaise, Simply Delicious, 91
  Bourbon- Mustard Cream, 377
  Brown Sugar Basting, 383
  Chile–Ginger–Green Onion, 318
  Chimichurri, 346–47
  Chipotle Dipping, 389
  Cilantro-Peanut Dipping, 389
  Cocktail, Nuevo Latino, 290–91
  Creamy Blue Cheese Dressing, 111
  Dried Sweet Cherry–Port, 237
  emulsion, about, 97
  Fennel and Orange Drizzling, 73
  Garlic, 321
  Garlic Dipping, 293
  Grilled Eggplant–Garlic, 126
  Grilled Peppers, Pick a Peck of,
    145–46
  Hollandaise, Food Processor or
    Blender, 97
  Horseradish, Spicy, 223
  Hot Fudge Ganache, 440–41
  Kimizu, 103
  Lemon Basil, 343
  Lemon Butter Drizzle, 87
  Lemon-Garlic Mayonnaise, 103
  Lemon-Soy, Spicy, 312
  Mango-Lemon, 92
  Mustard-Cornichon Beurre Blanc,
    100
  Mustard-Herb Dipping, 389
  Orange Mayonnaise, 278
  Peanut, Quick, 331
  Peanut Butter Dipping, 118
  Peppercorn Beurre Blanc, 102
  Pistachio-Pomegranate, 96
  Poblano Cream, 93
  Raspberry and Blood Orange, 92
  Raspberry Beurre Blanc, 101
  Red Wine–Shallot, 308
  Roasted Red Pepper, 94

  Smoked Butternut Squash, Fresh
    Sage, and Morel Cream, 158
  Smoked Chile Beurre Blanc, 99
  Smoked Garlic and Cilantro
    Cream, 93–94
  Sour Cream, Bacon, and
    Mushroom, 337
  Thai Green Curry, 290
  Thousand-Herb, 192
  Tomato-Chile, Spicy, 331
  Tomato-Fennel, 95
  Traditional Rotisserie Turkey
    Gravy, 229
  Tzatziki, 112
  Verte, 273
  Vietnamese Drizzle, 87
  Wasabi Mayo, 305
Sauerkraut
  BBQ Queens' Choucroute Garnie,
    405
  BBQ Queens' Choucroute Garnie
    with Smoked Bratwurst, 369
  Rustic Reuben, 360
Sausage(s)
  Grilled
    Chicken and Apple, with
      Honey-Almond Grilling
      Glaze, 365–66
    Hot Diggity Dogs, 365
    Pistachio, 372
    Seafood, with Cucumber and
      Tzatziki, 366
    Wisconsin Dilly Beer Brat
      Sandwiches, 366
  links, cooking tip for, 367
  Pork, Spicy, Rebecca's 'Que Queen
    Extraordinaire, 367
  Smoked, 368
    BBQ Queens' Choucroute
      Garnie, 405
    BBQ Queens' Choucroute
      Garnie with Smoked
      Bratwurst, 369
    Italian, and Artichoke Soup, 369
    Red Beans and Rice with, 369
Scallop(s)
  Grilled, 289–90
    with Fennel, Red Pepper, and
      Lemon-Tarragon Vinaigrette,
      291
    Skewers, Orange and
      Tarragon–Glazed, 261

  Skewers, Tequila-Lime, 269
    in Thai Green Curry Sauce, 290
  Stir-Grilled, Po'boy Sandwiches,
    298
  Stir-Grilled Shellfish, "Wonton"-
    Wrapped, 298
Scones, Campfire Skillet, 415–16
Seafood. See also Fish; Shellfish
  Sausage, Grilled, with Cucumber
    and Tzatziki, 366
Sesame and Soy Marinade, 389
Sesame-Soy Marinated Chicken,
    Smoked, 221
Shallot(s)
  –Red Wine Sauce, 308
  smoked, preparing, 140
  Vinaigrette, Hot, 85
Shellfish. See also Scallop(s); Shrimp
  Grilled
    Calamari, Stuffed, with
      Thousand-Herb Sauce, 291
    Clams with Lemon Butter
      Drizzle, 268
    Littleneck Clams with Pernod
      Butter, 288
    Lobster, 294–95
    Lobster, Italian-Style, 288
    Mussels, Garlic, and Parsley,
      Black Fettuccine with,
      288–89
    Oyster, Prosciutto, and Bay Leaf
      Skewers, 267
    Oysters, Clams, or Mussels in
      the Shell, 287
    Oysters in Pesto, 288
    Skewers, 259–60
    Squid, 289–90
    testing for doneness, 16, 17
  marinating times, 67
  Planked, 277
  Stir-Grilled, 297
    Squid Linguine with Amogio,
      298
    "Wonton"-Wrapped, 298
Shrimp
  Baby, Grilled Chiles Rellenos with,
    143–44
  Cedar-Planked, Chimichurri, 278
  Grilled, 289–90
    Aussie, on the Barbie with
      Orange-Ginger Baste, 261
    Deviled Eggs with, 380–81

with Nuevo Latino Cocktail
Sauce, 290–91
Prosciutto and Basil–Wrapped,
with Garlic Dipping Sauce,
293
in Thai Green Curry Sauce, 290
Stir-Grilled, 297
Stir-Grilled Shellfish, "Wonton"-
Wrapped, 298
Stovetop Smoked, 37
Silver Queen Corn Queen, 202
skewers, 7, 29–32
Slather, Mustard-Mayo, 66
slathers, about, 46
Slaws
Blue Cheese Coleslaw, 79
Broccoli, Crunchy, with Thai
Chile-Peanut Dressing, 80
Frozen Asset, 82
Layered Vinegar, 80–81
Red Cabbage and Apple, 83
Summer Squash, Mediterranean,
81
types of, 78
Smith, Kathy, 340
smoke flavor
adding to charcoal grill, 11
adding to gas grill, 12, 13–14, 20
"kiss of," gas grilling with, 13–14
non-wood, types of, 23
for plank cooking, 42, 43
wood, types of, 21–24
smokers. *See also* electric smoker
ovens; water smokers
adding smoke flavors, 21, 24
adjusting temperature in, 25
competition-style, 20
judging temperature of, 25
placing food in, 25
selection criteria, 18
stovetop, 21, 34–36
types of, 18
smoking foods, 18–28
bastes for, 26
compared with grilling, 2
doneness chart for, 28
glazes for, 26
heat temperatures for, 19–21
lid position for, 25
methods and tips for, 25–26
plank cooking, 42–43
preparations for, 19, 24–25

preparing food for, 25
smoke-roasting, about, 406
smoking time, estimating, 26
smoking timetable, 27
stovetop smoking, 34–36
utensils for, 6–7, 41
S'mores, 262
S'mores, Breakfast, 416
Sorbet, Mandarin Orange, 442
Sorbet, Pineapple, in Grilled
Pineapple Rings, 442
Soup
Green Chile and Smoked Chicken,
216
Grilled Gazpacho, 155
Smoked Duck and Wild Rice,
239
Smoked Italian Sausage and
Artichoke, 369
Smoked Mushroom Bisque, 136
Smoked Potato, 153
Sour Cream, Bacon, and Mushroom
Sauce, 337
Spinach
Baby, Sautéed, with Olive Oil and
Garlic, 275
BBQ Queens' Smoked Stuffed Leg
of Lamb, 439
Cheesy Wild Rice, 371–72
Creamed, Classic, 319
Grilled Cheese in a Sarong, 128
Grilled Corn Layered Salad, 120
Pasta Salad with Rotisserie Lamb
and Eggplant, 432
Pesto–Stuffed Leg of Lamb, Rustic,
430
Strawberry, and Toasted Almond
Relish, Springtime, 425
Spreads
Eggplant, Sonoma Farmers'
Market, 124–25
Salmon, Happy, Happy, Happy
Hour, 286
Smoked Fish Pâté with Dill and
Lemon, 276
Squash. *See also* Summer Squash;
Zucchini
Smoked, 157
Smoked Acorn, Spicy, 159
Smoked Butternut, Fresh Sage, and
Morel Cream Sauce, Linguine
with, 158

Squid
Grilled, 289–90
Grilled, Linguine with Amogio,
298
Grilled Stuffed Calamari with
Thousand-Herb Sauce, 291
stir-grilling, technique for, 32
stovetop smokers
adding wood chips to, 21
checking food in, 35
cleaning, 36
description of, 34
recipes for, 36–39
smoking foods in, 34–35
Strawberry, Toasted Almond, and
Spinach Relish, Springtime,
425
Summer Squash. *See also* Zucchini
Grilled, 154
Balsamic-Marinated Vegetables
on the Grill, 314–15
Char-Grilled Baby, 155
Vegetable Platter with Fresh
Basil Vinaigrette, 129–30
Vegetable Ribbon Skewers, 156
Slaw, Mediterranean, 81
Smoked, 157
Vegetable Confit, 158
Vegetable Confit on Country
Bread with Tapenade and
Goat Cheese, 158
Stir-Grilled
Balsamic-Thyme Vegetables,
167
Chicken and Summer Vegetable
Pasta with Fresh Basil
Vinaigrette, 199
with Fresh Herbs, 167–68
Tequila-Lime Chicken, 199
Sweet Potato(es)
Grilled, 147
Grilled, and Red Onion Skewers,
151
Homemade Vegetable Crisps
with Smoky Cheese Dip,
170–71
Smoked, 152
Smoke-Roasted, with Garlic and
Rosemary, 408
Swordfish, Lime-Grilled, with
Charred Tomato-Chipotle
Salsa, 272

T

Tamarind and Yogurt Beef Kabobs with Warm Pita Breads, 331
Tandoori Marinade, 74–75
Tarragon and Orange Glaze, 261
Tarragon Grilled Turkey Breast, 223
Tarragon Rotisserie Chicken, French, 218
Tarts
    Blueberry-Peach, with Macaroon Crust, 295–96
    Fresh Fruit, 374–75
    Grilled Vegetable, 149
    Smoked Onion, 141
    Tomato, Late-Harvest, 209
temperature, in grills, 13
temperature, in smokers, 25
Tequila-Lime Chicken, Stir-Grilled, 199
Tequila-Lime Marinade, 73
Tequila-Lime Scallop Skewers, 269
Teriyaki Glaze, Gingered, 196
Teriyaki Marinade, Homemade, 69
thermometers, 7, 41
Tio, Celina, 314
Tofu
    Stir-Grilled Asian Lettuce Wraps, 168–69
    Thai-Style Stir-Grilled Vegetables in Lemongrass Marinade, 167
Tomatillo, Grilled, Salsa, 163
Tomato(es)
    Charred, –Chipotle Salsa, 162–63
    -Chile Sauce, Spicy, 331
    and Corn Salad, Fresh, 203
    -Fennel Sauce, 95
    Fire-Roasted, and Olive Topping, Grilled Pizza with, 180
    Fresh, A Platter of, 206–7
    Garlic, and Chile Chutney, 428
    Grilled, 159
        BBQ Queens' Grilled Antipasto Platter, 144
        "Burgers" with Herbed Cream Cheese, 160
        Goat Cheese, 160
        Provençal, 160–61
        Provençal, Indoor, 161
        Roma, with Anchovy, Garlic, and Parsley, 160

Vegetable Platter with Fresh Basil Vinaigrette, 129–30
    Zucchini-Stuffed, with Basil, 270
Grilled Gazpacho, 155
Jersey, Grilled Bruschetta with, 294
and Mozzarella Salad with Two Dressings, 354–55
Picadillo Olive Salsa, 192
Pine Nut, and Caper Relish, Summer, 425
Roasted Cherry, with Frizzled Herbs, 208
Roma, Salad, Italian, 207
Sliced, Smoked Corn, and Slivered Red Onion Salad, 122
Smoked, 161
    Aioli, 110
    and Basil Butter, Rustic Bread with, 177–78
    and Garlic, Fettuccine with, 165
    and Gouda Pasta Salad, 173
    Greek Stuffed, 164
    and Grilled Red Onion Relish, 324
    Grits, 164
    Rotisserie Leg of Lamb with Smoked Ratatouille, 432
    Stovetop, 37–38
    with Tuna, Lemon, and Herbs, 165
    Vegetable Confit, 158
    Vegetable Confit on Country Bread with Tapenade and Goat Cheese, 158
Smoked Beef BLT, 339
Smoked Mozzarella, and Fresh Basil Salad, 173
Stewed and Scalloped, 322
Stir-Grilled
    Balsamic-Thyme Vegetables, 167
    Chicken and Summer Vegetable Pasta with Fresh Basil Vinaigrette, 199
    Chicken and Vegetables, 198
    Tequila-Lime Chicken, 199
    Vegetables, Thai-Style, in Lemongrass Marinade, 167
Tart, Late-Harvest, 209
Torte, Cranberry-Almond, with Cranberry Drizzle, 394–95
Trout, Apple Cider–Smoked, with Horseradish Cream, 286–87

Trout, Smoked, Benedict with Confetti Hash, 273–76
Tuna
    Burgers, Asian, with Wasabi Mayo, 305
    Lemon, and Herbs, Smoked Tomato with, 165
    Steaks, Peppercorn, Oak-Planked, with Orange Mayonnaise, 278
    Steaks, Seared Rare, with Toasted Sesame Oil, 272
Turkey
    Grilled
        Burgers, 303
        Burgers, Fourth of July Pilgrim, with Dried Cranberry Relish, 305
        Roulade with Lemon-Basil Sauce, 343–44
        testing for doneness, 16, 17
    Grilled Breast
        Fillets, Bacon-Wrapped, 223
        Steaks with Spicy Horseradish Sauce, 223
        Tarragon, 223
        Tenderloin Steaks, 222–23
    Rotisserie, 228–29
        Gravy, Traditional, 229
        Sandwich, Day-After, 229
    Smoked
        Apple-, 233
        Hash, 231
        and Monterey Jack Club Sandwiches, 231
        testing for doneness, 28
        timetable for, 27
        Whole, 230
    Smoked Breast
        Apple-, 233
        Boneless, 226
        Brie and Basil–Stuffed, 227
        with Cranberry-Orange Salsa, 227
        Goat Cheese Cream Sauce, and Sun-Dried Tomatoes, Penne with, 227
    Stir-Grilled Asian Lettuce Wraps, 168–69
Tzatziki, 112

U

utensils, for grilling, 6–7, 41

V

Veal, grilled, testing for doneness, 16, 17

Vegetable(s). *See also specific vegetables*
Grilled
Balsamic-Marinated, 314–15
BBQ Queens' Grilled Antipasto Platter, 144
and Goat Cheese Terrine, 130–31
Platter with Fresh Basil Vinaigrette, 129–30
Ribbon Skewers, 156
Skewered, 149–50
Tart, 149
testing for doneness, 16, 17
marinating times, 67
rotisserie cooking, 40
Smoked
Confit, 158
Confit on Country Bread with Tapenade and Goat Cheese, 158
and Grilled Corn Pudding, 120
Stir-Grilled, 166
Balsamic-Thyme, 167
and Chicken, 198
Thai-Style, in Lemongrass Marinade, 167
Venison, Drunk, 242–43
Vinaigrettes
Balsamic-Thyme, 84
Basil, 355
Basil, Fresh, 85
Caper, 309
Chipotle, 86
Citrus Caesar, 84
Lemon-Sumac, 279–80
Lemon-Tarragon, 75–76
Mustard-Shallot, 327–28

Orange-Cumin, 313
Orange-Fennel, 280
Saffron, 76
Shallot, Hot, 85
using as marinade, 67
Wheat Beer, 77

W

Wasabi Mayo, 305
water smokers
adding smoke flavors to, 24
charcoal, lighting, 19
description of, 5, 8
electric, lighting, 10, 20
electric, smoking times on, 26
gas, lighting, 10, 20
grilling foods in, 8, 12, 19
smoking foods in, 8, 12, 19–20, 26
Weaver, Candy, 240
Weber kettle grills, 4
Wells, Carolyn, 232
Wine
Red, Marinade, Provençal, 70
Red, –Shallot Sauce, 308
Red, Vinegar, and Herb Marinade, 377
Sangria!, 250
woks, 32
"Wonton"-Wrapped Stir-Grilled Shellfish, 298
wood chips, 21, 24
wood chunks, 24
wood flavors. *See* smoke flavor
wood pellet grills
adding smoke flavors, 24
adjusting temperature in, 13
description of, 5
electric-fired, lighting, 9–10
indirect grilling in, 12
smoking foods in, 12, 21

wood pellets, 5, 24, 41
wood "sticks" or logs, 24
Worcestershire Marinade, 391

Y

Yogurt
Tandoori Marinade, 74–75
Tzatziki, 112

Z

Zucchini
Grilled
Balsamic-Marinated Vegetables on the Grill, 314–15
Char-Grilled Baby Summer Squash, 155
Gazpacho, 155
Summer Squash, 154
Vegetable and Goat Cheese Terrine, 130–31
Vegetable Ribbon Skewers, 156
Mediterranean Summer Squash Slaw, 81
Smoked, 157
Rotisserie Leg of Lamb with Smoked Ratatouille, 432
Vegetable Confit, 158
Vegetable Confit on Country Bread with Tapenade and Goat Cheese, 158
Stir-Grilled
Balsamic-Thyme Vegetables, 167
Chicken and Summer Vegetable Pasta with Fresh Basil Vinaigrette, 199
Chicken and Vegetables, 198
Summer Squash with Fresh Herbs, 167–68
Tequila-Lime Chicken, 199
-Stuffed Tomatoes with Basil, 270